I0815336

Word

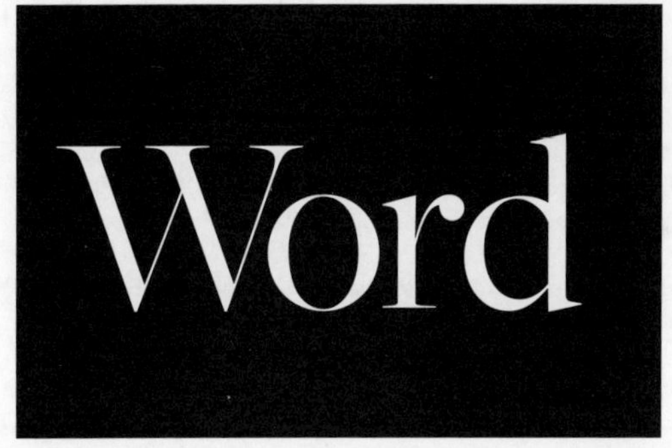

MALCOLM B. YARNELL III

978-1-0877-8071-9

Published by B&H Publishing Group
Brentwood, Tennessee

Dewey Decimal Classification: 231.2
Subject Heading: GOD / JESUS CHRIST / CHRISTIANITY—DOCTRINES

Cover design by Brian Bobel. Author photo by his family.

1 2 3 4 5 6 • 29 28 27 26

This second volume is dedicated to my beloved family, all the adults of whom worship the Eternal Word who became flesh for us. May the resurrected God–Man be pleased with our generations:

Karen Annette Yarnell,
Truett and Ashlyn and Lucas and Lydia,
Matthew and Victoria and Zion and Eden,
Graham and Gracie,
Kathryn,
Elizabeth

Contents

Preface

THE BIBLE BEGINS ITS ENLIGHTENING discourse with the foundational claim that God created everything by breathing and speaking. Reflecting on this creative activity, orthodox Christians conclude the Lord God made the heavens and the earth by his Spirit and by his Word. God "created" (Gen. 1:1) while his Spirit was "hovering" over the nothingness (v. 2) and his Word "said" things with power (v. 3).[1]

Every time "the LORD God" spoke his Word during those first six days, that which was previously nothing became something (Gen. 2:4). God repeatedly said, "Let there be," with perfect authority. And whatsoever he spoke about, that thing came into being (1:3, 6, 9, etc.). At the same time, God's eternal Spirit executed the perfect will he was proclaiming (v. 2). The one Lord God thereby brought every creaturely reality, including the space which marks the world's physical extension and the time which marks its progress, into existence.

Afterward, God revealed further truths about his Word through the prophets. Calling Israel to find comfort in the Lord, the prophet Isaiah reminded them of God's power amidst their frailty. "All humanity," he said, is like the grass which "withers" and like the

1. The truth that God is Trinity, while not personally defined in the first chapter of Genesis, was nevertheless disclosed through his Trinitarian activity as Creator. The truth of God as Trinity was fully disclosed in the New Testament (e.g., Matt. 28:19; 2 Cor. 13:13). Malcolm B. Yarnell III, *God*, vol. 1, Theology for Every Person (B&H Publishing, 2024), 71–94.

flowers which "fade" (Isa. 40:6–7).[2] But by contrast, while the world begins and ends, "the word of our God remains forever" (v. 8). He also disclosed that God sends his Word into the world to engage it intimately with his power and authority. The Lord God is above and beyond our conceptual capabilities (55:8–9), so his Word comes to us like "rain and snow." The Word descends from above, as an act of utter grace, to give life to the earth and its inhabitants (v. 10). From these Old Testament passages, we come to realize three profound truths about the Word of God: The Word is eternal. The Word creates all things. And the Word sustains life.

We then hear further stunning news: The eternal Word is more intimately involved in human life than through original creation and continuing sustenance. God continued speaking through the prophet, "My word that comes from my mouth will not return to me empty, but it will accomplish what I please and will prosper in what I send it to do" (v. 11). Yet more truth about the Word of God is hereby revealed: The Word comes from God and is sent into the world. The Word is distinct from God. The Word exercises personal agency. And the Word successfully accomplishes the will of God.

Isaiah also revealed how God would redeem his people through the suffering of his elect "servant" (Isa. 52:13–53:12). However, the connection of this Servant with the eternal Word, and with the powerful "son of man," who would reign over the universe forever from the divine throne (Dan. 7:13–14), was not yet clearly perceived. Even the immediate disciples of Jesus did not understand the world-altering truth about the Word and the Servant until after Jesus conquered death, reconstituting our humanity through his resurrection. Nevertheless, the facts of the New Testament's eternal gospel—that the Word of God is both God and with God, that he became a human being to redeem humanity by his death and resurrection, and that he reigns forever—was already revealed to the Old Testament prophets.[3]

---

2. The Spirit of the Lord is the source of both life and death in Isaiah 40:7 (cf. Gen. 2:7; 6:3; 7:22; Ps. 104:29–30). We shall have more to say about the third Person of God the Trinity in the final volume of this series. That volume, to be titled *Spirit*, will be dedicated to explaining who God the Holy Spirit is and what he has done, is doing, and will do alongside the eternal Father and the eternal Word.

3. The confluence of these great truths about the Word and the Servant should cause little wonder, then, that the book of Isaiah has been called "the fifth Gospel." John F. A. Sawyer, *The Fifth Gospel: Isaiah in the History of Christianity* (Cambridge University Press, 1996).

According to the New Testament, this Word, the only begotten Son of God, is Jesus the Christ, the Son of Man and suffering Servant (Matt. 16:16; Mark 14:61–63; 15:28 NASB1995, 39; John 1:1, 18). This One, who is truly God and truly man, recapitulated or perfected our humanity, working our salvation through his atoning death and victorious resurrection for us (Matt. 16:21; Eph. 1:10; Heb. 2:9–10). The risen Lord explained this transformative truth about himself from holy Scripture to the apostles (Luke 24:25–32, 44–48). He then disseminated the good news to the world through his church's proclamation. This proclamation focuses on his person as the Word who became flesh and his work to provide us with salvation (John 1:14; Rom. 1:1–4; 10:9–10).

It was only after the resurrection, when Jesus explained the mystery of the good news of salvation to his disciples, that this revelation became clear to mankind.[4] The mystery of the divine plan worked through the Word, which was previously made known in the Old Testament, thus it includes at least seven profound truths:

1. The Word of God is eternal, powerful, and personal.
2. The Word created all things.
3. The Word sustains all things.
4. The Word came into the world.
5. The Word worked wonders in the world.
6. The Servant suffered vicariously for our sins and conquered death.
7. The Son of Man reigns over everything forever from the divine throne.

There is so much more which needs to be said about the Word of God. This is why he constitutes the central and continually dominant subject of this book. We will learn together of how the Word is the eternal Son of God the Father. And of how he is our Creator and Providential Lord with the Father and the Spirit. How he created us in his image and continues to love us despite our sin. How he remains the electing God even as he becomes the Elect One, the Son of Man, Jesus Christ. How he walked before us to blaze the trail into life through his atonement on the cross and his resurrection

4. John Behr, *The Mystery of Christ: Life in Death* (St. Vladimir's Seminary Press, 2006), 15–44.

from death. How he is the One who now confers grace by calling sinners to believe in him, to be born again, and to become his disciples. How he is our predecessor, guide, and intercessor through this life. How he will ensure that we come through every danger, even death itself, into the very throne room of God.

And we will finally learn together how, on the "day of the LORD," before his glorious throne, every knee shall bow, and every tongue shall confess that "Jesus Christ is Lord" (Amos 5:18–24; Phil. 2:11; 1 Thess. 5:2). Even now, true believers confess his glorious Person and his saving work. These profound truths, derived from the mystery planned and hidden in the eternal will of God, prompt us to pray:

> To you, our one and only Lord Jesus Christ, truly God and truly man, we direct our worship. We, your disciples, even now bend our knees and ask you to open our minds, to mold our hearts, and to free our tongues so that we may obey you and confess to every creature that you, in your fullness of deity and in your assumed humanity, save us from our sins. You are our Creator, Sustainer, and Redeemer. You are the Beginning and the End of all things. You became a man for us, you died on the cross for our sins, and you arose from the dead for our justification. You are our eternal Prophet, Priest, and King. You, eternal Word, are our sole, sufficient, and sovereign Lord. With the Father and with the Spirit, we worship you, the One God.

Dear reader, with this prayer and with a glimpse of the glorious vision of the divine throne before your mind's eye, let's continue the journey we began together in the first volume of Theology for Every Person. Join with me as we discover the profound truth about the eternal Word. Let us marvel at his wondrous love for the world that he created, that he preserves, and that he will one day judge.

In this second volume, the various chapters focus on the work of Jesus Christ, the second Person of the blessed Trinity. First in order, however, we must learn of the One from whom the Word proceeds, God the Father. With the Father and his Son, the center and circumference of all Christian dogma, we must also consider the doctrines of creation and providence, as well as the doctrines of humanity and sin, and of the many works of Christ. As we travel together and converse about Jesus Christ, let us keep our eyes firmly glued upon the Word who became man, for he alone is "the pioneer and perfecter of our faith" (Heb. 12:2).[5]

After his resurrection from death, Jesus came and walked alongside two of his disciples as they took the journey to Emmaus. The risen Lord explained how the truths about his glorious Person and his perfect work were already revealed in his written Word. As we listen to his Word, we should not be surprised if our hearts begin "burning within" us just like the hearts of those disciples burned (Luke 24:32). And as our hearts burn for the eternal Word, who is "the only begotten God" (John 1:18 NASB1995), let us worship him together. Then, like the early disciples, let us excitedly get up, run, and tell others everything we have learned about him (Luke 24:33–35).

5. The first Greek term which describes Jesus in this verse, "pioneer" (*archegon*), indicates the person who both starts a journey and takes the lead during that journey. Another way to translate this term is "author." The second Greek term, "perfecter" (*teleioten*), indicates the person who both sets the example and brings to completion. The Lord Jesus Christ both fosters and finishes the Christian's journey into eternal relationship with God. This one Person, Jesus Christ, is at the same time the perfect God who calls us and the perfect man who completes us.

CHAPTER ONE

Who Is God the Father?

THE PRINCIPAL REALITY OF GOD as Father has not always received the attention it should in Christian theology, especially in recent centuries.[1] This lack of attention to the Father really should cause a great scandal. After all, our Lord emphasized prayer to him. At the beginning of his model prayer, Jesus reminds us to worship God as we confess him to be eternal, holy, and royal. Alongside our creed of theology proper, Jesus commands us to confess the work of the Father in election, providence, and redemption:

> "Therefore, you should pray like this: Our Father in heaven, your name be honored as holy. Your kingdom come. Your will be done on earth as it is in heaven. Give us today our daily bread. And forgive us our debts, as we also have forgiven our debtors. And do not bring us into temptation, but deliver us from the evil one.
>
> "For if you forgive others their offenses, your heavenly Father will forgive you as well. But if you don't forgive others, your Father will not forgive your offenses." (Matt. 6:9–15)

1. Peter Widdicombe, *The Fatherhood of God from Origen to Athanasius* (Oxford University Press, 1994), 1.

"The Lord's Prayer" provides us with a summary of the Person of the eternal Father and of his divine work, while reminding us of our utter dependence upon him. Let us continue our journey into the good, the true, and the beautiful by recalling our faith in the first Person of the divine Trinity.

The following two truths should orient our minds and hearts as we address the immediate question before us: "Who is God the Father?" To answer this important question, first, let us remember what "theology" means. Second, let us remind ourselves that God offers human beings salvation theologically, that is, through his Word about himself.

After these two truths (the reality of God and his salvation of us by his Word), we should rehearse the truth that the Father is God. As God the Father, he sources the Trinity, even as he is not the only Person of the eternal Godhead. We must also recall the distinction between God in himself and his actions toward his creatures. Afterward, we will survey the biblical witness regarding the Person of the Father. Finally, we must pay special attention to the ways in which he acts with paternal love toward his human creatures.

God and His Word

Theos and Logos

Remember that our important word, *theology*, derives from two Greek terms: *Theos*, which means "God," and *Logos*, which means "word." Theology means, quite literally, word, or thought or speech, about God. Holy Scripture emphasizes both *logos* and *theos*, and it places the terms in close relationship.

Regarding the second Person of the Trinity, Scripture says the Word is, always and at once, both "God" and "with God" (John 1:1). "The Word" is, in substance, the one eternal God, and, by distinction, the eternally begotten Son of God (John 1:18; Heb. 1:5–6). On the one hand, everything that God is, this is also his Word, eternally and entirely and equally (John 10:30; 14:10–11; 16:15). On the other hand, the Word is distinct from God the Father, as we shall see, through eternal generation.

Regarding the work of God, Scripture says God speaks to us through his Word. The Word is the revelation of God to humanity. Indeed, the only way we can know that God is God comes through his revelation of himself as Word. When taken together, these two Greek words, *theos* and *logos*, indicate both the irreducible unity and the personal relation between God and his Word.

We should also consider theology from a twofold perspective, the divine outlook and the human response: "Theology" is, from the divine perspective, first and foremost and forever, a set of personal relations. The eternal relation between God the Father and God the Son is metaphorically described as "generation" or "being begotten."[2] The second eternal relation, between God the Father with the Son and God the Holy Spirit, is called "procession" or "spiration."[3] These terms—*generation* and *procession*—thus technically describe distinct divine relations.

From the human perspective, "theology" is both a revealed "word about God" and the human "study of God." Because God remains unknown to us apart from revelation, God must first reveal himself to us by grace. Our thoughts about God, our theologies, are entirely responsive, entirely secondary. "First theology" is God's knowledge of his triune self, while "second theology," human knowledge about God, comes from God's revelation of himself.[4]

In the last book, we focused on the being of God the Trinity and on his revelation of his eternal Word to the prophets and apostles by his Holy Spirit. In this book, we focus upon the eternal Word of God in his eternal relation to his Father, on his incarnation as the One who is truly God and truly human, and on his works of creation and providence and redemption.

The Word Saves

Remember, moreover, that you are personally invited to come on the journey of knowing God. Every person, upon hearing the Word of God, must follow the incarnate Word into a saving relationship with the eternal God. In our prior discussion about divine revelation,

---

2. The term *generation* is borrowed from biology, but when applied to the eternal relation between God the Father and his Son (cf. John 1:14, 18; 3:16; Heb. 1:5; 5:5), it does not suggest biological movement.

3. *Procession* describes the relation between the Father and the Spirit (cf. John 15:26). *Spiration* is sometimes used in theological literature to describe this same eternal relation.

4. On "first theology," "second theology," and "third theology," see Malcolm B. Yarnell III, "Systematic Theology," in *Theology, Church, and Ministry: A Handbook for Theological Education*, ed. David S. Dockery (B&H Academic, 2017), 267–68, 278.

we learned God's revelation of himself is personal and propositional. Revelation is personal, in that each of us are called into an encounter with God face-to-face. Revelation is also propositional, for we come to know about God through truths stated in words.[5]

We are responsible for hearing God's saving Word, believing it in our hearts, and confessing it with our mouths. The Word of God is centered on this saving truth: Jesus Christ is the Lord God. He is the eternal Word who became flesh, died on the cross for our sins, and arose from the dead for our justification (Rom. 4:25; 10:9–10). Through his incarnation and passion, the Word perfected and recapitulated our humanity so that we may approach God (Heb. 2:10, 14–18; Eph. 1:10).[6]

The preaching of the Word offers us faith and union with Christ by coming near our hearts and tongues through our ears (Rom. 10:8, 17). A person's positive answer to the proclaimed Word will save that person (v. 13). If we believe in Christ, we are brought into a saving relationship with God (John 3:16). Good theology presumes a person has made a faithful intellectual and heartfelt response to God's Word.

So, who is this Word? Finding the answer to the all-important question, "Who is the Word of God?" can be broken down into an examination of "God" on the one hand and of his "Word" on the other. To identify the reality of God and his Word, we must look to Scripture's witness to the Father and to the Son. In this first chapter, we must examine the identity of God as the Father. In the second, we shall develop our theology of the Father and his work. In the third chapter, we take up our primary aim in this book, glorifying the eternal Word.[7]

---

5. For further discussion about these two necessary aspects of divine revelation—the personal and the propositional—see David S. Dockery and Malcolm B. Yarnell III, *Special Revelation and Scripture*, Theology for the People of God (B&H Academic, 2024), 25–41.

6. *Recapitulation* is a somewhat literal translation of the Greek *anakephalaiosasthai* used in Ephesians 1:10. It indicates a summing up again, a reconstruction, or a reconstitution. This theme shall be developed further in the last chapter of this book.

7. Of course, we glorify the Son, not exclusive of the Father and the Spirit. Rather, we glorify the Father with the Son with the Holy Spirit, for he is one God in three Persons.

He Is "God"

To understand what we mean when we say, "God the Father," we must examine who God is and who the Father is. After identifying "God" and designating "the Father," we must consider the various relationships that the term "Father" indicates when it is applied to God. First, we note that the Father is God.

The Mystery and Revelation of God

We can learn much about God and the proper attitude we should have toward him through the experience of a man in the Ancient Near East. The patriarch Job suffered so severely from God's permissive providence that he and his friends wondered why these tragedies fell upon him. After Job found the answers offered by his friends unhelpful, he pressed the matter in his prayer to God: "Let the Almighty answer me" (Job 31:35b).

The Lord's response to Job's demanding prayer overwhelmed that man with the knowledge of how great and powerful God is. Job learned how small and utterly dependent human creatures are.

> Then the Lord answered Job from the whirlwind. He said: "Who is this who obscures my counsel with ignorant words? Get ready to answer me like a man; when I question you, you will inform me. Where were you when I established the earth? Tell me, if you have understanding." (38:1–4)

The questions which the Lord shot back to Job reminded the man that he was dealing with One who remains beyond his capability to comprehend. At this point, the patriarch rightly humbled himself before God.

> Then Job replied to the Lord: "I know that you can do anything and no plan of yours can be thwarted. You asked, 'Who is this who conceals my counsel with ignorance?' Surely I spoke about things I did not understand, things too wondrous for me to know. You said, 'Listen now, and I will speak. When I question you, you will inform me.' I had heard reports about you, but now my eyes

> have seen you. Therefore, I reject my words and am sorry for them; I am dust and ashes." (42:1–6)

We learned in the previous volume that we must be very careful never to speak of God apart from God's revelation of himself. Job learned this lesson, as did his friends (42:7–9). Among his unwise friends, only Elihu seemed to exercise some restraint in his speeches about God. Elihu confessed, "The Almighty—we cannot reach him—he is exalted" (37:23a). A little later, Elihu reminded the assembled men that God gives no ground to presumptuous people. "He does not look favorably on any who are wise in heart" (v. 24b).

The only possible answer to the question, "Who is God?" is this: "God is who he reveals himself to be." We must remain humble and continually recall our entire dependence upon God's grace of self-revelation as we consider answering the ultimate question of divine reality.

Moreover, we ought never distort the revelation of God's reality, neither by adding to his Word nor by subtracting from his Word. Those things which God reveals about himself we must affirm wholeheartedly; those things which he does not unveil must remain a mystery to us. Human speech about God must be humbly dependent, wisely circumspect, and joyfully worshipful.[8] Thankfully, God chose to reveal himself, so that we can know definite truths about him. God the Father discloses himself in his Word and by his Spirit.

God the Trinity

So, then, who is God? Jesus provided the most complete answer in the Great Commission he gave to his church. The one true God must be named in the initial Christian confession of baptism, "the Father and of the Son and of the Holy Spirit" (Matt. 28:19). Paul repeated this truth in his confessional prayer at the end of his second letter to the church of Corinth: "The grace of the Lord Jesus Christ, and the love of God, and the fellowship of the Holy Spirit be with you all" (2 Cor. 13:13). In other words, both Christ and his apostle command us to confess God is Trinity.[9]

---

8. On the origin and limitations of theological language, see Yarnell, "Systematic Theology," 261–64, 268–70.

9. For a theological exegesis of these biblical confessions of the Trinity, see Malcolm B. Yarnell III, *God the Trinity: Biblical Portraits* (B&H Academic, 2016), 1–56.

First, we must learn to confess that the one Lord God is the Father. Most scholars agree that when *theos* is used in the New Testament, the term typically refers to the Father. Karl Rahner concluded from his studies of the use of *theos* in the New Testament that the term does not merely sometimes indicate the Father. Rather, the New Testament use of *ho theos* "signifies the First Person of the Trinity" without exception.[10] "God," therefore, always refers to the Father.

However, *theos* also encloses the identity of the Son and the Holy Spirit with the Father. Diminishing the identification of God as Father is improper. To diminish him is to pervert the truth of the Trinity. Rahner restated a classic theological distinction from this profound reality: On the one hand, "the word and concept 'God' signifies the Person to whom the divine nature is proper." On the other hand, "'God' can stand for each of the three Persons who possess this nature, or again 'God' can stand for all three Persons together."[11]

In the second place, therefore, we must affirm that the Son, too, is the one Lord God. At the high point of the Gospel of John's witness to the deity of Christ, the apostle Thomas responded to Jesus with the greatest confession about the deity of the Son. After he saw Jesus truly was the resurrected Son of God, this previously doubtful disciple proclaimed in deep reverence, "My Lord [*kurios*] and my God [*theos*]" (John 20:28).

As we shall see, this remains a necessary confession for every orthodox Christian regarding Jesus Christ. Jesus Christ, the eternal Word, the Son, is both "Lord" and "God." With those who fostered the Nicene Creed, orthodox Christians have learned to confess the Father possesses the divine nature "unoriginately," while the Son possesses the same nature "by eternal generation."[12] Orthodox Trinitarianism requires affirmation of the eternal relations of origin.

Thirdly, the Holy Spirit is likewise the Lord God. In the Old Testament, "the Spirit of the Lord" often acts with power. The apostle Paul states rather directly, "the Lord [*kurios*] is the Spirit [*pneuma*]" (2 Cor. 3:17). Similarly, according to the apostle Peter, to sin against "the Holy Spirit [*to pneuma to hagion*]" is to sin against "God [*theos*]" (Acts 5:3–4).

---

10. Karl Rahner, *Theological Investigations*, vol. 1, *God, Christ, Mary and Grace*, transl. Cornelius Ernst (Helicon Press, 1961), 126–27.

11. Rahner, *Theological Investigations*, 1:126.

12. Rahner, *Theological Investigations*, 1:146.

To summarize the necessary confession of the eternal relations of origin, we must learn to say three things: the Father is the Lord God without origination; the Son is the Lord God by eternal generation; and the Holy Spirit is the Lord God by eternal "spiration" or "procession" (cf. John 1:14, 18; 15:26).[13] Having rehearsed these indispensable truths about the Trinity, we must now further explore the truth that God is the Father.

He Is "the Father"

Scholars variously use terms like "theology proper" or more rarely "patrology" to describe the doctrine of God the Father.[14] When we speak of "theology proper," we may either be referring to God in his nature, which is entirely and equally the possession of all three divine Persons, or we may be referring with more particularity to God as Father in his Person. As with every linguistic claim, context determines meaning.

In the previous volume, we learned to correlate God's ontological or immanent perspective with our economic or functional perspective.[15] By "ontology" or "immanence," we refer to the reality of God in his own eternal being. By "economy" or "function," we refer to God's actions toward his creatures. In academic contexts, ontology is often used to describe the reality of something, while economy is used to describe how something works. When these terms are applied to God, the first set of terms considers who God is, while the second set considers what God does.

The divine economy, it will be remembered, includes God's great works of creation, revelation, redemption, and consummation. Moreover, God himself is "pure act," so the distinction between divine economy and divine ontology is human shorthand intended

---

13. Rahner, *Theological Investigations*, 1:146. Most scholars now disagree with Rahner regarding the so-called de Régnon thesis, which posits a significant difference between the emphases of the Cappadocians and Augustine (Rahner, *Theological Investigations*, 1:146–47).

14. "Patrology" also indicates the study of the early church fathers. Johannes Quasten, *Patrology*, 4 vols. (reprint, Christian Classics, 1983–1986). "Theology proper" includes the perfections or attributes of God, which were introduced in the first volume of Theology for Every Person.

15. Malcolm B. Yarnell III, *God*, vol. 1, Theology for Every Person (B&H Publishing, 2024), 90–91.

to help our limited minds comprehend God better. The distinction between ontology and economy should never be used to posit any partition or division in God's eternal reality.[16]

When we talk about the "immanent Trinity," we address God's one eternal nature and the internal relations of the three Persons. When we talk about the "economic Trinity," we address God's grace toward his creatures. The economic Trinity reveals the immanent Trinity truly if not exhaustively.[17]

Knowing the Father Immanently

We would be wise to learn, first, to say certain things about the Father from the perspective of the immanent Trinity. Within the Triune Godhead, the Father is the eternal and never-ending source of the Son (John 13:3) and of the Holy Spirit. Through the eternal generation of the Son (1:18) and the eternal procession of the Spirit (15:26), the Father is wholly and undividedly One with the Son and with the Holy Spirit. The Father's eternal generation of the Son, and the eternal procession of the Spirit, are known as "the eternal relations of origin."

The Trinitarian doctrine of the eternal relations of origin verifies that the entirety of the one Godhead is shared simply, or equally and indivisibly and eternally, by the three Persons. These truths were revealed by the Lord himself. First, Jesus proclaimed, without any further qualification, "Everything the Father has is mine" (16:15a), thereby explaining what he meant when he said, "I and the Father are one" (10:30). Second, Jesus taught that the Holy Spirit also participates with full sovereignty in the perfection of God (16:15b).

From such revelation about the exalted nature of the Three as One, we should be concerned never to diminish nor to distort the divine being. Nor should we ever diminish any of the three Persons. The unity of the divine nature includes the truth that God has one divine will and one divine authority. Early orthodox theologians thereby confessed the true deity of God with the Father's eternal

16. Scholastic theologians spoke of God as "pure act," indicating there is no unrealized potential in God. Thomas Aquinas, *Summa Contra Gentiles*, Book One, God, transl. Anton C. Pegis (University of Notre Dame Press, 2000), 100–101. God's essence ought not be diminished by us, and his actions ought not be divided from his being.

17. Yarnell, *God the Trinity*, 173–74.

generation of the Son and eternal procession of the Holy Spirit. The Son possesses "the entire fullness of God's nature" with the Father, although "bodily" by virtue of the economy of his incarnation (Col. 2:9), as does the Holy Spirit (Acts 5:3–4).

Knowing the Father Economically

Second, we should also learn to say certain things about the Father from the perspective of the economic Trinity. The economic Trinity concerns how God works. According to Jesus and to his brother, the apostle James, the Father is the source of all created goodness or blessedness (Luke 18:19; James 1:17). Divine blessedness indicates all God's works are good, right, and proper.

The works of the Father include all the works of God. God the Father is involved in the great divine works of creation, redemption, and the final consummation. Of course, the Son and the Holy Spirit are invariably involved in each of these divine works, too. God the Father also works inseparably with the Son and the Holy Spirit in providence and revelation. The unity of the three Persons in one essence is mirrored in the triunity of God's work. Let us now dig deeper into Scripture's witness to the ontological and economic blessedness of God the Father.

The Biblical Revelation of the Father

Scripture reveals God is Father. The Old Testament emphasized how God was fatherly in his actions toward his people. The New Testament brings clarity to the doctrine of God the Father by showing that he is Father in a unique way to his only Son and that he eternally relates to the Son by generation and the Holy Spirit by procession. Moreover, God the Father has a twofold paternity, one by nature or directly within the Godhead, and one by grace or derivatively toward creation.[18] Regarding the latter, Scripture affirms that God is fatherly in general toward his human creatures, and that he becomes Father to the redeemed through faith in his Son.

---

18. Gilles Emery, *The Trinitarian Theology of St. Thomas Aquinas* (Oxford University Press, 2007), 160–61.

The Old Testament Revelation of the Father

In the Old Testament, Yahweh is fatherly in his actions toward his own people. He creates his human children (Deut. 32:6; Mal. 2:10). He loves his children passionately (Ps. 103:13) and knows his children intimately (Jer. 31:9). He provides for his children (Deut. 1:31) and protects his children (Exod. 4:22–23; Ps. 68:5). He expects loyalty from his children (Jer. 3:19), so he disciplines them when they fail (Deut. 8:5). He also offers redemption to his sinful children (Isa. 63:16; Hosea 1:10). In the Old Testament, the Lord acts in a fatherly way toward his creatures. He not only produces his children; he loves them intimately, providing for them and protecting them, disciplining them and redeeming them.

In the Old Testament, the Messiah is also revealed as "Father." The Messiah is, furthermore, named "Mighty" and "Eternal" as well as "Prince," even "God" (Isa. 9:6). The Old Testament thus locates the Messiah with "God" as "Father." While some may wish to drive a wedge between the divine Father and his Son to preserve both Persons, such texts deny any such division. Thomas Aquinas thus argued that when we speak of internal divine relations, "Father" means the first Person. However, "When we use the name 'Father' to signify God's relation to the world, this word actually indicates the whole Trinity."[19] The Messiah thus told Philip, "The one who has seen me has seen the Father" (John 14:9b). And Hebrews thus treats the people of God both as Christ's "children" and as his "brothers and sisters" (Heb. 2:12–17; cf. Isa. 8:18 LXX).[20]

To describe God as fatherly also points to his omnipotence. Ancient Near Eastern rulers were often referred to as fathers. Isaiah's prophecy that the Messiah would be named "Eternal" and "Father" points not only to the Messiah's own participation in the Father's reality but also to his divine right to rule.[21] The prophet Daniel was likewise given a revelation of the "everlasting dominion" of the Son with "the Ancient of Days." The title "Ancient of Days" alternated

---

19. Emery, *The Trinitarian Theology of St. Thomas Aquinas*, 164. In other words, from our creaturely perspective, to contemplate God as "Father" or "fatherly" is to contemplate the Three, but within the Godhead, the Father generates the Son while the Spirit proceeds. The operations of the Three are, moreover, inseparable.

20. The people of God are the children of Christ by virtue of his divine works of creation and redemption, the brothers and sisters of Christ by virtue of their union with his humanity.

21. John N. Oswalt, *The Book of Isaiah, Chapters 1–39* (Eerdmans, 1986), 247.

with "Most High" (Dan. 7:18–27) to identify the inhabitant of the divine throne as Yahweh.[22] The Messiah, named "Son of Man," rules with the Ancient of Days, from the eternal throne, hereby indicating his entire participation in divine authority (vv. 13–14).

Subsequently, in the New Testament, God was definitively named "Father." This name for God, particularly for the first Person, was first revealed to us by Jesus Christ, the second Person, who came in flesh and assumed our human nature. In the New Testament, God the Father is also described according to three different relationships: He is the Father in a unique way to his only begotten Son; he is fatherly in a general way to all human beings; and he is fatherly in a narrower way to Christians.

He Is Uniquely Father to His Begotten Son

God is *uniquely* Father, by way of eternal generation, to his only begotten Son, Jesus Christ. The Father revealed Jesus was his "beloved Son" (Matt. 3:17; 17:5; 2 Pet. 1:17). In return, "'Father' was the most frequent way in which Jesus directly addressed God."[23] Christ's relationship with the Father was unique, for he addressed him in prayer as "my Father" (Matt. 26:39, 42) and in the very intimate form of "Abba" (Mark 14:36).[24] The Son's relationship with the Father is so unique that knowledge of the Father is simply unavailable to those who do not know Jesus (John 8:19).

The Gospel of Mark distinguishes Jesus, who is God's "beloved son," from the prophets, who are merely God's "servants" (Mark 12:1–12; 13:32). "This clearly implies Jesus' superiority to the prophets who came before him and therefore his unique identity as God's Son."[25] From the perspective of salvation, the only way for human beings to come to the Father is through his Son (John 14:6; Acts 4:12).

The Gospel of John declares its purpose is propagating faith in Jesus as "the Messiah, the Son of God" (John 20:31). It reveals

---

22. Roland K. Harrison, "Ancient of Days," in G. W. Bromiley, *International Standard Bible Encyclopedia*, rev. ed., vol. 1 (Eerdmans, 1979), 122.

23. Adam Winn, "Son of God," in Joel B. Green, Jeannine K. Brown, and Nicholas Perrin, eds., *Dictionary of Jesus and the Gospels,* 2nd ed. (IVP Academic, 2013), 888.

24. Jesus was the first to use such a title of "familiarity" in prayer to God. Joachim Jeremias, *The Prayers of Jesus*, transl. John Bowden, Christoph Burchard, and John Reumann (Fortress Press, 1967), 62.

25. Winn, "Son of God," 890.

that the Father and the Son comprehend one another with a knowledge shared only by the Holy Spirit (10:15; 11:25; 16:14, 30; 17:25; 21:17). The Father shares his whole being and activity with the Son (16:15). Their relationship of knowledge is, moreover, grounded in a unity of being: "I and the Father are one" (10:30).

John reveals the unity of being between the two Persons in numerous ways: The Father and the Son have the same name (17:11; 18:5–9), the same will (14:13–14), the same love (14:21, 23; 15:9), and the same glory (11:4; 13:31–32; 17:5). The Father and the Son also have the same authority (16:23; 17:20; 19:11), the same truth (14:6; 17:17, 19), and the same words (8:38; 12:49–50; 14:10). The Father and the Son work the same works (5:19; 9:3–4; 14:31), give the same revelation (7:16–17; 8:18), and exercise the same judgment (5:22, 30; 8:16). The Father and the Son together send the Holy Spirit (14:26; 15:26; 20:22)—God sending God.

The only distinction between God the Father and the Son is the latter's personal and eternal generation by the former (John 1:18; 3:16). The Son, moreover, alone among the Three assumes our humanity (1:14; 17:4). These two distinctions, personal generation and human assumption, never separate the Father from the Son. The divine Persons always remain "in" one another (14:10–11, 20; 17:23).

The divine unity of the Father with the Son requires men both to confess the Son is "Lord" and "God," and to worship the Son with the Father (John 9:38; 12:26; 20:28). Jesus taught his disciples both to pray to the Father "in my name," and to pray to himself as the Son (14:13–14). Positively, to know the Son is to know his Father (8:19; 16:3). Negatively, to reject the Son is to reject God. Properly honoring the deity of the Son determines one's eternal destiny: "The Father, in fact, judges no one but has given all judgment to the Son, so that all people may honor the Son just as they honor the Father. Anyone who does not honor the Son does not honor the Father who sent him" (5:22–23).

The Son's divine generation requires us to affirm the unity of the divine nature of the Father and the Son, even as it distinguishes the divine Persons from one another (John 1:1, 14; 3:16–18; Heb. 1:5). Scripture also leads us to confess the unity of the Person of Christ in two natures: As "God the only Son," Christ possesses the deity of the Father (John 1:18), and as a human being, Christ depends on the Father (Matt. 26:39–42; Luke 23:46).

"Fount of the Godhead"

Orthodox theologians have long recognized God the Father is the "fount of the godhead," to use a catchphrase from the early church.[26] This phrase summarizes the biblical descriptions of God the Father as eternally generative of the personal relations of the eternal Trinity. In the Old Testament, God personally described himself as "the fountain of living water" (Jer. 2:13). In the New Testament, Jesus taught that the Father, who is the principle of life, gives that same principle to his Son (John 5:21), a principle that the Holy Spirit also possesses (6:63).

God is eternally One, and the Person of the Father eternally, immanently, and personally generates the Person of the Son. Moreover, the Holy Spirit eternally, immanently, and personally proceeds from the Father (15:26). Western theologians confess that the Spirit also proceeds from the Son. God, the Father and the Son and the Holy Spirit, uniquely possesses the principle of life by nature. Therefore, from God the Trinity, who is the Father and the Son and the Spirit, both our created lives and our resurrected lives derive by grace.

Reflecting the influence of the classical Christian theological interpretation of Scripture upon his own exegesis, the eighteenth-century Baptist theologian John Gill also affirmed the doctrine of God's eternal relations of origin. Gill began his discussion of the divine personal relations thus: "Since there are Three who are the one God; and these Three are not one and the same Person, but three different Persons, there must be something which distinguishes them from each other; and the distinction between them is not merely *nominal* [but] *real* and *personal*."[27]

Gill showed from Scripture that the distinctions between the Persons are "eternal and immutable" and do not "depend on any works done by them." The divine personal relations are not an act of the divine will but necessarily express his divine nature. The eternal relations also establish that the Three fully share one nature.[28] These

26. Widdecombe, *The Fatherhood of God from Origen to Athanasius*, 5.

27. John Gill, *A Body of Doctrinal Divinity; Or a System of Evangelical Truths, Deduced from the Sacred Scriptures*, new ed. (London, 1839; reprint, Paris: The Baptist Standard Bearer, n.d.), 140–41.

28. Gill, *A Body of Doctrinal Divinity*, 141–42.

"personal relations, or distinctive relative properties" alone distinguish the Persons from one another.[29]

Gill says "paternity" is the distinctive personal relation of the first Person, while "filiation" belongs to the second Person, and "spiration" to the third Person. In plain English, the eternal relation of "begetting" belongs to the Father alone. That the Father generates or begets the Son distinguishes him from both the Son and the Spirit. Divine generation "gives him, with great propriety, the name of Father."[30]

The Father's generation of the Son derives not only from the New Testament, as we shall see, but also the Old. Alluding to the Second Person, wisdom literature reveals that "Wisdom" was "born" or "given birth" before creation (Prov. 8:24–26).[31] Speaking from eternity in a royal psalm, God said he had "begotten" "my Son" (Ps. 2:7 KJV; cf. Heb. 1:5).[32] Moreover, the prophet Micah revealed the Messiah's human generation was of "Bethlehem" in "Judah," while his divine generation was "from everlasting" (Hebrew *'olam*; Micah 5:2 KJV).[33]

The heavenly doctrine of the Father's generation of the Son must be detached from earthly or physical conceptions of begetting. The biblical revelation of the Father's generation teaches that Christ is "a distinct divine person in the Godhead," "the true and natural Son of God, begotten in the divine essence by the Father," and "in a way and manner not to be comprehended or conceived of by us."[34] It is "a great mystery of godliness" above our ability to conceive.[35]

---

29. Gill, *A Body of Doctrinal Divinity*, 142.

30. Gill, *A Body of Doctrinal Divinity*, 142.

31. These verses contain "five determinations" that "wisdom preexisted the cosmos." Bruce K. Waltke, *The Book of Proverbs, Chapters 1–15* (Eerdmans, 2004), 412.

32. Nancy de Claissé-Walford, Rolf A. Jacobson, Beth LaNeel Tanner, *The Book of Psalms* (Eerdmans, 2014), 69.

33. Calvin says the plural "goings forth" elides with a singular meaning, denies the Rabbis' creation of the Messiah according to an eternal decree, and affirms eternal generation. John Calvin, *Commentaries on the Twelve Minor Prophets*, transl. John Owen, 3 vols. (reprint, Baker, 1996), 3: 299–300. This older reading of eternity proper is disputed, although not necessarily as a denial of eternal generation itself. C. F. Keil and F. Delitzsch, *Commentary on the Old Testament*, transl. James Martin, 10 vols. (reprint, Eerdmans, 1984), 10: 479–81.

34. John Gill, *The Doctrine of the Trinity Stated and Vindicated* (London, 1731; reprint, Fareham, UK: Bierton Particular Baptists, n.d.), 102.

35. Gill, *The Doctrine of the Trinity Stated and Vindicated*, 105.

The Father guarantees the entire participation of Christ in deity by nature with eternal generation.[36]

The unique and eternal paternal–filial relation of the Father to the Son prompted New Testament Christians to worship the Trinity. One recent study found that the first disciples "gathered in Jesus' name for worship, prayed to him and sang hymns to him, regarded him as exalted to a position of heavenly rule above all angelic orders, appropriated to him titles and Old Testament passages originally referring to God, sought to bring fellow Jews as well as Gentiles to embrace him as the divinely appointed redeemer, and in general redefined their devotion to the God of their fathers so as to include veneration of Jesus."[37]

The apostles both prayed to the Father through the Son and prayed to the Son together with the Father.[38] They explicitly worshiped the Son and the Holy Spirit with the Father in baptism at the command of the Son (Matt. 28:19) and in prayer as inspired by the Holy Spirit (2 Cor. 13:13, rendered as 13:14 in many other translations). The first Christians worshiped the one and only God, who is the Father with his Son and with the Holy Spirit, at the command of Christ and led by the Spirit. And so must we!

The Relationship of God the Father to Humanity

God the Father relates immanently and, therefore, eternally and immutably, *by nature*, with his only begotten Son and with his proceeding Holy Spirit, as we have seen. However, Scripture also teaches that God the Father acts in paternal ways, *by grace*, toward those whom he made in his image. God is the Father to all human beings in general as a result of his creative love. But God is Father to those who believe in his Son as a result of his redemptive love.

---

36. Gill, *A Body of Doctrinal Divinity*, 144.

37. Larry W. Hurtado, *One God, One Lord: Early Christian Devotion and Ancient Jewish Monotheism*, 2nd ed. (T&T Clark, 1998), 11.

38. Josef A. Jungmann, *The Place of Christ in Liturgical Prayer*, transl. A. Peeler (The Liturgical Press, 1989), 127–40.

He Is the Father of All Human Beings

A creative set of paternal–filial relations with God was disclosed in the New Testament.[39] Unlike the eternal relations of origin wherein the Father and the Son and the Holy Spirit have the same nature, this set of relations is a created grace. Another way to say this is that while Christ is *uniquely* the Son of God the Father, God is also *generally* "the Father" of all human creatures. Where God is eternally and immanently the Father of the Son by divine nature, God is the creaturely Father of all human beings by his divine economy of grace.

The fatherhood of God, because it is grounded in the activity of creation, includes all human beings. Angelic creatures are also sometimes described as "sons of God" (Job 1:6; 2:1).[40] Scripture indicates that God's paternity to his rebellious human children continued even after we began pursuing our own evil desires (Matt. 5:45; Luke 15:11–32). Paul favorably cited Aratus, one of the Greek poets, who said of God, "For we also are his offspring" (Acts 17:28–29). Paul seems to have meant by this that every human being is created by God "in his own image."[41]

God reveals himself to all human beings as their loving caregiver (Acts 14:15–17). And all human beings are required to render exclusive worship to God for his possession of deity, for his creation of humanity, and for his paternal care for humanity (Acts 14:15; 17:22–23, 30–31; Rom. 1:25). These passages indicate that God is fatherly toward all human beings *by way of creation*. He is also fatherly, although in a different manner, to some human beings *by way of redemption*.

---

39. *Filial* means "relating as a son." It can describe relationships that are similar in some way to the direct Father–Son relation.

40. Aquinas notes God is also Father to creatures even if they have "reason only of a trace," based on Job 38:28. St. Thomas Aquinas, *Summa Theologica*, vol. 1, transl. Fathers of the English Dominican Province (Christian Classics, 1981), 175. The options proposed for the identity of "the sons of God" in Genesis 6:2 include angels, kings, sons of Seth, and sons of Cain. "Suffice it to say, it is impossible to be dogmatic about the identification of 'sons of God' here." Victor P. Hamilton, *The Book of Genesis, Chapters 1–17* (Eerdmans, 1990), 262–65.

41. F. F. Bruce, *The Book of the Acts*, rev. ed. (Eerdmans, 1988), 339–40.

He Is the Father of the Redeemed

In another distinct set of paternal–filial relations, God is *more narrowly* identified as "our Father" in reference to Christ's personal disciples (Matt. 6:9). This more restricted group of human beings have been "adopted" into sonship by God the Father through faith in the Son, a grace applied by the Holy Spirit (John 1:12–13; Gal. 4:5–6; Rom. 8:14–17).

The Lord Jesus Christ is the only human Mediator between God and humanity (1 Tim. 2:5). Only he can share the benefits of his unique relationship to God the Father, and he shares this relationship with believing human beings (Matt. 10:32–33; John 8:42; 14:21, 23). As Lord, Christ grants "mercy" to those who believe (Matt. 9:27–29; 15:21–28; 17:14–18). As the only Son of God, who came from and returns to his Father, he prays to the Father for those who believe in him and the truth about him (John 17).

Through the justifying and sanctifying work of the Son and the Spirit, "all" believers are said to "have one Father" (Heb. 2:11). This adoptive sonship brings great privileges, including access to the throne of God (Heb. 4:16; Rev. 3:21) and co-heirship with Christ (Rom. 8:17; Gal. 3:29). The disciples of Jesus may now address God as "our Father," but only through their union with the Son (Matt. 6:9; John 16:26). The redeemed may even pray to the Father with the intimate name, "Abba," through union with Christ (Rom. 8:15; Gal. 4:6).[42]

The eternal Son's relationship with "my Father" remains eternally and ontologically different than the disciple's adoptive relationship with "your Father" (John 20:17). Moreover, just as the Father and the Son are one, so the disciples of Christ must be one (17:11, 22). Christian unity with both God, primarily, and with one another, derivatively, is possible only because Christ is the only one who is simultaneously "in" the redeemed and "in" God (17:23). He is in the redeemed as the perfect human being and in God as the divine Son.

In summary, God the Father works in paternal love toward all those whom he created in his image. And God the Father works in paternal love toward those whom he redeems through faith in his Son by the regeneration of his Holy Spirit. The creative fatherly work of God and the redemptive fatherly work of God involve the Son and the Holy Spirit as well as the Father, as noted above.

---

42. "In this way, Jesus gave them a share in his relationship with God." Jeremias, *The Prayers of Jesus*, 63.

Conclusion

Clive Staples Lewis was shocked by the beauty and profundity of God's fatherhood. First, he noted that being begotten and being created are radically different movements. "To beget is to become the father of; to create is to make." In eternity, "Christ is begotten, not created." This locates the Son with God rather than creation. "What God begets is God."[43] The Son is, therefore, God of God. The Son is eternally one with the Father, and God is not the Father apart from the Son.[44]

Second, even before a human being can be united with Christ by faith, "in a certain sense, no doubt we are sons of God already. God has brought us into existence and loves us and looks after us, and in that way is like a father."[45] Lewis hereby confirms God acts in a fatherly way toward his creatures, in both his creation of them and in his continuing provision for them.

Third, in a redemptive sense, "by attaching ourselves to Christ, we can 'become Sons of God.'" This is, moreover, "the point in Christianity."[46] God the Father wills human salvation through faith in his only begotten Son. The fourth Gospel promises, "But to all who did receive him, he gave them the right to be children of God, to those who believe in his name, who were born not of natural descent, or of the will of flesh, or of the will of man, but of God" (John 1:12–13).

Believing in the teachings of the prophets and the apostles, early Christians recognized we cannot know God as our Father by our own natural devices. John of Damascus, the last of the early church fathers, and the great compiler of patristic theology, declared, "The divine is therefore ineffable and incomprehensible."[47] However, from the depth of his perfect blessedness God chose to reveal himself to us by grace.

From the teachings of holy Scripture, Christians have learned to confess their faith in "one Father, the principle and cause of all things, not begotten of anyone, who alone exists as uncaused and

---

43. C. S. Lewis, *Mere Christianity* (HarperCollins, 2000), 156–57.

44. Lewis, *Mere Christianity*, 166–67, 172–73.

45. Lewis, *Mere Christianity*, 156–57.

46. Lewis, *Mere Christianity*, 156.

47. John of Damascus, *On the Orthodox Faith: Greek Critical Text and English Translation*, transl. Norman Russell (St. Vladimir's Seminary Press, 2022), 59.

unbegotten, the maker of all things, and by nature Father of his one and single only begotten Son, our Lord and God and Savior Jesus Christ, and originator of the all-holy Spirit."[48]

So, as you ponder the reality and activity of God as Father, Father in his unique divine Person within the Godhead, and Father in his triune identity toward his creation, may you see that he is the one true God. May you embrace the truth that he is our holy and almighty Creator, the fount of all goodness. And may you know with certainty the blessed comfort of salvation which comes from our heavenly Father through faith in his only begotten Son and regeneration by his Holy Spirit.

Let us follow the apostle Paul's lead and praise the Father: "Blessed be the God and Father of our Lord Jesus Christ, the Father of mercies and the God of all comfort" (2 Cor. 1:3). Let us praise the Father with our whole being due to his sovereign, righteous, and enduring love for us. Those who want to be redeemed come to the Father by the grace of the Spirit alone through faith alone in the only Christ and only true Mediator, Jesus of Nazareth, the eternal Word of God. The Father sent his Son to become a human being, to die on the cross for our sins, and to arise from the dead for our justification (Rom. 4:25).

An old Swedish hymn may help you express praise to the Father for his blessings. While you worship God the Father, remember also that we are made in his image. As he is the Blessed One, the source of all goodness, so may we be channels of mercy and comfort to his children.[49]

Children of the heavenly Father
Safely in His bosom gather;
Nestling bird nor star in heaven
Such a refuge e'er was given.

God His own doth tend and nourish;
In His holy courts they flourish.
From all evil things He spares them;
In His mighty arms He bears them.

---

48. John of Damascus, *On the Orthodox Faith*, 72.

49. David and Amanda Erickson, *The Flourishing Family: A Jesus-Centered Guide to Parenting with Peace and Purpose* (Tyndale, 2024).

Neither life nor death shall ever
From the Lord His children sever;
Unto them His grace He showeth,
And their sorrows all He knoweth.

Though He giveth or He taketh,
God His children ne'er forsaketh;
His the loving purpose solely
To preserve them pure and holy.[50]

Study Questions

1. What is the relationship of God the Father in the eternal Trinity? Describe both his being and his personal relations.

2. In the Old Testament, how is God described as being fatherly toward his creatures? In the New Testament, how is God described as being fatherly toward the redeemed?

3. Is God the Son also described as the Father? How is God the Son fatherly to human beings?

Suggested Resources

- John Gill, *The Doctrine of the Trinity Stated and Vindicated*
- C. S. Lewis, *Mere Christianity*
- David S. Dockery, ed., *Theology, Church, and Ministry*

50. Caroline V. Sandell-Berg, "Children of the Heavenly Father," transl. Ernst W. Olson, in Wesley L. Forbis, ed., *The Baptist Hymnal* (Convention Press, 1991), 55.

CHAPTER TWO

Who Is He to You?

IN THE LAST CHAPTER, WE learned the ways in which Scripture describes "God" as "Father." We discovered that God is Father, primarily and uniquely, through the eternal generation of his only Son. Second, he is also fatherly through the graces of creation and providence toward his creatures, especially human beings. Third, we learned he is fatherly in a special redemptive way to those who believe in his only begotten Son.

In this chapter, we will consider both how the revelation of the Father has been understood and how he should be understood. First, respecting the contributions of other believers, we review the reception of the Father in the history of the church. Second, we survey recent debates over divine fatherhood. Third, we begin crafting a doctrine of God as Father. Finally, we will confess together, "one God the Father Almighty, Creator of heaven and earth."

The question driving this discussion can be stated personally: "Who is God the Father to you?" This is simultaneously a personal question and a communal question, for God has revealed himself as Father to all believers; indeed, to all creatures in some sense.

The Father in Christian History

Christian reflection upon the truth about God the Father developed through the centuries from being primarily concerned with both his nature and his work to becoming primarily concerned with his work. The early church explored how we should think of the Father's reality and work, but the modern church restricted its study to his economy. With this restricted outlook, the gains previously made in patristic theological exegesis of Scripture were often forgotten.

Especially harmful have been the modern denials that we might receive knowledge of God with any certainty. These denials about human access to divine reality, which have influenced both liberals and conservatives in the West, were soon followed by heated arguments over the relationship of the divine Father to human gender. These arguments have sometimes detracted from the blessing of divine fatherhood.

For centuries, the church has contended with various heresies and errors regarding God the Father. Paying attention to ancient errors and modern debates becomes necessary so that we can help our churches craft appropriate and helpful responses to gross overstatements emanating from various camps. Restoring to the church its knowledge that God is eternally Father, who looks at us with love and concern, seems particularly important in today's harsh environment, wherein fatherly abuse and filial neglect has become rampant.

The Foundational Doctrine of God the Father

Among the early Christians, the church in Alexandria, a city established by Alexander the Great and now located in the modern nation of Egypt, developed the doctrine of God the Father. Origen, an Alexandrian theologian born in the second century of the church and martyred in its third, placed the Father at the center of his ruminations about God. Expositing Scripture, he learned God the Father is coextensive with the divine nature. Moreover, analogous to human generation, Origen taught that the Father generates the Person of the Son eternally. Finally, he said God created the world as Father, reveals himself to his human creatures as Father, and redeems believers in his Son as Father.

Origen derived his doctrine of salvation from Paul and John. Peter Widdecombe summarizes his theological soteriology in this way:

> We come to know God as Father through a step-by-step progression to the status of adopted sons

> and thus to a share in the eternal relationship of the Father and the Son. Origen portrays this progression as a spiritual pilgrimage from the condition of fear, servitude, and ignorance which characterizes the Lord–servant relationship to that of filial knowledge and love which characterizes the Father–Son relationship. This pilgrimage involves a corresponding development in our moral behaviour: as we become morally pure, we grow in our knowledge of Wisdom and in our degree of sonship.[1]

Through the influential ministry of Origen, early Christian theologians learned to teach that God is Father by nature, that he is Father in the generation of his coeternal Son, and that he is Father in the procession of his coeternal Spirit. God is eternally Father precisely in that he has an eternal Son, and the divine Persons are essentially inseparable. God is immanently, eternally, and relationally Father to his Son and his Spirit.

God also acts in a fatherly way, by means of grace rather than by eternal generation or by eternal procession, toward his creatures in creation, revelation, and redemption. "The Father–Son relation is the means by which creation is brought into being, and it is also both the means and the model for the subsequent restoration of that creation to the knowledge of God."[2]

These basic doctrines about God the Father, defined by Origen and disseminated from the ancient cosmopolitan city of Alexandria, were received as broadly true across the early church. However, one theologian, subsequently decried as the greatest heretic, denied the eternal generation of the Son. This man, known as the greatest of the heretics to appear in Christian history, thereby both dishonored Christ and endangered human salvation.

The Heresy of Arianism and the Athanasian Response

The greatest heresy in Christian history was formalized by Arius, a popular priest in fourth-century Alexandria. This heresiarch

---

1. Peter Widdecombe, *The Fatherhood of God from Origen to Athanasius* (Oxford University Press, 1992), 93.

2. Widdecombe, *The Fatherhood of God from Origen to Athanasius*, 63.

("leading heretic") set out to exalt God the Father, like theologians before and after him, but he exalted the Father at the atrocious price of dishonoring the Son.[3] Arius was trained in philosophy when Middle Platonism was ascendant. That pagan worldview portrayed God as an absolute distant Monad mediated by "a secondary 'divinity' who was, so to speak, the divine mind in action."[4] Arius similarly portrayed the Father as absolute and distant. He maintained God's otherness by subordinating the Son and the Holy Spirit.

The heresiarch described the Father as "the Superior" in his popular extended hymn, "Thalia,"[5] wherein he reformulated theology to make God into "a hierarchical Trinity."[6] He earlier described the Father as "one God, alone Ingenerate, alone Everlasting, alone Unbegun, alone True, alone having Immortality, alone Wise, alone Good, alone Sovereign."[7] Despite correction by his bishop, however, Arius doubled down on his view of the Father's superiority and the Son's inferiority. Arianism's base innovation was to impose a hierarchy upon God, denying the Father and the Son were "equal."[8]

Arius divided the Father from the Son by repeatedly subordinating the Son. Infamously, he claimed the Son's nature was different from the Father's nature, by means of his generation. He presumed generation and creation were identical movements. Arius used an important Greek philosophical term in an adverse way. He denied the Son was *homoousios*, of "the same nature," with the Father.[9] Among Arians, the Father's nature was deemed "unbegotten" in

---

3. Frances M. Young, *Nicaea to Chalcedon: A Guide to the Literature and Its Background*, 2nd ed. (SCM, 2000), 47.

4. Rowan Williams, "Athanasius and the Arian Crisis," in G. R. Evans, ed., *The First Christian Theologians: An Introduction to Theology in the Early Church* (Blackwell, 2004), 158. See also Rowan Williams, *Arius: Heresy and Tradition*, rev. ed. (Eerdmans, 2002).

5. The *Thalia* (Greek "Banquet") is available in fragments in the works of Athanasius of Alexandria. Cf. Athanasius, *De Synodis* 15, in Archibald Robertson, ed., *Select Writings and Letters of Athanasius, Bishop of Alexandria*, Nicene and Post-Nicene Fathers, 2nd series, vol. 4 (reprint, Hendrickson, 1994), 457–58; and Athanasius, *Against the Arians* 1.5, in Robertson, ed., *Select Writings and Letters of Athanasius*, 308–9. The text in *Against the Arians* is fragmentary and interspersed with opposition commentary.

6. Young, *Nicaea to Chalcedon*, 48.

7. Letter of Arius to Alexander of Alexandria, in Athanasius, *De Synodis* 16.

8. Arius, "Thalia," ll. 2, 9. See the modern translation of the *Thalia* in Williams, *Arius*, 101–3.

9. Arius, "Thalia," ll. 3, 9.

essence, while the Son's nature was deemed "begotten" in essence. Arius diminished the Son by ascribing a separate essence to him. This false teaching required an answer.

Athanasius, the formidable African champion of Christian orthodoxy, countered that generation and creation were two different movements—one being eternal, the other economic. First, God the Father beget his Son eternally. Second, God the Father and the Son created the world, establishing its temporal course.[10] Athanasius placed the Son on the divine side of the stark divide between Creator and creation through recalling Scripture's ascription of generation to God (cf. John 1:18; 3:16; Heb. 1:5–6). When a human being is begotten, he receives the fullness of human nature. Similarly, God shares all that he is by nature with the Son.[11]

Due to God's perfection, Athanasius argued the Father's begetting of the Son must not be circumscribed or reduced by crude reference to creaturely generation. Divine fatherhood must rather be considered according to divine perfection. God the Father beget eternally God the Son in the perfection of one divine nature. Moreover, God's perfect fatherhood is forever the standard of limited creaturely fatherhood, not vice versa. Human fatherhood is measured by God, "for of him 'is every fatherhood in heaven and earth named.'"[12]

Refusing correction, however, Arius continued to diminish the Son by ascribing to his preexistent person creaturely limitations. Arius certainly elevated the Son above creation, and he even allowed the Son to be named "God," but only with equivocation. For Arius, Christ was God but not "true God."[13] The heresiarch thoroughly subordinated the Son to the Father. For instance, he infused eternity with temporal qualities, arguing, "God was not eternally a father," and "the Son did not always exist."[14] Arius also ascribed change to the divine Son.[15] He went on to intrude a difference or "degree" in authority between the Father and the Son,[16] as well as to ascribe

---

10. Athanasius, *Against the Arians* 57–60.

11. Athanasius, *Against the Arians* 14.

12. Athanasius, *Against the Arians* 23; Eph. 3:15.

13. Williams, *Arius*, 101.

14. A modern translation of Athanasius's commentary on *Thalia* may be found in Williams, *Arius*, 100–1.

15. Williams, *Arius*, 100.

16. Arius, "Thalia," l. 15.

to the Trinity differences in "glory," "subsistence,"[17] existence, will,[18] "wisdom," and "understanding."[19]

In summary, Arius tried to elevate God the Father by diminishing the Son in essence and authority. However, subordinating the eternal Son in any way necessarily also diminishes the eternal Father.[20] Jesus warned the Jewish leaders that humanity cannot honor the Father by dishonoring the Son. The Father himself glorifies the Son, because the Son possesses the name and identity of the great "I am" (John 8:48–59; cf. 5:23; 17:4–5). In subsequent Christian history, the baleful influence of Arianism persisted. Arians and "Semi-Arians" continued to diminish Christ in diverse ways well into the fourth century, and even to this very day.[21]

The Christian Creeds

Arius divided the early church by rejecting the discipline of Alexander, the bishop of his church in Alexandria, and appealing to other bishops, so the Council of Nicaea gathered and rebuked his heresy in 325. However, the Arian myth of hierarchy continued to attract those seeking power over others, including emperors and their clerical ideologues alike.[22] During the middle decades of the fourth century, various groups sought ways to promote Arian ideas, while typically denying they were Arian.[23] Some affirmed Nicaea in name but continued to reduce the Son either by altering or ignoring Nicaea's central claim that the Son is "true God from true

---

17. Arius, "Thalia," ll. 16–17.

18. Arius, "Thalia," ll. 20–21.

19. Arius, "Thalia," ll. 23, 34.

20. Arius may not have recognized that in saying the Son was mutable, he necessarily concluded God is not eternally Father. He thereby surrendered the divine transcendence he sought to protect.

21. The history of the mid-fourth century attempts to correlate Arianism with orthodoxy are described in Athanasius, *De Synodis* 21–31. Cf. R. P. C. Hanson, *The Search for the Christian Doctrine of God: The Arian Controversies* (T&T Clark, 1988), 318–81.

22. The Emperor Constantius especially sought this. George Huntston Williams, "Christology and Church-State Relations in the Fourth Century," [two parts] *Church History* 20.3 (1951): 3–33, and 20.4 (1951): 3–26.

23. Williams, "Athanasius and the Arian Crisis," 162. This reluctance to admit one's Arian doctrines continues into the present. "Those who follow his theological tradition seldom or never quote him, and sometimes directly disavow connection with him." Hanson, *The Search for the Christian Doctrine of God*, xvii.

God," having substantial unity (Greek *homoousios*) with and unique personal generation (Greek *monogena* and *gennathenta*) from the Father. Others outright denied orthodox divine ontology or banned its consideration.[24]

The Nicene Creed reached its universally received form at the Council of Constantinople in 381. This brilliant dogmatic statement summarized the orthodox fathers' careful reading of Scripture. Nicene exegesis was refined in response to heretics like Arius of Alexandria and Marcellus of Ancyra, but Nicene theologians like Athanasius were demonstrating the deity of the Father and the Son and the Holy Spirit through biblical interpretation both before and after the rise of the Arian heresy.[25] The theological exegesis of the Cappadocians, who included Basil of Caesarea, Gregory of Nazianzus, and Gregory of Nyssa, solidified Trinitarian orthodoxy.

Both Athanasius and the Cappadocians powerfully defended the Nicene settlement, honoring God the Father by honoring his only begotten Son in primarily scriptural terms. The classical creeds of the ancient church, such as the Nicene Creed, the Apostles' Creed, and the Athanasian Creed, drew upon Scripture to confess the Trinity. They developed the triune structure of the Christian's first formal confession, made during baptism (Matt. 28:19). Because the Father came first in the baptismal confession, they highlighted his being and activity. First, they affirmed the Father is the one God. They also taught directly or by implication his unity with the Son and the Spirit even as he remains distinct by his generation of the Son and procession of the Spirit. They also described his perfection of power and his work as Creator.

The Apostles' Creed begins the first of its three articles with the confession, "I believe in God the Father, omnipotent, Creator

---

24. These groups offered alternative terms to distinguish the Father from the Son. Semi-Arians said the Son was *homoiousion* ("of like nature") with the Father. Arians opined he is *anomoios* ("dissimilar") to the Father, while others said he is merely *homoios* ("like") the Father. Constantius sought to ban all language of *ousia*, but this proved impossible. A substantial group of Semi-Arians ultimately recognized the need for Nicaea. Mark Delcagliano, "The Emergence of the Pro-Nicene Alliance," in Young Richard Kim, *The Cambridge Companion to the Council of Nicaea* (Cambridge University Press, 2021), 256–81.

25. Athanasius had previously developed a high Christological hermeneutic in *On the Incarnation*. His later *Against the Arians* merely sharpened his theological exegesis in correction of the heresy.

of heaven and earth."[26] The Nicene Creed provided a fuller statement, taking into account his creation of both the realm of the spiritual as well as the physical universe: "We believe in one God the Father Almighty, Maker of heaven and earth, of all things visible and invisible."

In 381, Nazianzus led the Council of Constantinople, which formalized the Nicene Creed. His famous *Theological Orations* disclose the orthodox theological conclusion about the reality of God the Father: The name "Father" identifies him as the source of the eternal divine relations. "'Father' designates neither the substance nor the activity, but the relationship, the manner of being, which holds good between the Father and the Son."[27] The truth of the eternal relations of origin thereafter became widely accepted.

While the truths which God revealed about himself required reception, defining divine reality apart from revelation required rebuke. Against those who presumed they could define the nature of God as "unbegotten," Gregory replied that humanity cannot know "what God is in his nature and essence." We simply know that God is.[28] Gregory also affirmed the Father's eternal generation of the Son without presuming to define that mystery. "God's begetting ought to have the tribute of our reverent silence. The important point is for you to learn that he has been begotten."[29]

Summarizing this universal orthodoxy as it was received in the West, the so-called Athanasian Creed[30] confessed the Father is "one person," who is "equal in glory" and "coeternal in majesty" with the Son and the Spirit. The "one Father," moreover, is "uncreated," "infinite," "eternal," and "omnipotent" with the Son and the Spirit. While he shares "deity" simply and entirely with the Son and the Spirit, the Father remains distinct in person. Drawing directly upon the language of the New Testament regarding the eternal relations, this creed affirms the Son is "begotten" of the Father, while the Spirit is "proceeding." "The Father is neither made nor created nor

---

26. For modern translations of the three ancient creeds, see Malcolm B. Yarnell III, *God the Trinity: Biblical Portraits* (B&H Academic, 2016), 240–43.

27. Gregory of Nazianzus, *On God and Christ: The Five Theological Orations and Two Letters to Cledonius*, transl. Frederick Williams and Lionel Wickham (St. Vladimir's Seminary Press, 2002), 84.

28. Nazianzus, *On God and Christ*, 49.

29. Nazianzus, *On God and Christ*, 76.

30. This creed can be traced to the early sixth century. J. N. D. Kelly, *The Athanasian Creed: Quicunque Vult* (Adam and Charles Black, 1964).

begotten."[31] Among the classic creeds, the Athanasian Creed provides a strong defense against the Arian heresy and its children and is therefore commended to the reader.

Medieval Orthodoxy

Prior to the severe diminishing of theological orthodoxy during and after the Enlightenment of the eighteenth century, the classic credal statements of the Great Tradition held sway for more than a millennium. During the medieval period, the biblical foundations and dogmatic implications of the creeds were repeatedly explored and affirmed as necessary for Christian proclamation. The writings of the last major theologian of the classical period, Augustine of Hippo, were carefully studied for their presentations of God, Christ, and the Spirit, as well as creation, humanity, and salvation.

One of Augustine's admirers was Peter Lombard (ca. 1095–1160), the bishop of Paris. Lombard's four books of *The Sentences* became "the standard theological textbook in the West. Only in the sixteenth century were they gradually replaced by Thomas Aquinas's *Summa theologicae*."[32] According to the Parisian theologian, the Father and the Son and the Holy Spirit possess equally and entirely every divine attribute and action. For instance, "none of these persons excels another in might." "The omnipotence which the Father has, the Son also took by being born and the Holy Spirit by proceeding."[33] In other words, the divine relations of origin—the eternal generation of the Son and the eternal procession of the Spirit—guarantee the unity of deity and the personal equality of the Three.

The greatest medieval theologian Thomas Aquinas, in his studies of God the Father, characterized divine paternity with five truths: First, God the Father has "affectivity and love" for his eternal Son by nature and for their creatures by grace. Second, God and his Son share mutual knowledge of one another. Third, the two act in and with one another. Fourth, with eternal generation, the Son receives

31. Yarnell, *God the Trinity*, 242.

32. "There is no piece of Christian literature that has been commented on more frequently—except for Scripture itself." Philipp W. Rosemann, *Peter Lombard* (Oxford University Press, 2004), 3.

33. Peter Lombard, *The Sentences*, Book 1, *The Mystery of the Trinity*, transl. Giulio Silano (Pontifical Institute of Mediaeval Studies, 2007), 116.

by nature the fullness of deity. Fifth, traits which human beings typically perceive as maternal are also ascribed in Scripture to God the Father, including "conception, childbirth, and caring for the child."[34]

Reformation Orthodoxy

During the Reformation, orthodox divine ontology, including the Personhood of the Father and his eternal relations with the Son and the Spirit, was typically presumed. However, two shifts in emphasis occurred. First, attention became focused upon the work of God, especially his work of revelation as salvation. The being of God receded into the background.[35]

In a second shift, the role of the Son dominated confessional discourse, and the Father was more passively considered. For instance, in the Thirty-Nine Articles adopted by the Church of England, the Son was described as "the Word of the Father, begotten of everlasting of the Father, the very and eternal God, and of one substance with the Father." But the English Reformers focused mostly on human salvation: The Son was incarnate, died, and arose from the dead so that he might "reconcile his Father to us."[36]

The Reformers remained orthodox in their view of God the Father. However, heresy and error began to challenge the Trinitarian consensus as the Reformation continued in subsequent decades. Newer forms of both Arianism and Sabellianism arose, the Socinians being foremost among the latter. Addressing theology proper, the Socinians isolated the Father from the Son and the Spirit. Addressing salvation, they said the Son merely shows us the way to God by example.[37]

---

34. Gilles Emery, *The Trinitarian Theology of St. Thomas Aquinas*, transl. Francesca Aren Murphy (Oxford University Press, 2007), 155–56.

35. Both Philip Melanchthon and John Calvin, however, were criticized for some ambiguities in their doctrines of the Trinity. Scott R. Swain, "The Trinity in the Reformers," in Gilles Emery and Matthew Levering, eds., *The Oxford Handbook of the Trinity* (Oxford University Press, 2011), 228, 234–35.

36. The Thirty-Nine Articles, art. II, in Philip Schaff and David S. Schaff, eds., *The Creeds of Christendom*, vol. 3, 6th ed. (Baker, 1993), 488.

37. Stanislas Kot, *Socinianism in Poland: The Social and Political Ideas of the Polish Antitrinitarians*, transl. Earl Morse Wilbur (Starr King, 1957). Cf. "The Rise and Fall of British Arianism," in Maurice Wiles, *Archetypal Heresy: Arianism through the Centuries* (Oxford University Press, 1996), 62–164.

These new Arians divided God the Father from his Son and diminished the Son, both in his being and in his activity. Presuming to comprehend divine reality, they contradicted the orthodox dogmas that God is incomprehensibly one yet three, and that he is simple, immutable, and pure act.[38] Francis Cheynell, among others, stepped forward to defend orthodoxy, while scholars like Faustus Socinus, Baruch Spinoza, and William Chillingworth argued for a self-guided rationalist reading of Scripture. The latter form of Bible study led to modern infidelity.[39] For instance, new Arians like Thomas Emlyn and William Whiston in the early eighteenth century stressed the Father's authority was greater than that of the Son.[40]

The Shift in Modern Consciousness

More recent confessions, including those favored by conservative evangelicals, reflect a deepening reluctance to address divine reality. Modern theologians' broad retreat from classical Trinitarianism was accompanied by modern philosophy's attack on human access to metaphysical reality. Any discussion of divine ontology became suspect in the academy, and orthodox discourse was demeaned.[41]

Preachers commonly followed suit in the late seventeenth century, having been advised to avoid studying the Trinity. After the Enlightenment, proclamation of the Trinity and thus of God the Father was suppressed among both liberals and evangelicals. In particular, conservatives demonstrated reluctance to preach Trinitarian ontology, perhaps influenced by preference for simplistic readings of Scripture, by ignorance of orthodox tradition, and by dogmatic uncertainty about the essentials of the Christian faith.[42]

---

38. Sergiej Saverio Slavinski, *Francis Cheynell: Polemic and Piety* in The Divine Trinunity of the Father, Son, and Holy Spirit (1650) (Brill, 2024), 77–117.

39. Slavinski, *Francis Cheynell*, 38–54.

40. Malcolm B. Yarnell III, "'The Point in Question' at Salters' Hall," in Stephen Copson, ed., *Trinity, Creed and Confusion: The Salters' Hall Debates of 1719* (Centre for Baptist Studies in Oxford, 2020), 132–33, 140–41, 156.

41. This shift in consciousness became widely recognized among recent theologians through David Steinmetz's essay, "The Superiority of Pre-Critical Exegesis." Cf. Yarnell, *God the Trinity*, 86–105.

42. Malcolm B. Yarnell III, "Preaching," in Brandon D. Smith, ed., *The Trinity in the Canon: A Biblical, Theological, Historical, and Practical Proposal* (B&H Academic, 2023), 377–84.

Following the Southern Baptist Theological Seminary's *Abstract of Principles*, for instance, *The Baptist Faith and Message* (1925, 1963, 2000) failed to affirm the generation of the Son and the procession of the Holy Spirit.[43] Instead, when this modern confession does speak of God, it focuses on divine action: "God as Father reigns with providential care over His universe, His creatures, and the flow of the stream of human history according to the purposes of His grace. He is all powerful, all knowing, all loving, and all wise. God is Father in truth to those who become children of God through faith in Jesus Christ. He is fatherly in His attitude toward all men."[44]

Modern Christians have been reluctant to confess God the Father in his being, even while they readily discuss his work. This reluctance explains how certain sectors of evangelicalism have slipped toward Arianism and Semi-Arianism.[45] Debates among members of the Evangelical Theological Society over the relationship of the Son to the Father in 2016 jolted evangelicalism into reconsidering classical dogma.[46]

Recent Debates about the Father

Assisted by the precipitous decline in the use of the classical creeds, certain proposals regarding God as Father have sparked debate over the last century. First, theologians considered the ways in which "father" describes different relationships. A second

43. The New Hampshire Confession, which provided the structure for the first half of *The Baptist Faith and Message*, by contrast, affirmed "the personal and relative distinctions of the Father, the Son, and the Holy Spirit," who are "equal in every divine perfection." *The New Hampshire Confession*, art. II, in William L. Lumpkin and Bill Leonard, *Baptist Confessions of Faith*, 2nd ed. (Valley Forge, PA: Judson Press, 2011), 379.

44. *The Baptist Faith and Message*, art. II, in *Baptist Confessions of Faith*, 513.

45. Jehovah's Witnesses are almost universally recognized to be Arians. Steven A. McKinion and I agree that forms of Arianism constitute the greatest threat to the faith today. McKinion and Yarnell, "For Baptist Confessionalism," *Baptist Press* (January 4, 2024). Cf. Andrew Brown, Stephen Lorance, McKinion, and Yarnell, "The Need for the Creed," *Credo Magazine* (May 30, 2024). For more on Semi-Arianism, see chapter 13.

46. Emily McFarlan Miller, "'Heresies' of 2016: A Banner Year for Christian Controversies," *The Washington Post* (December 30, 2016); Kate Shellnut, "The Complementarian Women Behind the Trinity Tussle," *Christianity Today* (August 2016).

conversation centered on the proper translation of *kephale* in God the Father's relation to his Son. Third, argument arose over feminist efforts to apply female language to God. A fourth dispute then developed over masculinist appropriation of Scripture's ascription of male language to God.

Paternal–Filial Relations

First, how do we correlate the diverse biblical testimony which treats God uniquely as the Father of Christ, generally as the Father of all human beings, and narrowly as the Father of the redeemed? Some twentieth-century theologians disagreed over the best way to interpret the diverse witness of Scripture. However, these three meanings—that God is uniquely Father to his Son, that God is fatherly in a general way toward all human beings, and that God is fatherly by way of adoption to the redeemed—were nonetheless generally accepted.[47]

But why did the distinction between the general and redemptive meanings arise in the first place? Alas, another "father" long ago vied for and won human allegiance. Man accorded divine honor to an angelic usurper. The deceptions of this false father, the ancient serpent, corrupted humanity's once good relationship with God (Gen. 3:1–7). When the Pharisees questioned Christ's paternity, Jesus told them they did not truly know "my Father" (John 8:19). Instead, the adopted "father" of the Pharisees is "the devil." Their rebellion against the true Father led them to reject his divine Son when he appeared (vv. 42–44).[48]

God remains the Father of all human beings, even in our rebellion against him, for he made us in his image, and he still loves us. Some have now received God the Father's offer of reconciliation to him through his Son's recapitulation of humanity (Rom. 5:12–21; 1 Cor. 15:22, 45–49; Eph. 1:10). But others have chosen to remain under their evil "father," Satan. Restoration to a right relationship

---

47. See chapter 1 above regarding the biblical witness to these three types of divine fatherhood. On the history, see James Leo Garrett Jr., *Systematic Theology: Biblical, Historical, and Evangelical*, 2nd ed. (BIBAL Press, 2000), 299–30.

48. "Jesus does not, of course, here deny that the Jews, like all men, are children of God the Creator, like Paul's offspring of God for all men in Acts 17:28. What he denies to those Pharisees is that they are spiritual children of God who do his will." Archibald Thomas Robertson, *Word Pictures in the New Testament*, vol. 5 (Broadman, 1932), 153–54.

with the Father in union with Christ is available through "adoption" by the Holy Spirit (Rom. 8:9–11, 14–17).

Interpreting Kephale

Debate has swirled around Paul's description of the Father as the *kephale* of Christ. By the end of the late twentieth century, scholars settled on three major options for translating 1 Corinthians 11:3, which states, "But I want you to know that Christ is the head of every man, and the man is the head of the woman, and God is the head of Christ." *Kephale* can be interpreted as "head" in the sense of authority, in the sense of origin or source, or in the sense of preeminence in place.[49]

A problem with the first interpretation, which favors a difference in power, arises if it is applied to intra-Trinitarian relations. We not only lack corroborating evidence for the Father's "authority over" the eternal Son but possess contrary evidence, for the Father and the Son share entire power and authority as the One God. Paul earlier said those who are truly called believe Christ is "the power of God" (1 Cor. 1:24; cf. John 16:23; 17:20; 19:11). The translation "head" in the sense of authority was, tellingly, favored by Arian heretics.[50] Despite this doubtful pedigree, a modern evangelical scholar reordered the relations of the passage into a "hierarchy of headships." He then deployed his stringent "chain of subordination" against "feminism."[51]

The second interpretation, head in the sense of "origin" or "source," agrees with Paul's subsequent affirmation that woman came from man. Source, moreover, conveys Paul's apparent use of *kephale* elsewhere in his corpus (Eph. 4:15–16; Col. 2:19).[52] The immediate context in 1 Corinthians 11 concerns human social placement

49. Anthony C. Thiselton, *The First Epistle to the Corinthians: A Commentary on the Greek Text* (Eerdmans, 2000), 811–22.

50. Athanasius's *Against the Arians* contains detailed exegesis of passages discussing divine ontology. Thiselton, *The First Epistle to the Corinthians*, 811, 816. Protestations to the contrary are summarily critiqued by Fee. Gordon D. Fee, *The First Epistle to the Corinthians* (Eerdmans, 1987), 502n–503n.

51. George W. Knight III, *The Role Relationship of Men and Women: New Testament Teaching*, rev. ed. (P&R Publishing, 1985), 1–6, 20–21. Wayne Grudem later contributed an appendix for this interpretation, 49–80.

52. Moisés Silva, ed., *New International Dictionary of New Testament Theology and Exegesis*, 2nd ed., vol. 2 (Zondervan, 2014), 670–71.

(vv. 2–7). Paul's discussion about the origination of persons comes immediately afterward (vv. 8–12). "Woman came from man," Paul concluded, and now "man comes through woman." Yet both man and woman, indeed, "all things come from God" (v. 12).

Rejecting both the "authority" and "source" options, Anthony Thiselton argued for a third interpretation, *kephale* as "preeminent" or "foremost." Thiselton underscored the immediate context of the term in 1 Corinthians 11. He also appealed to the subtle exegesis of the early Greek-speaking church father, John Chrysostom. Chrysostom argued "that a parallel between men/women and God/Christ should not give 'the heretics' grounds for a subordinationist Christology." Instead, men and women, like God and Christ, "are of the same mode of being."[53] *Kephale* indicates neither "authority over" nor "source," but dignity of place.

Whether one chooses to emphasize authority, source, or place, any interpretation of *kephale* that makes God the Father superior to the Son contradicts the Nicene tradition. As is well known, the ecumenical council of Nicaea in 325 clearly affirmed the unity of essence between the Father and the Son with the homoousion. And the bishops gathered for the ecumenical council of Constantinople in 381 asserted the Three possess "a dignity deserving the same honour and a co-eternal sovereignty."[54] In other words, all three options err if the Father is divided from the Son. Any change concerns the humanity assumed by the Word.

Standing in the classical tradition, Anselm of Canterbury recognized the divine Persons share equally in every divine property, including supremacy and ontology: "the Father, on his own, totally is the supreme spirit, and the Son, on his own, totally is the supreme spirit, . . . in such a way that they are not two spirits but one spirit."[55] John Calvin agreed, saying of the Son: "Being of one essence with the Father, he is his equal."[56] A lesser authority or eminence applies

53. Thiselton, *The First Epistle to the Corinthians*, 818–19.

54. Greek *synaidiou tas basileias*; Latin *imperium coaeternum*. Norman P. Tanner, ed., *Decrees of the Ecumenical Councils*, 2 vols. (Georgetown University Press, 1990), 1:28.

55. Anselm, *Monologion* 43, in Brian Davies and G. R. Evans, eds., *Anselm of Canterbury: The Major Works* (Oxford University Press, 1998), 56.

56. Christ can be seen as "inferior" only "inasmuch as he assumed our nature." John Calvin, *Commentary on the Epistles of Paul to the Corinthians*, vol. 1, transl. John Pringle (Baker, 1996), 353. Fee similarly limits "source" to the incarnation. Fee, *The First Epistle to the Corinthians*, 505.

only to the humanity of Christ in his humiliation. That his human title, "Christ," is used in 1 Corinthians 11:3, rather than his divine name, is significant. Modern evangelical proponents of "eternal functional subordination," alas, continue to challenge the orthodox consensus.[57]

The God of Feminism

In the late twentieth century, feminist theologians sparked a third controversy by renaming God "Mother." One denomination declaimed "use of masculine-biased language applied to the Trinity," including the masculine names "Father" and "Lord." The National Council of Churches called God both "Father and Mother."[58] Mary Daly criticized Scripture's masculine language, writing, "If God is male, then the male is God."[59] Drawing upon "feminist consciousness," Elizabeth Johnson called God "Mother of us all" or "Spirit Creatrix."[60] She appealed to the Hebrew for "Spirit," *ruach*, which is a feminine noun. Against Johnson, however, it should be noted that the pronoun for Spirit is always masculine when used of God.[61]

Donald Bloesch was among the first evangelical theologians to counter these feminist arguments. He noted how radical feminism mirrors various ancient and modern errors, including pagan goddess worship, syncretistic Gnosticism, and the racist German Christian

57. Wayne Grudem claims agreement with Nicaea yet introduces a new distinction, "equality in essence and subordination in role." Grudem, *Systematic Theology: An Introduction to Biblical Doctrine*, 2nd ed. (Zondervan Academic, 2020), 306–7. Bruce Ware divided eternity into temporal categories, claimed the Father has eternal authority over the Son, and ascribed greater glory to the Father. Bruce Ware, *Father, Son, and Holy Spirit: Relationships, Roles, and Relevance* (Crossway, 2005), 65, 71. In 2016, Grudem and Ware repented of their denial of the eternal generation of the Son but continued to subordinate the Son in authority. Communications Staff, "ETS 2016: Ware defines Trinity view; Mohler urges conviction and compassion on transgender issues," The Southern Baptist Theological Seminary (November 18, 2016).

58. Donald G. Bloesch, *The Battle for the Trinity: The Debate over Inclusive God-Language* (Wipf and Stock, 2001), 2–3.

59. Mary Daly, *Beyond God the Father: Towards a Philosophy of Women's Liberation* (Beacon, 1973), 19. For a short history of the feminist movement to rename God, see Spencer Miles Boersma, *The Father and the Feminine: Exploring the Grammar of God and Gender* (Cascade, 2024), 5–8.

60. Elizabeth A. Johnson, *She Who Is: The Mystery of God in Feminist Theological Discourse* (Herder and Herder, 2002), 121, 133.

61. The Greek equivalent, *pneuma*, is neuter; the Latin *spiritus* is masculine. Bloesch, *The Battle for the Trinity*, 33; Johnson, *She Who Is*, 83.

movement. Arguments for the gendered God of feminism have failed to convince most evangelicals.[62]

While the refashioning of God in a feminist vein has neither gained nor should gain widespread approval, we must recognize that Scripture applies feminine analogies to God. For instance, Moses said God hovered like a bird over and "gave birth" to Israel (Deut. 32:11, 18; cf. Ruth 2:12; Pss. 17:8; 36:7). Responding to Job, the Lord compared his creative work both to begetting like a father and bearing like a mother (Job 38:28–29). The prophet Isaiah repeatedly used feminine analogies for divine action, likening his care for Israel to that of a mother bird, a woman in labor, and a mother nurturing her child (Isa. 31:5; 42:14; 49:15; 66:13). Jesus Christ applied the divine metaphor of a "hen" to himself as redeemer (Matt. 23:37–38; Luke 13:34).[63]

Scripture ascribes neither a feminine name nor a feminine pronoun to God even as it employs feminine metaphors for his activity of blessing. Scripture does not, therefore, justify the presentation of God as a woman, nor as "bisexual or androgynous."[64] God, who is eternal Spirit, transcends the bodily analogies we have for him. He is bound neither by space nor by time, nor is he subject to our limits. The Creator, who is pure and eternal spirit, cannot be confined by his creation, nor by its temporal or physical categories, including biological gender.

In its human sense, we must admit, "God the Father is not male."[65] However, neither is he female. Rather, as the apostle Paul reminds us, the "one God and Father" is transcendently and irreducibly "above all," even as he is immanently and sovereignly "through all and in all" (Eph. 4:6). Any attempt to represent God in our image, whether male or female or some other aspect of creaturely reality, constitutes "idolatry" (Rom. 1:23).[66]

---

62. Bloesch, *The Battle for the Trinity*, 9–12, 39–41, 48–49, 69–88.

63. The apostle Paul likens his gospel ministry to both a "nursing mother" and a "father" (1 Thess. 2:7, 11).

64. Bloesch, *The Battle for the Trinity*, 54.

65. Amy Peeler, *Women and the Gender of God* (Eerdmans, 2022), 4.

66. D. W. McNutt, "Idolatry," in *New Dictionary of Theology: Historical and Systematic*, ed. Martin Davie et al. (InterVarsity Press, 2016), 436–37.

The God of Masculinism

A fourth controversy arose in reaction to the previous one.[67] Proponents of eternal functional subordination have been accused of "tampering with the Trinity,"[68] so that they might create a patriarchal "paradigm for gender roles."[69] Their masculinist model portrays the Father as having "absolute and uncontested supremacy, including authority over the Son and Spirit."[70] Arguments for anthropological "masculinity,"[71] often based on Trinitarian subordinationism, continue to foster disputes between evangelicals. John Piper rightly noted that Scripture's language about God gave "Christianity a masculine feel." But controversy erupted with his applications.[72]

Michael Bird sought to bring clarity to the conversation. He asked, "Is God *really*, *truly*, and *literally* a Father? If so, does that

---

67. This modern movement, which achieved institutional form in the Council of Biblical Manhood and Womanhood, was formed to refute Feminism. A recent search of their website found over 250 articles, journals, videos, and papers dedicated to its rebuttal: https://cbmw.org/resources/. Cf. John Piper and Wayne Grudem, eds., *Recovering Biblical Manhood and Womanhood: A Response to Evangelical Feminism* (Crossway, 1991, 2006).

68. Millard J. Erickson, *Who's Tampering with the Trinity? An Assessment of the Subordination Debate* (Kregel, 2009), 238–42.

69. Matthew Barrett, *Simply Trinity: The Unmanipulated Father, Son, and Spirit* (Baker, 2021), 221.

70. Ware, *Father, Son, and Holy Spirit*, 153.

71. Piper and Grudem decried the term *hierarchalist* because it emphasizes "structured authority" and lacks "mutual interdependence." "Preface (1991)," in *Recovering Biblical Manhood and Womanhood*, xv. Piper nonetheless provides a hierarchical structure with base terms like "lead" and "receive." Piper, "A Vision of Biblical Complementarity," in Piper and Grudem, eds., *Recovering Biblical Manhood and Womanhood*, 35. This author's view of the male–female relation more closely correlates with Gregg R. Allison, *Complementarity: Dignity, Difference, and Interdependence* (B&H Academic, 2025).

72. Cf. Aimee Byrd, *Recovering from Biblical Manhood and Womanhood: How the Church Needs to Rediscover Her Purpose* (Zondervan, 2020), 18–23, 99–132; Barrett, *Simply Trinity*, 213–59. Papers at the annual Evangelical Theological Society often focus on debates over God and gender. Some eight papers proposed to address the issue at the 2024 annual meeting: https://etsjets.org/?s=Gender. Christians for Biblical Equality was developed as a standing evangelical organization to rebut patriarchal theology: http://www.cbeinternational.org. On Piper, see Boersma, *The Father and the Feminine*, 1. Peeler likewise recognized the "unrelenting masculine language for God in Israel's Scriptures, the New Testament, and Christian theology," but this does not indicate God is "simply male." Moreover, Jesus Christ is "male like no other," and the centrality of Mary in the incarnation indicates the abiding importance of the female. Peeler, *Women and the Gender of God*, 2–6.

mean that maleness is a part of God's essence, his being, or his nature?"[73] Moreover, does a woman bear the image of God like a man? Bird answered that "all theological language is analogical," and that one should not "literalize metaphors like fatherhood."[74] The biblical term "Father" stands as the normative name for God, but "the danger of essentializing gender" in God must be recognized.[75] It is an egregious error to refashion God to justify any social anthropology.[76] And those who carry the image of God include all human beings, both male and female.[77]

While Scripture describes God with masculine terms and attributes, and generation is a bodily analogy, God remains Spirit. He must not be delimited by physical gender. Anselm pointed a way forward in such conversations. He affirmed the Father's begetting of the Son, but qualified his claim by observing divine generation is "superlatively" true.[78] When generation is applied to God, we must acknowledge that he transcends any creaturely connotations. For example, while the physical generation of a human being requires both a male and a female, the eternal generation of the divine Son involves only the divine Father (John 1:18).[79]

Ultimately, "there is no sexual differentiation" between God the Father and his Word.[80] Our doctrine of divine fatherhood must be elevated above creatureliness, including the distinction of sexuality, and purified of any crude or demeaning associations. God alone defines fatherhood in its perfection, just as he self-originates all perfection. It remains perilous to impose human gender ideology, whether feminist or masculinist, upon God.

We might take literally the command of Jesus, "Do not call anyone on earth your father, because you have one Father, who is in

---

73. Michael F. Bird, *Evangelical Theology: A Biblical and Systematic Introduction*, 2nd ed. (Zondervan Academic, 2020), 196.

74. Bird, *Evangelical Theology*, 198. Bloesch develops this important point with more detail in response to feminist theology. Bloesch, *The Battle for the Trinity*, 13–27.

75. Bird, *Evangelical Theology*, 199–200.

76. Yarnell, "From God to Humanity: A Trinitarian Method for Theological Anthropology," in Keith S. Whitfield, ed., *Trinitarian Theology: Theological Models and Doctrinal Application* (B&H Academic, 2019), 63–94.

77. A corollary question arises: How do we keep the well-documented failures and abuses of some human fathers from diminishing our view of God as Father?

78. Anselm, *Monologion*, 41.

79. Anselm, *Monologion*, 40.

80. Anselm, *Monologion*, 42.

heaven" (Matt. 23:9). God in his fatherliness is characterized by perfect love, righteousness, and holiness, while every human father (and mother) is delimited by natural creatureliness and moral fallenness. The real limits of human beings and our disappointments in one another may be overcome in those hearts and minds which reserve loyalty for God in Christ alone.

A Systematic Theology of God the Father

Clive Staples Lewis once protested that Christians in his day were turning from the biblical truth taught in the classic creeds and adopting novel teachings about God. He said the novelties were merely new versions of ancient errors. "For a great many of the ideas about God which are trotted out as novelties today are simply the ones which real Theologians tried centuries ago and rejected."[81] The following four conclusions summarize what may be said about the Father from a classical theological perspective.

The Mystery and Revelation of God the Father

From the earliest sections of Scripture to its last, we learn that God the Father is beyond our natural ability to see or understand. God told Moses, "You cannot see my face, for humans cannot see me and live" (Exod. 33:20). The prophet Isaiah was overwhelmed by his guilt and doom upon seeing the divine throne (Isa. 6:1, 5). Indeed, the thoughts and ways of God are beyond human comprehension (55:8–9). In his separate vision of heaven, the apostle John could only describe the "someone" seated on the divine throne in terms of radiance (Rev. 4:2–3). Jesus agreed, "No one has ever seen God" (John 1:18a).

How then can we know God? After all, Jesus promised, "Blessed are the pure in heart, for they will see God" (Matt. 5:8). Isaiah said that God descends to us by the grace of his Word (Isa. 55:10–11). Jesus explained that the Father reveals his ineffable self, but only through the Son: "The one and only Son, who is himself God and is at the Father's side—he has revealed him" (John 1:18b). He told Philip that his disciples may now see the divine Father but only in

81. C. S. Lewis, *Mere Christianity* (HarperCollins, 2000), 155.

the human face of Jesus, "The one who has seen me has seen the Father" (14:9b).

Anselm said knowledge of God is "a sublime mystery, which stretches well beyond the horizon of human understanding."[82] The Cappadocian Fathers warned against heretics like Eunomius, who assumed he could define the being of God the Father as "unbegotten." We can never know the nature of God. We may perhaps say we can see God, but only "scarcely," like an "averted figure," and through his purifying grace.[83] The apostle Paul said the only way we can have knowledge of our "God and Father" is through his decision to bless us "in Christ" (Eph. 1:3). It is only in the humanity of the Son that we have access to the Father.

The Divine Perfections of the Father

Everything we learned about the perfections of God in the first volume of Theology for Every Person must be said about the Father. The Father is both "Lord" and "God," and known by many other exalted names. He is a mystery, infinite, simple, and of himself. He is "the Blessed One," sufficient, spiritual, and personal. He is at once transcendent and immanent.[84]

Moreover, the Father is holiness, which includes his eternity, immutability, wisdom, omniscience, omnipotence, and omnipresence, as well as his jealousy, anger, wrath, and glory. He is righteous. He is love, which includes his patience, grace, faithfulness, kindness, compassion, mercy, and his impassibility. Also, he is free.[85]

God the Father is rightly ascribed all the divine perfections, even as he remains the one God. Everything said about God is the Father. Moreover, he is the source of every perfection that we perceive through his creation. Finally, his perfection may not be delimited by creaturely analogy.

---

82. Anselm, *Monologion*, 64.

83. Gregory of Nazianzus, *On God and Christ: The Five Theological Orations and Two Letters to Cledonius*, transl. Frederick Williams and Lionel Wickham (St. Vladimir's Seminary Press, 2002), 38–39.

84. Yarnell, *God*, chapter 6.

85. Yarnell, *God*, chapter 7.

The Father and the Trinity

Early theologians began referring to the Father as "unbegotten," due to his generation of the Son. However, seeking to define the Father's nature as "ingenerate" or "unbegotten" like Arius and Eunomius, as if the nature of the Father was superior to the nature of the Son, both exceeds and contradicts the biblical revelation.[86] It also claims more for human knowledge than can be justified. We know that the Person of the Father generates the Person of the Son due to divine revelation, but generation does not give the Son a different nature. Moreover, we are not told how divine generation occurs. Likewise, we know that God has a nature, but we cannot circumscribe and apportion his exalted nature with our words.

Sustained reflection upon biblical revelation led orthodox theologians to proclaim "the eternal relations of origin" in this way: First, God the Father is the eternal source of the Trinity (Jer. 2:13; John 5:26). Second, the Father begets the Son eternally. The Father then sends the Son on his temporal mission into the world to become incarnate (John 1:18; 3:16; Heb. 1:5–6). Third, the Holy Spirit eternally proceeds from the Father. The Spirit is then sent on mission by the Father and the Son into the world (John 14:16; 15:26).[87]

The eternal generation of the Son and the eternal procession of the Spirit from the Father correlate with the Nicene belief that the three Persons share the Godhead simply, that is, without division, without diminishing, and without temporality. When the Nicene Creed confesses that the Son is "begotten of the Father" and "of one substance with the Father," it means the Son is truly "God," even as he is "from God." And by offering singular worship to the Spirit with the Father and the Son, the unitary deity of the Three, grounded in the "one God the Father," is further confessed.

86. For more detail, see the three 2025 Griffith Thomas Lectures delivered at Dallas Theological Seminary. Malcolm B. Yarnell III, "The Biblical Genius of the Nicene Creed: Spirit and Structure," "The Biblical Genius of the Nicene Creed: Content," "The Contemporary Relevance of the Nicene Creed: The Need for and Challenges to Its Retrieval," *Bibliotheca Sacra* 183.

87. Western Christians commonly argue from the twofold sending of the Spirit that he proceeds from both the Father and the Son. This will be discussed in more detail in volume 3 of this series.

The Equality of the Father

The Father and the Son and the Holy Spirit: Here is our One Lord God. The Father shares in the fullness of divine being with his Son and his Spirit. Nothing about being God is held back. Jesus claimed, "Everything the Father has is mine" (John 16:15a). The Spirit likewise "takes" the divine nature shared by the Father and the Son (John 16:15b). Paul identified divine perfections like "wisdom" and "power" with the being of God and the person of Christ (1 Cor. 1:24).

The divine nature belongs entirely to the Three as One. As Matthew Barrett explains, "Scripture always emphasizes the Son's equality with the Father, without any qualification. And when I say always, I mean *always*."[88] The Three are distinguished as divine persons by the eternal relations of origin alone. There is no division of the divine attributes, including divine omnipotence and omniscience and omnipresence, between the Three. God is simply God, and this encompasses the Father as well as his Son and his Spirit. We shall rehearse the Father's work as God in subsequent chapters, focusing particularly on creation and providence.

Your Confession

Our original question was, "Who is God the Father to you?" Please allow me to commend the Nicene answer. It provides helpful statements derived from Scripture. These statements will solidify in your mind and assist you in confessing with your mouth your belief in God the Father. When you pray, according to the command of Jesus, "Our Father in heaven" (Matt. 6:9), let the Nicene Creed's summary of the biblical witness to his being guide you.

Notice how the creed confesses the unity of the Father, his deity, his power over, and his creative relation to all creatures. Notice also both his eternal relations of generation of the Son and of procession of the Holy Spirit, alongside the one substance of the Father with the Son with the Holy Spirit. Notice also that these profound truths are intended to prompt our worship of God the Father with the Son together with the Holy Spirit.

---

88. Barrett, *Simply Trinity*, 235.

> We believe in one God the Father Almighty, Maker of heaven and earth, of all things visible and invisible.
>
> We believe in one Lord Jesus Christ, the only begotten Son of God, begotten of the Father before all ages, God from God, . . . begotten not made, being of one substance with the Father . . .
>
> We believe in the Holy Spirit, the Lord and Giver of Life, who proceeds from the Father [and the Son], and who with the Father and the Son together is worshiped and glorified . . .

Study Questions

1. What did the heresiarch Arius teach about God as Father? What did the defender of orthodoxy, Athanasius of Alexandria, say in response?

2. What are the eternal relations of origin as taught by orthodox theologians?

3. How would you respond to contemporary efforts to define God according to gender? Address the modern movements both of feminism and of masculinism.

Suggested Resources

- Gregory of Nazianzus, *On God and Christ*
- Anselm of Canterbury, *Monologion*
- Donald G. Bloesch, *The Battle for the Trinity*

CHAPTER THREE

Who Is the Word?

CHRISTIAN THEOLOGY IS SHAPED BY the most exciting story ever heard. The good news it rehearses takes the tedious monotony and utter insanity of this present world and turns it upside down. It does so with the seemingly incredible assertion that the eternal God became a man and died on the cross to atone for the sins of the world. This world, which he originally created, had revolted against God. It then killed the very Son whom the Father lovingly sent to reconcile the world with himself. However, God is deterred neither by rebellion nor by death, for the murdered Son "swallowed up" death, thereby destroying it "forever" (Isa. 25:8 NIV; 1 Cor. 15:54).

Dorothy Sayers famously corrected the dull preaching of the English clergy, reminding them of the foundational narrative of the gospel, a narrative that should be emphasized in all Christian proclamation: "the dogma is the drama."[1] Christian dogma discloses the world's drama, whose principal actor is the divine Son who became man, and whose principal action is every divine act and every perfect human act. "The plot," she wrote, "pivots upon a single character, and the whole action is the answer to a single central problem, *What think ye of Christ?*"[2] Sayers joins a long line of orthodox theologians

1. Dorothy Sayers, *Letters to a Diminished Church: Passionate Arguments for the Relevance of Christian Doctrine* (Thomas Nelson, 2004), 1, 14–20.

2. Sayers, *Letters to a Diminished Church*, 1, 56–57.

who have recognized the Bible focuses on the revelation of the cosmic mystery of the one Lord Jesus Christ, the eternal Word.[3]

A Preliminary Sketch of the Word

Exactly who is this Word who dominates the divine drama? He both grants reason to all creatures and makes sense of every word uttered in creation, revealing God perfectly. Orthodox Christians believe the Word is our Lord Jesus Christ, the Son of God. He is the eternally begotten Son, one God with the Father and the Holy Spirit. Sadly, during the Enlightenment, access to his revealed divine reality was deemed inaccessible. Recently, however, New Testament scholars have begun to reconsider Christ's divine reality.[4] We welcome their efforts.[5] The truth of Christ's divine personhood must be recovered. I will be arguing in this chapter that Christ possesses deity absolutely according to the biblical text.[6]

Christ is God in his being, and thus also God in his economy: The triune God created all things. He created humanity "in our image, according to our likeness" (Gen. 1:26). The second Person of the Trinity, the eternal Son or Word, is "the exact expression" of God the Father (Heb. 1:3). After humanity fell into sin, the eternal Word assumed our humanity to save us by recapitulating our humanity

---

3. Cf. St. Maximus the Confessor, *On the Cosmic Mystery of Jesus Christ*, transl. Paul M. Blowers and Robert Louis Wilken (St. Vladimir's Seminary Press, 2003), 123–29; Leonhard Schiemer, "The Twelve Articles of the Christian Faith," in John D. Rempel, ed., *Jörg Maler's Kunstbuch: Writings of the Pilgram Marpeck Circle* (Pandora Press, 2010), 237–56; John Behr, *The Mystery of Christ: Life in Death* (St. Vladimir's Seminary Press, 2006); Gerald R. McDermott, *A New History of Redemption: The Work of Jesus the Messiah Through the Millennia* (Baker, 2024).

4. See David S. Dockery and Malcolm B. Yarnell III, *Special Revelation and Scripture* (B&H Academic, 2024), 303–8, 323–24.

5. E.g., Michael F. Bird finds evidence of absolute divine ontology being ascribed to Jesus by Paul (Phil. 2:6; Col. 2:9), John the Elder (1 John 5:20), the author of Hebrews (Heb. 1:3; 13:8), and John the Seer (Rev. 1:8, 17; 21:6; 22:13). He also affirms the ontological importance of the Logos in the Gospel of John, which we develop in more detail below. Bird, *Jesus Among the Gods: Early Christology in the Graeco-Roman World* (Baylor University Press, 2022), 41–84.

6. "Absolute divine ontology" must be distinguished from a subordinating "relative divine ontology." The latter sees divinity as an honorific earned to join a hierarchy of heavenly beings rather than a real possession of the one divine nature. Bird, *Jesus Among the Gods*, 43–46.

(Eph. 1:10). Without distorting his person or diminishing his divine perfection whatsoever, he took upon himself our human nature. The Word became flesh in Jesus of Nazareth, the Christ.

The Word adopted our nature, becoming one with us, except that he never sinned. Christians have come to recognize he is the one human Person with whom we must unite, for he is truly God and truly man. He alone is our Mediator (1 Tim. 2:5). The Word died on the cross to atone for the sins of the whole world. But death and the grave could not contain him. The one who is God and man conquered death by rising again, promising to justify "everyone who believes in him" (John 3:16).

After conveying this true interpretation of Scripture to his apostles (Luke 24:25–27, 44–47), the Lord commissioned them to disciple the world with this truth (Luke 24:48; Matt. 28:16–20). He then ascended to the right hand of the Father (Acts 1:9–11; Rev. 5). He now intercedes for us on the very throne of God, but one day "the Word of God" will return to "trample the winepress of the fierce anger of God" (Rev. 19:13, 15). The Kingdom of our Lord Jesus Christ, who remains the perfect Word of God even as he brings to perfection our humanity in himself, will never end (2 Sam. 7:13; Ps. 145:13; Dan. 4:3, 34; 6:26; 7:14, 27; Micah 4:7; Luke 1:33; John 18:36).

To perceive well the contours of this life-giving and wrath-dispensing worldwide drama, we must consider the eternal Word of God: who he is, and what he does. The Word in his Person and work constitutes the central, indispensable, and unalterable dogma of the Christian faith. He ought to be believed and proclaimed everywhere, always, and by all. He should never be diminished! His inspired apostles and prophets tell us how we can know him and his provision of reconciliation to God.

We begin our portrait of Jesus Christ by surveying the biblical presentation of his Person. His divine names include "Word," "Son of God," "Son of Man," and "Lord," among others. Over the next few chapters, we will review the Christian faith's striking portrayal of this divine and human Person, as well as his work. As the magnificent, exulting, and terrifying scriptural portrait of our King, Priest, and Prophet is progressively unveiled, I pray we will grow in appreciation for both his holy Person and his sacrificial love. We begin our review of our one Lord Jesus Christ by focusing on his name, "Word."

The Cross-Cultural Background of the New Testament Logos

English scholars and Bibles typically translate the Greek *Logos* with "Word," but it has a broader meaning of "speech" or "message." John's use of the term in the prologue to his Gospel (John 1:1–18), widely recognized to be a key Christological text, brought together major intellectual patterns from two diverse cultures, the Hebrew and the Greek. The New Testament doctrine of the divine Logos is simultaneously rooted in the Old Testament and conversant to Greek philosophy.

The Hebrew Scriptures pictured the divine Word as the agent of creation. In Genesis 1, God created as he "spoke" (*dabar*; Gen. 1:3, 6, 9, etc.). The psalmist later declared, "By the word [*dabar*] of the Lord the heavens were made, And by the breath of His mouth all their host" (Ps. 33:6 NASB1995). "Wisdom" (*chakma*, Prov. 8:12), a personified synonym for sage speech, was similarly with God "from eternity" or "before" creation (vv. 22–26 NASB). Proverbs 8 clearly locates Wisdom prior to the origin of creation.[7] Wisdom then worked joyfully with God in crafting the world (vv. 27–31). Word, or Wisdom, exists and operates on the divine side of the Creator-creature divide.

The personal agency of divine speech did not cease with creation, for "the word of our God [*dabar elohim*] remains forever" (Isa. 40:8). Isaiah described the divine Word's continuing sovereignty over creation: "My word [*dabar*] that comes from my mouth will not return to me empty, but it will accomplish what I please and will prosper in what I send it to do" (55:11). The Hebrew presentation of Word or Wisdom suggests an eternal, creative, and personal agent. The Septuagint, the Greek version of our Old Testament, translates the Hebrew *dabar* as *logos*.

As the Old Testament prophets concluded their contributions to sacred Scripture, the Logos as the intellectual center of the universe took

7. Proverbs 8:23 uses three different Hebrew terms for the eternality of Wisdom. Wisdom is from *'olam*, "everlasting," from *rosh*, "the beginning," and from *qedem*, "the earliest." The threefold repetition of the temporal terms *panim*, "before," *terem*, "before," and *ad-lo*, "before," also points beyond the origin of creation (vv. 22, 25, 26). Verses 23–25 refer to Wisdom as being *nasak*, "formed," *chul*, "born," and again *chul*, "given birth," in eternity. Verse 27 begins, more simply, "I was there when he established the heavens."

a central role in Greek philosophy. In the sixth century BC, Heraclitus, a pre-Socratic philosopher of "enormous influence,"[8] described the Logos as "the omnipresent wisdom by which all things are steered." Among the Stoics who came to prominence in the late fourth century BC, Logos was the law that guides nature like a divine fire.[9] In the first century of the present era, Philo of Alexandria, "the outstanding representative of Hellenistic Jewish culture,"[10] described the Logos as "the agent of nature," "the medium of divine government in the world," and "the means by which man may know God."[11]

In the Wisdom of Solomon, a popular Jewish text written between the close of the Old Testament and the opening of the New, the Word of God was portrayed as moving with personal agency and powerful vigor: "Thy all-powerful word leaped from heaven, from the royal throne, into the midst of the land that was doomed, a stern warrior carrying the sharp sword of thy authentic command." This Word acted as a divine intermediary, "[touching] heaven while standing on the earth" (18:15–16 RSVCE). Among rabbis in the New Testament era "Word" and "Wisdom" became dynamically intertwined.

After reviewing this rich multicultural background, George Beasley-Murray concluded, "The employment of the Logos concept in the prologue to the Fourth Gospel is the supreme example within Christian history of the communication of the gospel in terms understood and appreciated by the nations."[12] Thorleif Boman detected the Hebrew stream of *dabar/logos* merging with the Greek stream of *logos* in the New Testament: Where the Hebrews emphasized his activity, and the Greeks emphasized its thought, the apostle John involved the divine Logos in both "reason" and "deed."[13]

John correlated the personal agency of the Hebrew tradition with the intellectual activity of the Greek tradition. He associated Logos with that "Light" (Greek *phos*), which "gives light to

8. Anthony Kenny, *Ancient Philosophy*, A New History of Western Philosophy, vol. 1 (Oxford University Press, 2004), 11–17.

9. Kenny, *Ancient Philosophy*, 96–100.

10. Kenny, *Ancient Philosophy*, 105.

11. George R. Beasley-Murray, *John*, Word Biblical Commentary, vol. 37 (Word, 1987), 6.

12. Beasley-Murray, *John*, 10.

13. Thorlief Boman, *Hebrew Thought Compared with Greek* (SCM Press, 1960), 58–69.

everyone" and "was coming into the world" (John 1:9). A close synonym of *logos*, "message" (Greek *rhema*), was likewise both used in the Septuagint and applied in the New Testament to Christ and the proclamation about Christ. Paul wrote, "The message [*rhema*] is near you, in your mouth and in your heart. This is the message [*rhema*] of faith that we proclaim" (Rom. 10:8). "So faith comes from what is heard, and what is heard comes through the message [*rhema*] about Christ" (Rom. 10:17; cf. Isa. 55:11; Heb. 11:3; 1 Pet. 1:25).

Identifying the Logos

The Christological truth garnered from the biblical presentation of the eternal Word of God and of his incarnation emphasizes three major truths about him: his personal unity, his true deity, and his true humanity. The unity of the two natures in Christ, effected by the divine Word's economic assumption of humanity, is technically known as "the hypostatic union."[14] When one considers the identity of Christ, we must hold these three truths together:

Figure 1: Three Truths About the Identity of Jesus Christ

- Personal Unity: The Word is one Person, even as the fullness of his being is revealed by many names, titles, and actions.
- True Deity: The Word is the eternal God. He is the only begotten God, one with God the Father and the Holy Spirit. His deity is eternal, absolute, and unqualified.
- True Humanity: The Word became a man, assuming our human nature, body and soul, to his Person. He became human in totality, except for sin, to redeem our humanity by

14. E.g., Bernard Lonergan, *The Ontological and Psychological Constitution of Christ*, transl. Michael G. Shields (University of Toronto Press, 2002), 109.

> recapitulating and perfecting it in his own Person.

These three truths are sufficiently narrated in the first four books of the New Testament canon, the Gospels. The Synoptic Gospels—Matthew, Mark, and Luke—portray Christ in narrative form according to the perspective of the disciples who possessed immediate knowledge of his humanity. The first disciples gradually came to the knowledge of his deity alongside his humanity. Scholars refer to their approach as a "Christology from below," that is, from the perspective of his humanity.[15] The first recorded Christian sermon, preached by the apostle Peter, also presented Christology from below (Acts 2:22–24).

By contrast, the Gospel of John focuses on showing that Jesus was God from eternity. Because he starts by highlighting his divine nature, theologians call John's teaching about Christ a "Christology from above." John looks at Jesus first from the perspective of him being God.[16] However, John also taught that the disciples came to a fuller knowledge of his Person by degrees, receiving the truth of his life-producing deity only after seeing him conquer death (John 2:21–22). The letters of Paul and the books of Hebrews and Revelation present similar Christologies from above (cf. Col. 1:15–20; Phil. 2:5–11; Heb. 1:1–4; Rev. 1:9–20).[17]

The immediate method by which a theologian decides to approach the Person of Christ, whether "from above" or "from below," is a matter of wisdom and freedom. Scripture manifests both approaches. "The ultimate question is the outcome, the final or completed Christology."[18] Daniel Akin calls also for Christology to be developed "from behind," recognizing the importance of Old Testament messianic prophecy.[19] We might add that Christology can

---

15. Millard J. Erickson, *Christian Theology*, 2nd ed. (Baker, 1998), 684–87.

16. Erickson, *Christian Theology*, 682–83.

17. Paul is primarily concerned with Christ's soteriological work. Gordon D. Fee, *Jesus the Lord According to Paul the Apostle: A Concise Introduction* (Baker Academic, 2018), 3. As a result, Paul's ontology of Christ must be discovered through his treatment of the divine economy. Malcolm B. Yarnell III, *God the Trinity: Biblical Portraits* (B&H Academic, 2016), 161.

18. James Leo Garrett Jr., *Systematic Theology: Biblical, Historical, and Evangelical,* vol. 1, 2nd ed. (BIBAL Press, 2000), 611.

19. Daniel L. Akin, "The Person of Christ," in Akin, Bruce Riley Ashford, and Kenneth Keathley, eds., *A Theology for the Church,* rev. ed. (B&H Academic, 2014), 391.

be developed "from ahead," by receiving his apocalyptic and eschatological revelation of himself.

Those who wish to incorporate the full witness of Scripture and maintain the claim to be orthodox will accept each of these methods to develop their Christology: from above, from below, from behind, and from ahead. They will thereby be led to affirm the full truth about the Person of the Word by maintaining his personal unity, his true deity, and his true humanity.

The Logos Is the One Lord Jesus Christ

The New Testament consistently ascribes to the Lord personal unity, just as Jesus Christ always identified himself as "one." There is no evidence whatsoever that he was perceived as two or more persons. Paul emphasized Christ is the "one [*heis*] mediator between God and mankind" (1 Tim. 2:5). The Lord said of himself, "No one [*oudeis*] has ascended into heaven except the one [*ho*] who descended from heaven—the Son of Man" (John 3:13; cf. 6:62; 17:4–5). Jesus and his apostles hereby maintained Christ's personal unity from his divine preexistence through his human incarnation and human ascension to the divine throne.

In the Old Testament, the Lord God was named "the Righteous One" (Prov. 21:12; Isa. 24:16). The earliest leaders of the church, from Peter to Stephen to Ananias, extended the same divine identity to Jesus Christ by naming him, "the Righteous One" (Acts 3:14; 7:52; 22:14). The apostle John also called him, "the righteous One" (1 John 2:1), while simultaneously affirming both his humanity and his deity. The Righteous One "has come in the flesh" (4:2), and "God remains in him and he in God" (4:15).

The apostle Paul named him, "one [*heis*] Lord, Jesus Christ" (1 Cor. 8:6). He elsewhere located Christ's deity inextricably in personal unity with his humanity: "For the entire fullness of God's nature dwells bodily in Christ" (Col. 2:9). An early Christological hymn rehearsed by Paul similarly began with the Lord as a divine Person and incorporated his human life therein.[20] Known as "the mystery of godliness," this Jewish Christian song presumed Christ's

20. Jerome D. Quinn and William C. Wacker conclude this "gem" is a "creedal hymn," which with 1 Corinthians 15:3–5 can be dated linguistically to the first or second decade of the church of Jerusalem. Quinn and Wacker, *The First and Second*

personal unity from his divine preexistence through every aspect of his human life, including his incarnation, death, resurrection, and ascension. The ancient Jerusalem church's six-stanza creed preserved in song Christ's unity of Person with both his eternal deity and assumed humanity:

> He who was revealed in human flesh,
> was made victorious in the Spirit;
> he who was seen by God's messengers,
> was heralded to the pagans;
> he who was received in faith, in the world,
> was taken up in glory. (1 Tim. 3:16b)[21]

As we shall see in our review of historic Christology, the unity of Christ's Person required subsequent defense against various heresies. For instance, in a pair of opposing heresies, the Nestorians disastrously compromised the unity of Christ, while the Eutychians overemphasized his unity to the detriment of his two natures. Again, through another set of differing errors, both Adoptionists and Apollinarians maintained his unity but only by diminishing one of his natures; Adoptionists diminished his deity; Apollinarians, his humanity. In the Modern era, Kenoticism exalts his unity but diminishes his deity.

The Chalcedonian Formula helpfully maintained the truth of the unity of Christ's Person, even while it upheld his two distinct natures. The ecumenically received Council of Chalcedon, which gathered in 451, confessed our Messiah's unity repeatedly while denying any division in his Person. He is "one and the same Son, our Lord Jesus Christ." He is "one and the same Christ, Son, Lord, only begotten." He is "a single person and a single subsistent being." In conclusion, "he is not parted or divided into two persons but is one and the same only begotten Son, God, Word, Lord Jesus Christ."[22]

The sixth century Athanasian Creed similarly confessed Christ is "one Son" and "one Christ; one moreover not because he has converted divinity into flesh but because he has assumed humanity into God; one entirely not by confusion of substances but by unity of

---

Letters to Timothy: A New Translation with Notes and Commentary, Eerdmans Critical Commentary (Eerdmans, 2000), 315–48 (esp. 316, 318, 321).

21. Quinn and Wacker, *The First and Second Letters to Timothy*, 315–16.

22. Yarnell, "Christology in Chalcedon: Creed and Contextualization," *Southeastern Theological Review* 11 (2020): 17.

person. For as the rational soul and body are one man, thus God and man is one in Christ."[23] Scripture, interpreted by orthodox believers, thus proclaims the complete unity of Jesus Christ, even as it maintains both his eternal deity and his assumed humanity.

The Logos Is the Only Begotten God

The Gospel of John identifies the Word with God and grants the Word divine agency. Regarding his divine nature, it repeatedly expresses the profound truth that the Logos is the eternal God. Grounding his entire outlook in God's sovereign creation of the world and humanity, John taught that the eternal Word possesses a twofold identity: As God, he is one with God, yet he is also in relation to God. On the one hand, the Word is directly ascribed the reality of God, for he simply "is God" (John 1:1c). On the other hand, the Word is distinguished by relationship, for he is "with God" (1:1b). The Word is identical to God yet distinct with God.

Nearly two dozen names or titles are used to designate the Word in John's first chapter. These descriptors may be divided into three types. Some establish his deity, and others his humanity, while yet others reveal both his deity and his humanity. First, John clearly emphasizes Christ's deity with names like "Word" (John 1:1, 14); "God" or "himself God" (vv. 1, 18); "life" (v. 4); "light" (vv. 4–5, 7–9); "the only begotten" or "only begotten God" (vv. 14, 18 NASB1995); and "the Son of God" (vv. 34, 49). Second, some are human titles. These are discussed in the next section. Third, in the Johannine literature, yet other titles touch upon both his deity and his humanity, thereby reinforcing his personal unity. The first chapter alone mentions "the Lamb of God" (v. 29); "the one who baptizes with the Holy Spirit" (v. 33); "the one Moses wrote about in the law" (v. 45); and "the Son of Man" (v. 51).

In the Gospel of John, the Son's identity with and relation to the Father is indicated not only through names of paternal–filial relation. John ascribes divine reality to the Son and his personal relation with the Father in numerous ways. The divine reality of the Son with the Father and the personal mutuality between the Father and the Son are guaranteed by the dogma of eternal generation. The

23. Yarnell, *God the Trinity*, 242–43.

dawning realization that Jesus is the Lord God rightly prompted his disciples to worship the Son with the Father.

The divine reality of the Word revealed in the written Word can be discussed under four headings: He is the One Lord God; he is with God; he is God by eternal generation; and we worship him as God.

He Is the One Lord God

The fourth Gospel establishes the full possession of the divine nature, will, and character between the Father and his Son. First, referring to the wholeness of the Son's unity of nature with God, the apostle wrote, "The Father loves the Son and has given all things into his hands" (John 3:35). Among the "all things" is included the inescapable and primary divine reality of having "life in himself" (5:26). Jesus went even further, stating without qualification, "Everything the Father has is mine" (16:15a).[24]

Next, the Son identified his "will" entirely with the will of the Father (4:34; 6:38–40). The one will of God shared by Father and Son includes both the prerogative to grant life and resurrection through Christ's words and the prerogative to render eternal judgment upon those who fail to honor God as Father and as Son (5:24–29). The will of the Son and the will of the Father are indivisible (5:30). This unity of will is eternal in nature, simply because it is the common property of the divine nature (8:29).

Jesus also gave himself the divine name, "I am," meanwhile placing himself temporally "before" Abraham (8:58). Scandalized by the theological implications of Jesus's self-description using the highly revered divine name, the Jewish religious leaders tried to stone Jesus for equating himself with God (8:59).[25] With regard to the Son's divine nature, will, and character, every true believer must confess with the apostle Thomas that Jesus Christ is "My Lord and my God" (20:28).

---

24. Alongside the unity of perfections between the Father and the Son, the Spirit also possesses the fullness of divine knowledge (John 16:15b). This indicates the unity of nature between the Three.

25. In the first chapter of this book, we summarized the multitude of ways in which the Son is identified with the Father in name, nature, and activity, and we refer the reader back to that discussion.

Thomas F. Torrance said early Christians were driven to affirm the *homoousios* of Nicaea, because they realized "that without that mutual togetherness and oneness in being and act between the incarnate Son and the Father, the Gospel message would be empty of saving significance for humanity."[26] We must affirm an "unbroken oneness" between the Father and the Son in the life, the passion, and "the ultimate executive authority" of Jesus Christ.[27] "When we look into the face of Jesus Christ and see there the very face of God, we know we have not seen and cannot see God anywhere else or in any way but in him, for he is God himself become human, and there is no God except the God who has come and meets us in Jesus."[28]

He Is "With" God

Jesus is certainly the one Lord God, but he also located himself in unique relational identity with God. He referred repeatedly to his personal location and distinction vis-à-vis God. He demonstrated this personal relationship with the Father in several ways, including his movement of descent and ascent, the prepositions of origin and return, the activity of sending and going, and that he personally faces God the Father.

John 3:13 provides the paradigm for locating the Son during his earthly ministry: "No one has ascended into heaven except the one who descended from heaven—the Son of Man." The Son's origin of being is "from above." He is not originally "of this world" (8:23). The Son and the Father, moreover, have their being "in" one another (14:10, 20).[29] The Son has shared eternal "glory" with the Father before, during, and after his incarnation (8:54; 17:5). During his incarnation and earthly ministry, the Son had "come" "from" the Father in heaven (6:32–33, 38, 50–51; 7:29; 8:14). Afterward, he was "going" back "to" the Father in heaven (6:62; 7:33; 8:14).

---

26. Thomas F. Torrance, James B. Torrance, and David W. Torrance, *A Passion for Christ: The Vision that Ignites Ministry* (Wipf and Stock, 2010), 11.

27. Torrance et al., *A Passion for Christ*, 12–15.

28. Torrance et al., *A Passion for Christ*, 14.

29. Patristic scholars referred to this intimate and eternal mutual indwelling between the divine Persons as *perichoresis*. The eternal, and thus ontological, truth of perichoresis includes the Holy Spirit, too. Being with the Father and the Son eternally, the Spirit is then sent "from" the Father and the Son to dwell with the disciples of Jesus economically (14:17, 26; 15:26).

In eternity, the Father and the Son always "face" one another as distinct persons.[30] The Son alone has "seen the Father" (6:46). And if a disciple has "seen" the Son, he has also "seen the Father" (14:9). The Son's sight of the Father is unique, so his relationship to the Father is radically differentiated from human relationships (8:38). Jesus denied that his eternal personal relation to the Father could belong to anyone else (8:21). His uniqueness is reinforced by the ascription to him of eternal generation by God.

Eternal Generation

At the conclusion of his majestic prologue, the apostle John furthered our knowledge of the divine reality of the eternal Son of God: "No one has seen God at any time; the only begotten God who is in the bosom of the Father, He has explained Him" (John 1:18 NASB1995).[31] The doctrine of the Son's eternal generation, clearly revealed here, is mentioned elsewhere in Scripture too (cf. Prov. 8:25; Ps. 2:7; John 1:14; 3:16, 18; 5:26; Heb. 1:5; 5:5; 1 John 4:9). The eternal generation of the eternal Logos has a dual function. It reveals his relational distinction from the Father, and it demonstrates his real unity with the Father.[32]

In his Gospel prologue, John used the Hebraic literary form of an inclusion, which restates an important matter at the end as at the beginning of a discourse. By beginning and ending with affirmations of both the Word's unity with God and his distinction from God, this Jewish apostle emphasized the twofold reality of the one Word. At the beginning of the prologue, John proclaimed that the Word was both God and with God; at the end of the prologue, he declared the Word is *monogenes theos*, "the only begotten God."[33]

---

30. On the way the "face" establishes the "I-You" distinction and relationality between persons, see Roger Scruton, *The Face of God: The Gifford Lectures 2010* (Continuum, 2012), 76–78.

31. Many translations influenced by scholars in the twentieth and twenty-first centuries have downplayed the meaning of generation. More recently scholars began to question the denial of generation. Yarnell, *God the Trinity*, 121–22; Fred Sanders and Scott R. Swain, eds., *Retrieving Eternal Generation* (Zondervan, 2017).

32. Josh Malone classifies the dogmatic function of eternal generation under three headings: "essential unity," "personal distinction," and "relational order." Malone, "Eternal Generation: Pro-Nicene Pattern, Dogmatic Function, and Created Effects," in Sanders and Swain, eds., *Retrieving Eternal Generation*, 273–77.

33. Textual critics agree the alternative reading, "only begotten Son," is later. Bruce M. Metzger, *A Textual Commentary on the Greek New Testament* (United Bible Societies, 1971), 198.

In John 1:18, the noun *monogenes* (Greek "only begotten") is placed in apposition with *theos* (Greek "God"), reinforcing the truth that the Word is divine. The Son is, literally, "the only begotten God" or, in a looser translation, "himself God."[34] The Word is "God," absolutely (John 1:1), and "the begotten God," personally (v. 18 NASB1995). The great New Testament textual scholar, Fenton John Anthony Hort, rightly said this verse possesses "exquisitely exact language."[35] The phrase *monogenes theos* can only be said of one Person, the Lord Jesus Christ. Due to John's revelation of the "only begotten God," who is both eternal Word and eternal Son, we also know more clearly about the eternal Father.[36]

The eternal relation of generation between God the Father and his unique Son is strengthened in the same verse by John's intimate imagery of the only Son of God as being "in the bosom of the Father." The Greek word *kolpon* may be translated as "lap" or "bosom." Through this relational metaphor of a "continual fellowship" between persons, John allowed no conceivable means by which one might separate God the Father from his Son.[37]

Biblical theologians point to other biblical metaphors which support the doctrine of eternal generation. These include God the Father's grant of the divine "name" to the Son (John 17:11–12),[38] the eternal possession by the Son of "the Father's glory" (Heb. 1:3),[39] and the Father's personal grant to the Son to claim possession of "life in himself" (John 5:26).[40] The Son is the eternally begotten God as seen in his name, his glory, and his personal possession of the principle

34. Charles Lee Irons, "Only Begotten God: Eternal Generation, a Scriptural Doctrine," in Matthew Barrett, ed., *On Classical Trinitarianism: Retrieving the Nicene Doctrine of the Triune God* (IVP, 2024), 401–18.

35. Fenton John Anthony Hort, *Two Dissertations: I on Monogenes Theos in Scripture and Tradition, II on the 'Constantinopolitan' Creed and Other Eastern Creeds of the Fourth Century* (Macmillan, 1876), 14.

36. Hort, *Two Dissertations*, 15.

37. Archibald Thomas Robertson, *Word Pictures in the New Testament*, vol. 5 (Broadman, 1932), 17. Cf. Yarnell, *God the Trinity*, 121–26.

38. R. Kendall Soulen, "*Generatio Processio Verbi, Donum Nominis*: Mapping the Vocabulary of Eternal Generation," in Sanders and Swain, eds., *Retrieving Eternal Generation*, 140.

39. Scott R. Swain, "The Radiance of the Father's Glory: Eternal Generation, the Divine Names, and Biblical Interpretation," in Sanders and Swain, eds., *Retrieving Eternal Generation*, 40.

40. D. A. Carson, "John 5:26: Crux Interpretum for Eternal Generation," in Sanders and Swain, eds., *Retrieving Eternal Generation*, 82.

of life, an incommunicable attribute that may be said only of the Creator.

John's term for the Word's personal generation, *monogenes*, occasioned controversy in the early church. Arius denied the true meaning of generation, which indicates the continuity of being. Denying the common being of the Father and the Son, the heresiarch said that Christ had a beginning in some type of eternity past and that he received a lesser nature by the will of God.[41] Nicene theologians responded by affirming the Son was "begotten from the Father before all the ages, light from light, true God from true God, begotten not made, one essence with the Father."[42] While remaining a mystery in its full sense, the analogy of generation applied to God means the Word "proceeds as subsisting in the same nature" as the Father.[43]

Worship Him

Due to his divine identity and his subsistence in the eternal relations within the Trinity, truths which are reinforced by the disclosure of his eternal generation and his participation in every divine act, redeemed humanity must learn to worship the Son with the Father, along with the Spirit. Jesus alluded to the worship empowered and sought by the Trinity in his conversation with the woman at the well. The Son as the embodiment of divine "truth," together "in spirit," which is only possible through the Holy Spirit, enables people to act as "true worshipers" of God (John 4:24–25).

The Jewish leaders were incensed that Jesus made himself "equal" to God by claiming God was his Father (5:18). However, Jesus reinforced his claim to deity when he disclosed the foundational Christian liturgical principle: "That all people may honor the Son just as they honor the Father" (v. 23). Jesus later revealed to the man healed from blindness that he is truly "the Son of Man." He also received the man's worship of him as "Lord" (9:35–38). Jesus likewise received the worship of Thomas, when this formerly skeptical disciple confessed that Jesus was "my Lord and my God" (20:28).

41. Rowan Williams, *Arius: Heresy and Tradition*, rev. ed. (Eerdmans, 2001), 101–3.

42. Yarnell, *God the Trinity*, 241.

43. St. Thomas Aquinas, *Summa Theologica*, vol. 1, transl. Fathers of the English Dominican Province (Christian Classics, 1981), 149.

No higher demonstration of the deity of the incarnate Word is possible than the worship that the early church offered to him in the written Word. Larry Hurtado found six ways in which monotheism came to include Jesus Christ. The New Testament evidence of worship being offered to Christ includes the singing of early Christian hymns; prayers directed to Christ; invocation of the name of Christ as divine, as with baptism; the celebration of the Lord's Supper; recorded confessions of Jesus Christ as "Lord," "Son of God," and "Christ;" and prophetic revelation from the risen Christ in heaven.[44]

The Logos Became Man

"'But you,' he asked them, 'who do you say that I am?'" (Matt. 16:15). The directly personal question of the man standing before them prompted the disciples to consider the human identity of Jesus even as they began recognizing his divine identity. They had no doubt that Jesus was human. For instance, in the first chapter of his Gospel, John refers to him with the human name "Jesus" (John 1:17, 29, 45) and with human titles like "Christ" or "Messiah" (vv. 17, 20, 25, 41), "the Prophet" (vv. 21, 25), "a man" (v. 30), "Rabbi" or "Teacher" (v. 38), and "the King of Israel" (v. 49).

However, even as we focus on the truth of his humanity, we must never lose sight of his deity; and vice versa. The apostle Peter said more than he fully understood at the time when he properly confessed that Jesus is both the human "Messiah" and "the Son of the living God" (Matt. 16:16; cf. vv. 21–23). Similarly, Paul's first description of the gospel to the church of Rome included the twofold claim that Jesus Christ is both the human "descendant of David" and the divine "Son of God" (Rom. 1:1–4). The apostles affirmed two significant claims about the one Person Jesus Christ: his true deity and his true humanity.

In the first significant claim, the apostles agreed that Christ is the Lord. He is the eternal Word who became flesh. They continually maintained his deity even as they affirmed his humanity. They said that in his eternal deity, Christ was "equal to" or possessed "equality" with God (John 5:18; Phil. 2:6). As we shall see, the apostles repeatedly claimed Christ was the Creator. James said

44. Larry W. Hurtado, *One God, One Lord: Early Christian Devotion and Ancient Jewish Monotheism*, 2nd ed. (T&T Clark, 1998), 100–14.

"every good and perfect gift" comes from "the Father of lights" by the Logos (James 1:17–18). The apostolic consensus was that the Word, the Son, belonged permanently on the eternal side of the Creator-creature divide.

In a second significant claim, the apostles also agreed that the Lord "became flesh" in Jesus Christ (John 1:14). John used a form of the common Greek root word *ginomai*, which could be translated as "be," "come to pass," or "be made." Paul used the same root word to confess Christ was "being made" (*ginomenos*; Phil. 2:7b). Paul also described his humanity as that which the Lord was *labon*, "taking" or "assuming," to himself (Phil. 2:7a). The humanity of Christ was manifestly a created reality, in contrast to his uncreated deity.

The mystery of the incarnation forms the background belief of the entire New Testament. However, certain passages stand out as particularly helpful in perceiving the portrait of the divine human, Jesus Christ. Daniel Akin identified a "quintessential quartet" that explicitly teaches "both the deity and humanity of Jesus."[45] We shall add one passage in our review of rich Christological texts in the New Testament. These texts are found in John 1, Ephesians 1, Philippians 2, Colossians 1, and Hebrews 1. There are numerous other New Testament texts that could have been added to this Christological quintet, but space limits us here.

John 1:1–18

Building on our previous discussions of the fourth Gospel's prologue, we can summarize the teachings of John about the identity of the Son with seven statements. First, he is divine and a divine Person, being both "God" and "with God" (John 1:1). Second, he is the begotten divine Person, identified by the prologue both as "only begotten," emphasizing his uniqueness, and "only begotten God," emphasizing his deity (vv. 14, 18 NASB1995). Third, the Word is the eternal Creator. "All things were created through him, and apart from him not one thing was created that has been created" (v. 3). Fourth, the Word as Creator preexisted his entrance into the world, a truth rejected by his own people (vv. 10–11).

Fifth, the Word became human in Jesus Christ: "The Word became flesh and dwelt among us" (v. 14). Cyril of Alexandria denied that any change may be ascribed here to his divine nature. In

45. Akin, "The Person of Christ," 400.

his deity, the Word remains eternal and immutable. "Become" indicates that the Word permanently, rather than temporarily, united human nature to himself. "Dwelt among us" reinforces his human orientation. The Word's assumption of our nature continues forever so that we may receive his blessings forever. "He came down into that which was in slavery, not to do anything for himself but to give himself to us 'that by his poverty, we might become rich' (Phil. 2:7; 2 Cor. 8:9)."[46] "Become" indicates the perfecting of humanity, not the diminishing of God.

Sixth, the Word is the illuminating Person, identified by both the apostle John and John the Baptist as "the light" (John 1:4–9). He is the eternal light who "gives light to everyone" but also came into the world (v. 9). Seventh, he is the enlivening Person, who is named "life," indicating his ability to give eternal life to those who receive him (vv. 4, 12–13). Elsewhere, John confessed the *Logos* was from the one who is "the beginning," but that he had now been "seen," "observed," and "touched" (1 John 1:1).

Ephesians 1:7–12

The whole Trinity is represented in Ephesians 1:3–14 in his economic work. The heart of the passage is focused on the Son (vv. 7–12), even as the Father acts through the Son (vv. 3–6) and the Spirit applies the work of the Son (vv. 13–14). Daniel Trier noted this passage's "overwhelming Christ-centeredness."[47] In the middle Christological section alone, the Son is presented as taking center place in three divine activities: redemption, recapitulation, and predestination.

According to verses 7–8, we are united "in him," by the instrumentality of his blood, for "the forgiveness of our trespasses." According to verses 9–10, the divine "plan," or "the mystery" of God's will which derives from "his good pleasure," intends "to bring everything together in Christ." This is the meaning of "recapitulation." According to verses 11–12, "we who had already put our hope in Christ" are predestined to receive an "inheritance" for the purpose

46. Cyril of Alexandria, *Commentary on John*, vol. 1, transl. David R. Maxwell, ed. Joel C. Elowsky, Ancient Christian Texts (IVP Academic, 2013), 63–64.

47. Daniel J. Treier, *Lord Jesus Christ*, New Studies in Dogmatics (Zondervan Academic, 2023), 53.

of glorifying God in Christ. In summary, Christ himself sovereignly summarizes everything in heaven and on earth (v. 10).

Philippians 2:5–11

Scholars have also identified Philippians 2:6–11 as an early Christian hymn. This song, taken from the worship of the first Christian generation, provides readers today "significant evidence of an early incarnational Christology."[48] Paul used the hymn to offer a lesson about how Christians should adopt the same humility that Christ demonstrated (v. 5). Its larger structure is twofold, focused on the descent of Christ Jesus (vv. 6–8) followed by his ascent (vv. 9–11).

The descent begins with an "ontologically revealing" claim about Christ. He possesses "equality with God," such that he need not grasp for it. His equality with God derives from his "existing in the form of God" (v. 6). The Greek term *morphe*, translated as "form," "reveals an essential reality."[49] In verse 7, we are told that he "emptied" himself by "assuming" the *morphe* of a servant.[50] The eternal Word's assumption of human reality should not be taken as an addition or a subtraction to God, for God is immutable. Rather, humanity is transformed by the assumption. In verse 8, Christ "humbled himself" further, receiving death into himself.

The ascent begins with an affirmation of the divine activity which followed Christ's second human humbling. God "highly exalted" Jesus by giving him "the name [*onoma*] that is above every name [*onoma*]" (v. 9). *Onoma* here alludes to the divine name, Yahweh, the "I am," as is made clear when the exaltation of Christ is taken up by "every tongue." The universal confession will be, "Jesus Christ is Lord."

Believing and confessing that Jesus Christ is the "Lord" (Greek *kurios*) constitutes a saving confession for people today. This base confession can only be truly said through the grace of the Holy Spirit (Rom. 10:9–10; 1 Cor. 12:3). "Jesus is Lord" is the fundament, the very ground, of all true Christian creeds. It can only be confessed in truth if he is both your "one Lord" (1 Cor. 8:6) and truly the

---

48. Trier, *Lord Jesus Christ*, 190.

49. Trier, *Lord Jesus Christ*, 192.

50. We will discuss the mistranslation of *ekenossen* in the historical section on Kenoticism in chapter 13.

master of your life (Matt. 6:24; Luke 6:46).[51] Christ's eternal kingdom, about which we will have more to say, derives from his absolute and unique being as "Lord."[52]

Colossians 1:15–20

Paul commonly circumscribed creation by God rather than circumscribing God by creation (cf. Acts 17:28). Using a holistic series of prepositions of agency, which could only be ascribed to God, he wrote the Colossian church about the revelation of Christ both as Creator and as Redeemer.

Paul said that all things were created "by him" and "through him" and "for him" (Col. 1:16). The Lord Jesus Christ, in his divine Person, is located "before" creation and continually holds creation together (v. 17). While his work is described as that of creation and preservation, his personal reality is described as the "image [*eikon*] of the invisible God" (v. 15).

While he was the "firstborn" [*prototokos*] or divine heir of creation in his deity (v. 15), he was also the "firstborn" [*prototokos*] to arise from death in his humanity (v. 18). "In sum, by speaking of Christ as firstborn, Paul affirms the preexistent sonship of Christ and his authority over all creation—He is the eternal Son of God."[53] Through the dual use of this single term, the hymn to the centrality of Christ in Colossians 1:15–20 divides into two sections, the first focusing on his deity (vv. 15–17), the second, his humanity (vv. 18–20).

Even in the section on Christ's humanity, the divine origin of his activity is reinforced. He acts as God in creation and in redemption, the latter divine work identified also with his humanity: "For God was pleased to have all his fullness dwell in him, and through him to reconcile everything to himself" (vv. 19–20a). Through his redemptive activity as the one who is both God and man, he alone can claim to be the "head" of the church. He thus retains "first place in everything" (v. 18).

---

51. Malcolm B. Yarnell III, *The Formation of Christian Doctrine* (B&H Academic, 2007), 79–82; Malcolm B. Yarnell III, *God*, vol. 1, Theology for Every Person (B&H Academic, 2024), 99.

52. Karl Heim, *Jesus the Lord: The Sovereign Authority of Jesus and God's Revelation in Christ*, transl. D. H. van Deelen (Philadelphia: Muhlenberg Press, 1961), 43–63.

53. Brandon D. Crowe, *The Lord Jesus Christ: The Biblical Doctrine of the Person and Work of Christ* (Lexham Academic, 2023), 96.

Whether we consider him in his deity or in his humanity, Jesus is the one Lord.

Hebrews 1:1–6

The book of Hebrews speaks similarly to the other apostles. The Son of God, the one begotten in the eternal present (Heb. 1:5; cf. Ps. 2:7; 2 Sam. 7:14), is both the Creator and the "heir" of creation (Heb. 1:2). The ontological metaphors are then stacked up to indicate the fullness of the Son's deity. He is "the radiance of God's glory" (v. 3a), a metaphor that indicates neither a beginning nor an end of a reality.

The Son is also "the exact expression [*charaktar*] of his nature [*hypostaseos*]" (v. 3b). *Charaktar* is a near term for *eikon*, indicating a perfect representation, while *hypostasis* can be translated either as "nature" or as "person." Either translation buttresses the orthodox conclusion that the Person of the Son is united with the Person of the Father in divine nature. Moreover, God continues to sustain creation "by his powerful word" (v. 3c).

And "when," subsequent to his divine preexistence so to speak, he came into the world, the Father sealed the ascription of deity to his incarnate Son by commanding the angels to worship him (v. 6). Through his incarnation, he made "purification for sins" by the shedding of his blood (v. 3d). He then ascended again to "[sit] down at the right hand of the Majesty on high" (v. 3e), indicating his right to the eternal throne over his everlasting kingdom.

Elsewhere, the book of Hebrews maintains both the eternality of Jesus Christ and his humanity. In his eternal deity, he is perfect: "Jesus Christ is the same yesterday, today, and forever" (Heb. 13:8). In his incarnate humanity, he suffers, dies, and arises: God made "the [source] of their salvation perfect through sufferings" (2:10).[54]

At the end of the preface to the Hebrews, Christ's humanity was said to have become "superior to the angels, just as the name he inherited is more excellent than theirs" (1:4). The eternal Word always possessed the name. His humanity became known as the bearer of the divine name through his victorious ascent. Humanity, created lower than the angels, became superior to the angels through

54. On the eternal generation of the Son in Hebrews, see Madison N. Pierce, "Hebrews 1 and the Son Begotten 'Today,'" in Sanders and Swain, eds., *Retrieving Eternal Generation*, 117–31.

the union of God with man in Christ (Heb. 2:7–9; cf. Ps. 8:1–9). The only way this letter can be read properly is by maintaining the personal unity of Jesus Christ and distinguishing, though not separating, the eternal divine nature from his assumed human nature.

The Humanity of Christ

We have witnessed to the divine reality of the Son through Scripture's ascription of the eternal relation of generation between the Father and the Son. From our review of five major Christological texts, we must also acknowledge his humanity is part of the divine economy. When Jesus says the Son of Man "descended from heaven" or was "sent" by the Father (John 3:13, 34; 17:3) and that he "ascended into heaven" or is "coming" to the Father (3:13; 17:13), he was not limiting the divine ontology of the Son but describing his divine economy. The Word is not limited in his eternality by his incarnation; rather, the Word elevates humanity into eternity.

Moreover, Jesus Christ was revealed, after his resurrection, to have become man eternally. Responding to Mary Magdalene, he affirmed both his unique divine relation to the Father and his human relation to God. First, he told Mary that he is "ascending" to "my Father," indicating his unique divine relation (John 20:17). Second, because he had reconciled the holy God with fallen humanity, he also told Mary, God is now "your Father." In Christ's humanity, the Father is "my God" and, by the extension of divine grace through Christ's union with humanity, the Father is now "your God" (v. 17).[55]

Due to his personal unity, with God on the one hand and with humanity on the other hand, Christ has become the eternal "high priest" who can mediate the grace of restoring human unity with God to believers in him (Heb. 2:17; 3:1; 4:14–15; 5:5–6; 7:1, 26; 8:1; 9:11; 10:21).

Conclusion: Who Do You Say That He Is?

The Chalcedonian Formula, crafted amidst great debate over the identity of Jesus Christ, has proven to be a helpful statement of the identity of Jesus Christ. As you read this confession from

55. A necessary by-product of the unity of believers with God in Christ is the unity of believers with one another (John 17:21–23).

the fourth ecumenical council, please note how it consistently maintains the unity of the Person of Christ, the truthfulness of his eternal divine nature, and the truthfulness of his assumed human nature.

> So, following the saintly fathers, we all with one voice teach the confession of one and the same Son, our Lord Jesus Christ: the same perfect in divinity and perfect in humanity, the same truly God and truly man, of a rational soul and a body; consubstantial with the Father as regards his divinity, and the same consubstantial with us as regards his humanity; like us in all respects except for sin; begotten before the ages from the Father as regards his divinity, and in the last days the same for us and for our salvation from Mary, the virgin God-bearer as regards his humanity; one and the same Christ, Son, Lord, only-begotten, acknowledged in two natures which undergo no confusion, no change, no division, no separation; at no point was the difference between the natures taken away through the union, but rather the properties of both natures is preserved and comes together into a single person and a single subsistent being; he is not parted or separated into two persons, but is one and the same only-begotten Son, God, Word, Lord Jesus Christ, just as the prophets taught from the beginning about him, and as the Lord Jesus Christ himself instructed us, and as the creed of the fathers handed it down to us.[56]

Study Questions

1. What are the three basic truths which must be remembered when we consider the identity of the Lord Jesus Christ?

---

56. Norman P. Tanner, ed., *Decrees of the Ecumenical Councils*, 2 vols. (Georgetown University Press, 1990), 1:86–87.

2. Where in Scripture would you go to defend the personal unity of our Lord Jesus Christ? Be specific.

3. Where in Scripture would you go to defend the deity of the Lord Jesus Christ? Be specific.

Suggested Resources

- Dorothy Sayers, *Letters to a Diminished Church*
- Michael Bird, *Jesus Among the Gods*
- Fred Sanders and Scott Swain, eds., *Retrieving Eternal Generation*

CHAPTER FOUR

Who Is the True Christ?

IN THE FIRST TWO CHAPTERS of this book, we considered the truth about God the Father. We first surveyed what Scripture had to say about the Father. Second, we heard the witness of other Christians through the centuries about the Father. Third, we offered our own systematic theology of God the Father. We are now following the same method regarding the truth about God the Son. In the last chapter, we surveyed the biblical witness about the Son. In this chapter, we will listen to the witness of other Christians, especially during the first centuries of the church, about the Son or Word of God.

Honor the Word

From first to last, Scripture warns against those who dishonor the Word of God. The serpent's first recorded words distorted the Word of God (Gen. 3:1). Moses warned against adding to or subtracting from the Law of God (Deut. 4:2; 12:32). Jeremiah repeatedly proclaimed judgment upon prophets pretending to have God's spoken Word and condemned a king for mutilating God's written Word (Jer. 14:11–16; 23:16–22, 31–32; 28:15; 36:1–32; cf. Ezek. 33:17). Jesus, the incarnate Word, affirmed the written Word is unalterable (Matt. 5:18). The incarnate Word also warned that "false messiahs" and "false prophets" would seek "to lead astray, if possible, even the elect" (Matt. 24:24). His apostles rebuked teachers who misinterpret the written Word to "bring in destructive heresies" with their "made-up stories" (2 Pet. 2:1–3; cf. 2 Tim. 4:3–4; Titus 3:9–11; 2 John 7–11; Jude 3–4). The biblical canon concludes with a reminder the divine Word will return to judge. He will invariably punish those who subtract from or add to his written Word (Rev. 19:13; 22:18–19).

Identifying the "false christs," along with their "false prophets" and "false teachers," helps the churches honor Christ. The apostles faced the danger of false christs, and the early church fathers faced it, too. It would be wise to obey the words of the former and pay attention to creeds of the latter. While the Chalcedonian Formula, provided at the end of the last chapter, captures the basics of true Christology, it is advantageous to see how the orthodox dogma of the true Christ developed. Both before and after that council, numerous heresies and errors were manufactured to mislead God's people and draw them away from Christ. The battle to glorify Christ by defending the truth about him continues to this day. It is incumbent upon Christians to discern clearly and speak carefully about the true Christ.

Scripture brings four additional reasons to know the true Christ, alongside the ongoing phenomenon of false christs, to mind. In the second place, the New Testament is very clear that only the true Christ can bring a person into the kingdom of God (Matt. 7:21–23; Luke 13:25). There is no salvation available through any other person, in any other name, or under any other truth (John 14:3; Acts 4:12). Apart from the one true Christ, we have no hope to be saved. He is our "one mediator" (1 Tim. 2:5–6).

Third, Christians are called to be "ambassadors" of the true Christ, so we must speak of him boldly (2 Cor. 5:20; Rom. 10:14–15). We must also be extraordinarily careful never to "distort" his gospel while proclaiming it. Perverting the gospel of the true Christ brings condemnation upon the proponents of that false gospel (Gal. 1:7–9). Christological heresy and error must be rebuked, and the truth of Jesus must be maintained in his true church.[1]

1. For the definitions of *dogma*, *orthodoxy*, *heresy*, and *error*, please review Malcolm B. Yarnell III, *God*, vol. 1, Theology for Every Person (B&H Publishing, 2024), 242–44.

Fourth, fallen minds easily change Scripture's presentation of the true Christ by glibly presuming to define God. Men forget that Christ's divine thoughts and ways exist beyond our conceptual ability (Isa. 46:5, 9; 55:8). In the fourth century, the Cappadocian fathers repeatedly rebuked the last great Arian heretic, Eunomius of Cyzicus, for defining God with unbiblical terms, for presuming he could define God's very nature, and for imposing a hierarchy of substance and power upon the divine Persons.[2]

In the fifth century, Cyril of Alexandria, the great champion of Christological orthodoxy, argued that heretical efforts to push the biblical witness beyond its own statements fail to respect the mysterious truth of Christ being both God and man. "The method of these things is altogether ineffable, and there is no mind that can attain to such subtle and transcendent ideas." Instead, we must point with humility and prayer beyond human analogies to God in his transcendence.[3] Scripture says Christ's humanity is like a "veil" which conceals his deity (Heb. 10:20 NASB), so it would be wise to recognize the limits of our human conceptual abilities and refuse to read our conclusions into the text.[4]

Fifth, we must worship the true Christ. Recall the contours of the saving gospel of Jesus Christ which prompt Christians to worship him: God the Word took our human nature to himself to "perfect" it for us (Heb. 2:10). His incarnation involved neither subtraction nor addition to his divine person, for either would impose change upon the immutable One (13:8). Rather, he "took" or "assumed" (Greek *labon*) our form and likeness (Phil. 2:7). Jesus is henceforward embodied. As man, Christ is historical. He embraced our history, so that human beings may come to know him. However, as

2. Gregory of Nyssa, *Against Eunomius* 1.3–16, in Philip Schaff and Henry Wace, eds., *Gregory of Nyssa: Dogmatic Treatises, etc.*, Nicene and Post-Nicene Fathers, 2nd series, vol. 5 (1893, reprint Hendrickson, 1994), 36–54. Cf. Malcolm B. Yarnell III, "The Contemporary Relevance of the Nicene Creed: The Need for and Challenges to Its Retrieval," *Bibliotheca Sacra* 183 (forthcoming 2025).

3. "The force of any comparison falters here and falls short of the truth, although I can bring to mind a feeble image of this reality which might lead us from something tangible, as it were, to the very heights and to what is beyond all speech." Cyril of Alexandria, *On the Unity of Christ*, transl. John Anthony McGuckin (St. Vladimir's Seminary Press, 1995), 130.

4. Likewise, a "veil" or "curtain" (Greek *katapetasmotos*) hid the outer court from the temple on the one hand, and the temple from the holy of holies on the other (Mark 15:38; Heb. 6:19; 9:3).

God, he remains eternally above history. The divine Son is unknowable, except through his gracious self-revelation in his incarnation. The power behind his mystery prompts us to worship him in his transcendence. But God also faces us in Christ (John 14:9), so in Christ's human face, we must worship the incomprehensible and ineffable God.

Many errors and heresies in church history arose as men persuaded others not to honor Jesus Christ. Glibly presuming that he can grasp the totality of Christ, or that he can define Christ's generation, the heretic distorts the truth of the Word. Some compromise the irreducible truth that Christ is God who became and remains man. Others deny that in his humanity, he died and arose from the dead. Others fail to see that even while the nails held him on the cross, he continued to uphold creation. Some compromise his deity, others his humanity, yet others his personal unity. One apostle condemned all Christological heresy under the rubric of "denying Jesus Christ, our only Master and Lord" (Jude 4).

By contrast, true believers affirm the human Jesus of history is the Christ of faith. He is the eternal Word of God who became flesh and remains an embodied human being, experiencing for us not only incarnation but also undergoing death. He then arose from the dead for our justification (Rom. 4:25), and ascended to the right hand of the Father, where he intercedes for believers today (Heb. 4:14–16). Jesus Christ is one person, both God and man, and his glorious ontology ought never be diminished, distorted, or denied.

The Earliest Heresies

Our goal in this chapter is to detect the true Christ by rejecting the false christs. The false messiahs whom the apostles and their earliest followers identified and rebuked were multiple. The Ebionites, a sect concurrent with the Judaizing heresy, said Jesus was the human son of Joseph and Mary (Acts 15:1; Rom. 3:20; Gal. 1:6–9; 2:16, 21; Titus 1:10–14; 3:9–11).[5] By contrast, the Docetists (from the Greek *dokeo*, "appear" or "seem") said the humanity and sufferings of Christ were only apparent (1 John 4:2–3).[6] Theodotus, an Adoptionist, said

5. J. N. D. Kelly, *Early Christian Doctrines*, rev. ed. (HarperCollins, 1960), 139–40.

6. 2 Clement to the Smyrnaeans, 9.5; Johannes Quasten, *Patrology*, 4 vols. (Allen, TX: Christian Classics, 1995), 1:51.

Jesus was a mere man who received divine power when the Spirit, or Christ, came on him at baptism.[7]

Even more sophisticated Christological heresies developed during the second and third centuries. Gnosticism, a mythology evident in various religions, found Christian proponents in Valentinus, Basilides, and Marcion. They claimed a special *gnosis* (Greek "knowledge") about how human beings fell from God into the world and can return to God. They said the Demiurge, the Creator of the world, was an *aeon* (Greek "age") who emanated from the remote Divine Being and fell. The Divine Being sent Christ with a secret to enable *pneumatikoi* (Greek "spiritual men") to return through matter to the Divine Being. Paul rebuked such "myths" in his pastoral epistles (1 Tim. 1:3–7; 4:1; 6:20; 2 Tim. 2:16–18, 23; 3:7; 4:4, 14).[8]

Later, in the third century, Modalism became prominent and diminished Christ by confusing his Person with the Father. Praxeas of Rome, according to Tertullian, "makes a heresy out of unity," by teaching "that the Father himself came down into the virgin, himself was born of her, himself suffered." Noetus of Smyrna, according to Hippolytus, said, "Christ was the Father himself, and the Father himself was born, suffered, and died." Among these Patripassians, who taught that the Father suffered on the cross, Sabellius was their leading proponent.[9] Arius gained momentum for his opposing heresy of subordinationism by vilifying the heresy of Sabellianism.

The Christological heresies of the first centuries directly compromised Christ's deity, humanity, or unity. Subsequent heresies increased in their subtlety but still presented false christs. These more developed heresies typically compromised Christ in some aspect of his personal reality, either by diminishing his deity, his humanity, and/or his personal unity. In contrast to these false christs, the widely accepted dogmatic portrait of the true Christ was developed through the teachings of the church fathers. Orthodox dogma was formed through debates with countless heresies as adjudicated in the ecumenical councils.

---

7. Kelly, *Early Christian Doctrines*, 116–17. Paul of Samosata, a bishop of Antioch condemned in 268, seems to have taught that the "Son" was a mere man. Kelly, *Early Christian Doctrines*, 117–19, 140.

8. Willis Barnstone and Marvin Meyer, eds., *The Gnostic Bible* (Boston: Shambhala, 2003), 1–19.

9. Kelly, *Early Christian Doctrine*, 119–23.

The Logos According to the Church Fathers

Due to its basis in biblical revelation and its multicultural background, the concept of the *Logos*, "Word," whose biblical meaning we reviewed in the last chapter, proved helpful to early Christian apologists and theologians. The church historian Hans von Campenhausen found that, "the acceptance of the Greek legacy was spiritually inescapable and a vital factor in what we now call theology."[10] Two prominent writers, Justin Martyr and Augustine of Hippo, among other church fathers, explored the meaning of Christ as the Logos. Reviewing their thoughts will help us perceive Christ as he was understood in the first five Christian centuries.

Justin Martyr

The earliest post-apostolic Christian writers, including Clement of Rome, Ignatius of Antioch, and Justin Martyr, confessed that Christ is God.[11] Seeking to reach unbelievers after his conversion from paganism, Justin explored the confluence between the biblical testimony to the Logos and the Greek philosophers' ruminations about Christ. Active in the mid-second century, Justin is "the first theologian" whose writings have come down to us in somewhat full form.[12] Christ's personal ontology, his divine economy, our human salvation, and the need to worship Christ were simply but thoroughly integrated into his theology.

Justin explained the person of Christ to the Emperor Antoninus in his *First Apology*. He explained that God is "most true," and that in the human Christ "abides the seed of God, the Word."[13] He later informed the Roman Senate in his *Second Apology* that Christians worship the Word with the Father, because he is "from the unbegotten and ineffable God." He entered the world to save us from sin

---

10. Hans von Campenhausen, *The Fathers of the Greek Church*, transl. W. Kohlhammer and L. A. Garrard (Black, 1963), 5.

11. Michael F. Bird, *Jesus Among the Gods: Early Christology in the Greco-Roman World* (Baylor University Press, 2022), 10.

12. Justin was a resident in the major Eastern city of Ephesus before moving to Rome. He lived and died for Christ in the second century. Von Campenhausen, *The Fathers of the Greek Church*, 5.

13. Martyr, *First Apology*, in *The Apostolic Fathers with Justin Martyr and Irenaeus*, Ante-Nicene Fathers, vol. 1, eds. Alexander Roberts, James Donaldson, and A. Cleveland Coxe (Hendrickson, 1994), 164; Martyr, *Second Apology*, 193.

and death. The Logos "became man for our sakes, that, becoming a partaker of our sufferings, He might also bring us healing."[14]

Justin believed the Word reveals himself to all men in some sense. However, people receive his truth variously, by "degrees of participation or sharing."[15] When the Old Testament prophets were delivering their inspired prophecies, they were most clearly moved "by the Divine Word."[16] Christ taught the first Christians the meaning of these allusive prophecies, for the Old Testament's messianic declarations "were not yet understood."[17] Justin also appealed to Greek philosophers, poets, and historians, including Socrates, Plato, and the Stoics, as evidence for the existence of the Logos.[18] He even speculated Plato "took" truths from Moses.

Justin argued that wise persons will pay attention to and develop the "seeds of truth" about God and Christ that have been dropped "among all men." However, when people "assert contradictories" to the Word's revelation of God, they show they do not "accurately understand" the truth.[19] Justin, "the Martyr," perhaps the greatest early apologist for the Christian faith, was later killed for refusing to compromise his worship of the one true God and his incarnate Word.[20]

Augustine of Hippo

At the end of the patristic period, Augustine of Hippo, the leading theologian of the Latin-speaking West, also considered how Scripture and society intersect. In his *Confessions*, Augustine addressed the problems that come from pagan reflection upon the Word. Even as he decried pagan error, he lauded some of their basic findings.

First, Augustine spoke positively about what pagan philosophers taught him: "In them I read—not, of course, word for word, though the sense was the same and it was supported by all kinds of

---

14. Justin Martyr, Second Apology, in *The Apostolic Fathers*, 193.

15. Eric Osborn, "Justin Martyr," in G. R. Evans, ed., *The First Christian Theologians: An Introduction to Theology in the Early Church* (Blackwell Publishing, 2004), 118.

16. Martyr, *First Apology*, 175.

17. Martyr, *First Apology*, 173.

18. Martyr, *First Apology*, 164.

19. Martyr, *First Apology*, 177.

20. Osborn, "Justin Martyr," 120.

different arguments—that at the beginning of time the Word already was; and God had the Word abiding with him, and the Word was God."[21] Augustine believed that any agreement between the wisest pagans and Scripture was due to divine grace. "But the Word, who is himself God, is the true Light, which enlightens every soul born into the world."[22] Citing John 1:9, Augustine developed a doctrine of general human intellectual illumination by the Word.[23]

Second, Augustine also discussed the profound differences between the Word's general illumination and inspired biblical revelation. While the philosophers were sometimes perceptive, they lacked the saving knowledge of the Word. Regarding the incarnation, "I did not find it written in those books that he came to what was his own." Nor did he find in the pagan writings "that the Word was made flesh and came to dwell among us." "They do not say that he dispossessed himself and took the nature of a slave." And as for Christ's crucifixion, "there is no word in those books to say that in his own appointed time he underwent death for us sinners."[24]

Due to these important differences between the contents of biblical revelation and the contents of pagan rumination, Augustine argued general Logos philosophy invariably leads to idolatry. For followers of other religions to be saved, they need to hear of the special revelation of Jesus Christ. He therefore contrasted "the most outrageous pride" of Platonism with "the way of humility when the Word was made flesh and came to dwell among the men of the world."[25]

Still, Augustine saw some good in paganism. Like the Israelites who despoiled the Egyptians during the Exodus, he received "the gold" available in their learning. But he advocated accepting their ideas only with great care. Before his conversion, pagan learning told him, "there was something to be seen." Alas, he lamented, "I was not yet able to see it."[26] Pagans misuse the general knowledge of

---

21. Saint Augustine, *The Confessions*, transl. R. S. Pine-Coffin (Penguin, 1961), 144.

22. Augustine, *The Confessions*, 144. Cf. John 1:9.

23. Gareth B. Matthews, "Knowledge and Illumination," in Eleonore Stump and Norman Kretzmann, eds., *The Cambridge Companion to Augustine* (Cambridge University Press, 2001), 180–81; Mary T. Clark, *Augustine* (Continuum, 1994), 19–25.

24. Augustine, *The Confessions*, 144–45.

25. Augustine, *The Confessions*, 144.

26. Augustine, *The Confessions*, 147.

God they receive by grace. They exchange the truth "for idols and all kinds of make-believe."[27]

Thankfully, however, through the divine Word revealed to the prophets and the apostles in holy Scripture, Augustine was introduced to the truth. He ultimately rejected pagan idolatry, which misuses the illumination of God provided in nature and conscience. Through the preaching of the church, he heard and followed the incarnate Word in humility and faith.

The True Christ in Orthodox Thought

Two other prominent early church fathers were particularly instrumental in developing the outlines of orthodox Christology even further. Both men paid careful attention to the truth about the eternal Word, who became human, died on the cross, rose from the dead, and ascended to heaven, and will return to establish his kingdom forever. Both also served as bishops of the same large and powerful multicultural city in north Africa, the port of Alexandria at the entrance to the Nile Delta.

During the early fourth century, Athanasius of Alexandria discerned and defended biblical teaching about the person of Christ as the Arian controversy unfolded. During the early fifth century, Cyril of Alexandria discerned and defended biblical teaching about the person of Christ as the Nestorian controversy unfolded. Both advanced the Nicene dogma of Jesus Christ. Along with Maximus the Confessor, who was active toward the end of the great period of Christological development, they serve as exemplars of orthodox teaching about the one Lord Jesus Christ, true God and true man.

Athanasius of Alexandria

Athanasius cautiously explored the New Testament's description of the eternal Logos who became flesh. Before entering the fray against Arianism, Athanasius exegeted the doctrine of the generation of the Son from Scripture historically, linguistically, and canonically. His careful biblical hermeneutic helped him defend a high doctrine of the person of Christ. The eternal Word, he often recalled, is "in the Father" (John 14:10), "equal to God" (Phil. 2:6),

27. Augustine, *The Confessions*, 146.

and "one with the Father" (John 10:30). "The Son, being from the Father and belonging to his essence, is inalterable and unchangeable as the Father himself."[28]

Like Justin and Augustine, early in his theological career Athanasius sharpened his doctrine of the eternal Logos by exegeting Scripture. He also debated with both Jewish rabbis and pagan philosophers.[29] Maintaining the difference between the Creator's eternal nature and our creatureliness, he noted that in the biblical text the eternal Word was on the divine side of the Creator–creature divide.[30] He was persecuted by imperial forces at the behest of Arian heretics and chased into exile five times. But Athanasius stood courageously by "his central conviction," garnered from Scripture, that genuine Christianity "stands or falls by the confession of the full divinity of the Word."[31]

Scripture's revelation of the divine reality of the Word, who is both one with God and related to God through eternal generation, led Athanasius to defend Nicene doctrine even at great personal cost. Scripture prompted him to confess: "that the Word of the Father is Himself divine, that all things owe their being to His will and power, and that it is through Him that the Father gives order to creation, by Him that all things are moved, and through Him that they receive their being."[32]

The Word who created all things also redeems his creatures, "for the One Father has employed the same Agent for both works, effecting the salvation of the world through the same Word Who made it in the beginning."[33]Athanasius believed only the Word could save fallen humanity, for only he was both God and man. Man is created "in the image of God," but the Word is "the Image Absolute."[34] "The Saviour of us all, the Word of God, in His great love took to Himself a body and moved as Man among men, meeting their senses, so to speak, half way."[35]

---

28. Athanasius, *Orations Against the Arians*, 1.36, cited in Khaled Anatolios, *Athanasius* (Routledge, 2004), 93.

29. Athanasius, *On the Incarnation: The Treatise De Incarnatione Dei Verbi*, transl. C. S. M. V. (St. Vladimir's Seminary Press, 1996), 25, 64–94.

30. Anatolios, *Athanasius*, 40–41, 67.

31. Anatolios, *Athanasius*, 39.

32. Athanasius, *On the Incarnation*, 25.

33. Athanasius, *On the Incarnation*, 26.

34. Athanasius, *On the Incarnation*, 38.

35. Athanasius, *On the Incarnation*, 43.

Against those who diminish the Word through the incarnation, Athanasius espoused his deity. "The Word was not hedged in by His body, nor did His presence in the body prevent His being present everywhere as well."[36] Christ's divine immutability was not compromised by his assumption of human mutability. Athanasius's point was reinforced by the anathemas against Arianism, which were attached to the creed of the Council of Nicaea in 325.[37]

Athanasius promoted the "partitive exegesis"[38] of Scripture to help believers understand how Christ can be described in truly divine terms and truly human terms without compromising his personal unity. The Word always is God and acts as God, even as he assumes human nature and acts as man. He is the one Christ, who is God and man. Partitive exegesis, also known as the "double hermeneutic," distinguishes the divine and the human aspects of the one Christ. Athanasius noted how the various texts in Scripture address Christ from one of two perspectives:

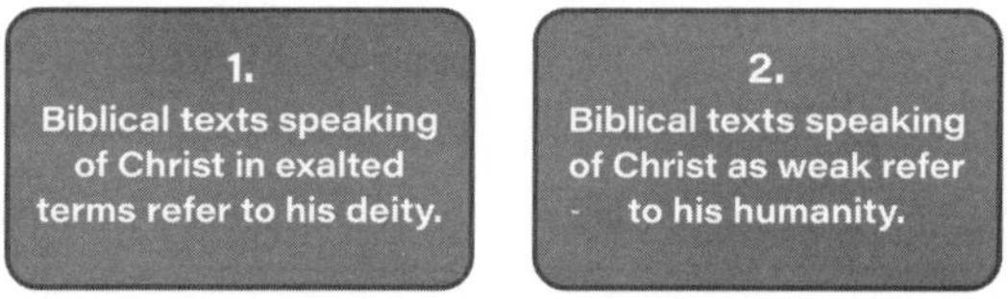

1. Biblical texts speaking of Christ in exalted terms refer to his deity.	2. Biblical texts speaking of Christ as weak refer to his humanity.

Figure 2: The Twofold Christological Scope of Scripture

First, regarding Christ's humanity, Athanasius said, "You must understand, therefore, that when writers on this sacred theme speak of him as eating and drinking and being born, they mean that the body, as a body, was born and sustained with the food proper to its nature." Second, regarding Christ's deity, Athanasius said, "God the Word, who was united with [humanity], was at the same time ordering the universe and revealing himself through His bodily acts as not man only but God."[39]

36. Athanasius, *On the Incarnation*, 45.

37. Norman P. Tanner, *Decrees of the Ecumenical Councils*, 2 vols. (Georgetown University Press, 1990), 1:5.

38. The ancient practice of "partitive exegesis" has been described as explaining "how we read Scripture with attention to the two natures of Christ concurring in one person." Stephen O. Presley, *Biblical Theology in the Life of the Early Church: Recovering an Ancient Vision* (Baker Academic, 2025), 100.

39. Athanasius, *On the Incarnation*, 46.

In other words, the deity of the eternal Word who became human was neither diminished nor distorted through his incarnation. Moreover, Christ's humanity was not compromised but maintained by the power and glory of his deity. Rather, our human nature was perfected in the humanity of the Word through his incarnation, death, and resurrection. He perfected human nature, so that we might be able to come into the saving presence of God.

Athanasius helpfully explained the mystery of the personal union of the divine nature with the human nature in the incarnation. He showed that both his humanity and his deity are preserved intact and entire in Christ. The fact that Jesus Christ is one with God yet also one with humanity enables him to serve as the one Mediator for our salvation. Christ is able to sanctify our nature by his personal union of both God and man.

> His body was not for Him a limitation, but an instrument, so that He was both in it and in all things, and outside all things, resting in the Father alone. At one and the same time—this is the wonder—as Man He was living a human life, and as Word He was sustaining the life of the universe, and as Son He was in constant union with the Father. Not even his birth, therefore, changed him in any way, nor was he defiled by being in the body. Rather, he sanctified the body by being in it.[40]

Cyril of Alexandria

While Athanasius wrote *On the Incarnation* near the beginning of his ministry, Cyril composed his great work, *On the Unity of Christ*, toward the end of a long career of exegeting the written Word of God and defending the incarnate Word of God. Cyril's struggle to teach the true Christ against the innovative heresy of Nestorianism was approved by the ecumenical Council of Ephesus in 431.[41] But what was it that originally prompted Cyril to launch what became a centuries-long struggle to define orthodox Christology?

40. Athanasius, *On the Incarnation*, 45–46.

41. McGuckin, "Introduction," in Cyril, *On the Unity of Christ*, 15.

A rival school of biblical interpretation to that of Alexandria had established itself at Antioch. One of Antioch's leading teachers, Diodore of Tarsus, said the incarnation was composed of "Two Sons," one divine and one human.[42] Theodore of Mopsuestia, another leading Antiochene, said Christ was "two persons" joined in a "moral union" or "community of thought and will." Theodore divided Christ again by asserting, "The one who assumed is not the same as the one who was assumed."[43]

Theodore's "exaggerations," "omissions," and "dangerous tendencies"[44] were popularized by Nestorius, a controversial bishop of Constantinople, and his chaplains. The Nestorians, sundering the divine Christ from the human Christ, came to deny the orthodox belief that Mary could be *Theotokos*, the woman who "carried God" in her womb.[45]

Cyril's voluminous biblical studies and keen theological insights helped him defend the unity of the person of Christ against Nestorianism's division of Christ. The Nestorians portrayed Christ as composed of two subjects, while Cyril consistently depicted him as one subject. Cyril perceived how Nestorianism carried on the dishonorable project of Arianism, which diminished Christ before the incarnation. For their part, the Nestorians now diminished Christ in the incarnation.

In response, Cyril reminded them that Scripture named Christ, "Emmanuel," "God-with-us" (Matt. 1:23; Isa. 7:14). Christ is God, and he was conceived as a man in the womb of the Virgin.[46] Cyril said the Nestorians "bankrupt the economy of salvation" by denying the same Son who was eternally begotten of the Father had become incarnate. "In short, [Christ] took what was ours to be his very own so that we might have all that was his" (cf. 2 Cor. 8:9).[47]

Only the one who is the Word become man could reconcile holy God with sinful man: "The Word who is God came down from out of heaven and entered our likeness, that is to say submitted to birth from a woman according to the flesh, while ever remaining

42. Diodore had led the charge against the paganism of Julian the Apostate and defended the deity of Christ. Quasten, *Patrology*, 3:397–98.

43. Theodore of Mopsuestia, *Homily* 8, in Quasten, *Patrology*, 3:415.

44. Quasten, *Patrology*, 3:417.

45. Quasten, *Patrology*, 3:514.

46. Cyril, *On the Unity of Christ*, 50–52.

47. Cyril, *On the Unity of Christ*, 59.

what he was, that is one from on high, from heaven, superior to all things as God even with the flesh."[48]

Cyril also repeated the partitive exegesis of Athanasius, assigning both divine acts and human acts to the one Christ. He refused to allow these distinct actions to be assigned to anyone but the one Christ. "For there is only one Son, the Word who was made man for our sake. I would say that everything refers to him, words and deeds, both those that befit the deity, as well as those which are human."[49] In summary, "Christ is in no way divided."

While emphasizing the unity of Christ, Cyril never lost sight of Christ's two natures. Christ is both God and man, and not a third thing. His deity is not diminished by the incarnation, nor is his humanity. "He suffers in his own flesh, and not in the nature of the Godhead."[50] Cyril recognized that holding these great truths about Christ requires humility, for God as transcendent remains beyond our conceptual grasp. The two natures of the one Christ are a scandal to the carnal mind, but the great mystery of Christ prompts true believers to worship him.

Finally, Cyril taught that the incarnation, death, resurrection, and ascension of the eternal Word is the only way humanity could be saved. Drawing on the difference between Adam, who was "a living being," and Christ, who is "a life-giving spirit" (1 Cor. 15:20–22, 45), Cyril said, "There was no other way for the flesh to become life-giving, even though by its own nature it was subject to the necessity of corruption, except that it became the very flesh of the Word who gives life to all things."[51]

Human salvation depends upon orthodox Christology. Because of the precise exegetical insights of Cyril, his writings became the touchstone of orthodoxy in the later councils, which focused primarily on Christology.

---

48. Like Athanasius, Cyril continually maintained the deity of Christ after the incarnation. "He remained Lord of all things even when he came, for the economy, in the form of a slave and this is why the mystery of Christ is truly wonderful." Cyril, *On the Unity of Christ*, 61.

49. Cyril, *On the Unity of Christ*, 107.

50. Cyril, *On the Unity of Christ*, 130.

51. Cyril, *On the Unity of Christ*, 126, 132.

Conciliar Christology

It will help bring clarity if we review the development of orthodox Christology through the ecumenical councils. It is wise to hear the voices of believers in the universal church. The dogmatic declarations of the seven most widely received gatherings honored God by expositing the foundational, central, and indispensable Christian doctrines of Trinity and of Christ. These Christians were compelled to identify through careful exegesis, to contend in vigorous argumentation, and to preserve in worshipful profession "the faith that was delivered to the saints once for all" (Jude 3).

"Conciliar Christology" examines the teachings about Christ approved by the gatherings of bishops in councils. These large gatherings became possible only after the state persecution of Christianity stopped in the early fourth century. Seven "ecumenical councils," which gathered from the fourth through the eighth centuries, have been widely regarded as teaching the true faith.[52]

The members of these councils felt providentially led to develop orthodox dogma in response to the deceptions of "false teachers" with their "destructive heresies" (2 Pet. 2:1–3). Christ and his apostles prophesied the coming of "false christs" taught by "false prophets" and "heretics" (Matt. 24:24; 1 Cor. 11:19; Titus 3:10), and the early church was compelled to correct them. These orthodox Christians discerned the revealed truth about God in Scripture, then confessed him in their creeds, even as false teachers misconstrued the written Word and dishonored the eternal Word with their human contrivances.

The first ecumenical council, comprised of more than three hundred Christian bishops assembled in a lakeside basilica at Nicaea, emphasized the deity of Christ. The second, which formalized the Nicene Creed, also discerned and confessed his humanity, while defending the deity of the Son and the Holy Spirit.[53] The third ecumenical council then found it necessary to defend the unity

52. "Ecumenical" indicates the human world according to its known extent. These councils are deemed ecumenical, because churches all over the known world have received and taught their interpretations of Scripture.

53. Some historians divide the ecumenical councils between the Trinitarian and the Christological, with the first two being focused on Trinity. However, the first two councils were also supremely interested in the person of Jesus Christ. Cf. Kelly McCarthy Spoerl, "Apollinarius and the Nicene Homoousion," in Young Richard

of his person. Subsequent councils preserved the biblical revelation of Christ by defending the personal union of his divine nature and will with his human nature and will. Together, the ecumenical councils[54] progressively unfold "the mystery of the ultimacy of Jesus Christ."[55] They demonstrate how early believers were passionate to know Christ and glorify him.

Nicaea, 325

The Council of Nicaea anathematized Arianism for diminishing the Son. Arius dishonored the Son by denying he had the same nature, glory, and authority as God. Reducing divine eternity by subdividing it with created time, he placed the Son in a time before the creation of all other things. The heresiarch taught that the Son came into existence by the Father's will. Arius also denied the Son should be worshiped equally with the Father.[56]

Alexander, the bishop of Alexandria, corrected Arius. He showed from Scripture both the equality of the Son in every way, and his likeness through generation with the Father. For instance, Alexander recalled John 5:23, wherein Christ said we must honor the Son to honor the Father. Because the Son is truly God, Christians worship the Son with the Father as one God.[57] Alexander also argued that, while the Son's eternal generation is ultimately incomprehensible to humanity, Scripture establishes his equality with the Father through his generation (Prov. 8:25; John 1:14, 18; 3:16; Heb. 1:5; 5:5). The

---

Kim, ed., *The Cambridge Companion to the Council of Nicaea* (Cambridge University Press, 2021), 303.

54. The seventh ecumenical council, which met at Nicaea in 787, confessed that images of Christ may be venerated but only God may be adored. The rise of iconoclastic tendencies in Christian-ruled territory and in Islam without prompted orthodox believers to recognize Christ may certainly be represented, for he is human. Nicaea II thus reaffirmed the true humanity of Jesus by allowing artistic representation of his human body. Many were still reluctant to picture the Father. Francis Dvornik, *The Ecumenical Councils* (New York: Hawthorn, 1967), 36–40.

55. Tibor Horvath, *Jesus Christ as Ultimate Reality and Meaning: A Contribution to the Hermeneutics ofOunciliar Theology* (Toronto: Regis, 1994), 23.

56. Arius, *Thalia*, in Rowan Williams, *Arius: Heresy and Tradition*, rev. ed. (Eerdmans, 2001), 101–3.

57. Alexander of Alexandria to Alexander of Constantinople, in Theodoret, *Ecclesiastical History* 3, in Philip Schaff and Henry Wace, eds., *Theodoret, Jerome, Gennadius, Rufinus: Historical Writings*, Nicene and Post-Nicene Fathers, 2nd Series, vol. 3 (Hendrickson, 1994), 39.

Son is "without beginning" and has "a perfect likeness in all things to his Father," the only distinction being his generation.[58]

Alexander's basic insights about the full deity of Christ and the eternal generation of his Person, and that Christ's deity requires us to worship him, was deemed universal church dogma by the Council of Nicaea. The bishops who gathered from churches across the world crafted the Nicene Creed to confess Christ and condemn Arius's diminishing of his deity. Alexander's orthodox successors in the African city of Alexandria, especially Athanasius and Cyril, became intrepid defenders of our one Lord, the man Jesus.

Constantinople, 381

More than fifty years later, a second ecumenical council gathered in the imperial capitol of Constantinople to consolidate the gains made in divine Christology and divine Pneumatology at Nicaea. They also addressed new heresies about both Christ and the Holy Spirit. For instance, wayward doctrines of Christ were taught by Marcellus of Ancyra and Apollinaris of Laodicea. Both affirmed Nicaea and opposed Arianism, but both of these heretics then proceeded to diminish the Word of God in other ways. Their teachings shocked orthodox theologians into action during the decades leading into the second ecumenical council.

The first errant theologian, Marcellus, lacked a doctrine of eternal generation to explain the personhood of the Son. He compared the Word to a breath which has its beginning in God and returns into God. He limited the incarnate Christ to the time between his incarnation and the supposed end of his kingdom. He said 1 Corinthians 15:28—"the Son himself will also be subjected to the one who subjected everything to him"—meant Christ's kingdom will cease.[59] Marcellus was so focused on preserving the unity of God that he denied the Word is an eternal Person and limited his humanity. Christ, he argued, has only a "partial kingship."[60]

58. Alexander of Alexandria to Alexander of Constantinople, 39–40.

59. Contrary to the Kingdom Cessation viewpoint, Christ restores the universe to its proper place of submission with his humanity. Creation becomes subject to Christ as God through Christ as Man. Numerous biblical texts, as we saw in the last chapter, identify the kingdom of Christ as eternal rather than as temporary.

60. Khaled Anatolios, *Retrieving Nicaea: The Development and Meaning of Trinitarian Doctrine* (Baker Academic, 2011), 86–92.

Semi-Arian theologians like Eusebius of Caesarea were the first to condemn Marcellus, doing so in personal writings and through various synods. Upon further reflection, other pro-Nicene theologians also withdrew support from him.[61] Marcellus was formally condemned in the first canon of the second ecumenical council, held at Constantinople in 381.[62] A new clause was also added at the end of the Christological article of the Nicene Creed: "His kingdom shall have no end."[63] This key addition, based on the numerous passages which demonstrate Christ's Kingdom is forever (cf. 2 Sam. 7:12–16; 1 Chron. 17:11–14; Pss. 2:8; 45:6–7; 110:1–4; Isa. 9:7; Dan. 7:13–14; Matt. 26:62–64; John 18:36; 1 Cor. 1:24; Phil. 2:9–11; Eph. 1:20–22; Col. 1:16; 2:9–10; 3:1; Heb. 1:5–13; 13:8; Rev. 5:13; 7:15–17; 19:16; 22:3–5, 13),[64] simultaneously preserved the eternality of the personhood of the Word and the ascent of his humanity to his eternal throne.

The second errant theologian, Apollinaris, had defended the deity of Christ but at the price of the "mutilation" of his humanity.[65] The bishop of Laodicea even criticized Marcellus, but he dishonored Christ, too, although in a different way. Adopting Plato's tripartite anthropology, he taught that the Word of God took a human body and irrational soul at the incarnation but not a human spirit or mind. Following Platonism's restrictive meaning of *sarx* (Greek "flesh"), Apollinaris promoted a Word-body Christology which reduced Christ's human nature.[66]

Contrary to the Greek philosophical anthropology used by Apollinaris, the New Testament follows the Old Testament in

61. Lewis Ayres, *Nicaea and Its Legacy: An Approach to Fourth-Century Trinitarian Theology* (Oxford University Press, 2004), 62–69; Khaled Anatolios, *Deification Through the Cross: An Eastern Christian Theology of Salvation* (Eerdmans, 2020), 186; Philip Schaff, *History of the Christian Church*, vol. 3, 5th ed. (1863; reprint, Hendrickson, 1996), 651–53. Christian friendship does not countenance heresy.

62. "Council of Constantinople," Canon 1, in Norman P. Tanner, ed., *Decrees of the Ecumenical Councils*, 2 vols. (Georgetown University Press, 1990), 2:31; Quasten, *Patrology*, 3:197–201.

63. Malcolm B. Yarnell III, *God the Trinity: Biblical Portraits* (B&H Academic, 2016), 241.

64. See the further reasons this clause is required in Yarnell, "The Contemporary Relevance of Nicaea."

65. Quasten, *Patrology*, 3:382.

66. J. N. D. Kelly, *Early Christian Creeds*, 3rd ed. (Longman, 1972), 332–37.

typically using "flesh" to mean "the whole person."[67] Moreover, the biblical witness repeatedly demonstrates the truthfulness of Christ's entire humanity. Not only the Gospels, but the rest of the New Testament reveals the existence of his human mind or spirit, by which he exercised human thought, will, and speech (cf. Matt. 24:36; 26:39; Mark 13:32; Luke 2:40; 8:45–46; 22:44; 23:46; 1 Cor. 2:16; Heb. 2:10–14, 18; 4:14; Rev. 1:18; 5:6–7).

Gregory of Nazianzus responded that Christ had to assume the fullness of our humanity to save us. The first part of his famous Christological axiom stated, "For that which He has not assumed He has not healed." If Christ does not have a human mind, the human mind cannot be saved, and our whole human nature needs to be reconstituted by Christ.

In the second part of his axiom, Gregory turned from Christology proper to Christ's importance in salvation. Gregory said humanity can be reunited to God only through the union of the two natures in the one Mediator: "But that which is united to his Godhead is also saved." For orthodox theologians like Gregory, the divine Christ had to assume our human nature in order to redeem us. The One who is eternally God "assumed Manhood also for our salvation."[68]

Gregory, the bishop of Constantinople, chaired the Council of Constantinople for a time. The council followed his lead and condemned the heresies of both Apollinaris and Marcellus.[69] Alongside the necessarily negative condemnations of heresies, the positive confessions of the Nicene Creed—that the eternal Son "descended," "became flesh," and "became human"—also provide an effective

67. "Flesh" in the Old Testament (Hebrew *batsar*) often indicated "humanity as a whole," "the whole being," "the person as a whole," or "the whole person." The New Testament received and expanded the Septuagint's translation of *batsar* with the Greek *sarx*. Moisés de Silva, *New International Dictionary of New Testament Theology and Exegesis*, 5 vols. (Zondervan, 2014), 4:253. "Thus John [1:14] asserts the deity and the real humanity of Christ. He answers the Docetic Gnostics who denied his humanity." Archibald Thomas Robertson, *Word Pictures in the New Testament*, 6 vols. (Broadman Press, 1932), 5:13.

68. Gregory also condemned Apollinaris for portraying the Trinity as a hierarchy of power, thereby undermining divine sovereignty. Apollinaris said the Three are "Great, Greater, and Greatest." Gregory Nazianzus, Epistle 101, in Philip Schaff and Henry Wace, eds., *Cyril of Jerusalem, Gregory Nazianzen*, Nicene and Post-Nicene Fathers, 2nd series, vol. 7 (Hendrickson, 1994), 439–40, 442.

69. Council of Constantinople, Canon 1, in Tanner, ed., *Decrees of the Ecumenical Councils*, 2:31.

antidote to theologies which limit the fullness of Christ's assumption of humanity. Christ in his incarnation assumed and perfected our whole human nature.

Both Marcellus and Apollinaris demeaned the dignity of the eternal Word, who is truly God and truly Man. Marcellus compromised Christ's personhood and humanity through denying his eternal reign. Apollinaris compromised Christ's humanity through denying his possession of a human spirit or mind. Diminishing Christ's humanity also contradicts the way that God provides human salvation. Because the one Mediator between God and humanity must be simultaneously human and divine (1 Tim. 2:5–6), diminishing Christ's humanity compromises our salvation just as much as the Arian diminishing of Christ's deity. Subsequent councils therefore continued to condemn the heresies of both Marcellus and Apollinaris along with the heresy of Arius.

Ephesus, 431

The third ecumenical council gathered in Ephesus to uphold Christ's Person. They honored Christ by confirming Cyril's doctrine of Christ's personal unity and condemning Nestorius's division of his Person. Nestorius had tried to avoid "the attribution of the human experiences of Christ to the divine Word."[70] Cyril cooperated with orthodox Antiochene theologians like John, the bishop of Antioch, to reaffirm Nicaea and Constantinople and confess belief in Christ as a single subject with two natures rather than as two different persons.

While they preserved Christ's unity, both Cyril of Alexandria and John of Antioch recognized Scripture's differentiation between Christ's exalted divine nature and his assumed human nature. They said, "the only begotten Son of God," a single subject, is comprised of two perfections, "perfect God and perfect man." His human nature, moreover, is entire, being both "of a rational soul and body." Their Formula of Union, which united orthodox theologians from both the schools of Alexandria and Antioch, also affirmed the divine narrative of the incarnation: In "unconfused union," "God the Word

70. Anatolios, *Deification Through the Cross*, 196.

took flesh and became man and from his very conception united to himself the temple he took from her."[71]

Cyril emphasized the unity of Jesus Christ, but without compromising his divine attributes, and he affirmed his divine attributes, but without diminishing his human attributes. On the one hand, he said the deity of Christ was preserved at the incarnation, because "although he assumed flesh and blood, he remained what he was, God in nature and truth." On the other hand, he said the humanity of Christ was not obliterated in the incarnation. "We do not say that his flesh was turned into the nature of the godhead."[72] Christ's two natures remain united in his one Person.

Human salvation is utterly dependent on the personal union of God with man in Christ. It is only through Christ's personal union with us as human beings that we can come to know God, for only Christ is both God and man. "We know only one Christ, the Word from God the Father with his own flesh."[73]

Chalcedon, 451

Two decades later, the Council of Chalcedon recalled the teachings of Cyril and affirmed that Christ is one person in two natures, with each nature retaining its own qualities.[74] The council applauded Cyril's writings for preserving the truth that Christ was not "a mere man."[75] Chalcedon also lauded the *Tome* of Pope Leo, which held in balance both the single subject Christology of Cyril with the two natures Christology emphasized by orthodox Antiochenes. Chalcedon, in turn, condemned the error of Eutyches, an Alexandrian who went beyond Cyril to teach that there were two natures before the personal union but only one afterward.[76]

---

71. Council of Ephesus, *Formula of Union*, in Tanner, ed., *Decrees of the Ecumenical Councils*, 1:69–70.

72. Council of Ephesus, Cyril to Nestorius, Third Letter, in Tanner, ed., *Decrees of the Ecumenical Councils*, 1:53.

73. Council of Ephesus, Cyril to Nestorius, Third Letter, in Tanner, ed., *Decrees of the Ecumenical Councils*, 1:51.

74. Cyril of Alexandria, Letter 40: To Acacius, in *St. Cyril Letters 1–50*, transl. John I. McEnerney (Catholic University of America Press, 1987), 162.

75. Council of Chalcedon, Definition of the Faith, in Tanner, ed., *Decrees of the Ecumenical Councils*, 1:85.

76. Henry Chadwick, *The Church in Ancient Society: From Galilee to Gregory the Great* (Oxford University Press, 2001), 553–55.

Pope Leo's letter to Flavian, the Patriarch of Constantinople, is noteworthy for the way in which it summarizes and explains the unity of the person of Christ without diminishing either his humanity or his deity. Like the theologians of Nicaea, Constantinople, and Ephesus beforehand, Leo rehearsed the gospel narrative of the divine economy of salvation, placing the divine Word in human history: "Thus was true God born in the undiminished and perfect nature of a true man, complete in what is his and complete in what is ours."[77]

Leo taught that Christ's deity is entirely one with the Father's deity. The Son is "co-eternal with him, in no way different from the Father, since he was born God from God, Almighty from the Almighty, co-eternal from the Eternal, not later in time, not lower in power, not unlike in glory, not distinct in being."[78] In other words, from his divine ontology to his divine economy, everything the Father has, so has the Son (cf. John 16:15).

In turn, Christ's humanity is as complete as our humanity. The union of humanity with deity in Christ did not diminish that humanity. "As God is not changed by showing mercy, neither is humanity devoured by the dignity received." The activity of Christ's humanity remained human. There was, however, an "enhancing" of humanity by Christ.[79] The matter of this "enhancing" became clearer in subsequent councils.

Leo appropriated the teachings of the apostles to uphold the unity of Christ's person even as he maintained his true deity and his true humanity. His review of their writings led him to state: "The same one is both the Son of God and also the Christ." There is only one Christ in two natures according to the apostolic testimony. "And to have believed that the Lord Jesus Christ was either only God and not man, or solely man and not God, was equally dangerous."[80] Leo's careful exegetical theology was precisely stated in the formula adopted at Chalcedon, reviewed at the end of the last chapter.

---

77. Council of Chalcedon, Leo to Flavian, in Tanner, ed., *Decrees of the Ecumenical Councils*, 1:78.

78. Leo to Flavian, 77.

79. Leo to Flavian, 78–79.

80. Leo to Flavian, 80.

Constantinople II, 553

At the Second Council of Constantinople in 553, mediating theologians sought to maintain the unity of the church from being damaged by radicals in the Antiochene tradition. The school of Antioch was teaching that the balance previously achieved at Chalcedon in 451 contradicted both the Alexandrian tradition and Cyril's emphasis upon the unity of Christ.

In response to the misinterpretations of Scripture and orthodoxy by the Antiochene theologians, the writings of three prominent Antiochene theologians were examined. Theodore of Mopsuestia, Theodoret, and Ibas were found to be deficient and were condemned by the council. Cyril's work at Ephesus and Leo's work at Chalcedon were reaffirmed, and the dogmatic decrees of the four previous ecumenical councils were likewise reaffirmed.[81]

Constantinople II emphasized the hypostatic union of Christ against various alternative unities which diminished Christ. They noted how the type of unity advocated by Apollinaris and Eutyches had confused the natures. Conversely, the type of unity advocated by Theodore and Nestorius was too weak to maintain true unity, for it was "a union only by affection." Instead of this weak communion between the two natures, the council declared the true unity of Christ was "a union between the Word of God and human flesh which is by synthesis, that is by a union of subsistence." The Greek phrase translated into Latin as *unitionem . . . subsistentiam* was *tan henosin . . . kath' hypostasin*. These ancient phrases may be translated woodenly into English as "subsistent union" and "hypostatic union," or more loosely as "personal union."[82]

Constantinople III, 680–681

At the Third Council of Constantinople in 680, Christ's wills and principles of energy became a critical concern. Efforts to heal the ongoing rivalry between the two major schools of Antioch and Alexandria continued, but some proposed solutions created difficulties too great for truly orthodox teachers to ignore.

81. Council of Constantinople II, Sentence Against the Three Chapters, in Tanner, ed., *Decrees of the Ecumenical Councils*, 1:110, 113.

82. Council of Constantinople II, Anathema 4, in Tanner, ed., *Decrees of the Ecumenical Councils*, 1:115.

Sergius, the bishop of Constantinople, proposed bringing the hypostatic union and two natures into easy conceptual grasp by affirming Christ had "one energy." Honorius, the bishop of Rome, added that Christ had "one will." Heraclius, the Emperor, liked the one will idea and condemned any teaching that Christ might have two wills.[83] The solutions of Sergius, Honorius, and Heraclius did not receive universal approval.

Stepping forward to defend orthodox Christology, Maximus the Confessor argued that, whatever those leading churchmen might think, a contextual reading of Matthew 26:36–42 requires the orthodox believer to affirm Christ has two wills. In the garden of Gethsemane, Christ concluded through deep personal struggle, "Yet not as I will, but as you will" (Matt. 26:39; cf. John 5:30; 6:38).

The two wills under consideration here could not be that of the eternal Son vis-à-vis the Father. Any doctrine of multiple wills or multiple energies belonging to one God would undermine divine unity. Apostolic testimony had already depicted Father and Son as possessing one word, one will, one work. Christ said he spoke "God's words," does "the will of him who sent me," and does "the works of him who sent me" (John 3:34; 4:34; 9:4; cf. 5:17–18, 30, 38; 6:45–46; etc.). Repeating the testimony of the apostles, Athanasius the Great likewise taught that the Father and the Son had one will and one work.[84]

With the conciliar tradition of biblical exegesis, Maximus sought to preserve the "perfect" and "whole" unity of the Three.[85] He believed that when the Word assumed humanity, humanity was granted personhood in the Word.[86] As a human person, Christ must have a human will and do human works. Following Nazianzus, a favorite theologian of his, Maximus believed what Christ does not

83. Douglas W. Johnson, *The Great Jesus Debates: Four Early Church Battles About the Person and Work of Christ* (St. Louis: Concordia, 2005), 117; Paul M. Blowers, *Maximus the Confessor: Jesus Christ and the Transfiguration of the World* (Oxford University Press, 2016), 159.

84. "For the will of the flesh had to be moved, and yet to be subjected to the divine will, according to the most wise Athanasius." Cyril, again, is also lauded. Council of Constantinople III, *Exposition of Faith*, in Tanner, ed., *Decrees of the Ecumenical Councils*, 1:128–29.

85. Maximus the Confessor, *Two Hundred Chapters on Theology*, transl. Luis Joshua Salés (St. Vladimir's Seminary Press, 2015), 104–7.

86. He learned this doctrine, known as *enhypostasis*, from Leontius of Jerusalem and Leontius of Byzantium. Blowers, *Maximus the Confessor*, 152.

assume, he does not heal. As with the mind (Greek *nous*), so with the will (Greek *thelema*). To redeem the human will, Christ must necessarily assume a human will.

Maximus argued that when Christ began his prayer with, "if possible, let this cup pass from me," he showed potential "resistance," just like any human would in the face of death. In the biblical context, the primary will under consideration was that of Christ's humanity. And against those who presume God can oppose himself, the divine will has no potential of resistance, for the Father and the Son and the Holy Spirit have one will by nature as God.[87]

Maximus concluded that "with the duality of his natures there are two wills and two operations respective to the two natures."[88] Christ's will and work as human was not placed in opposition to his will and work as God but brought into collaboration. Unlike fallen man, who opposed God's will, Christ submitted the human will into harmony with God. Christ corrected humanity's ability to exercise the will properly in a garden, reversing Adam's perversion of the human will in another garden.

When Christ submitted to God's will, he was bringing the human will into "perfect harmony and concurrence" with God through his obedience as a man. Maximus said the struggle in the garden occurred within this human will of Christ. Christ overcame natural human desire through his obedience to the Father. And he went on to secure the redemption of humanity through his bodily sacrifice. Christ surrendered his natural human will to the one divine will he possessed with the Father and the Spirit.[89] With the will, as in numerous other ways, Christ mediated the way back to God for humanity.[90]

When Maximus refused to surrender these powerful exegetical and theological insights, the imperial authorities mutilated him bodily. He died from his wounds in 662. However, some two decades later, the sixth ecumenical council gathered in Constantinople to

---

87. Maximus, *Opusculum* 6, in *The Cosmic Mystery of Jesus Christ: Selected Writings from St. Maximus the Confessor*, transl. Paul M. Blowers and Robert Louis Wilken (St. Vladimir's Seminary Press, 2003), 173.

88. Maximus, *Opusculum* 6, 174.

89. Blowers, *Maximus the Confessor*, 163.

90. Blowers, *Maximus the Confessor*, 142–44. "By the voluntary character of his suffering, Christ broke the pattern of human nature warring against itself, so also 'reconciling us through himself to the Father and to one another.'" Blowers, *Maximus the Confessor*, 155–58.

correct the heresy of the emperor (and the patriarch and the pope) and uphold the martyr's theology. They proclaimed with Maximus that Christ has "equally two natural volitions or wills in him and two natural principles of action which undergo no division, no change, no partition, no confusion, in accordance with the teaching of the holy fathers."[91]

Maximus envisioned the restoration of the universe occurring in Christ. Christ must be truly human, which requires both a human will and human energy, to reconcile humanity. He must also be truly divine, which requires both a divine will and divine energy to reconcile humanity with God. Constantinople III vindicated Maximus, saying, "We hold that two natural wills and principles of action meet in correspondence for the salvation of the human race."[92]

If one denies the human nature its principle of activity, which a "one energy" solution would surrender, Christ could not be truly human. Conversely, if one denies the divine nature its energy and will, Christ would not truly be divine. Without one Christ who, subsequent to the incarnation of the eternal Word, remains truly human and truly divine, human salvation becomes impossible. Gregory's perceptive axiom, "that which He has not assumed He has not healed," has far reaching implications, indeed.

Conclusion: The Classical Doctrine of Jesus Christ

As we have seen, orthodox soteriology depends upon orthodox Christology, which in turn derives from proper biblical interpretation. The doctrines of Christ, biblical authority, and salvation are interwoven. From his careful reading of Scripture, the first great patristic theologian, Justin, understood that Christ in his Person determines how he saves us in his actions. Insightful accounts of the Person of Christ subsequently developed through the tussle of theological debate. The proponents of the true Christ often paid a great price for defending him. The last great patristic theologian, Maximus, died a martyr for truth, just like the first, Justin.

91. Council of Constantinople III, *Exposition of Faith*, 128.
92. Council of Constantinople III, *Exposition of Faith*, 129–30.

These early believers' conclusions about the identity of Christ were captured in the dogmatic decrees of the great councils. These dogmas are received by Christians around the world, as the term "ecumenical" indicates.[93] The orthodox reception of knowledge about Christ's Person, and the impact of their discoveries upon our understanding of salvation, must not be glibly dismissed as tangential. The councils believed the Spirit was leading them, for Christ promised the Spirit would guide his followers "into all the truth" (John 16:13). Historically, churches have deemed their Christology biblically based, Spirit-led, and dogmatically necessary.

The Reality of Jesus Christ

We described the biblical consensus about the ontology or being of Christ as being comprised of three rules. After rehearsing the struggles of the early church to refute those who diminished Christ, we can now describe these three rules as follows. When speaking of his reality, we must affirm the following three truths together: Jesus Christ is one Person, who is truly God and truly human.

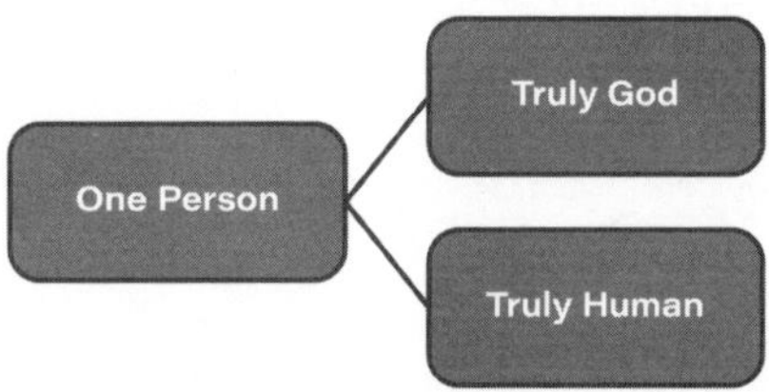

Figure 3: The Reality of the Eternal Word, the Lord Jesus Christ

1. Our Lord Jesus Christ is *one Person* eternally. His personal union includes both his eternal deity and his assumed humanity. Both natures are perfectly united in his Person, even while retaining their distinctive qualities. He is not two persons, but truly one Person.

93. The Eastern Orthodox received the first seven ecumenical councils. Roman Catholics agreed but added 14 more. Most Protestant scholars receive the first seven. Some pay attention only to the first four.

2. The eternal Word is *truly God*, differentiated only by his eternal generation from the Father. His deity remains wholly his in being and act. His deity was not diminished through his incarnation. He eternally exists and acts as God, before, during, and after his incarnation. God has one nature and one will, and his operations are inseparable.
3. Jesus Christ, the eternal Word who became flesh, is *truly human*. His humanity, like ours, is constituted of a body and a soul in entirety, including the properties of mind, will, and operations. His humanity is not diminished by union with the divine Word, although he certainly resurrects our humanity by divine activity. He obeyed God in all things. Through his incarnation and resurrection, Christ became a human person forever.

Our Salvation in Jesus Christ

In a similar way, the patristic consensus about the doctrine of salvation, which should be identified with the economic work of Christ, has recently been described as comprised of three rules:

1. The two natures of Jesus Christ are united in his one Person.
2. This personal union occurred through God's economic taking of our human nature to Christ's person. In other words, the eternal Word became human to work our salvation.
3. Human beings are invited into the presence of the triune God through spiritual union by faith. People are saved as the Holy Spirit mysteriously causes our spiritual union with the human Christ by grace, who himself possesses personal union with God by nature.[94]

94. Khaled Anatolios, *Deification Through the Cross*, 168. Cf. Richard Hooker, *The Word Made Flesh: A Treatise on Christology and the Sacraments*, eds. Brad Littlejohn, Patrick Timmis, and Brian Marr (Davenant Press, 2024), 61.

Christ and human salvation are inseparable, just as the two natures of Christ became inseparable through the divine work of incarnation. The Christian gospel depends upon the one true Christ. Only Jesus Christ is the way, the truth, and the life (John 14:6). Salvation is found only in his name (Acts 4:12). There is no other Mediator (1 Tim. 2:5–6). In other words, proclaiming the gospel requires proclaiming Christ. There is no other Christ and no other gospel. To proclaim another Christ is to proclaim a false gospel.[95] My prayer is that you and I will be faithful worshipers of the one true Christ, truly God and truly man, and that we will be faithful to proclaim his cross as alone sufficient for our salvation (1 Cor. 2:2).

Study Questions

1. What three truths about the identity of Jesus Christ were emphasized in the teachings of Athanasius of Alexandria and of his successor, Cyril of Alexandria? Provide an example from Scripture supporting each truth.

2. What heresies about Jesus Christ were condemned at the Council of Constantinople in 381? What truths were affirmed in response to the heresies?

3. What did Maximus the Confessor teach about the will(s) of Jesus Christ? What was the premiere biblical text to which he appealed?

Suggested Resources

- Athanasius of Alexandria, *On the Incarnation*
- Cyril of Alexandria, *On the Unity of Christ*
- Maximus the Confessor, *The Cosmic Mystery of Jesus Christ*

---

95. Cf. Gal. 1:6–9. Other false "christs" who appear in human history will be identified in chapter 13.

CHAPTER FIVE

Where Do We Begin?

◆ ◆

IN THE PREVIOUS CHAPTERS, WE considered the truth of God the Father and his only begotten Son, Jesus Christ. We listened carefully to the teachings of Holy Scripture about both the Father and his Son. We also listened to the conversations of other believers about their understandings of God and Christ. We then offered systematic summaries, of the doctrine of God the Father at the end of chapter 2, and of the doctrine of God the Son at the end of chapter 4.

Now, we must consider how God works in relation to those who are not God. The whole divine economy includes God's creation, providence, redemption, and consummation of all things, as well as his revelation of himself to his creatures. "Creation" covers both the initial act of the divine economy and the creatures he created. Providence explores his ongoing rule over his creatures. Redemption concerns his rescue of his creatures from evil. And at the consummation, God will require a final account from his creatures for how they used the gifts he initially granted them. Before proceeding to answer the question, "Where do we begin?" or "Where did we come from?" recall three axioms mentioned earlier and further developed below.

Three Axioms

Trinitarian Action

First, when God acts, he does so as the one God who is Trinity. The reality of God as Trinity is manifested in the way he acts as Trinity. In other words, the God who is Three in One reveals himself as the One who is Three. From the perspective of his one essence, because all divine action derives from God's one being, the divine economy necessarily involves the Father, the Son, and the Holy Spirit in every action. And from the perspective of the divine Persons, Scripture demonstrates that God the Father originates every divine work, while God the Son speaks it, and God the Holy Spirit perfects it.

The Creator–Creature Divide

Second, God is the transcendent, free, all-powerful, and good Creator of all that exists. God created the world by his own free will, and he created us from the blessed pattern of his triune love to be good and free, like himself. Even as the world received the good gifts of God at its origination, it remains dependent upon him in its progression and for its final completion. Scripture's transcendent God always retains his absolute self-sufficiency, and creation always remains utterly dependent on God. Divine independence and creaturely dependence mark a permanent divide between God and his creatures. This profound Creator–creature divide can be bridged only by divine action (cf. Deut. 30:12–13; Rom. 9:6–7).

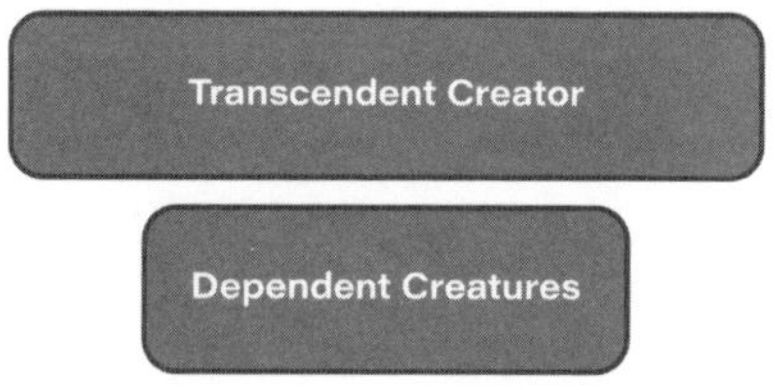

Figure 4: The Creator–Creature Divide

The Progress of the Cosmos

Third, from the perspective of his creatures, God's activities may be described historically according to the great events of creation, redemption, and consummation. These events are perceived from within history as a temporal progression, but the all-knowing God is always aware of his creatures' every action.[1] Throughout these dogmatic volumes, God's economy will be discussed under the headings of his three great actions toward his time-bound world: First, God created all things. Second, God is redeeming the world. Third, God will bring all things to their end. These three truths will be developed further as we continue turning our attention from the being of God to the work of God.

In this chapter, all three axioms are demonstrated in the first of the great works of God, creation. We demonstrate the first axiom by establishing the biblical basis, historical development, and theological contours of the inseparable operations of God the Trinity in creation. The remaining axioms will become apparent as we survey God's first great act. The truth of God as Creator ultimately reminds us that his creatures are obligated to worship God the Father with his Son with his Holy Spirit. God the Father is the font of triune personhood and the originator of the divine economy of creation, even as the Son with the Spirit is also Creator. God the Trinity is also the end of creation.

In the Beginning

The two oldest classical creeds of the church universal begin by confessing our Christian faith in "God the Father." They then proceed to discuss his work as "Creator of heaven and earth."[2] Both the Nicene Creed and the Apostles' Creed also include the Son and the Holy Spirit in the divine act of creation by confessing the Son is God and the Spirit is God. The Nicene Creed gives more detail, adding that the Father is Creator of "all that is seen and unseen."

1. God is eternal. The historical progress of his creation is present to him immediately, while creatures experience him mediately from within the creaturely limits of time and space. The doctrine of providence, with which the next chapter is concerned, is a subsidiary doctrine of creation.

2. Malcolm B. Yarnell III, *God the Trinity: Biblical Portraits* (B&H Academic, 2016), 240–41.

It also adds that the Son is he "through whom all things came into existence," and that the Spirit is "the Lord and Life-Giver."[3] However, the Father clearly leads in this unique divine act.

The classic Christian creeds confess God the Trinity is the one Creator, because this is a fundamental teaching of the Bible. Sacred Scripture begins by presuming the reality of God and by describing the divine act of creation:

> In the beginning God created the heavens and the earth. Now the earth was formless and empty, darkness covered the surface of the watery depths, and the Spirit of God was hovering over the surface of the waters. Then God said, "Let there be light," and there was light. (Gen. 1:1–3)

The first words of the biblical canon provide the basis from which all biblical dogma flows.[4] "The idea that God is the Creator of all things is the indispensable foundation on which the other beliefs of the Christian faith are based." "On this affirmation logically depends all that Christians say about God, about the world they live in, and about their own history, destiny, and hope." Not only is God the logical foundation of creation, human salvation depends on his being Creator, too. "Without the idea of God's creation of the world, of history, and of man, the Gospel of the redemption of man's life from sin becomes meaningless, self-contradictory, and vain."[5]

The first three verses of Scripture reveal the One who initiates all created reality. They also disclose the primary characters in creation. In short order, Genesis 1 introduces the primary actor (God),

---

3. Both creeds, which take their threefold form from the Christian's primary baptismal confession (Matt. 28:19), treat all three Persons as divine in confession and worship. The Nicene Creed makes this claim more explicit with ascriptions such as "God of God" to the Son and "together worshiped" to the Spirit.

4. The title of the first book of Scripture, "Genesis," derives from the Greek word for "origin" or "beginning" or the Latin word for "birth."

5. Langdon Gilkey, *Maker of Heaven and Earth: A Study of the Christian Doctrine of Creation* (Doubleday, 1959), 15–16. Perhaps due to contentious debates over evolution and world history, some systematic theologies underplay the doctrine of creation, while others emphasize it. James Leo Garrett Jr. cites Lewis Sperry Chafer, Walter Thomas Conner, and Helmut Thielicke as examples of the former; Norman R. Gulley exemplifies the latter. Garrett, *Systematic Theology: Biblical, Historical, and Evangelical*, vol. 1, 2nd ed. (BIBAL Press, 2000), 347n; Norman R. Gulley, *Systematic Theology: Creation, Christ, Salvation* (Andrews University Press, 2012).

the primary action (creation), and the primary beneficiaries of divine action (human beings). Next to God, human beings may be the most important creatures in creation, but they are not the only creatures. Moreover, their purpose is not their own to decide. Beginning where Scripture begins, let us consider what the Bible teaches us about God as Creator, especially that he is the Trinity, and what it teaches us about his act of creation.

God the Creator

Orthodox Christians understand that the Creator is one God in three Persons and that he preexists his creation of all other things. He exists eternally. To use temporal and spatial metaphors, we can say that God is "above" and "beyond" time and space. These creaturely metaphors do not limit God but point beyond our limits toward the unlimited God. God the Father, the Son, and the Holy Spirit both ontologically preexist creation and share equally in the initial divine act of creation. The utterly transcendent Creator provides the creaturely denizens of his created world with their origin, their progress, and their end.

These truths are sufficiently if summarily revealed in the first verses of Genesis 1. Verse 1 says "God" (Hebrew *'Elohim*) created all things. Verse 2 says the "Spirit" (Hebrew *Ruach*) of God was hovering over the chaos. The movement ascribed to the Spirit here was later ascribed to the Lord in his Shekinah glory as he formed the free nation of Israel out of a people once enslaved in Egypt (Exod. 13:21–22; 14:19–20).[6] It is significant that God and his Spirit together perform the work of creation. "The *ruakh* is on *'elohim*'s side of the Creator–creature divide."[7]

God and his Spirit are ontologically affirmed in Genesis 1:1–2 both by name and by activity. In contrast to the direct naming of God and his Spirit, his divine Word is not named but allusively revealed through his divine acts of speaking in verses 3, 6, 9, 14, 20, 24, and 26. While the personal realities of the divine Spirit and the divine Word are intimated here, the personal agencies of both are made explicit. The eternal personhood of the Word and the eternal

---

6. Yarnell, *Who Is the Holy Spirit? Biblical Insights into His Divine Person* (B&H Academic, 2023), 9–11.

7. Peter J. Leithart, *Creator: A Theological Interpretation of Genesis 1* (IVP Academic, 2023), 190.

personhood of the Holy Spirit are more thoroughly disclosed later in the canon.[8]

The third and subsequent verses reveal that when God spoke words during the first six days of creation, the thing about which he spoke received its reality. The agent of creation in the six days of creation, divine speech, came to the foreground of divine action at the conclusion of the introduction. Because the things spoken did not possess existence until after the divine word was spoken, the voice of God, who is named "Word" in the New Testament (cf. John 1:1–3), is also located with God and his Spirit on the one Creator's side of the Creator–creature divide. The creaturely reality spoken into existence and its temporal run in creation began only after God the Trinity created that reality with his words.

While Genesis 1:1–3 does not explicitly affirm the doctrine of the Trinity, the One who is Three nevertheless exercises a unitary personal agency before the foundation of creation. The divine economy of creation thus evinces a proto-Trinitarian shape in the first chapter of the biblical canon.[9] Each divine Person, later revealed by his distinct eternal relation in the Godhead, also takes a distinct role in the one work of creation: God "created" (Hebrew *bara'*), the Spirit "was hovering" (Hebrew *rahap*, "moving"), and the Word "said" (Hebrew *'amar*). The simple act of divine creation encompasses origination, proclamation, and administration.

Figure 5: The Trinitarian Act of Creation

The Creator Is God the Trinity

Other Old Testament texts reinforce the revelation of creation in Genesis 1 as formed by a Trinitarian act. Psalm 33:6 includes

8. On the personhood of the Spirit in Genesis 1, see Yarnell, *Who Is the Holy Spirit?*, 8–9. On the personhood of the Word, see chapters 2–4 above.

9. The prefix "proto" is used here in emulation of the common theological claim that the promise made by God after the Fall, that Eve's "offspring" would conquer the serpent, is an early form of the gospel, a "proto-evangelium" (Gen. 3:15).

both the Word and the Spirit with God at creation: "The heavens were made by the word [*dabar*] of the Lord [*Yahweh*], and all the stars, by the breath [*ruach*, literally 'Spirit'] of his mouth." Proverbs 8 identifies Wisdom, taken by many exegetes to be a theological synonym for the Word, as the companion of God "before" creation (vv. 22–26). Wisdom delighted with God in "every day" of creation (vv. 27–31). Psalm 104:30a similarly ascribes creative agency to the Spirit: "When you send your breath [*ruach*, literally 'Spirit'], they are created."

The New Testament repeatedly identifies the Word as a divine Person and as the agent of creation. The prologue to the Gospel of John says, "all things were created through him," then reinforces his creative agency by stating it negatively (John 1:3). The personal inability of many in the world to recognize the Word as Creator at his incarnation does not invalidate his prior claim over the world (v. 10). Later, restating the foundational Old Testament confession of God, the apostle Paul confesses that all things are "from" God the Father and that they came "through" and continue to "exist through" the one Lord, Jesus Christ (1 Cor. 8:6; cf. Deut. 6:4–5). The author of Hebrews agrees: God "made the universe through him" (Heb. 1:2).

Colossians 1 contains "the most expansive claim"[10] about the Word as Creator: "For everything was created by him, in heaven and on earth, the visible and the invisible, whether thrones or dominions or rulers or authorities—all things have been created through him and for him. He is before all things, and by him all things hold together" (Col. 1:16–17). The eternal Son of God stands before, under, and after every creature in creation, upholding creation and directing his creatures to fulfill his divine purpose. Each Gospel begins by connecting the advent of Christ to the advent of creation.[11] The disciples came to their deep conviction that Christ is the Creator by seeing him exercise lordship over creation through healing the sick, stilling the seas, and casting out demons.[12]

The New Testament also identifies the Holy Spirit as a divine Person and as co-equal agent of creation. Encompassing all the creative work of the Spirit, Jesus declared plainly, "The Spirit is the one

10. John S. Hammett and Charles L. Quarles, *The Work of Christ* (B&H Academic, 2024), 174.

11. Sean McDonough, *Christ as Creator: Origins of a New Testament Doctrine* (Oxford University Press, 2009), 19–22.

12. McDonough, *Christ as Creator*, 24–36.

who gives life" (John 6:63a). Jesus also correlated the work of the Spirit with his work as the Word in the creation of life: "The words that I have spoken to you are spirit and are life" (John 6:63c). The apostle Paul said the Holy Spirit is "the Lord," meaning he is divine in the absolute sense of that term. The Spirit is also "of the Lord," meaning he is personally related to the Father and the Son (2 Cor. 3:17).

As Lord and God, the Spirit "gives life" again and again (2 Cor. 3:6). As the Giver of Life, the Spirit is Creator, but his work is not limited to the initial act of creation. In the Old Testament, the Spirit gave life to humanity originally by providing man with his "breath of life" (Gen. 2:7), and when the Spirit withdrew his breath, death ensued (Gen. 6:3; Ps. 104:29). The Spirit provided life at creation. And he recreates life through the graces of salvation (John 3:5–8; Rom. 5:5). He who raised the human body of Jesus from death will also raise us back to life at the final resurrection (Rom. 8:11–13).[13]

Creation

God, the personal subject who initiates creation, necessarily preexists the objects of his creative action. From both a grammatical and a logical perspective the being and the existence of the Creator precedes his activity of creation. Likewise, those who have been created derive their entire existence through God's activity of creation. In creation, God grants those things which exist below God their origin. This Creator, moreover, is "personal" rather than a process.[14]

The divine act of creation marks the start of creation with the simple term, "the beginning" (Hebrew *bereshith*). In Genesis 1:1, this term is "used absolutely,"[15] marking the temporal limit of creaturely reality (cf. Isa. 46:10). Later in the biblical canon, "the beginning" (Greek *arche*) was used to indicate the One who exists beyond the natural limit of creation and transcends unmediated human knowledge (John 1:1; 1 John 1:1; Rev. 22:13). The absolute use of "the beginning" vindicates the claim of Genesis to be "true and actual

---

13. On the Holy Spirit as both "Creator" and "Re-Creator," see Yarnell, "The Person and Work of the Holy Spirit," in Daniel L. Akin, Bruce Riley Ashford, and Kenneth Keathley, *A Theology for the Church*, rev. ed. (B&H Academic, 2014), 527, 531–32.

14. C. F. Keil and F. Delitzsch, *The Pentateuch*, transl. James Martin (Eerdmans, 1985), 41.

15. Keil and Delitzsch, *The Pentateuch*, 46.

history," placing it beyond the capability of reason to comprehend entirely or to contradict.[16]

Those things which exist as creatures and live in time are described comprehensively as "the heavens and the earth." The word "heavens" (Hebrew *samayim*) can indicate the physical space above the earth. It can also point beyond the physical horizon toward the perfection of eternal spiritual reality, where God dwells. Things on "the earth" (Hebrew *'erets*) participate in material reality. As we shall see, those creatures whom we call "angels" are spiritual in nature, while human beings are both spiritual and material in nature.

All God's creatures experience change. Whatever its natural relation to matter and spirit, every creature is mutable. Genesis 1 describes the changes which occur in creatures as temporal. Creaturely change is marked by the progress of days (Gen. 1:5) and in the progress of those who have physical bodies. Bodily creatures experience birth and proceed through life to death. It should be noted that angelic beings, although heavenly or spiritual in nature, also demonstrate the constraints of space and time (Job 1:6–7; Rev. 20:1–3). "Eternity" is the perfect preserve of God, who alone does not change.[17] "Time" is the run of created things.

Every creature, whether composed of matter, spirit, or both matter and spirit, is situated within the progress of time by virtue of its origin after "the beginning." "History" considers the import of the changes in creatures through time.[18] Sacred history, revealed by God in Scripture, demonstrates that the progress and the importance of time are determined by God. It also demonstrates that although God is intimately involved with his creation, he is not determined by his creation. Instead, he freely acts from his own perfect, eternal, unchangeable, and living being.

The first three verses form an introduction to the first narrative of creation, which is focused on the six days of creation in Genesis 1:1–2:3. The first of the two creation narratives highlights the divine activity of creation through speech. The second creation narrative, relayed in Genesis 2:4–25, reveals the origination and early lives of the human beings who capped creation on the sixth day (Gen. 1:26–31). According to the first creation narrative, God speaks to

---

16. Keil and Delitzsch, *The Pentateuch*, 40.

17. Augustine, *Confessions*, transl. R. S. Pine-Coffin (Penguin, 1961), 261–64. Cf. Yarnell, *God*, Theology for Every Person, vol. 1 (B&H, 2024), 49–70.

18. On *eternity*, *time*, and *history*, see Yarnell, *God*, 51–57.

himself, saying he made human beings, "in our image, according to our likeness" (v. 26). He gave his "male and female" human beings "rule" over the rest of the world (vv. 26–27). And he deemed his creation of humanity "very good indeed" (v. 31).

The Being and Work of God

Before proceeding to speak of the work of God in creation, we must remember to differentiate divine ontology from divine economy. We must also learn to affirm the inseparable operations and proper works of God the Trinity. Finally, we must honor God the Father as the personal source of the divine work of creation, indeed, of all the divine works. The Son and the Spirit perform every divine work with him, from creation through redemption to consummation.

Figure 6: From Ontology to Economy

The Being or Reality of God

Modern scholars, inhibited by our intellectual culture, are typically reluctant to discuss the being of God, considering divine ontology too speculative, even ridiculous. Any concern with "metaphysics," that reality which exists beyond the immediately verifiable physical world, was deemed inaccessible and insignificant by naturalist philosophers in the Enlightenment. Contrary to Modernity's man-centered biases,[19] Scripture clearly reveals that God, who is purely spiritual, also possesses both being and personhood. We must learn to speak of divine ontology, but with respect for the truth that we can never define his divine being. God has a nature, even as his nature cannot be comprehended.

19. Peter Gay, *The Enlightenment: The Rise of Modern Paganism*, rev. ed. (Norton, 1995).

Moses knew that man cannot see God but discovered he can be known personally in his goodness and graciousness (Exod. 33:18–20). Philip learned he also might see God the Father, but only in the human face of Jesus Christ (John 14:9). The Apocalypse of John describes the current sight of God on his throne allusively with vivid metaphors of light and sound (Rev. 4:2–3; 21:3). But Christ promised the purified in heart they will one day see God for who he is (Matt. 5:8). Paul said the redeemed will see God "face to face," knowing him truly, in the end (1 Cor. 13:12).

The New Testament refers to God's being, which we cannot see, with terms like "the Godhead" (Greek *theotes*) and "the divine nature" (Greek *theios* or *theias physeos*). Paul proclaimed that the divine nature is sought after by humanity (Acts 17:29). He also said God's nature is fully present in the body of Jesus Christ (Col. 2:9). But Peter said God's being is known by grace only to the redeemed. They know God through *koinonia* (Greek "participation" or "sharing") in the divine nature (2 Pet. 1:3–4). Completing Scripture's ontological description of God, the author of Hebrews says the Father has *hypostaseos* (Greek "nature" or "person"). The Son perfectly reflects the Father's Person in his own Person (Heb. 1:3).[20]

While Scripture demonstrates that we can and should speak about divine being, we must always remember to speak about God's nature with thorough humility. The error of Eunomius, the second greatest heretic after Arius, began with his presumption that a human being could define the divine nature.[21] We must also remember to distinguish speech about God in himself from speech about God in relation to his creatures. The Greek church fathers placed speech about God "in" himself under the rubric of *theologia*, "theology proper." Modern theologians similarly speak of divine being under the terminology of "divine ontology."

20. After the rise of the Enlightenment, New Testament scholars often denied the ability of Christians to speak of the divine nature, but these and other texts speak of God in his being. Peter uses the adjective *theias*, "divine," to modify the noun *physeos*, "nature," clearly indicating God possesses an ontology (2 Pet. 1:4). For an example of the grudging reluctance of liberal scholars to recognize divine ontology, preferring instead to speak of his actions, see Ethelbert Stauffer, "*Theos*," in Gerhard Kittel, *Theological Dictionary of the New Testament*, transl. Geoffrey W. Bromiley, vol. 3 (Eerdmans, 1965), 110–12; Kleinknecht, "*Theios*," in Kittel, *Theological Dictionary of the New Testament*, 3:122–23.

21. See chapter 4 above.

Alternatively, to speak of that which is "outside" God refers to his creatures. The church fathers treated God's relationship with creation under the rubric of *oikonomia*, "economy." The divine economy, or God in relation to the world outside himself, must remain distinct in our minds from divine ontology, God in himself. Technically, however, we must also learn to say that because God is the greater reality, we live and move and have our existence "in" him (Acts 17:28). Again, this is metaphorical language, so the limitless reality of God is greater than our limited perception of his reality.

In these volumes, when we speak of the reality or nature of God, or divine ontology or theology proper, we are referring to God in his being. Metaphorically, when we speak of the reality which is "inside" God, we are referring both to his one nature and to the three Persons who entirely share his nature. Metaphorically, when we speak of God's activity, the divine economy, or that which is "outside" God, we are referring to his relations with creation. Metaphors like "inside" and "outside" point beyond our immediate knowledge toward his transcendent and substantial spiritual reality.

Inseparable Operations

When speaking of the work of God, we must remember that the activity of God derives from his one nature. When we say God acts from his nature, we mean that God acts with integrity regarding who he is. The God who "created" is simply one—*bara'* in Genesis 1:1 is in the third person singular. The one God always works from his unitary nature without division, without opposition, and without domination between the Persons. The Three, moreover, participate fully and equally in one divine action. To use the language of Augustine of Hippo, the Trinity's work is "inseparable" or "indivisible" (Latin *indivisa*).[22]

Beyond creation alone, the inseparable operations of the three Persons are affirmed repeatedly in Scripture. In our review of the Christology revealed in the Gospel of John, we noted the unity of the words and the works of the Father and the Son. Adonis Vidu traced "the unity of operation" between the Father and the Son and the Holy Spirit in greater detail through chapters 5, 10, and 14 in the Gospel of John. The words of God, the works of God, and "the

22. St. Augustine, *The Trinity*, transl. Edmund Hill, ed. John E. Rotelle (New City Press, 1991), 175.

power and authority of God" reside as fully in the Son as in the Father. Moreover, "there is no tension between Jesus's equality with God and his dependency on the Father." The obedience ascribed to the Son, in other words, belongs entirely to Christ's human nature.[23]

The Father and the Son and the Holy Spirit—the Three are One. Orthodox Christians affirm that God is one in substance,[24] and that the Persons are eternally "in" one another.[25] We also affirm that God acts with unity from his one divine nature. "In the same way that the persons exist indivisibly, so they *act* undividedly."[26] The Son does everything that the Father does (John 5:19) and speaks whatever the Father speaks (14:24; 17:8). In Scripture's narratives of redemption and revelation, therefore, as in the narrative of creation, the Three always work as one.[27]

Likewise, dividing the one will of God into multiple wills would violate God's unity, simplicity, and immutability. Separating the activity of God into opposing works, such that the will and work of the Father is said to dominate the Son, or that the Son is said to dominate the Spirit—this too violates the unity, simplicity, and immutability of God. Because the Father and the Son and the Holy Spirit are eternally One, so the Three act in unity toward that which is without, that is, toward his creation.

According to the Athanasian Creed, those who have the true faith know "not three gods, but one is God." We confess "not three lords, but one Lord."[28] It also understands the three Persons as one God work together in one divine act. God's actions are inseparable between the Father and the Son and the Holy Spirit. The One is Three; and the work of the Three is One.

---

23. Adonis Vidu, *The Same God Who Works All Things: Inseparable Operations in Trinitarian Theology* (Eerdmans, 2021), 36–51.

24. The Nicene Creed affirms the Son is *homoousios* (Greek, "one essence") with the Father. Yarnell, *God the Trinity*, 241.

25. Following John of Damascus, theologians began to speak of *perichoresis*, as a way of indicating that the Three "mutually indwell" one another.

26. Gilles Emery, *The Trinitarian Theology of St. Thomas Aquinas* (Oxford University Press, 2010), 309.

27. The inseparable operations of the Trinity in Redemption are summarized in Ephesians 1:3–14, and the inseparable operations of the Trinity in judgment and renewal at the Consummation are summarized in Revelation 12–14, 21–22. Yarnell, *God the Trinity*, 186–90, 222–26.

28. The Athanasian Creed is also known as the *Symbolum Quicunque*. Yarnell, *God the Trinity*, 242.

Proper Operations

The Three are "one single Creator."[29] The one God works unitedly, simply, and immutably in all his divine works. The one God works inseparably in creation, in his revelation of himself to his creatures, in our redemption, and in the final consummation of the universe. However, the Three also work distinctly according to the internal relations of the eternal Trinity. The works of God are inseparable from the unity of God but are also properly appropriated to the three Persons.

The one work of the one God is seen in every divine activity, but his work is also properly ascribed to Three. Take creation as an example: God the Father creates (Gen. 1:1), but he does so "through" speaking his "Word" (Gen. 1:3; Ps. 33:9; John 1:3) and by "sending" the "breath" of his Spirit (Gen. 1:2; 2:7; Ps. 104:30). God initiates creation from the Father, performs creation through the voice of the Word, and executes his work by the Holy Spirit.

A second example of the Trinity's proper working is found in the divine work of Redemption: God the Father provided for human salvation by sending the Son to become a human being, "born of a woman, born under the law, to redeem those under the law." God then sent "the Spirit of his Son into our hearts," so that we could truly call God "Father" (Gal. 4:4–6). Just as grace descends from God through the Son and the Spirit, so the Spirit returns us to communion with the Father through the Son. "For through him we [Jew and Gentile] have access in one Spirit to the Father" (Eph. 2:18).

Gregory of Nyssa said the proper working of the Persons involves "a transmission of Power, beginning from the Father, advancing through the Son, and completed in the Holy Spirit."[30] He thereby grounded the proper works of the Three in divine simplicity and the inseparability of the divine operations.[31] The One and the Three must be simultaneously affirmed in being and in act: "Since, then, the character of the superintending and beholding power is one, in Father, Son, and Holy Spirit." Nyssa illustrated the proper works of God by saying they occur through the one divine act "issuing from

---

29. Emery, *The Trinitarian Theology of St. Thomas Aquinas*, 344.

30. Gregory of Nyssa, *On the Holy Spirit*, in Philip Schaff and Henry Wace, eds., *Gregory of Nyssa: Dogmatic Treatises, Etc.*, transl. William Moore and Henry Austin Wilson, Nicene and Post-Nicene Fathers, Second Series, vol. 5 (Hendrickson, 1994), 320.

31. Nyssa, *On the Holy Trinity*, in Schaff and Wace, eds., *Gregory of Nyssa*, 328.

the Father as from a spring, brought into operation by the Son, and perfecting its grace by the power of the Spirit."[32]

Based on biblical revelation and the excellent exegetical work of the early church fathers, subsequent theologians have come to speak of each divine Person as having "appropriated" to himself certain "proper" works. These works reflect the eternal mode of existence of that Person. These works also express the economic mission of the Person.[33] "Mode of existence" refers to the eternal relation of each Person to the other Persons. "Mission" refers to the special work of each Person as God acts upon the world.

Figure 7: Eternal Modes and Personal Missions

As for the *personal modes of existence* of the Three, we have already seen that God the Father eternally generates or begets the Son. Jesus also taught that the Holy Spirit eternally "proceeds from the Father" (John 15:26). Western theologians have traditionally reasoned that, because the Son sends the Spirit economically, the Spirit may be said also to proceed from the Son (14:16, 26; 15:26; 16:7). Both Eastern and Western theologians agree that God the Father alone is neither generated nor proceeds but remains the font or source of the Persons. Generation and procession from the Father mark the personal modes of existence, or eternal relations of origin, of the divine Persons.

As for the *personal missions* of the Three, God the Father sent the Son through the conception of the Holy Spirit into the world to redeem humanity (Matt. 1:20; Gal. 4:4–5). The one God accomplished our salvation, but only God the Son assumes our humanity (John 1:14; 2 Cor. 8:9; Phil. 2:6–7). The Son alone, therefore, died upon the cross, was buried, arose from the dead, and appeared

32. Nyssa, *On "Not Three Gods,"* in Schaff and Wace, eds., *Gregory of Nyssa*, 334.

33. A divine Person's "mode of existence" is grounded in his eternal relation of origin and issues forth in a distinct mission. This language originated in the East and was taken up in the West. Emery, *The Trinitarian Theology of St. Thomas Aquinas*, 353–55.

to the apostles (1 Cor. 15:3–8). The Father and the Spirit remain intimately involved in human redemption, but neither became flesh. To sanctify us personally, the Father and the Son send the Spirit to apply to our hearts the grace initiated by the Father and performed by the Son (Gal. 4:6; John 14:16; 15:26).

The proper works of the Three may never be said to contradict the inseparable operations of the One. Instead, God the Trinity's proper works proceed from his inseparable unity. The personal missions reflect the personal modes of existence. The three divine Persons act personally in unity.

The Father as Source and End

With the inseparable and proper works of the Trinity in mind, we can now state how God the Father is first given the title of "Creator" in the classical creeds. God the Father originates the one divine action performed by the Three. In the biblical witness, both the Father and the Son are said to send, and both the Son and the Spirit are sent, but the Father is never sent.

From an ontological perspective, the eternal relations of origin indicate the Father is "the principle of unity in the Trinity." And from an economic perspective, the Father is likewise "the principle and the end" of all the divine works.[34] God the Father thus describes himself as "the Alpha" and "the Omega," "the beginning" and "the end" (Rev. 1:8; 21:6).[35]

God the Father remains intimately involved, through origination and consummation, with the Spirit and the Son, in every divine work. We have seen this demonstrated in the great works of Creation and Redemption and Revelation. It remains now to establish this truth regarding the Consummation of all things: While the Son renders final judgment, the Father also sits upon the throne of heaven and judges all things with the Son (John 8:16; Rev. 20:11; 21:5–8). Likewise, the Holy Spirit executes the divine work of judgment "with fire" (Luke 3:15–17).[36]

---

34. Emery, *The Trinitarian Theology of St. Thomas Aquinas*, 173.

35. The Son also self-identified as the Alpha and the Omega, indicating he too participates in the origin and end of every creature (Rev. 22:13).

36. Rustin Umstattd, *The Spirit and the Lake of Fire: Pneumatology and Judgment* (Wipf and Stock, 2017).

All the divine works—from creation, providence, and revelation to redemption and consummation—derive from and involve the whole Trinity, inseparably and properly. Each divine work begins and ends with the Father and always includes the Son and the Holy Spirit. Drawing on the prepositions used by Paul in Romans 11:36, and citing Athanasius, Thomas F. Torrance summarized the reality of the unitary and distinct working of the Trinity in this way: "All three divine Persons have one Activity which is ever the same for 'the Father does all things through the Word and in the Spirit.'"[37]

In summary, both the inseparable work of the one God and the proper work of each divine Person must be acknowledged. Both divine ontology and divine economy drive us toward two conclusions: First, because the Father, the Son, and the Spirit are "in" one another (John 10:38; 14:10–12, 17–18, 20; 17:21) and mutually possess one divine "nature" (Rom. 1:20; Col. 1:19; 2:9), each Person thoroughly participates in every divine work. Both the unity of God and the mutual indwelling of the Persons require the inseparable operations of the One who is Three.

Second, from each divine Person's mode of existence and subsequent mission, each appropriates the work proper to himself. God the Father may be especially identified with the divine works of election, creation, and providence, for he originates every divine act. He likewise consummates all things for his glory with the Son and the Spirit. By virtue of his being their good Creator, the creatures of God are obligated to worship and glorify the Father, but they must always worship and glorify the Son with the Holy Spirit together with the Father as the one God.

The Beauty of God's Creation

The creation mythologies of modernity, like those of the ancient world, center upon creatures, including humanity.[38] Biblical

37. Thomas F. Torrance, *The Christian Doctrine of God: One Being Three Persons* (T&T Clark, 1996), 196.

38. Even the gods of the ancient creation mythologies repeatedly display human characteristics, limits, and failures. Both ancient and Enlightenment philosophy made human reason the measure of reality and tended to treat humanity as the end of the world. Olli-Pekka Vainio, *Cosmology in Theological Perspective: Understanding Our Place in the Universe* (Baker Academic, 2018), 11–17, 20–27.

revelation altogether contradicts these myths by foregrounding the Creator rather than the creature. The biblical creation account dignifies humanity but always in a secondary way, by ascribing to men and women a likeness to God. God remains primary. Some Christian theologians have chosen to focus on the creaturely in their approaches to creation, typically as an apologetic.[39] But systematic theology should be theologically oriented, satisfying the glory of the Creator rather than the mind of the creature.[40]

The creation accounts of the book of Genesis itself are "thoroughly theological." As a result, "actual cosmological details are not at the center of the story." "The focus is on God as the sole benevolent Creator, who creates an orderly, good world where humans can live."[41] Like James Leo Garrett Jr.,[42] I chose to emphasize God as Creator above, minimizing human speculation and maximizing divine revelation. Having highlighted the Creator, we now consider his creation. Our basic claim about creation has five aspects. God, who is perfect in every way, freely and sovereignly provides the universe with its origin, its goodness, its orderliness, and its end.

God Created in Correspondence with His Being

First, as a general principle, classical theology recognizes that God acts in concert with his perfections.[43] This principle applies to creation. "It is perfectly true, moreover, that when God brought the

---

39. E.g., Gulley, *Systematic Theology: Creation, Christ, Salvation*, chapters 1–8; A. A. Hodge, *Outlines of Theology* (1879; reprint, Banner of Truth, 1972), 237–48; Charles Hodge, *Systematic Theology*, 3 vols. (reprint, Hendrickson, 2001), 1:550–74; J. P. Moreland and William Lane Craig, *Philosophical Foundations for a Christian Worldview*, 2nd ed. (IVP Academic, 2017), 556–62.

40. On the need to recover the theological orientation of theology, see the "provoking" essay of John Webster. Swimming against the tide of academic liberalism, which sublimated theology to human canons, Webster delivered "Theological Theology" for his inaugural lecture as Lady Margaret Professor of Divinity at Oxford University. John Webster, *Confessing God*, Essays in Christian Dogmatics, vol. 2 (T&T Clark, 2005), 11–31. John was a serious anchor for me as an evangelical in a faculty succumbing to the history of religions approach.

41. Vainio, *Cosmology in Theological Perspective*, 17.

42. Garrett, *Systematic Theology*, 1:213.

43. Irenaeus among the church fathers and Stephen Charnock among the Reformed scholastics both affirmed this truth. Gerhard May, *Creatio Ex Nihilo: The Doctrine of 'Creation out of Nothing' in Early Christian Thought*, rev. ed., transl. A. S. Worrall (T&T Clark, 2004), 168–70; Stephen Charnock, *Discourses on the Existence and Attributes of God*, 2 vols. (Baker, 1979), 2:368.

universe into being He did not do so without reference to his own being."[44] Creation is commensurate with God's character in that it derives from his sovereign activity. His attributes are reflected in creation or contrasted with creation through his continuing relationship with it. Consider, for instance, the divine attributes of aseity, goodness, and transcendence.

Regarding divine aseity, note that God alone is self-sufficient. "Before the mountains were born, before you gave birth to the earth and the world, from eternity to eternity, you are God. You return mankind to the dust, saying, 'Return, descendants of Adam.' For in your sight a thousand years are like yesterday that passes by, like a few hours of the night" (Ps. 90:2–4). Creation contributes nothing to the constitution of God's own being; rather, creation derives entirely from his sovereign choice. The world is an expression of God's perfect will, and humanity remains utterly dependent upon God.

Regarding divine goodness, note that God is good, and that he blesses his creatures. God's goodness necessarily characterizes all God's works, including creation (Rom. 8:28; James 1:17; 1 John 4:8, 16). "God created the world because he loves us. The act of God's creating the world represents a going out of himself to engage with creation and with humankind."[45] As the creation of a good and loving God, creation participates in his goodness. Creation reveals his good order and fulfills his good purpose. A special but limited goodness was granted to humanity as the crown of his creation (Gen. 1:31). Human beings desire purpose, order, and goodness, because we were created in his image. God's goodness undercuts human legends of chaos and meaninglessness.

Regarding transcendence, note that while God communicates his goodness and reveals his glory to his creatures, his radical otherness remains undiminished. The prophet Isaiah cried out, "Do you not know? Have you not heard? The Lord is the everlasting God, the Creator of the whole earth. He never becomes faint or weary; there is no limit to his understanding. He gives strength to the faint and strengthens the powerless" (Isa. 40:28–29). "The Creator"

44. John Gresham Machen, *The Christian View of Man* (Banner of Truth, 1965), 85.

45. "He did not create the world out of any need, of self-expression or of communication; an 'Other' already existed in himself as Trinity. . . . God created humankind out of love." Anthony C. Thiselton, *The Thiselton Companion to Christian Theology* (Eerdmans, 2015), 347–48.

is eternal, immutable, and omniscient. He grants gifts of power to his creatures, but he delimits their abilities and constrains their authority with moral boundaries and the promise of final judgment. Human beings, even in the prime of their strength, remain limited and entirely dependent upon God (vv. 30–31). We must appreciate the radical difference between the Creator and his creation.

God Created the World Out of Nothing

Second, the radical transcendence and aseity of the eternal God prompt us to recognize the doctrine of *creatio ex nihilo*. Ancient philosophers to the contrary believed cosmic matter was eternal. Plato imagined that a *demiurge* (Greek "craftsman") fashioned things in the world according to their eternal forms. Aristotle abstracted creation from an existent substratum. The ideas of these respected philosophers attracted Gnostic heretics who recast the Christian faith with their myths. Pagan ideas also appealed to apologists eager to reach philosophers in the early Christian centuries.[46] However, the pagan concept of eternal matter contradicts biblical theology.

In contrast to the pagan eternalization of matter, the first Genesis creation account portrayed a unique opening act performed by a unique actor. "In the beginning God created the heavens and the earth." The Hebrew terms of the first verse are instructive: *Bereshith*, "in the beginning," indicates a simple starting point. *'Elohim*, the single subject, precedes creation and initiates the act from which all other actions in the cosmos follow. *Bara'*, "created," denotes unique divine initiative.[47] A related Hebrew term, *yatsar*, which specifies a fashioning from existing material, was not used here.[48] God, as the

46. Scholars disagree as to whether Justin Martyr held the idea of pre-existent matter. Clement of Alexandria seems to have accepted it but denied matter was a second principle of being. Stead, *Philosophy in Christian Antiquity*, 26–30; May, *Creatio Ex Nihilo*, 1–5, 118–47.

47. Isaiah 40–55 uses *bara'* sixteen times, and the Lord God is always the subject. He is "the everlasting God, the Creator of the whole earth" (Isa. 40:28). There is no other eternal principle than the Creator (Isa. 45:6d–7). He gave creation its good form and purpose: "The God who formed the earth and made it, the one who established it (he did not create it to be a wasteland, but formed it to be inhabited)" (Isa. 45:18).

48. In Genesis 2:7–8, *yatsar* describes God's formation of humanity from pre-existing matter, the dust of the ground. In Jeremiah 1:8, *yatsar* describes God's formation of the prophet in the womb.

sole actor, initiated the world, and everything, both "the heavens and the earth," derived from his originating act.

The Genesis account implicitly excludes the eternality of matter. Explicit reference to the doctrine of *creatio ex nihilo* (Latin "creation out of nothing") appears first in the intertestamental literature. During the Maccabean revolt against the Seleucid Empire, who sought to impose Hellenistic religion upon the Jews, the mother of seven Jewish martyrs appealed to God's absolute creative power. She called upon her youngest child to remain faithful even unto death, for God can create life by absolute fiat. "God did not make [the heavens and the earth] out of things that existed."[49] The apostle Paul argued similarly for the resurrection. God is "the one who gives life to the dead and calls things into existence that do not exist" (Rom. 4:17).

The book of Hebrews also affirms *creatio ex nihilo*, but as a faith proposition rather than as an apologetic to reason. "By faith we understand that the universe was created by the word of God, so that what is seen was made from things that are not visible" (Heb. 11:3). The author of the Apocalypse joined the chorus of faith in the transcendent Creator, claiming the existence of everything is due entirely to his authoritative will. "Our Lord and God, you are worthy to receive glory and honor and power, because you have created all things, and by your will they exist and were created" (Rev. 4:11).

Second-century Christian theologians deployed the doctrine of *creatio ex nihilo* against both the Gnostic heretics and the pagan philosophers. A Syrian Christian liturgy included the doctrine near the beginning of the second century. A few decades later, a Syrian church father named Tatian explicitly argued that God created matter.[50] Another Syrian theologian, Theophilus of Antioch, promoted the doctrine in his commentary on Genesis: "God has created everything out of nothing into being."[51] At the other end of the Roman empire, Irenaeus of Lyons concurred. He argued that *creatio ex nihilo* preserves divine freedom, power, and goodness.[52]

In subsequent centuries, the Christian dogma that God created the cosmos out of nothing was rarely denied. In the thirteenth century, church authorities quickly curtailed the resurgence of the

49. 2 Maccabees 7:28b RSVCE.

50. May, *Creatio Ex Nihilo*, 148–52.

51. Theophilus, *Autolycus* 1.4, in May, *Creatio Ex Nihilo*, 156.

52. May, *Creatio Ex Nihilo*, 164–78.

Aristotelian doctrine at the Sorbonne in Paris.[53] In the seventeenth century, both Jewish and Christian authorities rejected Baruch Spinoza's radical equation of nature with God, although his ideas have fed into the modern academy through his flawed method of Bible study.[54] Today, the Christian dogma of *creatio ex nihilo* reminds us that the universe of creatures is entirely temporal and remains entirely dependent upon God for its origination.

God Created the World in Goodness

Third, the early church also defended the biblical truth that the world was created by God who, by the perfection of his goodness, blessed his creatures. At several points during Moses's first creation account (Gen. 1:4, 10, 12, 18, 21, 25), God deemed his creation *tob* (Hebrew "good"). In a noteworthy solidification, after finishing his creative activity on the sixth day, God said his creation of humanity in his image was not merely good but *ma'ad tob* (Hebrew "very good"; v. 31).

In Genesis, moreover, the materiality of the world was not deemed a factor in the origin of evil. Rather, evil appears first with a creature later identified as a malevolent spiritual being (Gen. 3:1–5; Rev. 20:1–3). However, pagan dualists believed that matter was intrinsically unsound. Plato located the sources of evil in phenomenal reflections of nonspatial reality.[55] Gnostics believed matter came from Sophia, the lowest emanation of a high God. Upon his own entrance into the world, "Gnostic man is thrown into an antagonistic, anti-divine and therefore anti-human nature."[56] The elect, the Gnostics said, will find their way back above matter to the highest God through their cult's special "knowledge" (Greek *gnosis*).

---

53. G. R. Evans, *Philosophy and Theology in the Middle Ages* (Routledge, 1993), 67–72.

54. Expelled from his synagogue, Spinoza opined, "That eternal and infinite being we call God, or Nature [Latin *Deus, sive Natura*], acts from the same necessity from which he exists." Edwin Curley, ed., *The Collected Works of Spinoza*, vol. 1 (Princeton University Press, 1985), 544; Steven Nadler, *Spinoza: A Life*, 2nd ed. (Cambridge University Press, 2018), 270; cf. Spinoza, *Collected Works*, 1:434.

55. Harold Cherniss, "The Sources of Evil According to Plato," *Proceedings from the American Philosophical Society* 98 (1954): 23–29.

56. Hans Jonas, *Gnostic Religion*, 338; cited in Barnstone and Meyer, eds., *The Gnostic Bible*, 11.

Irenaeus, in his majestic work, *Against Heresies*, said the Gnostics divided humanity into groups characterized by one of three substances: "material," "animal," and "spiritual." Spiritual men are being "perfected;" material men cannot be perfected, and those in the middle may incline one direction or the other. Matter, the Gnostics said, "is incapable of salvation."[57] Irenaeus disagreed! To say that God's creatures are "the fruit of defect and the production of ignorance, is to be guilty of great blasphemy."[58] Irenaeus argued that creation participates derivatively in the goodness of its Creator. God is good, so he created his creatures with goodness. Creation is, therefore, not intrinsically evil.

Whence, then, came evil? Seeking to answer the Manichean heretics regarding the phenomenon of human evil, Augustine developed his doctrine of the libertarian free will. First, he affirmed the Christian tradition: God originally created all things good. Evil came later through disorder of the will, when creatures began placing their love of creation above love of God. "All sins come about when someone turns away from divine things that truly persist and toward changeable and uncertain things." "We do evil by the free choice of the will."[59] Evil, the church fathers taught, derives from the creature, not the Creator. God is good and created the world from his goodness.

God Created the World with Order

Fourth, that the good God created the world to bless it prompts us to confirm the orderliness of its relations. Both Christian theologians and natural philosophers have long recognized the widespread evidence of elements of order in the world. However, creation's order has required vigorous defense in the modern era.

Medieval theologians divided the six days of creation into two major creative movements. The first three days (Gen. 1:3–13) involved a work of division (Latin *opus divisionis*); the second three

57. Irenaeus, *Against Heresies*, in Alexander Roberts and James Donaldson, eds., *The Apostolic Fathers, Justin Martyr, Irenaeus*, Ante-Nicene Fathers (Hendrickson, 1994), 1:323–24.

58. Irenaeus, *Against Heresies*, 362.

59. Augustine, *On Free Choice of the Will*, transl. Thomas Williams (Hackett, 1993), 27.

days (vv. 14–31) were a work of ornamentation (*opus ornatus*).[60] Such a division of the creation order honors the beauty of God's creative activity and of the creation which resulted from it.

Take a moment to note the simplicity and the fittingness of the order in the six days of creation: On the first day, the energy of light was created (Gen. 1:3–5). On the second day, space was defined in the creation of the heavens (vv. 6–8). On the third day, the physical earth and its plants were created (vv. 9–13). On the fourth day, the courses of the stars, the sun, and the moon were set to mark time (vv. 14–19). On the fifth day, creatures were given the air and the water to inhabit and multiply (vv. 20–23). On the sixth day, animals were created to inhabit and fill the earth itself (vv. 24–25). On that same final day of creation, God made humanity in his image to rule the earth for him (vv. 26–31). The seventh day was marked by rest (Gen. 2:1–3).

Recognizing the orderliness in creation helped modern science develop from natural philosophy.[61] Biological order may be easily detected among higher (non-plant) life-forms through categories of "kind" (Hebrew *miyn*). The kinds of creatures in Genesis 1 encouraged the development of natural philosophy's language of "genus" and "species." "So God created the large sea-creatures and every living creature that moves and swarms in the water, according to their kinds. He also created every winged creature according to its kind" (1:21a). Later, "God said, 'Let the earth produce living creatures according to their kinds: livestock, creatures that crawl, and the wildlife of the earth according to their kinds.' And it was so. So God made the wildlife of the earth according to their kinds, the livestock according to their kinds, and all the creatures that crawl on the ground according to their kinds" (vv. 24–25a).

A most important distinction in creation was revealed on the sixth day. At the end of that final day of God's creative action, the height of creation and the beauty of its complexity were attained. According to verses 26–31, humanity was created in the image and likeness of God and made to be male and female. The man and the woman together were then given the responsibility to rule over the earth on God's behalf. They were also commanded to be fruitful,

---

60. Dale Moody, *The Word of Truth: A Summary of Christian Doctrine Based on Biblical Revelation* (Eerdmans, 1981), 144–45.

61. Herbert Butterfield, *The Origins of Modern Science 1300–1800*, rev. ed. (Free Press, 1997).

multiply, and fill the earth. Finally, they were granted the right to use the earth and its fruit.

The beautiful phenomena of orderliness in creation must be recognized, even as care must be exercised neither to impose an extrabiblical order upon the scriptural evidence nor to deny the order evident in the text. Imposition of order through over-schematizing the evidence of biblical revelation can lead to human abuse of creation; denial of the divine gift of orderliness can lead to the same. God makes distinctions in creation. These distinctions should be maintained. Yet it should also be recognized that creatures exist in a dynamic and delicate relation, and that this order was disrupted by sin. Humanity still bears responsibility to care for creation, even in its brokenness, after the Fall (Gen. 3:23).

For instance, reflecting the goodness of God, humanity was made the crown of creation on the sixth day. Man and woman were created to participate by grace in divine dignity, to live in equality with one another, and to exercise responsibility over the earth. However, the Fall introduced antinomies which continually work to undermine the harmony of the created order (Gen. 3:8–19). Historically, people have denied the dignity of other people, sought to impose authoritative hierarchies on others, and failed to steward creation properly. The disorderliness caused by human sin complicates our shepherding of God's good order.

God Created the World for His Purpose

Fifth, while lamenting the present sufferings in our world, we must remember the chief purpose for its creation. Our current experience, with its dysfunctions inherited through the moral deterioration of humanity, does not determine the end of creation but a passing moment in the progress of its history. The end of creation is determined by its Creator alone. "The goodness of creation is found neither in its present form nor in the judgment of man. It is good for the purpose of God."[62]

What does Scripture say about God's purpose or purposes for creation? In Genesis 1, the purpose for creation seems to be that God might bless it and delight in its goodness. God "blessed" (Hebrew *barak*) the animals, giving them the privilege to be fruitful and multiply (vv. 22–23). God blessed humanity, granting them not only

62. Moody, *The Word of Truth*, 145.

fruitfulness and multiplication, but the unique blessing of creation in God's image (vv. 26–28). That special blessing is then reflected in the derivative sovereignty given to the first human beings (v. 28). However, Scripture has yet more to say about the end of creation.

"It is manifest that the Scriptures speak on all occasions as though God made himself the end in all his works, and as though the same being, who is the first cause of all things, were the supreme and last end of all things."[63] The highest and chief end of creation is the same as the origin of creation, the Creator. The prophet Isaiah and the apostle John summarized this absolute truth with their repeated descriptions of the Lord God as "the beginning and the end," "the first and the last," and "the Alpha and the Omega" (Isa. 44:6; 48:12; Rev. 1:8, 17; 21:6; 22:13).

On the one hand, the benevolence, goodness, or love of God is shown in his blessing of creation. Because he loves the world he created (John 3:16), we understand the reason for its creation is simply his overflowing love. Showing his love to his creatures is one end that God has for his creation. On the other hand, Jonathan Edwards says the blessing of creatures constitutes a "subordinate end."[64] The subordination of creature to Creator is true. However, the love of God and the glory of God may never be subordinated to one another, for the being of God is unitary and simple.[65]

The God who "is love" (1 John 4:8, 16) certainly created the world to bless it, and our experience of God's love through his blessings in creation will find perfect fulfillment in our sight of God's glory in the final consummation (Matt. 5:8). The Old and New Testaments repeatedly point to God's original purpose and to his glory as the end of creation. Wisdom proclaims, "The Lord has prepared everything for his purpose" (Prov. 16:4a). Paul writes, "For from him and through him and to him are all things. To him be the glory forever. Amen" (Rom. 11:36).

---

63. Jonathan Edwards, "The End for Which God Created the World," in John Piper, *God's Passion for His Glory: Living the Vision of Jonathan Edwards* (Crossway, 1998), 183.

64. Edwards, "The End for Which God Created the World," in John Piper, *God's Passion for His Glory*, 125–36.

65. Charnock stated this truth in axiomatic form: "As above multitude there is an absolute unity, so above creatures there is an absolute simplicity." He then demonstrated the unity of eight of the attributes of God. Charnock, *Discourses on the Existence and Attributes of God*, 1:183–88.

In his study of the use of the canonical terms for "glory" (Hebrew *kabod*; Greek *doxa*), Edwards found a fourfold use: First, glory is inherent in God. Second, God communicates his glory to his creatures. Third, his creatures are intended to know his glory. Fourth, his creatures should express his glory.[66] All glory and blessing belong to the Creator's being, comes to us from the Creator, and returns to him through our praise. The pattern of the communicable attributes, described in the first volume of this series, repeats itself here.[67]

The scriptural canon provides a summary of the historical progress of divine glory through creation: The physical heavens offer continual if allusive expression to the glory of God (Ps. 19:1–3). But God's glory was revealed supremely and concretely in world history with his Son's obedient embrace of the cross (John 12:27–28). Today, his glory is seen in the obedience believers give to God (1 Cor. 10:31; 1 Pet. 4:11). Finally, God's glory will be manifested in its fullness when the redeemed are granted the beatific vision of the Trinity (Rev. 5:8–14; 21:22–27).

A Systematic Theology of Creation

Twelve truths must be maintained in the construction of a helpful doctrine of creation. The first eight truths, being more biblical and theological in orientation, have already been established. They can be summarily stated in one or two sentences based on the previous discussions. The remaining four truths are more apologetic in focus, dealing with cosmology, anthropology, and philosophy. Apologetic truth should be considered but must remain subordinated to theology, for theological truth derives from the teachings of Scripture.

1. The creative activity of God perfectly aligns with his nature as God.
2. Creation is one work of God the Trinity. The Father elects, the Word enacts, and the Spirit

66. Edwards, "The End for Which God Created the World," in John Piper, *God's Passion for His Glory,* 230. Edwards says the end of creation is "God's internal glory or fullness existing in its emanation." Edwards, "The End for Which God Created the World," 247.

67. Malcolm B. Yarnell III, *God,* vol. 1, Theology for Every Person (B&H, 2024), 104–5.

executes the one divine will to create the universe of creatures.
3. Creation participates by grace, and therefore according to divinely imposed limits, in God's goodness.
4. Creation is out of nothing. Neither the world nor its matter is co-eternal with God.
5. The goodness of creation must be maintained against dualism, which sees evil as a coexistent principle with good.
6. The orderliness of creation must be maintained against chaos on the one hand and falsely imposed order on the other.
7. The end of creation is God's glory and man's blessedness.
8. The Creator–creature divide must be maintained over against any tendency toward Pantheism, in its ancient or modern forms. Conversely, the Creator's continuing involvement in creation through providence must be maintained over against Deism.

Now, we may turn to apologetics. In the ninth place, the debates between "young earth" Creationists and "old earth" Creationists must be considered. The biggest difficulty for old earth Creationists to overcome with their theory is the fact that *yom* in Genesis 1 everywhere indicates a literal "day." In response, some old earth Creationists take the biblical text at less than face value, either as "myth" or as "saga."[68] Such interpretations can create problems, if they are allowed to diminish the verity of the inspired text.

Tenth, the Enlightenment theory of human evolution must be considered. Many modern proponents of evolution certainly are atheists, and their philosophical and cosmological ruminations rightly require Christian suspicion with Christian compassion. However, there are theistic evolutionists, including the early Darwin and many Roman Catholics. Millard Erickson, a leading evangelical, argues for "micro-evolution" within species while denying "macro-evolution" or cross-species evolution.[69]

---

68. Garrett, *Systematic Theology*, 1:342–44.
69. Millard J. Erickson, *Christian Theology*, 2nd ed. (Baker, 2001), 408–10.

Eleventh, modern science as a discipline has evinced an anti-divine bias, yet its roots are irreducibly dependent upon the theological foundation of a Creator initiating and sustaining nature according to the laws he gave to it. Indeed, the whole discipline of modern science developed out of natural theology and philosophy, as witnessed in the very architectural development of the Bodleian Library at the University of Oxford. Historically, modern science depends upon theological presuppositions about physical stability and temporal progress in the laws which govern the physical sciences.[70] Kenneth Keathley shows how faith and science need not remain in perpetual conflict.[71]

Twelfth, we must address modernist embarrassment over Scripture's teaching about creation. Friedrich Schleiermacher, the father of theological liberalism, sought to make Christianity acceptable to modernity's "cultured despisers of religion," in part by dismissing large portions of the biblical witness about creation. Unfortunately, he transformed the Christian religion. Leo Garrett responded well to liberalism, saying Christian "theologians should handle responsibly biblical texts." "Skepticism" toward biblical texts about creation "would make impossible any Christian theological system with deep roots in the Bible." Because "biblical statements about creation are essentially religious," creation's "essential religious nature must be preserved and recognized."[72]

Conclusion: Worship Your Creator

> The heavens declare the glory of God, and the expanse proclaims the work of his hands. Day after day they pour out speech; night after night they communicate knowledge. There is no speech; there are no words; their voice is not heard. Their message has gone out to the whole earth, and their words to the ends of the world. In the heavens he has pitched a tent for the sun. It is like

70. Butterfield, *The Origins of Modern Science*, 89–107.

71. Kenneth D. Keathley, *Faith and Science: A Primer for a Hypernatural World* (B&H Academic, 2024).

72. Garrett, *Systematic Theology*, 1:346–47.

> a bridegroom coming from his home; it rejoices like an athlete running a course. It rises from one end of the heavens and circles to their other end; nothing is hidden from its heat. (Ps. 19:1–6)

The purpose of creation is to declare God's glory. This is the message of creation itself, although humanity's ability to hear it well was diminished after the Fall. Indeed, too often, fallen humanity has confused its limited participation in glory with God's eternal glory.

Stated from a negative perspective, the Law of God restricts "worship" to the one true God, such that any deviation brings severe judgment (Exod. 20:3–6; Deut. 10:12; 11:16). The Lord Jesus reaffirmed our creaturely need for unique fidelity to God in his rebuke to the deceiver (Matt. 4:10). He later instructed the Samaritan woman that true worship is directed to "the Father" but also "in Spirit" and "in truth" (John 4:23–24). Scripture identifies all three divine Persons as "truth," but God the Son, who is "the truth," is the only way to worship the Father (John 14:6). Glorifying creatures is an act of idolatry (Rom. 1:22–23).

Stated from a positive perspective, the model prayer Christ provided to his disciples explicitly addresses prayer to "Our Father," who is our Creator. Even as it honors the name of the Father as "holy," Christ's form for prayer is uniquely intimate (Matt. 6:9). The apostles Paul, Peter, and John repeatedly called believers to praise our "God and Father," thereby removing any hint of a division between God and the Father (Rom. 15:6; 2 Cor. 1:3; 11:31; Gal. 1:4; Eph. 1:3; 4:6; Phil. 4:20; 1 Thess. 1:3; 3:11, 13; 1 Pet. 1:3; Rev. 1:6). Of the five biblical invocations to God mentioned by the great evangelical hymnwriter Isaac Watts, two explicitly name the "Father," while the remainder refer to his fatherly rule and to his fatherly dignity.[73]

Basil of Caesarea demonstrated through his careful exegetical reading of Scripture that Christian worship necessarily follows a twofold pattern. First, God the Father is the end of worship enabled in the Son by the Spirit. Second, the three Persons are worshiped equally together as the one and only God. Worship directed to God the Father is exemplified in Ephesians 2:18 and Galatians 4:6;

---

73. Isaac Watts, *A Guide to Prayer* (1715; reprint, Banner of Truth, 2001), 11.

worship to God the Trinity in Matthew 28:19 and 2 Corinthians 13:13.[74]

When we say, "God," we speak of the Father with the Son with the Holy Spirit, without any limitation on the deity of the Persons. And when we speak of the perfect work of the one God, we speak without any limitation on the divine activity of the three Persons. Orthodox Christians, ancient and contemporary alike, thus also render worship to God as Father and as Trinity.

Even as we address our prayers to "Our Father," the Creator, we worship the one God who is Trinity and has created us. With the saints and the angels gathered around the throne of the Creator, we must say, "Blessing and honor and glory and power be to the one seated on the throne, and to the Lamb, forever and ever!" (Rev. 5:13b). With the ancient Nicene Creed, we must confess the Father as our Creator, but we must also confess that the Holy Spirit, "together with the Father and the Son, is worshiped and glorified."

With the Dissenting theologian Isaac Watts, we must honor God both in his "unity of essence" and in "his inconceivable subsistence in three persons, the Father, the Son and the Holy Spirit, which mystery of the Trinity is a most proper object of our adoration and wonder."[75] True believers will one day join together with all of God's creatures in a chorus of eternal praise to the Father and the Son and the Holy Spirit, the one true Lord God, for he is our awesome and wonderful Creator (Rev. 4:9–11).

Study Questions

1. Do the works of God belong inseparably to all three Persons? Are certain acts appropriated by particular Persons?

2. Did God create the world out of nothing? Where do you find this teaching in Scripture?

3. Is the creation of God good or evil? Was it created good, then tainted by evil?

74. Basil of Caesarea, "On the Spirit," in Philip Schaff and Henry Wace, eds., *Basil: Letters and Select Works*, transl. Blomfield Jackson, Nicene and Post-Nicene Fathers, Second Series, vol. 8 (Hendrickson, 1994), 2–50.

75. Watts, *A Guide to Prayer*, 12.

Suggested Resources

- Gregory of Nyssa, *On the Holy Trinity*
- Adonis Vidu, *The Same God Who Works All Things*
- Herbert Butterfield, *The Origins of Modern Science 1300–1800*

CHAPTER SIX

Where Is He Taking Us?

IN THE FIRST TWO CHAPTERS of this book, we explored the truth of God the Father. We heard the biblical witness to him, evaluated the historic conversations about him, and offered a systematic summary of the doctrine of God the Father. In chapters three and four, we honored the truth of God the Son by exegeting Scripture's revelation of him, by exploring the early church's struggle against heretics who dishonored the Son, and by offering a systematic summary of the personal union of two natures in Christ, a union required for our salvation.

In the previous chapter, we began exploring the work of God, starting at the beginning of time with his creation of the universe. After expositing the biblical witness to God the Trinity as Creator, and to the truths Scripture teaches about his beautiful work of creation, we offered a systematic summary of the doctrine of creation. In this chapter, we continue our discussion of God's works. We now consider divine providence, which talks about how God is guiding creation to accomplish his ultimate purpose. God's providential work is centered in, and bounded by, Jesus Christ.

The Universal Christ

"Throughout history we can find examples of how the world's people have been concerned with ultimate or crucial questions."[1] Humanity's universal search for the ultimate meaning of life has motivated many thinkers. After examining the gamut of religious and secular responses to the question of the universe's ultimate meaning, philosopher John Newport argued that Scripture provides the only "comprehensive, coherent, creative, and personally satisfying" answer. While humanity remains responsible for its actions, God is bringing everything to its "consummation in the second coming of Christ" when "the fullness of God's kingdom" is universally experienced.[2] Evangelist Billy Graham spoke more personally: "I have spent my lifetime proclaiming one central truth: there is good news for the people of the world. At the heart of that good news is Jesus Christ."[3]

Christ the Center

The two theologians mentioned above were Southern Baptists, but theologians from all Christian traditions ground universal reality in Jesus Christ. Pope Benedict XVI said the divine–human Person of Christ is "the center" of the Christian faith tradition, while his death and resurrection constitute "the center of human existence."[4] From a quite different tradition, religious philosopher D. Elton Trueblood says the Quaker doctrine of the Inner Light actually refers to "Christ Himself."[5] Presbyterian pastor and theologian Mark Jones similarly grounds theology proper in the second Person of the Trinity: "Apart from Christ, the attributes of God remain meaningless to us. In Christ alone can we understand the true and living God."[6]

---

1. John P. Newport, *Life's Ultimate Questions: A Contemporary Philosophy of Religion* (Word, 1989), 1.

2. Newport, *Life's Ultimate Questions*, 95.

3. Billy Graham, *Storm Warning* (Word, 1992), 80.

4. Joseph Ratzinger, *Principles of Catholic Theology: Building Stones for a Fundamental Theology*, transl. Mary Frances McCarthy (Ignatius, 1987), 99, 189.

5. Quakers note the apostle John equated the universal Light with the eternal Logos. Elton Trueblood, *The People Called Quakers* (Friends United Press, 1966), 63, 69–70.

6. Mark Jones, *God Is: A Devotional Guide to the Attributes of God* (Crossway, 2017), 19.

Concluding his exhaustive treatment of the theology of the New Testament, the Lutheran biblical theologian Peter Stuhlmacher also inquired about the center of the entire canon. Against various academic presumptions, he found that many Old Testament scholars have concluded that "the one God of Israel" is "the Father of Jesus Christ." Similarly, the center of the New Testament is "the one God in Jesus Christ."[7] Stuhlmacher argued that the early church's analogy of faith captures Scripture's central message.[8]

We can certainly speak of Christ as the center of creation, because his work as Redeemer—through his human incarnation, death, resurrection, and eternal intercession—theologically orients history from within history. Christ centers universal history by virtue of his redemptive work. However, he also constitutes history from above and beyond the world.

Christ the Circumference

We must also speak of Christ as the circumference of creation, because his eternal sovereignty orients all history from his divine reality. As God, Christ is the Creator, Sustainer, and Consummator of the cosmos. He is the one God with the Father and the Spirit. Paul wrote, "For everything was created by him, in heaven and on earth, the visible and the invisible, whether thrones or dominions or rulers or authorities—all things have been created through him and for him. He is before all things, and by him all things hold together" (Col. 1:16–17). The gospel of John, the book of Hebrews, and the Apocalypse make similar statements about Christ, locating him before and after creation, upholding it from within, and ruling it from above (John 1:1–3; Heb. 1:10–12; Rev. 22:13).

Basil of Caesarea taught that the Word imagined, created, and rules the world with God from its creation to its consummation. First, "the supreme Artist," God the Trinity, from eternity "imagined the world such as it ought to be." His perfect intellectual crafting

---

7. Peter Stuhlmacher, *Biblical Theology of the New Testament*, transl. Daniel P. Bailey and Jostein Ådna (Eerdmans, 2018), 772–74.

8. Stuhlmacher sees six truths at the center of Scripture: Jesus Christ is one essence with the Father; his apostles preached his gospel; Christ died for our sins; he arose, ascended, and will come again; his church is the new people of God; and he gives them his Holy Spirit. Stuhlmacher, *Biblical Theology of the New Testament*, 774–78.

provided for the cosmos its "harmony" and "symphony."[9] Second, the Father and his Word with the Spirit created all things in an orderly and eternal manner.[10] Third, the Word, who is "intelligent reason," continues to provide for his creation "in the order of visible things" and to give guidance to "reasonable souls."[11] Finally, "the just Judge," in the end, "rewards all the actions of life according to their merit."[12] According to Basil, God works perfectly upon the world in his eternal counsel, in creation, through providence, and in the final consummation.

Center and Circumference

Jesus Christ is both the center and the circumference of the cosmos because he is one with God, the originator and consummator of all reality. Therefore, the second divine Person—and the work which he performs with the Father and the Spirit in creation, redemption, and consummation—orients history from without and within. In the lectures that follow, we shall see how the Son of God, the eternal Word who became flesh in Jesus Christ, rules universal reality through his perfect wisdom (cf. Prov. 8:22–31).

Four of the apostle Paul's statements to the church of Corinth demonstrate how Christ constitutes both the center and the circumference of the cosmos. First, Paul said "Christ is the power of God and the wisdom of God" (1 Cor. 1:24), demonstrating the Father does nothing apart from the Son. The divine governance of history, from its original creation to its final consummation, belongs to him. Second, Paul decided to teach them "nothing . . . except Jesus Christ and him crucified" (2:2). He thereby emphasized a twofold centrality, of Christ's Person and of his atoning work upon the Cross. Third, Paul reminded the Corinthians of their sure hope of resurrection in Christ, for "if Christ has not been raised, your faith is worthless" (15:17). Fourth, he recalled

---

9. Basil of Caesarea, "Hexaemeron" 2.2, in Philip Schaff and Henry Wace, eds., *Basil: Letters and Select Works*, Nicene and Post-Nicene Fathers, 2nd Series, vol. 8 (Hendrickson, 1994), 60.

10. Basil, "Hexaemeron," 2.6, in Schaff and Wace, eds., *Basil*, 62–63. "It is He whom Scripture vaguely represents [Gen 1:3], to show us that God has not only wished to create the world, but to create it with the help of a co-operator." Basil, "Hexaemeron," 3.2, in Schaff and Wace, eds., *Basil*, 65–66.

11. Basil, "Hexaemeron," 1.6, in Schaff and Wace, eds., *Basil*, 55.

12. Basil, "Hexaemeron," 1.5, in Schaff and Wace, eds., *Basil*, 54.

the Messiah's "everlasting" reign over his universal Kingdom (e.g., 2 Sam. 7:13, 16; Dan. 7:13–14). In his messianic role, and in his work of recapitulating humanity as the "second Adam," Christ exercises judgment over humanity (1 Cor. 15:20–26, 47–49). God the Son will bring all created things into their proper order and submit them to God the Father, with whom he inhabits the divine throne forever (1 Cor. 15:27–28; cf. Rev. 5:13; 7:17; 22:1–3).

Christ fills the concepts of reality and history with ultimate meaning. The Son is truly the Second Person of God the Trinity, who in his divine economy reigns over all creatures and over all time with perfect wisdom. He entered his creation at the Incarnation to reconstitute humanity from within. We might speak of Christ's universal rule and guidance of history through five divine titles: As the eternal Creator, he imagined, created, and sustains the cosmos. As the Promisor of a new covenant, he crafted for himself a covenant people to receive his gospel of redemption. As our Redeemer, he established the new covenant by his blood to offer the good news of salvation to all human beings. As the final Judge, he will come again to render judgment upon the living and the dead. Finally, as the eternal Heir, the consummation of all things comes under his everlasting rule, for he inherits creation. Christ Jesus, Son of God and Son of Man, provides the cosmos with its meaning from without and from within.

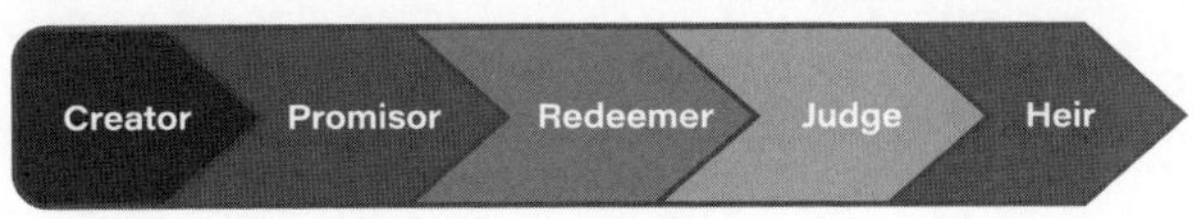

Figure 8: Christ the Center and Circumference of the Cosmos

The Divine Counsel

Where Basil spoke of God the Trinity "imagining" creation from his eternal perspective before its creation, theologians in the West often speak of divine "decrees" or divine "counsel." These terms are typically treated under the related doctrines of providence and election. When theologians speak of "providence," they consider the way in which God generally provides for his creatures and guides them toward the end he has for them. By "election," they typically focus on the salvation of human individuals.[13] As just demonstrated, however, we must be careful to ground our thoughts about the origin, progress, and end of every creature in the Person and work of Jesus Christ. This is as true for general provision as for personal predestination.

Divine Inscrutability and Our Dependence Upon Revelation

As we consider providence and election, we must be careful to assume nothing about the being and activity of God apart from divine revelation. In the ancient churches, some assumed a philosophical structure applies to God when they speak of the divine nature. In the history of the church, others assumed a philosophical structure might apply to his decrees. It is wise to take every theological claim about God's nature and God's work and make certain it is accompanied by a specific and relevant appeal to divine revelation. If not, that claim must be deemed speculative.

Scripture repeatedly warns against any human presumptions that God is like us. The Lord says, "You have done these things, and I kept silent; you thought I was just like you. But I will rebuke you and lay out the case before you" (Ps. 50:21). Again, "'To whom will you compare me, or who is my equal?' asks the Holy One" (Isa. 40:25). And again, "'For my thoughts are not your thoughts, and your ways are not my ways.' This is the Lord's declaration" (55:8).

Scripture also repeatedly warns against presuming we know God's hidden plans. The prophet Isaiah asked, "Who has directed the Spirit of the Lord, or who gave him counsel? Who did he consult? Who gave him understanding and taught him the paths of justice? Who taught him knowledge and showed him the way of understanding?" (40:13–14). God set Job back upon his heels for presuming to instruct him. "Who is this who obscures my counsel with ignorant words?" (Job 38:2).

The first set of texts demonstrates the incomparability of God vis-à-vis humanity. The second set of texts demonstrates the

13. Election will be discussed in more detail in *Spirit*, the third volume of Theology for Every Person.

inscrutability of God's divine decrees vis-à-vis human knowledge. The most dangerous presumptions in theology are made glibly by appeal to tradition or reason apart from specific and sustained attention to and submission before divine revelation, especially as it is conveyed to the church in the written Word of God. This is the error of too many speculative systems of metaphysics.

The Divine Counsel in Scripture

What do we know about the divine counsel through revelation? Three key Pauline texts reveal that God the Trinity planned to act in creation, redemption, and consummation. First, we know that God the Father is the origin and end of all things, and that all things also came into existence through his Son (1 Cor. 8:6). Second, we know that all things are being "summed up" or "recapitulated" in his beloved Son, Jesus Christ, according to the will of God (Eph. 1:10). Third, we know that the Holy Spirit, who has intimate knowledge of the divine counsel, reveals the "mystery," who is the Son, Jesus Christ (1 Cor. 2:6–16). Some infer from these passages at least an implicit revelation of an eternal Trinitarian "covenant of redemption."[14]

However, keep in mind both ontology and economy, as well as God's utter perfection and our human limitations. Ontologically, God is "pure act." He has no unrealized potential, and never lacks anything in himself. We, by contrast, are creatures and are in process. From our temporal perspective, his being precedes his activity. But from God's eternal perspective, his being and his act are necessarily one and the same. The divine economy and divine ontology are one, eternal, and simple, for God is self-sufficient, perfect, and complete in himself.[15]

Moreover, God's being precedes our being, for we are his creatures. And our being precedes our actions. Because of our placement in time, we distinguish ontology (being) from economy (function). We must do so without, however, imposing our temporal distinctions upon the eternal God. When God relates to his creatures, he plans and acts eternally in accordance with the character of his perfect

14. The most recent presentation of this influential theological paradigm was offered in Wang Yong Lee, *The Doctrine of the Covenant of Redemption According to John Gill (1697–1771)* (Wipf and Stock, 2025).

15. Malcolm B. Yarnell III, *God*, vol. 1, Theology for Every Person (B&H, 2024), 100–8.

being.[16] God also acts sovereignly in alignment with his attributes. Holiness, love, and righteousness drive the divine economy,[17] the moral application of his unlimited power. God's actions are never arbitrary.

God's actions do not function like an earthly physical mechanism, nor does his will act like an electronic computer program. His ways are qualitatively and infinitely superior (Isa. 55:8–9). Our Lord is a "living God," who engages personally and verbally with his creatures in a dynamic relationship of judgment or blessing marked by human prayers and divine speech (Deut. 5:26; Josh. 3:10; 2 Kings 19:4; Pss. 42:2; 84:2; Jer. 10:10). Jesus Christ is "the Messiah, the Son of the living God" (Matt. 16:16). Through his Son, the living God calls human beings to repent and enter filial relationship with him (Acts 14:15; Rom. 9:26; Heb. 3:12). This living God is inexorably drawing human beings back to himself, and we can either have our hearts cleansed by the Spirit or face terrifying judgment (Heb. 9:14; 10:31). "The Spirit of the living God" writes his will upon pliant human hearts rather than upon stone (2 Cor. 3:3).

As we discovered in the last chapter, the Trinity acts in dynamic unity even as the Persons appropriate, or take to their Person, certain actions. The Trinitarian missions reflect the Trinitarian processions. The Father, therefore, is typically seen as leading, not only in creation, but also in providence and election. Reviewing the biblical evidence regarding divine causation, Basil of Caesarea concluded the Father is "the initiating cause." But the Son and the Spirit are also involved in providence and election. The Son is "the operating cause" and the Spirit is "the perfecting cause" in all the divine actions.[18]

Ephesians 1:3–14 has long been recognized as perhaps the key passage in the Pauline corpus regarding divine causation. In summary, God the Father planned to bring all things together in and for his Son, sealing the redeemed with his Spirit. The Greek terms in this incredibly important passage reveal the divine plan or counsel:

- *Protithemi; prothesis:* God "purposed" all things in Christ (vv. 9, 11).

16. Yarnell, *God*, 49–70.

17. Yarnell, *God*, 109–26.

18. Basil of Caesarea, "De Spiritu Sancto," in Philip Schaff and Henry Wace, eds., *Basil: Letters and Select Works*, Nicene and Post-Nicene Fathers, 2nd Series, vol. 8 (Hendrickson, 1994), 21, 22, 38.

- *Mysterion:* He now reveals this "mystery" which he planned eternally (v. 9).
- *Thelema; boule:* God made known the mystery of his "will" (v. 9) and works all things according to the "decision" of his "will" (v. 11).
- *Anakephalaiosasthai:* Focusing on the central activity in the divine economy, Paul says God "recapitulated" or "summed up" all things in Christ. The verb, taken literally, indicates Christ "headed" the universe "again" by the divine will (v. 10).
- *Eklegomai:* God "chose" us in Christ before the foundation of the world to be "holy" and "blameless" (v. 4).
- *Proorizo:* God "predestined" us to be adopted through Christ (vv. 5, 11).

The Christological and theological orientation of the Greek prepositions in this passage is also highly instructive. Against hasty man-defined or world-centered readings, Paul demonstrates God's will is not enraptured with creation but with Christ. The divine plan certainly includes human creatures but derivatively. Instead, God's counsel is primarily "in" or "with" (*en*, used twelve times), "according to" or "in agreement with" (*kata*, five times), "for" or "to" (*eis*, four times), "through" (*dia*, twice), and "before" (*katenopiov*, once) Christ, God, and his glory. The divine plan is, secondarily, "on," "in," "until," and "for" (*eis*, used three times; *epi*, twice) humanity, creation, and time.

When coupled with the primary application to God in Christ of the terms for foreordination in Paul's great hymn to the Trinity in Ephesians 1:3–14, the contextual orientation of the prepositions in the same passage point to a theological and Christological understanding of the divine plan. God the Trinity is the origin, center, and end of his own plan, and humanity is certainly taken into that plan but derivatively and as a dependent recipient.

The Divine Plan

God's will for the world, according to Paul, originates with the Father, centers in Christ, and is completed by the Holy Spirit. God the Trinity plans, performs, and perfects his will in himself, and, by way of secondary inclusion, God plans the blessing of his creation. In the biblical revelation, the divine counsel is decidedly God-ordained and Christ-centered and Spirit-executed rather than man-defined and world-centered and humanly dependent. Our utter dependence again calls for humble circumspection on our part when we speak of God's eternal decree.

Sean M. McDonough has argued that the creation of the world, followed by its new creation, are not two different movements made necessary by the Fall. To give the Fall that type of priority would undermine divine sovereignty. The incarnation of Christ, as well as his cross and resurrection, followed by his ascension, second coming, and eternal reign from the throne of the New Jerusalem, are the plan of God from eternity. "The divine plan is not fractured even if the route to the city takes some unusual turns."[19]

Maximus the Confessor, in his famous work, *On the Cosmic Mystery of Jesus Christ*, discerned the narrative of Scripture carefully in conversation with the exegetical genius of the earlier orthodox theologians. For Maximus, the divine plan, "foreknown before the foundation of the world," is that God would work all things in himself.[20] All things came from God in Christ and must return to him. The Lord Jesus Christ is the divine agent in both creation and its recapitulation as the new creation. According to Maximus, "The termination of time is fixed within Christ."[21] "Rest" in God is the "ultimately desirable" state of all human beings, and God works in Christ to bring us to that rest.[22] To prepare us for our rest with God, Christ has come to recapitulate or reconstitute human desires on our behalf. Christ draws us through recapitulating us into a sanctified life with God.[23] In the eternal Word, our beginning and our end as intelligent creatures find unity.[24] Maximus, in other words, reinforces our claim that Christ is the center and circumference of creation.

---

19. Sean M. McDonough, *Creation and New Creation: Understanding God's Creation Project* (Hendrickson, 2016), 49.

20. Maximus, "On the Cosmic Mystery of Jesus Christ," *Ad Thalassium* 60, in Maximus the Confessor, *On the Cosmic Mystery of Jesus Christ*, transl. Paul M. Blowers and Robert Louis Wilken (St. Vladimir's Seminary Press, 2003), 123.

21. Maximus, *Ad Thalassium* 60, in *On the Cosmic Mystery of Jesus Christ*, 128.

22. Maximus, *Ambiguum* 7, in *On the Cosmic Mystery of Jesus Christ,* 46–52.

23. Maximus, *Ambiguum* 7, in *On the Cosmic Mystery of Jesus Christ,* 53–58.

24. Maximus, *Ambiguum* 7, in *On the Cosmic Mystery of Jesus Christ,* 59–72.

The Divine Decrees

What does God decree? We may speak of "divine decrees," but we must avoid careless impositions upon the biblical description of those decrees. Problems may arise when we construct important doctrines partly from Scripture and partly from speculation. Scholastic systems pose a "danger" when they compromise the theological foundation of the divine will and turn Christ into a mere instrument. "Even Christ cannot be the foundation of election on this understanding of the decrees."[25] Wise theologians avoid speaking hastily of the will of God apart from his revelation of that will.

Neither should we appeal to "mystery" only as a device to fill in the gaps of a partially theological and partially philosophical system. A review of what Scripture says about three important decretal concepts will help us discern the divine decrees while untangling them from post-biblical speculations. Consider the biblical revelation of "the mystery," "from the foundation of the world," and what is deemed "necessary."

"The Mystery"

In theological literature, the term "mystery" is sometimes employed when seeking to solve the philosophical conundrum of relating the predestinarian fate of human individuals to those same persons' libertarian free wills. However, the biblical terms for mystery focus on God's revelation in Christ. They are not intended to serve as an argument from silence to plug an embarrassing gap in a human system of thought.

"The mystery" (Aramaic *raz*, Greek *mysterion*, Latin *sacramentum* or *mysterium*) is the plan of God, once hidden but now revealed. Mystery in the biblical sense does not proceed in the way of a modern bookshop. Detective mysteries and spy novels ascribe to some human being the ability to extract the truth from a tangled web of evidence. By stark contrast, the apostle Paul, the most prolific user of the term, "does not apply *mysterion* to things he does not

25. Katherine Sonderegger, "Election," in John Webster, Kathryn Tanner, and Iain Torrance, eds., *The Oxford Handbook of Systematic Theology* (Oxford University Press, 2007), 111.

understand."[26] The biblical presentation of mystery concerns God's plan for creation. The mystery was previously unknown to humanity and partially veiled to the prophets. But his plan has now been definitively unveiled. Paul uses the term *mysterion* in two major ways: to describe the good news revealed about Jesus Christ, and to foretell the fulfillment of all things in Jesus Christ.

First, Paul uses "mystery" generally to denominate the proclamation of the gospel of Jesus Christ (Rom. 16:25; 1 Cor. 2:1; Eph. 6:19; Col. 4:3–4).[27] The term is applied to various elements of the gospel. These gospel elements include the Person of Christ (Col. 2:2–3), the previously hidden plan of God to send his Son (1 Cor. 2:7), as well as his incarnation (1 Tim. 3:16), crucifixion (1 Cor. 2:8), resurrection, and ascension (1 Tim. 3:16). The gospel of Jesus Christ, in its major elements and in its general proclamation, is "God's hidden wisdom in a mystery, a wisdom God predestined before the ages for our glory" (1 Cor. 2:7). The mystery of divine predestination is, therefore, God the Son come in the flesh to die for humanity.

Second, Paul also uses "mystery" to describe the current and future recapitulation of all things in Jesus Christ (Eph. 1:9–10). Positively, the mystery concerns the present union of the church with Christ (5:32). However, the mystery also has negative eschatological connotations, including the partial if temporary hardening of Israel (Rom. 11:25) and the lawlessness to be released before Christ's return (2 Thess. 2:7). Finally, the eschatological mystery includes God's plan to save the nations (Eph. 3:3–4, 8–9; Col. 1:25–27) and to cause the resurrection of the saints (1 Cor. 15:51–52).

"From the Foundation of the World"

Other apostles refer to the divine mystery which effects human salvation in various ways. With Paul, they focus on the work of God in Christ. They speak of how God prepares many things "from the foundation of the world" (Greek *apo katabolas kosmou*). For instance, the author of Hebrews said that God completes his providential work

---

26. T. J. Lang, "Mystery," in Scot McKnight, Lynn H. Cohick, and Nijay K. Gupta, eds., *Dictionary of Paul and His Letters: A Compendium of Contemporary Biblical Scholarship*, 2nd ed. (IVP Academic, 2023), 714.

27. Lang offers a different scheme for organizing the Pauline references: a first subset of various uses and a second subset of uses focused on the eschatological gathering of God's people. Lang, "Mystery," 715–16.

from the foundation of the world (Heb. 4:3). Conversely, the Son became incarnate once to complete his sacrificial work (Heb. 9:26).

Peter said Christ's death was "foreknown before the foundation of the world but . . . revealed in these last times." Christ's subsequent resurrection and ascension to the divine throne were likewise part of the unfolding divine plan (1 Pet. 1:20–21). Note the metaphorical language of "before" concerns the divine will, which as eternal is not limited by the progress of creation. The revelation of God's eternal will has now been offered "in these last times," that is according to those temporal realities which restrict creatures.[28]

Recognizing the importance of using metaphorical language, Christ revealed the truth of his gospel, which was "kept secret from the foundation of the world," in parables (Matt. 13:35). Matthew says Christ also taught that his kingdom was "prepared for you from the foundation of the world" (25:34). Paul added that the holiness of the saints "in Christ" is expected from the foundation of the world (Eph. 1:4). Finally, John revealed that the Book of Life, wherein the redeemed are enrolled with the Lamb, exists eternally, or "from the foundation of the world" (Rev. 13:8; 17:8).

As used by Christ and his apostles, the metaphorical language of "foundation of the world" refers to the eternity of God, who created time but is not limited by time. The New Testament phrase correlates eternity with time in the Person and work of Christ Jesus.

"It Is Necessary"

The Greek term *dei*, which means "it is necessary," applies to the will of God for his creation. The word is helpful for discerning what Scripture says about divine necessity. According to the Acts of

28. Most scholars avoid imposing creaturely temporal divisions upon divine eternity. Cf. David Abernathy, *An Exegetical Summary of 1 Peter*, 2nd ed. (SIL International, 2008), 48; Daniel C. Arichea and Eugene Albert Nida, *A Handbook on the First Letter from Peter*, UBS Handbook Series (United Bible Societies, 1980), 42; Edmund P. Clowney, *The Message of 1 Peter: The Way of the Cross*, The Bible Speaks Today (InterVarsity Press, 1988), 72; I. Howard Marshall, *1 Peter*, The IVP New Testament Commentary Series (InterVarsity Press, 1991), 1 Pet. 1:17–21; Thomas R. Schreiner, *1, 2 Peter, Jude*, The New American Commentary (Broadman & Holman, 2003), 87–88. Departing from this consensus, Wayne Grudem employed the Arian-like language of "eternity past." Wayne A. Grudem, *1 Peter: An Introduction and Commentary*, Tyndale New Testament Commentaries (InterVarsity Press, 1988), 90.

the Apostles, God made it "necessary," in fulfillment of Scripture, for Christ to atone for our sins, to ascend to heaven, and to save us from sin (Acts 1:16; 2:23; 3:21; 4:12). According to Jesus, "it is necessary" for the gospel to be preached (Mark 13:10). In those passages which clearly utilize *dei* in reference to the divine plan for his creation, the necessity thus appears to be twofold: First, God determined for Christ to save us. Second, God determined for Christians to obey him and to preach the gospel of atonement.

Walter Grundmann worked through the Greek, Jewish, New Testament, and early Christian uses of *dei*. He found the biblical usage differs from paganism by virtue of its grounding necessity in a personal God rather than in neutral fate. *Dei*, especially prominent in the writings of Luke, comprehends the rest of the New Testament idea: "The *dei*, which as an expression of the will of God is at all these points an expression of His saving will, finally reveals to man his state of loss and thus demands faith in God's act of salvation."[29]

Other biblical texts fortify this understanding of divine necessity as requiring human faith and repentance. The scriptural references to God's necessary plan for human lives include: David declaring that God knows everything about the human person from before his life begins (Ps. 139:1–18); Isaiah saying that God plans from the beginning, and that his plan will stand (Isa. 46:8–11); Jesus teaching that God plans human life in both its great movements and in its minor details (Matt. 6:25–34); and the author of Hebrews warning that God calls Christians to be diligent in pursuing faithful living (Heb. 2:1).[30]

As we will observe in subsequent chapters, Moses revealed that God created humanity with a real yet limited freedom (Gen. 1–2, 4). However, human freedom was lost through the personal choices of Adam and Eve to become slaves to Satan, sin, and death (Gen. 3). Paul treated the slavery of humanity in a dialectical fashion. The opposition between slavery and freedom concerns whose slave we are and whose freedom we have. God redeems us to bring us his perfect freedom (Gal. 5:1). To serve God, therefore, is to be free in

---

29. Walter Grundmann, "Dei," in Gerhard Kittel, ed., *Theological Dictionary of the New Testament*, transl. Geoffrey W. Bromiley, vol. 2 (Eerdmans, 1964), 23.

30. On the strong necessity laid upon the activity of the human mind and the human will in Hebrews 2:1, see David L. Allen, *Hebrews*, New American Commentary (B&H Publishing, 2010), 191.

truth (Rom. 6:15–23). Paul also believed that God desires for every person to be saved (1 Tim. 2:4).

The Trinity and the Elect One

It should be apparent by now that Jesus Christ is the center and circumference of the divine plan and that his Person encompasses, and his work constitutes universal reality. He is also personally focused upon fulfilling the plan of God to guide, redeem, and perfect creation. Motivated by divine love, Christ came to show his divine glory to his people. Jesus said, "Father, I desire that they also whom You gave Me may be with Me where I am, that they may behold My glory which You have given Me; for You loved Me before the foundation of the world" (John 17:24 NKJV). The source and the goal of divine action are disclosed in Christ's prayer to the Father. First, intra-Trinitarian charity, the love of the Father and the Son from "before the foundation of the world," is the source of God's "desire" for his people. Second, his goal is to grant his people the privilege of seeing his eternal "glory" (cf. John 3:16).

Paul likewise treated the predestination of believers as subsidiary to Trinity and Christology: "And we know that all things work together for good to those who love God, to those who are the called according to His purpose. For whom He foreknew, He also predestined to be conformed to the image of His Son, that He might be the firstborn among many brethren. Moreover, whom He predestined, . . . these He also justified; and whom He justified, these He also glorified" (Rom. 8:28–30 NKJV). The call to salvation has its source in the goodness of God the Trinity, whose goal is that humanity conform "to the image of His Son."

Glory with Love

The divine plan of God for eternity comes from God through Christ in the Spirit, and its goal is returning us to his eternity. Gregory of Nyssa referred to this as "a circle of glory." "You see the revolving circle of the glory moving from Like to Like. The Son is glorified by the Spirit; the Father is glorified by the Son; again, the Son has His glory from the Father; and the Only-begotten thus becomes the glory of the Spirit." By faith, both a grace given to a human being by divine love and a duty for the human being, we perceive his glory.[31]

When the doctrine of divine glory is brought into correlation with the doctrine of divine love, Nyssa's circle of glory becomes also "a circle of love." As we noted in the first volume, divine love is often and rightly treated as moving outward from God. However, it also is intended to be returned to God and reflected to others.[32] Glory is often and rightly treated as a moving inward of God, but God also invites the redeemed to see his glory. This indicates a moving outward of the Creator toward his creatures. Both Trinitarian movements, love and glory, center in the Person and work of Jesus Christ.

In eternity, God the Father loved God the Son in the Spirit and planned to bless humanity in himself. God created and redeems from the basis of his love—this is the metaphorical "moving outward" from God. God also created and redeems for the purpose of his glory—this is the metaphorical "moving inward" to God. God created and redeemed us in order that the redeemed may participate in his divine glory. His love is the motivation for his glory. Divine love and divine glory may neither be sundered nor opposed nor sublimated, for God is simple. But let us dig deeper into his glory and his love.

First, how shall we perceive divine glory? Some believe glory requires a self-centered God.[33] But the scriptural doctrine of divine love seems to portray God as self-giving. Is there a contrast between the "hedonist" definition of glory on the one side,[34] and the self-giving message of the cross of Jesus Christ on the other side? Martin Luther reminded Christians in his day of the perversions to which "a theology of glory" may tend. Fingering the overweening clericalism evident in Roman circles, Luther exhorted the believer to become "a

31. "In like manner, again, Faith completes the circle, and glorifies the Son by means of the Spirit, and the Father by means of the Son." Nyssa, *On the Holy Spirit*, in Philip Schaff and Henry Wace, eds., *Gregory of Nyssa: Dogmatic Treatises*, Nicene and Post-Nicene Fathers, 2nd Series, vol. 5 (Hendrickson, 1994), 324.

32. Yarnell, *God*, 117–21.

33. John Piper sees this as a necessary corollary of divine sufficiency and as a call to God-centeredness. "God's ultimate commitment is to himself and not to us." John Piper, *Brothers, We Are Not Professionals: A Plea to Pastors for Radical Ministry* (Broadman & Holman, 2002), 7.

34. John Piper, *Desiring God: Meditations of a Christian Hedonist* (Multnomah, 2003).

theologian of the cross."[35] This was the command of Christ (Matt. 16:24). The glory of the divine Christ is found in his humiliation (John 12:23–28). Whichever approach to divine glory one takes, it is wise to leave the glory of humanity to God.

Second, how shall we perceive divine love? While one tendency may press divine glory toward divine self-centeredness,[36] another may press divine love such that distinctions about salvation, heaven, and hell are downplayed. For instance, a second popular Christian preacher preferred a God who refrains from rendering divine judgment.[37] This tendency has also been criticized.[38] The solution seems to lay between the extremes of the self-centered God on the one hand and the justice-lacking God on the other hand. We must constantly affirm the twin truths, of divine love and of divine glory. It is a matter of theological wisdom to correlate the outgoing love of God with the incoming glory of God.

Christological Election versus Anthropological Election

Karl Barth criticized his own Reformed tradition for turning election in a man-centered direction. In his commentary on the confessions of Westminster and Dort, Barth found that the problem became acute after the first generation of Reformers: "They were thinking anthropologically rather than theologically when they made the 'absolute decree,' which is a profound statement about God, into a doctrine not just about humanity but about this or that person—even if they did so with logical consistency. The doctrine of a 'limited number' of the elect is, in particular, not good doctrine; it ties God down to particular people when the meaning of the entire doctrine is precisely the freedom of God."[39]

---

35. Martin Luther, "The Heidelberg Disputation," in Harold J. Grimm, ed., *Luther's Works*, vol. 31 (Muhlenberg, 1957), 41–53.

36. John Piper began correcting this tendency with *God Is the Gospel: Meditations on God's Love as the Gift of Himself* (Crossway, 2011).

37. Bell seems more concerned to deny traditional definitions than to offer new ones. Rob Bell, *Love Wins: A Book About Heaven, Hell, and the Fate of Every Person Who Ever Lived* (HarperOne, 2011).

38. Michael E. Wittmer, *Christ Alone: An Evangelical Response to Rob Bell's Love Wins* (Edenridge, 2011).

39. Barth deemed the Reformed doctrines of *decretum absolutum*, "the absolute decree," and *numerus clausus*, "the limited number" of the elect, irreconcilable because it was centered anthropologically. Karl Barth, *The Theology of the Reformed Confessions*, transl. Darrell L. and Judith J. Guder (Westminster John Knox, 2002), 216.

For any doctrine of election to be properly situated, it must be understood first, foremost, and finally as proceeding from, continually focused upon, and ending in the person of Jesus Christ. For instance, at the mount of transfiguration, the disciples of Jesus began to perceive the glories of God. However, the disciples mistook Jesus as merely one among other men. In response, God the Father spoke loudly and clearly to them, startling the disciples into silence: "This is my beloved Son, the Chosen One" (*eklelegmenos*, "the Elect One," Luke 9:35; cf. Ps. 89:3; Isa. 42:1; 49:7; Luke 23:35).

Christ's claims to be the Elect One unnerved the skeptics in his day. The unbelieving crowd sneered at Jesus for naming himself, "The Chosen One" (Luke 23:35).[40] Many have speculated about election according to anthropological categories, but the New Testament doctrine of election is clearly and repeatedly framed by Christ. Human beings are considered elect only insofar as they are "in Christ." Both Peter and Paul address the election of Christ.

The apostle Peter said divine election was fulfilled in Jesus Christ. He is the elect foundation of the people of God (Isa. 28:16; 1 Pet. 2:6). Jesus said, "the elect" (plural) are those "whom he chose" (*hous exelexato*; Mark 13:20). False disciples will be led astray, but the elect will be known at the eschatological gathering (Mark 13:22, 27). "In short, Jesus is God's Chosen One. The ultimate goal of all previous election was to prepare the way for him to be revealed."[41]

In Galatians 3, Paul excoriated those who trusted in a genealogy of election displayed in circumcision for their salvation. To the contrary, it is by the Spirit through "faith" in Christ alone that a person is justified (vv. 6–7, 9). The gospel of election came "through" Abraham (v. 8). The promise was to Abraham's "seed," not "seeds," and that seed is "Christ" (v. 16). Salvation comes to men by faith in the Promise of the Messiah, not in a law of election, including the Law of Moses (v. 18).

Similarly, in Romans 9, Paul makes it clear that salvation does not come to "children by physical descent" but to "children of the promise" (v. 8). Romans 9:13, "I have loved Jacob, but I have hated Esau," has been read abstractly and individualistically, as if God personally preferred one while denying the other opportunity for salvation. This interpretation raises important questions about whether

40. Luke 9:35 uses the term *ho eklelegmenos*; Luke 23:35, *ho eklektos*.

41. "Eklegomai," in Moisés Silva, ed., *New International Dictionary of New Testament Theology and Exegesis*, rev. ed., vol. 2 (Zondervan, 2014), 151.

God is arbitrary or just.[42] However, as the Old Testament background of the statement about Esau and Jacob (Mal. 1:2–3) and its immediate New Testament context (Rom. 9:4–33) indicate, it is better seen as part of the divine plan for the outworking of salvation in history.[43] The seed is "traced through Isaac" (v. 7), continues through Jacob rather than Esau "according to election" (v. 11), then transmits through "the remnant" (v. 27). That seed is Christ, who is the Promise himself (cf. 2 Cor. 1:20; Gal. 3:16). The human descent of the Messiah, who was promised to the Hebrew Patriarchs, culminates in the revelation of "the stumbling stone." This stone, who is Christ, may either be believed or rejected (Rom. 9:32–33). Salvation through faith in the Elect One is available to Gentiles, too (v. 30).

Jesus Christ is not merely the instrumental agent of the divine plan of God for human election, although he certainly works our salvation. Jesus Christ in his divine nature is also the God who elects. As the eternal Son of God, he originates the divine plan in his eternal decree to elect humanity in himself. He accomplishes his self-election to atone for the sins of the people by becoming incarnate in the line of Abraham, Isaac, and Jacob, then by taking up his cross, arising from the dead, and bringing his heavenly kingdom to earth. Jesus Christ as true God elects to redeem humanity; Jesus Christ as the true man is the elected human being who redeems humanity. Christ assumed our human nature (Phil. 2:7) to "recapitulate" (Eph. 1:10) or "perfect" (Heb. 2:10) humanity and to "conquer" the world (John 16:33), thereby making creation "new," reconciling the world by restoring it to its intended right relation with God (2 Cor. 5:17–19).

The Person of Jesus Christ is the eternal Elect One: He is the God who elects man; and he is the man who is elected. The good news of Jesus Christ being the Elect is the eternal divine plan for our salvation. Human beings are numbered among the elect through faith in him as the Elect One. B. H. Carroll taught that election must be defined Christologically: "In Christ, the beloved. The blessings

42. R. C. Sproul, *The Gospel of God: An Exposition of Romans* (Christian Focus, 1994), 165–66.

43. F. F. Bruce, *Romans: An Introduction and Commentary*, Tyndale New Testament Commentaries (InterVarsity Press, 1985), 192–93; Grant R. Osborne, *Romans*, IVP New Testament Commentary Series (InterVarsity Press, 2004), 245–47. Cf. Robert H. Mounce, *Romans*, New American Commentary (Broadman & Holman, 1995), 198–99; John R. W. Stott, *The Message of Romans: God's Good News for the World* (InterVarsity Press, 2001), 267–68.

that I am to receive as a Christian were not bestowed upon me, the hateful, but in Christ, the beloved. I will get in them by getting into him, and be complete in him."[44] Rejection of Christ as the Elect One brings condemnation. Election is, from beginning to end, a supremely Christological doctrine.

Historical Developments

Theological Terms

As we survey the historic conversation about election and providence, it may be helpful to define some common terms used in older and in more recent discussions. "Providence" has been used to indicate God's guidance or "foreordination" of history. Providence is typically divided into three categories: "general providence," God's guidance of all creatures; "special providence," God's guidance of human life; and "very special providence."[45] The third category concerns "predestination," God's oversight of human salvation in particular.

Caution must be exercised when considering human schemes of providence. Protestant confessions generally consent to providence,[46] but Anthony Thiselton notes the Greek term for providence, *pronoia*, was not applied to God in the New Testament. Narrative commentary in Scripture affirms God's foresight over (Matt. 10:29), benevolent care about (Ps. 145:9), provision for (Matt. 6:30), and guidance of (Gen. 50:20) all his creatures. However, "All this in no way undermines the reality of evil or freedom."[47] Care should be exercised before presuming divine providence sanctions particular human ideas or human movements. The enthusiastic affirmations of vicious dictators like Adolf Hitler and Josef Stalin exemplify

---

44. B. H. Carroll, *Colossians, Ephesians, Hebrews*, ed. J. B. Cranfill (Baker, 1948), 77.

45. G. C. Berkouwer, *The Providence of God* (Eerdmans, 1972), 180.

46. Berkouwer, *The Providence of God*, 10.

47. Anthony C. Thiselton, *The Thiselton Companion to Christian Theology* (Eerdmans, 2015), 699.

this danger.[48] However, some evangelicals still find it beneficial to address the doctrine at length.[49]

Within Western theology, "election" typically contemplates the positive aspect of predestination. Some believe God predestines exact individuals who collectively constitute "the elect."[50] However, election may be corporate rather than collective in meaning. The Old Testament doctrine of election emphasizes the people of Israel as a whole.[51] And the New Testament evidence for election has been variously interpreted as corporate or individual. Clear references to individual election are rare.[52] Nevertheless, Calvinists and Arminians emphasize the individual, even as they divide over schema.

"Reprobation" considers the negative aspect of predestination. It is sometimes taken to mean that God has eternally consigned certain persons to damnation.[53] The doctrine of "double predestination" affirms both election and reprobation.[54] In an alternative scheme, "preterition" affirms positive election but not negative reprobation.

---

48. Berkouwer, *The Providence of God*, 162, 164. During the First World War German theologians presumed providential support for their war. Christian nationalism was later coopted by Adolf Hitler, who appealed to providence and submission. Few theologians resisted the rise of Hitler. One exception was Dietrich Bonhoeffer, who "came to recognize the dangerous corrosive potential of nationalism within the church." Karl-Wilhelm Dahm, "German Protestantism and Politics, 1918–39," *Journal of Contemporary History* 3 (1968): 29–49; Benjamin Ziemann, *Hitler's Personal Prisoner: The Life of Martin Niemöller*, transl. Christine Brocks (Oxford University Press, 2024), 37–39; Mark Devine, *Bonhoeffer Speaks Today: Following Jesus at All Costs* (Broadman & Holman, 2005), 126.

49. Piper wrote more than 700 pages about the doctrine, offering ruminations on providence over nature, Satan and demons, kings and nations, life and death, sin, conversion, Christian living, and eschatology. John Piper, *Providence* (Crossway, 2020).

50. Dortian theologians presume "God's eternal election of certain persons to salvation." F. H. Klooster, "Elect, Election," in Walter A. Elwell, ed., *Evangelical Dictionary of Theology* (Baker, 1984), 348.

51. William W. Klein, *The New Chosen People: A Corporate View of Election*, rev. ed. (Wipf and Stock, 2015), 39–40.

52. *Eklektos* is "used only on one occasion of an individual church member (Rom. 16:13)." Silva, *New International Dictionary of New Testament Theology and Exegesis*, 2:149. Some theologians appeal to Acts 13:48 to support a doctrine of individual election, but the verse may simply mean the gospel has effective power to save. And in the context of Lukan theology, Hans Conzelmann was blunt: "Luke was not familiar with the idea of a fixed number of elect." Hans Conzelmann, *The Theology of St. Luke*, transl. Geoffrey Buswell (Fortress Press, 1961), 154.

53. W. S. Reid, "Reprobation," in Elwell, ed., *Evangelical Dictionary of Theology*, 937.

54. Klooster, "Elect, Election," 348.

God is said simply to have "passed over" the reprobate.[55] While preterition is popular with theologians who wish to emphasize that God "wants everyone to be saved and to come to the knowledge of the truth" (1 Tim. 2:4), it does not easily correlate with the precise logical schemes of Augustinianism and Calvinism.

The language of "divine plan" and "divine counsel" may be preferred to "divine decrees." The former terms encourage a more holistic and dynamic perspective. The latter term is often utilized for intramural debates among Calvinist theologians about how an ostensible "decree to save (elect) some and reprobate others" is related to God's "decree to permit the Fall." One scheme places the decrees for individual election and reprobation before the decree for the Fall; a second places them during the Fall; a third, afterward.[56] Ongoing debates, conducted among committed predestinarians, indicate the highly speculative nature of some decretal theologies.[57]

Historic Debates in the East and the West

Western Christians have a long history of sometimes rancorous discussion about providence and election. This is because, after Augustine, whose thoughts still frame our conversation, Western theologians typically focused on reconciling human freedom and human responsibility with divine predestination. Early in his career, Augustine offered an optimistic doctrine of human libertarian freedom. However, after Pelagius deployed an even more optimistic view of the free will, Augustine emphasized the radical impact of the Fall on the human will.[58]

Eastern Christianity struggled less than the West with the speculative relation between divine providence and human free will. On the one hand, Pelagianism was condemned in the East at the

---

55. Reid, "Preterition," in Elwell, ed., *Evangelical Dictionary of Theology*, 874.

56. These speculative systems are known respectively as supralapsarianism, infralapsarianism, and sublapsarianism. Millard J. Erickson, *Christian Theology*, 2nd ed. (Baker, 1998), 842n-43n.

57. Applying the temporal terms *before* and *after* to the eternal mind of God also presents difficulties, for God is not bound by time. Neither does appeal to logical progress rather than temporal progress solve the problem, especially when there is no clear revelation for a logical distinction. The human mind works progressively; the divine mind is eternal.

58. Augustine and Pelagius will receive deeper consideration in the third volume of this series.

ecumenical council of Ephesus in 431.[59] On the other hand, the East focused on Christ's reconstitution of the human will in the garden of Gethsemane. Maximus the Confessor said Jesus Christ brought the human will into "perfect harmony and concurrence" with the divine will.[60] Eastern Christians did not invest the human will with inherent power but weakness.

Major patristic and medieval theologians in the East and in the West offered less controverted models. Gregory of Nyssa argued that because God created us in his image, we are granted a measure of freedom: A free God creates free people. "We have decision in our power."[61] Thomas Aquinas argued that God created humanity to reach its end, which is likeness to him: God is free and created his human creatures to reach this perfection, requiring active human willing. Stoic fatalism, therefore, must be rejected.[62] However, Aquinas agreed that Pelagianism, the subordination of divine freedom to human freedom, should also be rejected.

Protestant Confessions

After the Reformation, which had to wrestle against late medieval semi-Pelagian models of salvation, Protestants addressed providence in different ways. The most detailed treatment came in the seventeenth-century *Westminster Confession of Faith*. This confession was received by Reformed churches and influenced Congregationalists and Particular Baptists. In the first article under its chapter on "Providence," it says God "doth uphold, direct, dispose, and govern all creatures, actions, and things, from the greatest even to the least," and according to his character.[63] In subsequent articles, the Westminster divines made more distinctions, some derived explicitly from Scripture, others implied by logic. As "the

59. Leo Donald Davis, *The First Seven Ecumenical Councils (325–787): The History and Theology* (Liturgical Press, 1990), 157–58.

60. Maximus, "On the Two Wills of Christ in the Agony of Gethsemane," in Maximus the Confessor, *On the Cosmic Mystery of Jesus Christ,* transl. Paul M. Blowers and Robert Louis Wilken (St. Vladimir's Seminary Press, 2003), 173.

61. Cited in McDonough, *Creation and New Creation*, 57.

62. Thomas Aquinas, *Summa Contra Gentiles*, Book 3: *Providence*, Part 1, transl. Vernon J. Bourke (University of Notre Dame Press, 1975), 244–46.

63. *The Westminster Confession of Faith* (1647), 5.1, in Philip Schaff and David S. Schaff, eds., *The Creeds of Christendom with a History and Critical Notes*, 6th ed., 3 vols., (Baker, 1993), 612.

first cause," a divine decree must invariably occur, but God may employ "secondary causes."[64]

Westminster argued that the Fall and human sin are providentially decreed by God, "yet so as the sinfulness thereof proceedeth only from the creature, and not from God."[65] God may give Christians over to sin to "chastise" and "humble" them.[66] He "doth blind and harden" the wicked by withholding grace, withdrawing gifts, exposing them, and giving them over to lust.[67] Finally, this influential confession distinguished "general" providence, by which God provides for all creatures, from "special" providence, which he intends only for his church.[68]

Reacting against colder logical treatments of providence, the Society of Friends tried a different approach with their doctrine of divine Light. They argued redemption is universally available, for God "delighteth not in the death of a sinner, but that all should live and be saved." God makes salvation accessible to every human being through "his only Son a Light."[69] Expanding the Protestant doctrine of "the first and common grace" of general revelation, Quakers said those "who receive and resist not that grace" have access to salvation apart from the "distinct outward knowledge" of the gospel. People "who by providence are cast into those remote parts of the world where the knowledge of history is wanting" may still respond to Christ, the universal Light of the world (cf. John 1:9).[70]

The General Baptists, in their most popular early confession, also set forward a warmer doctrine of providence. They agreed that every person has "a capacity" to be saved. However, they did not countenance the Quaker doctrine of universal redemptive Light. Instead, the gospel which saves people "should be preached to every creature."[71]

---

64. *The Westminster Confession of Faith*, 5.2–3.

65. *The Westminster Confession of Faith*, 5.4.

66. *The Westminster Confession of Faith*, 5.5.

67. *The Westminster Confession of Faith*, 5.6.

68. *The Westminster Confession of Faith*, 5.7.

69. *The Confession of the Society of Friends* (1675), 5, in Schaff and Schaff, eds., *The Creeds of Christendom*, 3:792.

70. *The Confession of the Society of Friends*, 6.

71. *The Standard Confession* (1660), 4, in William L. Lumpkin and Bill J. Leonard, eds., *Baptist Confessions of Faith*, 2nd rev. ed. (Judson Press, 2011), 207.

Contemporary Evangelical Responses

Four contemporary evangelical responses to the historical debates over providence, predestination, and election may now be summarized. We will not consider the Arminian position at length as yet, for it developed from and continues in conversation with the classical Calvinist position. Jacob Arminius and the Reformed Arminians adapted the logic of Calvinism while rejecting its "deterministic metaphysic" and "particular and irresistible grace."[72] Let us consider the positions of classical Calvinism, modified Calvinism, Lutheranism, and the free churches.

Classical Calvinism

Herman Bavinck's treatment of the divine counsel of God is particularistic. "God's absolutely sovereign will is the only ground of predestination, which includes both election and reprobation." He argued that anything less than double predestination indicates a heresy of some type, either Pelagian or semi-Pelagian. He also deemed any robust doctrine of human freedom a problem: "When affirming the determining counsel of God, the major theological issue facing Christian theologians concerns human freedom."[73]

Bavinck also found it necessary to integrate philosophy into his theology. He lamented critics who dismiss Reformed theology, because it "speculatively deduces predestination from an a priori, philosophically deterministic concept of God." However, Bavinck also appealed to Scripture. And he said his system was not primarily anthropological nor soteriological in orientation; rather, it is "theological—the glory of God."[74] Yet it remains still a philosophical theology.

Paul Helm, a more recent Calvinist theologian, speaks of three contexts in which God operates providentially in a meticulous or detailed manner: in the individual Christian life, in the Christian church, and in creation. Helm's model of providence distinguishes

72. J. Matthew Pinson, "Preface" and "Arminians and Jonathan Edwards? Really?" in Pinson, ed., *Jonathan Edwards: A Reformed Arminian Engagement* (B&H Academic, 2024), xiii, 11.

73. Herman Bavinck, *Reformed Dogmatics*, vol. 2, ed. John Bolt, transl. John Vriend (Baker, 2004), 337.

74. Bavinck, *Reformed Dogmatics*, 2:338.

God's direct interventions from his permissive guidance. He also recognized the problem with identifying any event as providential. Like Bavinck, Helm read Scripture deductively, bringing in philosophy.[75]

Calvinists have not always clearly differentiated their doctrine of meticulous sovereignty from Stoic fatalism. The close correlation between philosophical Stoicism and Christian Calvinism is rooted in the life and thought of John Calvin, who trained as a lawyer and wrote his first volume on *De Clementia* by Seneca, the Latin Stoic philosopher.[76] Those following the methods of Calvin, Bavinck, and Helm are continually required to synthesize philosophy with theology.

Modified Calvinism

Millard Erickson developed a nine-point plan with his "moderately Calvinistic model" of election.[77] We offer it here as a helpful model for evangelicals who lean in a Calvinist direction. If one adopts Erickson's model, it must also be admitted that God's plan, like his character, remains unknowable apart from his revelation of that plan. While often engaging philosophy, Erickson demonstrates restraint and seeks to be primarily biblical.

First, "God's plan is from all eternity." In eternity the divine plan was conceived, while in history the divine plan is revealed (2 Tim. 1:9). Second, God wills from the basis of his good pleasure (Isa. 40:13–14). Third, God's plan finds its fulfillment in his glory (Rom. 11:36). Fourth, God's plan considers everything (Eph. 1:11). Fifth, God's plan will not be thwarted (Isa. 14:24–27). Sixth, divine activity originates from the divine character and not vice versa. The divine plan primarily considers God. Seventh, human willing must be considered, "but only secondarily." Eighth, the divine plan comprehends human activity, both good acts (Acts 13:48; Eph. 2:10)

75. Paul Helm, *The Providence of God*, The Contours of Christian Theology (IVP Academic, 1994), 17–37.

76. Ulrich Zwingli, too, admired Seneca and Stoicism. François Wendel, *Calvin: Origins and Development of His Religious Thought*, transl. Philip Mairet (Baker, 2000), 27–37.

77. On this model, which includes "two different senses of God's will," see Erickson, *Christian Theology*, 382–88.

and evil acts (Acts 2:23).[78] Ninth, God's plan, like his character, is "unchangeable."[79]

Lutheranism

In his review of Romans 8:28, Martin Luther said that Paul "from this point on begins to discuss the matter of predestination and election, which is not as deep a subject as is commonly thought, but rather is a wonderfully sweet thing for those who have the Spirit, but a bitter thing and harsh above all things for the prudence of the flesh."[80] Lutheran and free church evangelicals have found elements of Luther's perceptive insights into divine providence worth retention.

John Theodore Mueller, a twentieth-century Lutheran theologian, identified two major biblical truths which must be held. Holding these two truths, without surrendering either one, may prove too much of a tension for those seeking to harmonize a doctrine of the divine plan. Because both statements are true, they require systematic affirmation:

- *Sola gratia* reminds us that individual persons are saved only by grace.
- *Universalis gratia* reminds us that God wills the salvation of all people.[81]

According to Mueller, our minds try to manufacture a missing link for correlating these two biblical truths, but "Scripture commands us not to draw conclusions from the unsearchable judgments of God, but to adore them with awe and reverence."[82] Different theological systems go beyond biblical revelation when they try to provide their own links. Mueller says that Calvinists exceeded Scripture with their "eternal decree of damnation," and that synergists denied the biblical truth of *sola gratia*.[83]

---

78. The greatest evil is to murder the Son of God, is it not?

79. Erickson, *Christian Theology*, 377–81.

80. Martin Luther, *Lectures on Romans: Glosses and Scholia*, in Hilton C. Oswald, *Luther's Works*, vol. 25 (Concordia, 1972), 371.

81. John Theodore Mueller, *Christian Dogmatics: A Handbook of Doctrinal Theology for Pastors, Teachers, and Laymen* (Concordia, 1934), 177.

82. Mueller, *Christian Dogmatics*, 609.

83. Mueller, *Christian Dogmatics*, 609, 611.

While crafting a philosophical link so that one might connect Scriptural doctrines may seem advantageous, the practice of treating a widely debated solution as indispensable dogma may needlessly alienate other believers. It would be wise to remember that on this side of the final resurrection, Christians "know only in part" (1 Cor. 13:9).[84]

Free Church Theologies

More recent free church confessions minimize disagreement over the doctrine of providence, especially the problem of anthropological election. *The New Hampshire Confession of Faith* avoided hard definitions, asserting that election is simultaneously "the gracious purpose of God" and "perfectly consistent with the free agency of man." Its doctrine of election also "promotes humility" and "encourages the use of means in the highest degree."[85] However, some Baptists still find the problem worthy of debate.[86] Other free church theologians find the Lutheran approach, with its deep respect for biblical truth and its call for human humility in the face of divine inscrutability, amenable.

Based on the biblical evidence and informed by previous historical discussions, this free church theologian's systematic conclusions about providence and election are fivefold:

1. Jesus Christ is the Elect One. He is both electing God and elected man.
2. The biblical evidence indicates a corporate understanding of human election is preferable, but individual persons are not excluded.
3. The election of salvation comes to human persons by faith in Jesus Christ.

---

84. For more about the difficulties in providing missing links and its impact upon systematic theology, see "Theological Inferences: Be Careful When Reaching Beyond the Bible," *Pro Gloria Christi* (https://www.malcolmyarnell.com/2012/06/theological-inferences-be-careful-when.html).

85. *The New Hampshire Confession of Faith* (1833), art. ix, in Lumpkin and Leonard, eds., *Baptist Confessions of Faith*, 381. Cf. *The Baptist Faith and Message* (1963), art. v, in Lumpkin and Leonard, eds., *Baptist Confessions of Faith*, 413.

86. E. Ray Clendenen and Brad J. Waggoner, *Calvinism: A Southern Baptist Dialogue* (B&H Academic, 2008).

4. God calls the church to proclaim the gospel to the world.
5. Choosing a system of providence belongs to each theologian as a matter of Christian freedom grounded in scriptural exegesis.[87]

The Anthropological Problem

Many are very concerned with the following question: How do we reconcile divine sovereignty with human libertarian free will?

Four qualifications must be noted before seeking to answer this question. First, Christians should have no difficulty in heartily affirming both God's perfect sovereignty and humanity's willful responsibility, because both are clearly revealed. The exact system of divine sovereignty may differ from one Christian interpreter to another, but these two truths must be affirmed. Second, while the answer to our question presents speculative problems, it is not the "mystery" of Scripture. The biblical "mystery" is Jesus Christ, his Person and his work. He has been revealed, and he must remain the center and circumference of Christian theology. Third, this is not a theological problem, for God is perfect and his revelation is sufficient. Rather, individual election is an anthropological problem. Fourth, it should not be presumed that one of two controverted anthropological doctrines—human libertarian free will and individual human predestination—derive from Scripture. Instead, they derive from the Augustinian hermeneutic.

Two sets of questions should be probed further as you approach anthropological election: First, exactly where is human libertarian free will taught in Scripture? Are the limits of human freedom properly defined? Should Augustine's robust doctrine of free will be presumed? Second, where are the contours of individual human predestination clearly stated in Scripture? How much are theologians assuming about providence and election from tradition instead of revelation? I have elsewhere argued that both divine sovereignty and

87. Using the analogy of faith and freedom, Ron Highfield develops a similar view. Ron Highfield, "God Controls by Liberating," in Dennis Jowers, ed., *Four Views on Divine Providence* (Zondervan, 2011), 141–64.

human freedom must be handled with more circumspection than is sometimes evident in Christian conversations.[88]

Historically, two major Reformed systems have sought to solve the anthropological problem in an individualistic manner: Calvinism and Arminianism. In their interpretation of the key text of Romans 8:29, Calvinists say God "foreknew" the elect, because he "predestined" them as individuals.[89] They can then speculate concerning double predestination and the order of the divine decrees. By contrast, Arminians solve the anthropological problem by saying God "predestined" persons, because he "foreknew" their individual choices.[90] A third group of theologians lauds the teachings of Luis Molina (1535–1600). Molina offered a mediating approach to individual election they deem both theologically and philosophically adept.[91]

Those who wish to join the speculative debate over meticulous divine sovereignty and human libertarian freedom should consider the major positions arranged along a spectrum in the table below. Evangelicals may adopt either Calvinist "compatibilism," Molinist "middle knowledge," or Arminian human "libertarian freedom." However, the philosophical systems of determinism, open theism, and process theology exceed the boundaries of evangelical orthodoxy by compromising, respectively, divine goodness, divine foreknowledge, or divine immutability.[92]

---

88. For a restrained doctrine of human freedom, see Yarnell, "Crucified Monergism: A Theological Interpretation of Justification in Galatians," in Steven Hoskins and David Fleischacker, eds., *Justified in Jesus Christ: Evangelicals and Catholics in Dialogue* (University of Mary Press, 2017), 83–100. On election and the divine plan, please consult two of my theological interpretations presented in the chapel of Southwestern Baptist Theological Seminary. The first on Romans 9, regarding the redemptive-historical or Christological view of election (https://equipthecalled.com/swbtsc-podcast/swbts-chapel-september-30-2009/), and the second on Ephesians 1, regarding the divine plan (https://equipthecalled.com/swbtsc-video/the-economy-of-the-trinity/).

89. Mounce, *Romans*, 188–89.

90. Osborne, *Romans*, 222. For a mediating view, see Leon Morris, *The Epistle to the Romans*, Pillar New Testament Commentary (Eerdmans, 1988), 332.

91. Calvinism and Arminianism will be treated in more detail in the forthcoming volume, *Spirit*. Regarding Molinism, see Kenneth D. Keathley, *Sovereignty and Salvation: A Molinist Approach* (B&H Academic, 2010).

92. Erickson, *Christian Theology*, 305–8, 442–44.

Determinist	Calvinist	Molinist	Arminian	Open Theist	Process
Arbitrary fate has sealed each person's destiny. No alternative remedy is available.	God is neither arbitrary nor unloving. He elected certain human beings to salvation from eternity. God either reprobates or passes over others.	God allows human beings limited freedom. He arranges their context so that they freely choose his will.	God grants human beings libertarian free will. He foreknows every person's response to the gospel. He elects based on his knowledge.	God does not know the future with certainty. However, he knows all the possible futures which may occur.	God is in the course of becoming along with creation.

Table 1: A Spectrum of Modern Views on the Anthropological Problem

Christian unity is compromised when believers allow one of these speculative constructs to sour their attitude toward other believers. Christians should happily agree that God provides humanity with a measure of freedom while he retains sovereignty. Providence does not place divine sovereignty in opposition to human freedom but in guidance of it. Neither collapsing sovereignty into freedom nor collapsing freedom into sovereignty are recommended.[93]

Conclusion: Theological Exhortations

Whichever system you choose to apply to the true revelation of divine providence and election, please consider these concluding exhortations: First, always pray for divine guidance in your theological constructions, especially in those matters which most people find difficult to systematize.

Second, stand resolute where you have a written revelation from God. Do not depart from the biblical text, just because it may be difficult for you. Work through antinomies and paradoxes carefully.

Third, admit when your extrabiblical inferences and divisions derive from beyond Scripture. Our speculative constructs do not carry divine authority. Moreover, human constructions are themselves subject to human deconstruction. Hold loosely to the inescapable elements of human philosophy in your system.

93. Take the example of an earthly adult whose hand directs a rebellious three-year old. The wise adult may guide the child gently away from oncoming vehicular traffic for that child's protection. At the same time, the child's growing sense of creaturely freedom must be respected.

Fourth, presume not that your system is entirely correct, nor that other systems are entirely incorrect. Be careful to treat other Christian brothers and sisters with love. Human systems are not made in the image of God, but human beings are.

Fifth, hold fervently to the hermeneutical rules of faith, hope, and love in your theological ruminations. The rule of hope seems particularly relevant to the experiences of many people. We all want to make sense of the evil we see in this fallen world, but sometimes we must simply trust his plan. The psalmist, Asaph, admitted his heart was embittered when he saw evil people prospering (Ps. 73:21). He learned, however, to pray with eyes of faith to God, "You will guide me with Your plan, And afterward receive me to glory" (v. 24 NASB).

Sixth, avoid presuming upon providence. Before, during, and after the Civil War in the United States, educated Christians taught opposing positions passionately. The Presbyterian slaveholder theologian, James Henley Thornwell, said God invariably "assigns to every man, by a wise and holy decree, the precise place he is to occupy." James Lynch, an African Episcopal minister, disagreed: "Divine Providence" decreed "the deliverance of the slave from bondage." President Abraham Lincoln also affirmed providence's rule over history but doubted human insights: "The Almighty has His own purposes."[94] Rather than conjuring events, wise Christians prioritize worship of the "Elect One," proclamation of his gospel, and love for their fellow human beings.

Seventh and finally, counsel those who doubt their election to trust in the goodness of God. Martin Luther spoke with great pastoral insight to those who were worried about the state of their eternal soul before the God who elects.

> Therefore, he who is overly fearful that he is not elect or is tested concerning his election, let him give thanks for this kind of fear and rejoice that he is afraid, for he knows with confidence that God, who cannot lie, has said: "The sacrifice acceptable to God is a broken," that is, a despairing "spirit; a broken and contrite heart, O God, Thou wilt not despise" (Ps. 51:17).[95]

94. Mark A. Noll, *The Civil War as a Theological Crisis* (University of North Carolina Press, 2006), 81–82, 84, 87–89.

95. Luther, *Lectures on Romans*, 377–78.

Study Questions

1. When you hear the words "election" or "predestination," is your mind drawn first to the glory of Christ or to the fates of individual men? Who does Scripture emphasize?

2. What does Scripture say are the objects of divine "necessity"?

3. Among the historical systems that correlate divine election with human freedom, which one do you believe provides the best solution? Which other system provides helpful solutions, and what are they?

Suggested Resources

- G. C. Berkouwer, *The Providence of God*
- John Theodore Mueller, *Christian Dogmatics*
- Philip Schaff and David S. Schaff, *The Creeds of Christendom*

CHAPTER SEVEN

Who Are We?

According to perhaps the oldest literature in Holy Scripture, "the morning stars sang together and all the sons of God shouted for joy" as God created the universe (Job 38:7). The melody of music at the origin of the world reinforces our claim in chapter 5 that creation was crafted by God to reflect his goodness, beauty, and orderliness. In chapter 6 we discovered that he did not then leave his creation to find its way on its own. Instead, the Lord is guiding his creatures to fulfill the ultimate end for which he designed the universe.

Having explored the majestic work of God in creation and providence, we must now turn our attention to those exalted yet limited creatures whom he blessed by creating them in his image. Human beings are so important within the plan of God for creation that we will devote the next three chapters to considering our relational personhood, our individual constitution, and our tragic Fall into sinfulness.

While God created the world in general with music-like beauty, harmonious notes were particularly evident during his creation of the first human beings on the sixth day. Scripture speaks about humanity's creation in ballads sung by God, Adam, and Solomon. The melodic qualities of this Hebrew poetry suggests truths about God's work in creating and guiding humanity that transcend the liminal border between eternity and time. This reminds us to exercise humility in our ruminations about what God has done and is doing with us.

We must listen carefully to all that God has revealed about us, and we must be careful neither to add to nor to subtract from his revelation.

The divine author of creation expressed his personal joy in his blessed creatures through inspiring linguistic descriptions which employ not only factual propositions but emotive artistry. Propositionally, God concluded that his special creature, the human being, whom he made in his image, was not merely "good" or "beautiful" (Hebrew *tob*; Gen. 1:12, 18, 21, 25). Raising us above the other creatures, God deemed the first human beings "very beautiful" (Hebrew *me'od tob*; Gen. 1:31). Poetically, the subjective cadence of the Hebrew reveals truths which surpass the capacity of objective human propositions alone to describe God's eternal will and action.

Three Old Testament songs disclose the reality of humanity. Two are found in the first chapters of Genesis, while an enlightening refrain from Ecclesiastes interacts with those earlier masterpieces to extend our knowledge of our creation in relation to God and to one another.

- The song of God (Gen. 1:26–27) dwells on the creation of man and woman in the image of God. This song answers the question, "Who are we?"
- The song of Adam (Gen. 2:23) expresses his appreciation for the woman with her strength and suitability. This song answers the question, "Who are you?"
- The song of Qoheleth (Eccles. 3) considers the individual human person in relation to the Creator and to his creation. This song answers the question, "Who am I?"

These ancient poetic descriptions of the divine activity of creation and providence captured the Christian imagination of three highly regarded British academics in the mid-twentieth century. In *The Magician's Nephew*, C. S. Lewis portrayed the creation of fictional Narnia according to Aslan singing his creatures into existence.[1] In *The Silmarillion*, J. R. R. Tolkien envisaged the design

1. Aslan is a fictional figure who represents the second Person of the Trinity. The witch, representative of the evil one, sought to change the tune. C. S. Lewis, *The Magician's Nephew* (HarperCollins, 1994), 116–38.

of his universe through heroic music which incorporated even the dissonance of evil into its beauty.[2] And in *Christianity and History*, Herbert Butterfield, a highly regarded historian and the vice chancellor of Cambridge University, portrayed providence as an orchestral masterpiece wherein God overcomes evil's contrary notes by his sovereign power.[3]

In this chapter, we begin our review of the symphony of humanity with the Song of God and the Song of Adam, marveling at our relationships with God and with one another. In the next chapter, we explore the truth of our individual existence in this world as it exists now "under the sun." Then in chapter 9, we turn our attention to the disharmonies brought into creation by our first parents' willful rebellion against God and to the consequences we bring upon ourselves with our own personal rebellion against God. In subsequent chapters, we consider how sin does not keep God in Christ from ruling over us and working our redemption through his sovereign rule.

The Song of God

There is much to learn from the structural language of God's counsel. The creation of humanity narrated in Genesis 1:26–27 (ESV), the first song of Scripture, contains three stanzas:

> Then God said, "Let us make man in our image, after our likeness. And let them have dominion over the fish of the sea and over the birds of the heavens and over the livestock and over all the earth and over every creeping thing that creeps on the earth."
>
> So God created man in his own image, in the image of God he created him; male and female he created them.

2. In the fiction of Tolkien's "Middle Earth," Melkor similarly sought to change the creative music of "the One." J. R. R. Tolkien, *The Silmarillion: The Myths and Legends of Middle-Earth*, ed. Christopher Tolkien (HarperCollins, 1998), 15–22.

3. Herbert Butterfield, *Christianity and History* (Scribners, 1950), 94–95.

Made in the Image and Likeness of God

During the larger history of creation relayed in Genesis 1, humanity is not mentioned until later in the sixth day. The creation narrative builds to a crescendo with the fashioning of humanity, for they are the only creatures on earth who are said to be made "in the image of God." A shift in divine speech from the earlier creative acts also portends "something momentous." Previously, God spoke consistently in the jussive mood, "Let there be." But now he speaks in the cohortative, "Let us make." The Lord moves from commanding abstractly to acting reflectively, indicating his intense personal investment in human beings.[4]

In theological terms, God engages in a complex personal act of divine counsel.[5] "Let us make" is neither a speech to the angels (for they are not creators), nor an address to the earth (for it is not sentient). Nor is the plural akin to the self-inflated styling of a petty early modern European tyrant, as some commentators have opined. Rather, "Let us make" is God the Trinity's eternal and perfectly wise act of design which issues forth in his temporal act of creating. Humanity is hereby given an unparalleled place in God's plan for his creation.

Martin Luther writes, "Moses points out an outstanding difference between these living beings and man when he says that man was created by the special plan and providence of God. This indicates that man is far superior to the rest of the living beings that live a physical life."[6] When he says, "Let us make," God plans especially for the personal reality of his image. He pours his character personally by the grace of creation into this exalted creature.

---

4. Victor P. Hamilton, *Genesis: Chapters 1–17*, New International Commentary on the Old Testament, (Eerdmans, 1990), 134.

5. In philosophical terms, where earlier there was "performative speech-act," there is now a self-deliberation on the part of the Creator included with the performative speech-act. Kevin Vanhoozer has applied speech-act theory to good effect in his ruminations on hermeneutics. He describes creation as the first act in "the Christian theodrama." Kevin J. Vanhoozer, *Faith Speaking Understanding: Performing the Drama of Doctrine* (Westminster John Knox Press, 2014), 96–97. Cf. idem, *Is There a Meaning in This Text? The Bible, the Reader, and the Morality of Literary Knowledge* (Inter-Varsity Press, 1998); idem, *The Drama of Doctrine: A Canonical Linguistic Approach to Christian Theology* (Westminster John Knox Press, 2005).

6. Martin Luther, *Lectures on Genesis: Chapters 1–5*, transl. Jaroslav Pelikan, *Luther's Works*, vol. 1 (Concordia, 1958), 56.

This divine poem evinces a rhythmic pattern of 3–5–3: The first stanza is comprised of three short lines in which God grants humanity its identity. The personal reality of humanity, through the grace of creation, mirrors the personal reality of God. God said he made man "in our image" and "after our likeness." The reality of the human creature is hereby determined, primarily and ultimately, by relation to the Lord God rather than by relation to other creatures.

The second stanza involves a change in tempo from 3 lines to 5 lines. This introduces a change in theme from human identity to human responsibility. The text describes the grant of representative authority to humanity. The Lord commands the human beings to act among the other creatures on behalf of God. The Hebrew verb for "dominion" (*radah*) is in the plural, indicating both the man and the woman rule together.[7] The representative structure of this appointment is important: the gift of authority includes accountability.

The third stanza contains three lines intoned by the inspired narrator. The subject reverts to human ontology. The song focuses again on the exalted identity of God's leading creature, even as it relates his economy. The first account of human creation thus began with God's own song but ended with the chorus: "So God created man in his own image; he created him in the image of God; he created them male and female."

The divine song's triadic structure applies both personhood and community to both God and humanity. God refers to himself with a plural three times: "us," "our," "our" (lines 1a, 1b, 1c). His singularity is also affirmed three times: "God," "he," "he" (lines 3a, 3b, 3c). Similarly, humanity is described as a singularity three times: "man," "man," "him" (lines 1a, 3a, 3b) and as a relational plurality three times: "them," "them," "male and female" (lines 2a, 3c).

The poetic parallels reinforce the impression that plurality and singularity characterize both the Creator's reality and his creature's reality. But human reality remains entirely dependent upon divine reality. From the divine side, the song begins with a plural reference to God and ends with a singular reference to God. Reversing the divine intricacy in unity, the song begins with human unity and ends with human plurality.

---

7. Scholars disagree over how the plural mandate should be applied. For instance, modern egalitarians and modern complementarians respond to hierarchy. Allison works through the options and offers a third way. Gregg R. Allison, *Complementarity: Dignity, Difference, and Interdependence* (B&H Academic, 2025), 191–202.

In the first song ever conceived and performed, therefore, God sang humanity into existence, granting certain characteristics of himself to humanity. He made man "in" (Hebrew *be*) his "image" (*tselem*) and "as" or "according to" (*ki*) his "likeness" (*demuth*). The sovereign and free triune God dispenses, by way of likeness, his essential unity and personal relationality upon his highly privileged creature. The Creator sang into humanity the grace of his likeness in simplicity and personhood. No other material creature was granted such an exalted gift.[8]

Discerning the Image

So exactly what is the image or likeness of God in humanity? To begin with, we must continually refer our conception of the image to the Creator rather than the creature. The preferred question, therefore, is not, "What is the image?" but "Whose is the image?" To say "in the image" relates man to God in three profound ways: by humility, by glory, and by mediation.

The image relates God to humanity, first, by way of *humility*, through humanity's creaturely dependence upon God as eternal Creator. The determining figure is God, not man. If you would know what the image of God is in humanity, you must first discern who God is. Once you know the reality of God, you will be better equipped to discern the reality of his image. Humanity is always relative to and contingent upon God, while God remains eternally self-sufficient.[9] This requires creatures to adopt an attitude of humble adoration towards the Creator.

The second way of relation is by *glory*, through humanity's reflection of God. Regarding glory or light, we must again have recourse to the reality of God. Divine Trinitarianism is implied in the song's references to the unity and plurality of both God and humanity. Humanity thereby reflects the glory of God's Trinitarian personhood. In addition, as with glory, all the communicable attributes of the divine nature are reflected in humanity rather than

8. John Calvin believed angels were created in God's image. Berkhof disagreed, since no biblical text describes such a grant, angels were not given dominion like humanity, and angels lack natural bodies in which to reflect his image. Louis Berkhof, *Systematic Theology*, 4th ed. (Eerdmans, 1941), 206–7.

9. On divine aseity, see Malcolm B. Yarnell III, *God*, vol. 1, Theology for Every Person (B&H, 2024), 102–3.

inherent to the human constitution. God granted his exalted human creature a share in his life, speech, and dominion, and in many other divine attributes.[10]

The third way of relation is by *mediation*. Humanity is not the image of God immediately. Humanity was created "in" the image of God or "according to" the likeness of God (Gen. 1:26). In other words, humanity is mediately related to God by virtue of creation. By way of contrast, Jesus Christ is himself uniquely "the image of God" and "the exact expression of his nature." He is the "one mediator," because he relates directly to God by nature and to humanity by the grace of incarnation (1 Tim. 2:5; 2 Cor. 4:4; Heb. 1:3). Due to the Fall, humanity must be restored in the Person of the incarnate Christ and perfected by his Holy Spirit. The reconstitution of the image will be considered later.

Luther corrected theologians who recast divine reality in human terms rather than orienting humanity toward God: "But we were made according to the image of those Makers who say, 'Let Us make.' These Makers are three separate Persons in one divine essence. Of these three Persons we are the image."[11] In the twentieth century, theologians began reconceiving the Trinity toward human social relations. Some portrayed God according to democratic equality. Others posited a hierarchy of God over his Son to justify a hierarchy of man over woman.[12] Rejecting both social paradigms, we must approach humanity from God's revelation of his own reality and remain careful never to impose our preferred anthropology upon God.[13]

Before proceeding, a further warning about the danger of formulaic innovations in anthropology must be issued. Luther

10. On the communicable attributes, see Yarnell, *God*, 104–5.

11. Luther, *Lectures on Genesis*, 58.

12. Contemporary Social Trinitarianism has two major streams: the democratic portrait of God drawn by Jürgen Moltmann and Catherine LaCugna, and the hierarchical portrait of God drawn by Bruce Ware and Wayne Grudem. The first has been compared with tritheism; the second, Arianism. Cf. Amy Peeler, "The Need for Nicene Exegesis: Eternal Functional Subordination's Hermeneutical Innovation," in Matthew Barrett, ed., *On Classical Trinitarianism: Retrieving the Nicene Doctrine of the Triune God* (IVP Academic, 2024), 704–5; Paul D. Molnar, "Classical Trinity: Catholic Perspective," in Jason S. Sexton, ed., *Two Views of the Doctrine of the Trinity* (Zondervan, 2014), 88.

13. Malcolm B. Yarnell III, "From God to Humanity: A Trinitarian Model for Theological Anthropology," in Keith S. Whitfield, ed., *Trinitarian Theology: Theological Models and Doctrinal Application* (B&H Academic, 2019), 63–94.

recognized the need for chaste parsimony in providing a theological definition of humanity. The Reformer related the human reception of the image to the Trinity, but he never schematized the image. Luther even rebuked the leading Western theologian, Augustine of Hippo, whom he often followed. He corrected Augustine for imposing a man-derived structure upon the image through his Neo-Platonic anthropology of "memory, intellect, and will." Luther believed Augustine's scheme of humanity's internal constitution was alien to Scripture and overwrought. His warning remains salient.[14]

Historic Interpretations of the Imago Dei

We must account for the diverse interpretations theologians have offered for the doctrine of the *imago Dei* (Latin "image of God"). Four systematic questions about the image shall guide our historical review: What are the traditional interpretations of the *imago Dei*? Can the interpretations be summarized and synthesized as types? What model accounts best for the fruit of biblical exegesis? And, what was the effect of the Fall on the Image?

In response to the first question, Leo Garrett identified seven prominent approaches to the image in Christian history: The image has long been identified with human dominion or lordship over nature (Gen. 1:26, 28). It has also been correlated with human reason, or the intellectual faculty. The image was more recently compared to the confrontation of man with woman, analogous to God's relational nature. The image has sometimes been identified with the spiritual and moral innocence of human beings in their original,

14. Luther, *Lectures on Genesis*, 60–61. Augustine also speculated about "the libertarian free will" of the human being. *On Free Choice of the Will* was his first major theological treatise and was written before his famous conversion experience. A philosophical exercise for considering the responsibility of humanity for the introduction of sin, Augustine's speculations about free will have had a huge impact on subsequent theological development.

A warning against over-schematization regarding the human being remains true, at so many levels, including with the subject of the will. Some conclusions about the human will must certainly be drawn by implication from the text. Discussions of the will should begin with the exposition of Genesis 2–4. The human will is limited and fallible, according to that historical narrative. The Christian doctrine of the human will cannot be divorced from history for the sake of abstract philosophical speculation vis-à-vis predestination.

"prelapsarian" state.[15] It has also been classified as the capacity for spirituality and morality. A few have said the image refers to man's erect bodily stature. Finally, the *imago Dei* has been compared to responsible creaturehood in the Old Testament and spiritual and moral conformity in the New.[16]

Anthony Hoekema offered a helpful answer to the second question: Can these various views be synthesized? Hoekema organized the various views of the image of God into two summary types, the structural and the functional. The *structural views* consider "what man is like." The *functional views* consider "what men do."[17] Dietrich Bonhoeffer effectively discerned a third type, the *relational views*. These consider the interactions between persons. Hoekema opted for a composite view that includes more than one ideological type: "Since the image of God includes the whole person, it must include both man's structure and man's functioning."[18] Bonhoeffer's relational view may be incorporated into Hoekema's composite.

In the Image of the Trinity

The best doctrine of the image will incorporate the fruit of biblical exegesis with orthodox Christian dogma. On this basis, the truth of humanity's creation in the image of God may be summarized in Latin as *imago Dei est imago Trinitatis*: "the image of God is the imago of the Trinity." The fullness of the *imago Dei* as the work of the one God who is the Father and the Son and the Holy Spirit derives from an explicitly Christian canonical-theological reading of Genesis 1:26–27.[19]

There are exegetical hints that the one God is three Persons throughout Genesis 1. These significant suggestions are confirmed as revelation progresses into the New Testament. In the first place,

---

15. *Prelapsarian* means "before the Fall of humanity into sin." It is used to describe what humanity was like in the state of innocence.

16. James Leo Garrett Jr., *Systematic Theology: Biblical, Historical, and Evangelical*, vol. 1, 2nd ed. (BIBAL, 2000), 454–63.

17. Anthony A. Hoekema, *Created in God's Image* (Eerdmans, 1986), 68–73.

18. Hoekema, *Created in God's Image*, 69; cf. Garrett, *Systematic Theology*, 1:463–64.

19. "For by the hands of the Father, that is, by the Son and the Holy Spirit, man and not [merely] a part of man, was made in the likeness of God." Irenaeus, *Against Heresies*, 3.6.1, in Alexander Roberts and James Donaldson, eds., *The Apostolic Fathers, Justin Martyr, Irenaeus*, Ante-Nicene Fathers, vol. 1 (1885; reprint, Hendrickson, 1994), 531.

the term translated "God" in the first verse of Hebrew Scripture, *Elohim*, is nominally plural yet paired with a singular verb. Divine singularity is compatible, therefore, with some sense of plurality, a plurality given fuller description as the canon proceeds. Second, Genesis 1:1–3 alludes to a threefold divine activity. The Creator, the subject who initiates creation, is described in three ways. He is "God" (v. 1) and "Spirit" (v. 2) and the One who "said" (v. 3). Third, as seen above, the poetry of Genesis 1:26–27 indicates both divine plurality and unity through triadic movements correlating humanity with God.

Alongside these exegetical hints suggesting the Trinity in Genesis 1, the Christian way of reading Scripture as a unitary canon requires Christian scholars to affirm that humanity was created in the image of God, and that this God is Trinity. The whole Bible was inspired by the one and only God and witnesses to this one God; and his unity should not be sundered in the rush to satisfy modernist academic divisions.[20] The one God of the Old Testament is the Trinity of the New Testament; and the Trinity of the New Testament is the one God of the Old Testament. There are not two Gods in the Bible; there is only "the one and only one living and true God."[21] A unitary canon which speaks of one God requires Christian scholars to affirm that humanity was created in the image of God the Trinity.

The Old Testament demands singular human devotion to the One Lord God (Deut. 6:4–5). He is, "The LORD, the God of your ancestors, the God of Abraham, the God of Isaac, and the God of Jacob. . . . This is my name forever; this is how I am to be remembered in every generation" (Exod. 3:15). Jesus extended God's singular identity into the New Testament, "Now concerning the resurrection of the dead, haven't you read what was spoken to you by God: I am the God of Abraham and the God of Isaac and the God of Jacob? He is not the God of the dead, but of the living" (Matt. 22:31–32). The one God who inspired and reveals himself in both the Old and

20. On the unfortunate divisions created by modern forms of biblical theology and the need to recall the theological point of Scripture and the unity of the canon grounded in the one God who inspired it, especially with regard to the God of Genesis 1, see Kevin J. Vanhoozer, *Mere Christian Hermeneutics: Transfiguring What It Means to Read the Bible Theologically* (Zondervan, 2024), 75–103, 196–98; David S. Dockery and Malcolm B. Yarnell III, *Special Revelation and Scripture, Theology for the People of God* (B&H Academic, 2024), 147–205, 314–27.

21. The phrase, "the one and only one living and true God," derives from *The Baptist Faith and Message*, Article II.

the New Testaments is, in the words of Christ himself, "the Father and the Son and the Holy Spirit" (Matt. 28:19; cf. 2 Cor. 13:13).

Identifying the God of the Hebrew Torah with the Trinity taught by Jesus Christ in the New Testament prompted Lutheran theologians to emphasize the unity of the God who saves human beings from their sin. They affirmed that the gift of "essential righteousness" brings *trinitatis inhabitatio*, "the indwelling of the Trinity," to the redeemed. "God the Father, the Son, and Holy Spirit" has come to dwell "in the elect" through the grace of personal faith. The primary Lutheran confession, *The Formula of Concord*, teaches that this triune indwelling of redeemed humanity happens "by grace" and "only because of Christ's obedience and merit."[22]

Werner Elert developed the biblical case for the idea that humanity participates in the Trinity by grace through faith. The Father, he said, makes his "home" with us and lives "in" us. But our unity with God comes only through Christ's personal unity of two natures. In his very own Person, God the Son unites humanity with himself (John 14:23; 17:21). The Son can thereby become "the vine" to which believers are attached as "branches" (John 15:1ff). He is "the head" and we are "his body." This unity of redeemed humanity with God through Jesus Christ is the "mystery" of the faith (Eph. 1:22ff; 5:23, 30, 32). And God the Holy Spirit unites believers to the Son with the Father in a unique and unbreakable bond (Ps. 51:12; 1 Cor. 6:17, 19).[23]

---

22. *The Formula of Concord* (1577), 3.54, in Robert Kolb and Timothy J. Wengert, eds., *The Book of Concord: The Confessions of the Lutheran Church*, transl. Charles Arand et al. (Fortress Press, 2000), 571–72.

23. Werner Elert, *The Structure of Lutheranism: The Theology and Philosophy of Life of Lutheranism in the Sixteenth and Seventeenth Centuries*, transl. Walter A. Hansen (Concordia, 1962), 154–60. The redeemed "participate" or "share" (Greek *koinonia*) by grace "in the divine nature" (2 Pet. 1:4), "in the blood" and "body of Christ" (1 Cor. 10:16), and "of the Holy Spirit" (2 Cor. 13:13). "An actual 'sharing' (*communio*) or 'participation' (*communitas*) takes place between Christ and those who are his." Elert, *The Structure of Lutheranism*, 157–59. God indwells humanity through the restoration of the divine image by union with Christ. He shares his life with humanity through the gift of his righteousness by faith, a gift that comes to us due only to his love. This indwelling leads to our imitation of the life of Christ in the power of the Spirit. Elert, *The Structure of Lutheranism*, 160–76. "But the love of God as such is perceived not only as a statement made by God. It calls the heart of the believer into union with itself. It calls the psyche. And the psyche answers. God remains the Other One. He is not the depth of the soul, as the mystics teach. He always remains the You—otherwise there could be no love relationship. But God's You and the I of the

Royal, Rational, and Relational

It may be helpful to speak of the *imago Dei* according to our intended participation in the acts of the triune God. As we have seen, Scripture describes God as Trinity according to his inseparable and proper working. Among those divine works which seem especially related to the image of God in the early chapters of Genesis are three: God rules his creation; God is reasonable; and God relates to his creatures. The *imago Dei* may, therefore, be described as royal, rational, and relational.

The image of God is *royal*. To speak of royalty is to speak of power in command. When God made man in his image, he immediately and twice indicated humanity must "have dominion over" the world on God's behalf (Gen. 1:26, 28). Humanity's rule as God's representative on earth reflects the Father, even as all three Persons possess and exercise entire sovereignty. Note, however, that human rule of creation is limited in three ways: First, our rule remains under God. Second, human rule must be wholly for God's purpose. Humans are granted provision from creation to facilitate our limited rule as his vice-regents, but we must respect God and his creation. Third, nothing in this text grants any human being the right to rule over other human beings but only alongside other human beings, who themselves likewise rule under God.[24] The coordination of humanity's wide-ranging sovereignty requires the constitution of various human covenants. We will have more to say of these covenantal arrangements.

The image is also *rational*. To speak of reason is to speak of power in thought. When God made man in his image, he opened communication with humanity through a word of blessing and a word of command (Gen. 2:16–17). God's opening command has been described as the "covenant of works." God also brought the animals to man, granting him the power of identifying creation with words (vv. 19–20). Man's logic and language reflect his creation in

psyche are connected through love, which makes of man and God 'one thing.'" Elert, *The Structure of Lutheranism*, 176.

24. John Locke, *Two Treatises of Government*, ed. Peter Laslett (Cambridge University Press, 1960), 141–55; Malcolm B. Yarnell III, "The Baptists and John Locke," in Thomas S. Kidd, Paul D. Miller, and Andrew T. Walker, eds., *Baptist Political Theology* (B&H Academic, 2023), 107–8.

the image of the eternal God, who is Word or reason.[25] Both limited creativity and limited freedom accompany humanity's creation in the image of God as Word. God created by fiat and *ex nihilo*; we create by imitation and out of materials which already exist. He is entirely free, constrained only by his own character; we are free, constrained by his gifts, our character, and his coming judgment.

Finally, the image is *relational*. To speak of relation is to speak of power in grace. While God was making man in his image, he formed him from the red dust of the earth from which Adam derived his name (Hebrew *'adam* means "red"). God gave "breath" (Hebrew *neshamah*) to the body of Adam, thereby conveying "life" (Hebrew *nephesh*, Gen. 2:7). For as long as the Person of the Spirit maintains the gifting of breath, a human person lives (6:3). But when the Spirit withdraws, and ceases to grant breath, the human dies (Gen. 7:22; cf. Ps. 104:29–30). Our lives and relations, both with the Creator and with other creatures, reflects humanity's entirely dependent relation upon the breath of God.[26] The work of the Spirit as Creator and Sustainer of human life through his constant relation of giving life must not be forgotten. Nor must the creative relation be confused with the Spirit's re-creative relation of new life by faith. We will have more to say of that renewed relationship with God later.

The *imago Dei* given to humanity reflects the proper and inseparable work of the Trinity as taught in the canon: the Father in his dominion with the Son and the Spirit, the Son in logic and language with the Father and the Spirit, and the Spirit in life and relation with the Father and the Son. The three Persons work upon God's blessed creatures inseparably and properly. Humanity is royal, relational, and rational because humanity, male and female, is made in the image of the God who is royal, relational, and rational. Humanity certainly reflects the characteristics of God in his works of ruling, relating, and reasoning. However, there is much more about humanity that reflects God. For instance, humanity was intended to participate by grace in the communicable perfections of God. We are called to be holy like God and to love like God (Matt. 5:48; John 13:34). We are also called to participate in God's righteousness (Rom. 1:16–17).

---

25. Thomas Aquinas, *Summa Theologica*, transl. Fathers of the English Dominican Province, 5 vols. (Christian Classics, 1981), 1:397.

26. Malcolm B. Yarnell III, "The Person and Work of the Holy Spirit," in Daniel L. Akin, Bruce Riley Ashford, and Kenneth Keathley, eds., *Theology for the People of God*, rev. ed. (B&H Academic, 2014), 527.

However, human reflection of these communicable divine attributes has obviously been compromised by the Fall, and severely so.

The Effect of the Fall

What was the effect of the Fall on the image? Opinions have diverged over this question. Some have said the *imago Dei* was lost, others that it was not. John F. Kilner classified the widespread belief that the image of God was damaged by the Fall under four subcategories: "completely lost," "virtually lost," "partly lost," and "compromised." Kilner himself once held a "damaged" or "lost" position regarding the image of God in humanity. However, sustained reflection on the historic consequences of a "lost" view led him to reconsider.[27]

Luther, examining the state of the image before and after the Fall, concluded humanity had devolved. Before the Fall, the image was "something far more distinguished and excellent, since obviously no leprosy of sin adhered either to his reason or to his will."[28] Subsequently, many Lutherans concluded the image was completely eradicated. John Theodore Mueller believed man "through the Fall has entirely lost the image of God in its proper sense, that is, his concrete wisdom, righteousness and holiness, so that his intellect now is veiled in spiritual darkness."[29]

However, numerous biblical texts indicate the image remains. In Genesis 9:6, God continued to accord protection to human persons after the Fall, referring explicitly to the image: "Whoever sheds human blood, by humans his blood will be shed, for God made humans in his image." Human dignity remains because humans were created in God's image. In the New Testament, the image again demands human respect: "With the tongue we bless our Lord and Father, and with it we curse people who are made in God's likeness" (James 3:9). From such texts, Kilner argued that the image of God in humanity is "undamaged." "All people, then, have the uncompromised status of being in the image of God."[30]

---

27. John F. Kilner, *Dignity and Destiny: Humanity in the Image of God* (Eerdmans, 2015), 159–60.

28. Luther, *Lectures on Genesis*, 62.

29. John Theodore Mueller, *Christian Dogmatics: A Handbook of Doctrinal Theology for Pastors, Teachers, and Laymen* (Concordia, 1934), 207.

30. Kilner, *Dignity and Destiny*, 147.

Despite strong statements for the "undamaged" image of God in fallen humanity, advocates of this position still admit certain antinomies. "To be clear, no one claims that the Bible explicitly teaches that God's image remains undamaged." The biblical evidence is not easy to systematize.[31] Kilner defined the image abstractly as "the standard of what people are created to be." This standard, he argued, is "not diminished."[32] Kilner was driven by concern that "the average person," who hears the image is damaged, may put human life and dignity "at risk."[33] Harrowing examples that diminishing the divine image allows include not only slave-traders and slaveholders but the German Christians under Adolf Hitler.[34]

Whether one uses the language of "damaged" or "undamaged" regarding the image of God after the Fall, two errors must be avoided: On the one side, if the language of "damage" is applied to the *imago Dei* in human beings, we must teach that everyone retains dignity before God. Humans must be accorded full dignity by other human beings, because all are created in the image of God. On the other side, if the language of "undamaged" is applied to the *imago Dei*, it must be remembered that humanity is fallen. Sinfulness robs us of righteousness, and harms the will, the emotions, and the body, endangering human destiny. Sin horribly damages every human and requires the judgment of death by God (Rom. 6:23).

Our very nature has clearly been perverted, as seen in the continuing presence of sinful impulses among us. *The Baptist Faith and Message* teaches that people "inherit a nature and an environment inclined toward sin." Alas, however, some have used the idea of the lost image to brutalize others with persecution, slavery, even murder. In response we must recall that every human being retains their human nature, and God treasures those whom he made in his image to carry that nature. It may be best to affirm simultaneously that both "imagedness" and "sinfulness" reside in humanity after the Fall and before the final resurrection.

Whether the image was damaged or not by the Fall is not the primary issue. Our need for personal and communal obedience to God is. God has clearly revealed that we must render him worship. He also commands respect for those whom he created in his image.

31. Kilner, *Dignity and Destiny*, 147.
32. Kilner, *Dignity and Destiny*, 134.
33. Kilner, *Dignity and Destiny*, 176.
34. Kilner, *Dignity and Destiny*, 17–37.

The impact of the Fall on the image does not change God's gift. His creative intent must be our central concern; he commands respect for the *imago Dei* after the Fall. Our theological classification systems for the image do not change his love for his creatures. Nor do our classification systems dispense with our need to obey God's command to live ethically in our relationships. We must ultimately depend upon our union with Christ to restore the image within humanity.

The Song of Adam

"Who are you?" is the question we ask as we face other human beings directly and personally. Adam's song, found in Genesis 2, answers this immediate and intimate relational question. Having established that the human being is made in the image of the Trinity, and having explored definitions of that imagery, we must now discuss an extraordinary aspect of humanity's "image" and "likeness," or "analogy" and "similitude," to God.[35] The likeness of humanity to God includes in some way the diversity of being male and female. Our embodied creaturely lives as men and women fix our human identity with one another. The initial human interactivity of these two persons reflects in important if allusive ways to God the Trinity's inextricable intertwining in three Persons. Human gender relations may be said to reflect both the Trinity's *perichoresis*, "mutual indwelling," and *taxis*, "orderliness."

Human reflections of divine reality are analogous by design. Analogies compare two objects which possess not only similarities but differences. The wise use of analogy recognizes its inherent

35. Most scholars recognize "image" and "likeness" function as synonyms in the Hebrew text. Irenaeus distinguished the image, which he equated with intelligence and freedom, from the likeness, or holiness of the first human beings. The image remained while the likeness was lost with the Holy Spirit in the Fall. Hoekema, *Created in God's Image*, 34; Irenaeus, *Against Heresies*, 3.6.1, in Roberts and Donaldson, eds., *The Apostolic Fathers, Justin Martyr, Irenaeus*, 532. Bonhoeffer used the Greek synonym *analogia* rather than the Vulgate's Latin *similitudenem*. Dietrich Bonhoeffer, *Creation and Fall: A Theological Exposition of Genesis 1–3*, ed. John W. DeGruchy, transl. Douglas Stephen Bax, *Dietrich Bonhoeffer Works*, vol. 3 (Fortress Press, 1997), 65. These terms—*image*, *likeness*, *analogy*, and *similitude*—may be taken synonymously in this context.

definitional limits.[36] Our ruminations about the relational nature of those made in the divine image should, therefore, not be over-schematized. Nor should any speculative social scheme be imposed upon either God or human beings. Our created lives as embodied souls, the place for the triune image, are lived with our feet on this corrupted earth even while our hearts yearn for the perfection of heaven. On earth, we see heaven as through an opaque glass, enigmatically (Greek *ainigma*, "dimly," 1 Cor. 13:12). It does not yet appear what humanity shall be in glory (1 John 3:2).[37]

Scripture often offers a different set of questions and answers than those presumed by human cultures. Wisdom prompts us to hear voices in our societies with discretion (Prov. 1:5; 12:15). But the Word is perfect, and it reminds us that human beings are fallen (Pss. 19:7–14; 119:1–7). Christians must exercise discernment about the sin which perverts every culture. This includes our own immediate communities, which effect us in ways of which we often remain unaware. Too often Christians have allowed either the broader human society or their own preferred subculture to provide key answers about our humanity. It is wiser to seek answers to our human problems from the Word in the Spirit. In our day, Christians are confronted by cultural polarizations which swing between self-centered individualism and abusive hierarchy.[38]

The Man Sings

Adam's song, recorded in Genesis 2:23, was simpler than that sung earlier by God. In his verse, Adam reflected upon the beauty of creation. His song brings into sharper focus the relationality of man vis-à-vis God. The divine persons are distinct and orderly, a truth expressed well in the Greek patristic term *taxis*, even as the divine persons are intertwined and unified, a truth expressed well in the Greek term *perichoresis*. Distinction and equality necessarily characterize the relations of those made in the image of the Trinity:

---

36. Paul Bartha, "Analogy and Analogical Reasoning," in Edward N. Zalta and Uri Nodelman, eds., *The Stanford Encyclopedia of Philosophy* (Fall 2024), https://plato.stanford.edu/archives/fall2024/entries/reasoning-analogy/.

37. Yarnell, "From God to Humanity," 93–94.

38. Joshua D. Chatraw and Karen Swallow Prior, eds., *Cultural Engagement: A Crash Course in Contemporary Issues* (Zondervan Academic, 2019).

> Then the man said, "This at last is bone of my bones and flesh of my flesh; she shall be called Woman, because she was taken out of Man." (ESV)

The song of the first man focuses on the first woman. Where the first song was composed of three poetic lines, the second is not as complete, composed only of two lines. Adam's twofold ballad reflects God's song, but it lacks triadic fullness. This linguistic turn subtly suggests the limits in humanity's reflection of God. Where the first song concerned God pouring aspects of himself into his creature by grace, the second song concerns the man reflecting upon the created natural relation of himself to his formidable correspondent, the woman.

There are three notes in Adam's song. These can be described both theologically and historically. First, the woman is a gift from God which man receives as a grace. Second, God's gift of relationality for humanity is manifested in history as Adam recognizes the woman's correspondence to himself. Third, the two ways of theology and history can be seen in God's gift of personal reality to human beings, and in the man's recounting of the woman's identity.

The Grace of Woman

The first note in Adam's song rejoices in man's reception of the woman as a gift. The operative expression for grace in the second song is Adam's ecstatic response. The Hebrew phrase *happa'am* means, "Now!" or "At last!" The same expression is found in Genesis 30:20, where Leah cries out in great joy and relief, "God has given me a good gift" of a child. The gifts of God prompt human recognition of praise for his provision.

The grace of woman from God to man is later described as both a blessing and an identity. The woman remained a blessing after the Fall: "On the day that God created man, he made him in the likeness of God; he created them male and female. When they were created, he blessed them and called them mankind" (5:1b–2). There are five ways in which this passage indicates the woman is a grace: In general, she is a blessing. In particular, the man and the woman receive a dual identity that is both shared and distinct. She is also necessary for man. She is predestined for man. And she is created by God.

In the first place, the woman is a *blessing*. A woman is not an external curse given to torment the man in his fleshliness.[39] Rather, she is a divine blessing to him, spiritually and physically. Woman is given to man to be a blessing in the bonding of man and woman as "one flesh" (2:24; 5:2). Luther saw the gift of the woman as a blessing in numerous ways: She brings "companionship" to the man; she brings "protection" against postlapsarian sin; and she allows for procreation, the gift of children.[40]

Second, the man and the woman receive a *dual identity* by grace. The "female" (Hebrew *neqeba*) is created alongside the "male" (*zakar*), receiving the image and likeness of God together with the male (1:27; 5:2). There is both distinction and unity here. The distinctions of sex and gender are given as "mirrors" of "God's own self-giving love."[41] Neither the gift of maleness nor the gift of femaleness have been placed under the authority of humanity. Rather, gender comes as a created grace of God. Contemporary claims that one may change one's gender contradict this grace of distinction. Human unity is rooted in the fact that both the woman and the man are identified by God as "humanity" or "mankind" (1:27; Hebrew *ha 'adam*).[42] Adam is also the name of the first human male (e.g., 2:20; 4:1; 5:3; etc.). We should not be confused by the dual application of *ha 'adam*, to the first person and to the entire species. While the gift of gender produces distinct identities for the man and the woman, the gift of human nature produces a common identity. This common reality includes the *imago Dei*. The blessing of being made in God's image may not be arbitrarily limited by social schemes. The man is truly human and truly male, just as the woman is truly human and truly female.

In the third place, the divine gift of the distinct and united nature of woman is a *necessary* grace. Apart from woman, man is *lo' tob* ("not good" or "not beautiful," Gen. 2:18). Man in his alone state remains, if you will, un-good and ugly. Man considered "alone"

---

39. Cf. Roger Barrier, "What to Do When Your Spouse Is Your Thorn in the Flesh," *Crosswalk*, March 2019, https://www.crosswalk.com/church/pastors-or-leadership/christianity-questions-answers/what-to-do-when-your-spouse-is-your-thorn-in-the-flesh.html.

40. Luther, *Lectures on Genesis*, 116–17.

41. Katie J. McCoy, *To Be a Woman: The Confusion over Female Identity and How Christians Can Respond* (B&H, 2023), 93.

42. Charles Sherlock, *The Doctrine of Humanity*, Contours of Christian Theology (InterVarsity Press, 1996), 35.

is not God's intent; human companionship is required. The gift of two complementary bodies creates the condition by which human communion becomes possible.[43] Man apart from woman also lacks a creative grace which reflects God's creativity. Only the man and the woman together as "one flesh" may foster human life (2:24).[44] Through procreation humanity reflects the life-giving quality of the Creator. This reflection requires both sexes. Human procreation does not naturally occur without the personal participation of individuals from both sexes.

Woman is, in the fourth place, a *predestined* grace. Woman as God's grace for man occurs through divine self-reflection. Where in the first song God said, "Let us make," now before the second song, he says, "I will make." The plural self-reference (1:26) becomes a singular self-reference (2:18), evoking again the triune quality of the divine plan. Woman is a grace, a predestined grace for man, a grace poured forth from the eternal counsel. Woman keeps man from being "not good." Woman is not a hurried afterthought of God concerning his creature's deficiency. Woman is foreordained to ensure human wholeness.

Fifth, woman is a *created* grace: "So the LORD God caused a deep sleep to come over the man, and he slept. God took one of the ribs and closed the flesh at that place. Then the LORD God made the rib he had taken from the man into a woman and brought her to the man" (2:21–22). The woman is brought to the man while he sleeps. Her creation was not his plan, nor was she in his power. It is important to remember that woman is a grace of God, created by God, owned by God. This should not have to be said, but in those cultures shaped by empire and slavery, it must be stated plainly: No human owns another, for no human created another. God alone is Lord of all, for he made them all in his image.[45]

Man does nothing to bring woman into existence. He is an entirely passive recipient of a gracious movement only the triune Creator can plan, speak, and implement. She is God's grace. Luther said that when God "brought her to the man," this was the first act

43. John Paul II, *Theology of the Body in Simple Language* (Philokalia, 2008), 21, 29.

44. John Paul II, *Theology of the Body*, 41.

45. Nyssa argued that human beings belong to God alone, for they are made in his image. David Bentley Hart, "The 'Whole Humanity': Gregory of Nyssa's Critique of Humanity in Light of His Eschatology," *Scottish Journal of Theology* 54.1 (2001): 51–69.

of betrothal.[46] This man and this woman are now husband and wife by the will of God. Woman first proceeds from the body of man. Man and woman are afterward generated from the body of man through the body of woman, but God alone brings each one into being (1 Cor. 11:12). Adam is neither the cause of himself nor the cause of the woman.

Humanity, comprised of the male and the female, manifests created grace in three sets of relations: First, humanity is a grace whom God created for communion with himself. The gift of his image prepares us for the blessing of relationship with him. Second, humanity is a grace of the male and the female to each other. The relationships of human beings with one another derive from the human relation with God. Third, humanity was intended to be a grace to the earth. We were meant to steward the earth for God (Gen. 1:26, 28) by serving and guarding it (2:5, 15). Every human relation depends upon the divine–human relation.

The Intimate Relationality of Humanity

The second note in Adam's song sounds through his recognition of his correspondence with the woman, of her relation to the man himself. God led Adam to survey the animals. While Adam noticed the animals had suitable partners, the man sadly did not (Gen. 2:20). Even before this became evident in time to Adam, God eternally determined the man would receive a fitting mate. The specific language of the divine plan is important: "I will make a helper corresponding to him" (v. 18). The two important Hebrew terms that God uses to describe his plan for man and woman are *'ezer* ("helper") and *kenegdo* ("corresponding to"). Together, they indicate both origin and equality, both dependence and contribution, both identity and relationality.

'Ezer means "one who gives aid" or "helper." It does not imply inferiority in quality. Indeed, the term is used of God as a helper to Israel, appearing in threefold couplets (e.g. Deut. 33:7, 26, 29; Pss. 33:20; 115:9–11). The verbal form, *'azar*, means "succor," "save from danger," and "deliver from death."[47] *'Ezer* implies neither the ontological inferiority nor the economic inferiority of the helper. Rather, the term indicates a movement of grace from one person toward

46. Luther, *Lectures on Genesis*, 134.
47. Hamilton, *Genesis*, 176.

another, either God toward humanity or one human person toward another human person.

Kenegdo, a derivative of *neged*, means "before", "against", "in the presence", or "about."[48] It is as if God is saying, I will give him a helper "as in front of him" or "according to what is in front of him." "It suggests that what God creates for Adam will correspond to him. Thus the new creation will be neither a superior nor an inferior, but an equal."[49] *Kenegdo* indicates that "which should be about him." By divine design, marriage becomes, therefore, "an inseparable relationship." "There the wife so binds herself to a man that she will be about him and will live together with him as one flesh."[50]

Bonhoeffer translates *kenegdo* simply as "partner." The woman "is a partner of the man in bearing the limit imposed upon him." She is, he says, "the other who stands beside me and constitutes a limit for me." She is not a limit in a negative way, but in a positive way, for she "is a piece of me." She is "the limit that I love and that I will not transgress because of my love."[51] *'Ezer* indicates movement toward the other; *kenegdo* indicates equality between the one and the other. Borrowing the Greek fathers' Trinitarian terms, we may therefore say again that humanity, like God, demonstrates both the dynamic of movement in *taxis*, "order," and the equality inherent to *perichoresis*, "unified mutuality."

The reinforcing nature of these two relational terms recalls several enlightening philosophical ruminations about personhood. The Jewish philosopher Martin Buber used the terms "I" and "Thou" to indicate our need to recognize the responsibility each person has toward others.[52] The English philosopher Roger Scruton argued for the necessity of seeing the other person in a "face-to-face" relationship.[53] Greek Orthodox bishop John Zizioulas defined a person as a "being in communion," asserting a "person cannot exist without communion."[54] German Catholic Martin Spaemann advanced

---

48. James Strong, *Enhanced Strong's Lexicon* (Woodside Bible Fellowship, 1995).

49. Hamilton, *Genesis*, 175.

50. Luther, *Lectures on Genesis*, 117.

51. Bonhoeffer, *Creation and Fall*, 98–99.

52. Martin Buber, *I and Thou*, transl. Roland Gregor Smith (Scribners, 2023), 19–20.

53. Roger Scruton, *The Face of God: The Gifford Lectures 2010* (Continuum, 2012), 73–111.

54. John Zizioulas, *Being as Communion: Studies in Personhood and the Church* (St. Vladimir's Seminary Press, 1997), 18.

Christianity's ancient language of personhood, recalling the profound distance between the sacred reality of "someone" and the mundane objectivity of "something."[55]

The theological ruminations of the twentieth-century Christian martyr, Dietrich Bonhoeffer, are also helpful. Bonhoeffer made certain connections which were later taken up by both Karl Barth and Emil Brunner. These connections have since become theological commonplaces.[56] First, Bonhoeffer correlated the image of God as Trinity in Genesis 1:26–27 with the male–female relation, arguing that personal relations provide the proper analogy for the human being made in the image of God. He continued that discussion in his commentary on Genesis 2:18–25. The human creature is both like and unlike God:

> The human creature is free in that one creature exists in relation to another creature, in that one human being is free for another human being. And God created them man and woman. The human being is not alone. Human beings exist in duality, and it is in this dependence on the other that their creatureliness consists.[57]

Bonhoeffer hereby revolted against the traditional Western structuring of humanity by individualist ontology. "The likeness, the *analogia*, of humankind to God is not *analogia entis* but *analogia relationis*."[58] He drew two major truths from this principle.

His first point was that relationship prioritizes theology. What the analogy of relation means to Bonhoeffer is, first and foremost, not the relationship of man to woman, but the relationship of both to God. The God–human relationship is primary; the man–woman relation is secondary. Theology has priority over anthropology, for man is governed by God. The likeness of God in human beings must be consistently referred to God for its proper meaning.

> This *analogia* must not be understood as though humankind somehow had this likeness in its

55. Robert Spaemann, *Persons: The Difference between "Someone" and "Something,"* transl. Oliver O'Donovan (Oxford University Press, 2006), 78–80.

56. Bonhoeffer, *Creation and Fall*, 65.

57. Bonhoeffer, *Creation and Fall*, 64.

58. Bonhoeffer, *Creation and Fall*, 65.

> possession or at its disposal. Instead, the *analogia* or likeness must be understood very strictly in the sense that what is like derives its likeness only from the prototype itself and is "like" it only in pointing to it in this way.[59]

His second point concerns the woman's strength. Bonhoeffer explains philosophically that which Adam's spontaneous song expresses poetically: "This one is bone of my bone and flesh of my flesh." Adam is pleased that the woman is unlike the animals which God previously brought before him. He discerned the difference between his nature and the nature of the animals, and he ascribed to them names which accorded their differences (Gen. 2:19–20).

Adam discerned that the woman was not of a different kind; rather, she shared human nature with him. The woman corresponded to the man as an equal. If "flesh" "conveys the idea of weakness, frailty, and perishableness," then "bone," conveys the ideas of power, strength, and solidity.[60] Prelapsarian woman had the same nature and, therefore, similar strengths and weaknesses to prelapsarian man.

Bonhoeffer was a single man, so his ruminations here should not be interpreted as requiring marriage to display the image.[61] The apostle Paul did not make marriage, for all its goodness, necessary. Indeed, he preferred singleness (1 Cor. 7:32–35). The divine image resides in and is manifested through humans flourishing in various communities. Even as God reveals his triune and holy character in the covenant of marriage, so aspects of his character apply to other covenants, but only through respect for consciences under Christ's Lordship.[62]

---

59. Bonhoeffer, *Creation and Fall*, 65.

60. Garrett, *Systematic Theology*, 1:500.

61. Ferdinand Schlingensiepen, *Dietrich Bonhoeffer 1906–1945: Martyr, Thinker, Man of Resistance* (T&T Clark, 2012).

62. Malcolm B. Yarnell III, "Free Church Dogmatics: A Dialectic of Covenant and Conscience," *Bibelseminar Bonn Journal* 2.1 (2021): 24–33; idem, "The Free Church Form of Dogmatics: Covenant and Conscience under Christ," *Southeastern Theological Review* 14.2 (2023): 115–29.

The Prelapsarian Nature of Humanity

Adam provided the woman her personal name only after the Fall (Gen. 3:20). He named her Eve, which means "mother of all living," as a way of admitting "his indebtedness to her for life's future."[63] The act of naming her may have been his way of accepting "responsible headship,"[64] a role he had previously failed to exercise at the temptation (vv. 4–6).[65] The husbandry later exercised by the perfect man, Jesus Christ, is focused upon demonstrating personal submission to, and offering sanctification by the Word of God (Eph. 5:26).

The third note in Adam's song regards the naming of the woman and the identity of humanity. Before discussing the last verse in Adam's song, remember the pristine context in which it was given. Contemporary objections to the biblical identity of humanity arise after the Fall. If we were still in the garden and the Fall had not occurred, we would not have existential anxiety about the problems of human tyranny, abusive patriarchy, radical feminism, perverse sexuality, abortion, transgenderism, and so on. This shift in context prompts us to offer a short theology of power, and to review the goodness of prelapsarian life.

Concerning *authority*, we must address its origin, its abuse, and its judgment.[66] First, all power derives from God. God originally gave powers and responsibilities to angelic, human, and natural entities. God is the King of creation. Second, with the fall of humanity into sin through the temptation of the serpent, creation itself was subjected to futility. Angelic and human powers rebelled against their King, and natural powers are now in subjection. The kingdom of God is under assault from the kingdom of this world, for now ruled by a usurper, the devil. Third, God sent his Son, Jesus Christ, to conquer the powers of sin in a mysterious way. He died on the cross to reconcile human rebels. Granted all power, he is now bringing the

63. Kenneth A. Mathews, *Genesis 1–11:26*, New American Commentary (Broadman & Holman, 1996), 254.

64. Mathews, *Genesis 1–11:26*, 254.

65. "So Adam should have discerned that the serpent was evil and should have judged the serpent in the name of God in the place of the judgment tree." G. K. Beale, *A New Testament Biblical Theology: The Unfolding of the Old Testament in the New* (Baker Academic, 2011), 35.

66. This paradigm will be developed more fully in the third volume of Theology for Every Person.

powers to heel. His second coming will usher in judgment. He will return the subjected powers to God.

Concerning the nature of *prelapsarian life*, we may speak of identity and order. The original order was without dysfunction, although due to the gift of freedom through humanity's creation in the image of God, who is free, it had the possibility of dysfunction. The descriptions of life in Genesis 1–2 precede the Fall in Genesis 3. After humanity's rebellion against divine authority, human relationships became filled with problems, problems intractable apart from divine intervention. Human disobedience brought the internal struggle of humanity against God, human against human, and humanity's external struggles with both demonic and natural powers.

There is little description of differentiated roles before the Fall. Rather, the common image and responsibility, and human relationality, preclude the formal discussion of roles. Equality and differentiation in relationship precede roles. However, a certain role for Adam appears in the description of prelapsarian life: Adam's responsibility seems to have been to lead by teaching, by conveying the Word of God to others, for he alone was given the promise and command by God (Gen. 2:16–17). God also taught him to discern and to speak (vv. 19–20). Like God, Adam even sang truth. Eve was not excluded from speaking, but Adam was first. He received the Word of God to be given to others.

Other aspects of the goodness and beauty that characterized the original prelapsarian identity of humanity appear. Human ontology before the Fall was marked by life-giving communion, righteousness, and love, as well as proper perspectives on holiness, freedom, and power.

Creation was originally characterized by *life-giving communion* between God and humanity. God brought the animals to man. He brought woman to man (v. 22). He walked with the man and the woman in the cool of the day (3:8). God spoke directly with humanity and deemed his creature very good. Communion with the living God, of course, also demonstrates that life is part of the goodness man received. Prior to its appearance, death was only contained in a word of warning. Life's fruit was free.

Creation was also originally marked by *justice*. The Augustinian tradition believes there existed an original righteousness in the human relationship with God. This constituted integrity of the soul, alas, was lost through the Fall.[67] Life was granted to man and might have been available perpetually to man, if he had not sinned. The command and the warning imply eternal life was available.

Love also characterized humanity before the Fall. When God brought the woman to Adam, he reacted with pure joy. According to Luther, Adam's cry of "at last" "expresses most beautifully the affection of a husband who feels his need for a delightful and full relationship or cohabitation in both love and holiness." It "indicates an overwhelmingly passionate love."[68]

Holiness and *freedom* were also present. That God warned against sin indicates that while God gave so much blessing to humanity, there was also limitation. Humanity's freedom to exercise its powers is intended to operate within the limits of God's holy purposes. The warning against taking the fruit of one tree is preceded by the freedom to participate in everything else. The blessing of "you are free to eat" precedes and provides the context for "but you must not" eat of this one tree (2:16–17). The right to eat widely demonstrated the great freedom God gave to man, even as a limit to eating demonstrates the holiness God demands of man.

Finally, the prelapsarian *power* of humanity may be seen in the ascription of *'ezer* to woman. Woman is given to man to "help" him fulfill the vocation God had given them both. Woman worked powerfully alongside man as they both served God. Humanity ruled creation for God. They served and protected his earth (v. 15). Humanity was empowered to do this freely through righteous communion with a holy God motivated by love.

This was the nature of prelapsarian human life. The man and the woman lived in communion with God and with one another sharing in and rejoicing over the divine gift of life. Both acted in righteousness and love for God's glory. The holy and loving man came first in time and received the Word of God. The free and powerful woman helped the man fulfill God's command for them both to rule the world.

Prelapsarian Relations Between Human Beings

The prelapsarian nature of humanity sheds light on God's intentions for the relation between the man and the woman. Genesis

---

67. Eugene TeSelle, *Augustine the Theologian* (Wipf and Stock, 2002), 317–18.

68. Luther, *Lectures on Genesis*, 136.

2–3 indicates several truths regarding intra-human relationships. Their relation included the man's responsibility of teaching and the priority of the family vis-à-vis other families, among other truths.

First, the man became the first human being to *teach truth*. The news about freedom and responsibility that humanity toward God were delivered first to the man, and he appears to have conveyed the truth to the woman. The first man's first stewardship of teaching the Word of God to his wife seems not to have included tyranny or abuse.[69] From the original grace of Word to the man, then the instrumental grace of the Word through man, both heard and spoke the Word of God. Both were communing with God through his Word.

Adam twice named his wife, before and after the Fall. First, in the song, Adam named her as one corresponding to him: "This one will be called 'woman,' for she was taken from man." Adam's general name for her is *'isha*, which means "woman" or "wife," depending on context. A "woman" is a "wife" to only one man in a covenant that begins in betrothal and ends in death (Rom. 7:2). This man and this woman entered a marriage covenant the moment the Lord gave her in betrothal until the moment one died. Note also that *'isha*, "woman," may be a derivative of *'iysh*, meaning "man" or "husband," again depending upon covenantal context.[70]

Why did Adam choose this general name and not another? He was perhaps inspired to discern and identify the woman in relation to himself as the man. She was his correspondent, his wife. She is both different from him yet simultaneously one with him. She is different in gender yet identical in humanity. Building on this seminal event, the foundation of the family by God is described in the next two verses. Regarding the family, in which the man became the first teacher, please consider these six additional truths derived from the words of the Spirit-inspired narrator, Moses: The priority of the family; distinct families; a new unity; a pure relation; life after the Fall; and the continuing relevance of the family.

Second, consider *the priority of the family* among human covenants. The foundation of the family precedes the appearance of both state and church. In the history of the world, "The family

---

69. Whether Adam or Eve recast the original command is unknown (cf. Gen. 2:17; 3:3).

70. William David Reyburn and Euan McG Fry, *A Handbook on Genesis* (United Bible Societies, 1998), 75.

remains the essential unit of human existence."[71] The state does not begin until human evil demonstrates it requires constraint (Gen. 4, 9; Rom. 13). The church does not begin until the Holy Spirit comes at Pentecost (Acts 2). The structure of the family is simply not for the state nor for the church to define—God already defined it. The church must certainly proclaim the family, and the state must protect it. Alas, churches may fail in their task of proclaiming the family and states may fail by seeking to redefine the family, for example through recognizing polygamy, divorce, or same sex unions.

Third, we must recognize *the distinction between families*. The family has often been challenged precisely because we fail to understand a marriage bond begins with betrothal. "This is why a man leaves his father and mother and bonds with his wife" (Gen. 2:24a). The marriage bond supersedes all other family bonds. Undue interference in the covenant by those who are not parties to that covenant should be avoided, even if a member of that covenant is one's child.

Fourth, *a new unity* is constituted by marriage. If leaving parents breaks an old bond, cleaving or "clinging" indicates the creation of a new covenant. The language may shock a hyper-individualistic culture, but the man "bonds with his wife, and they become one flesh" (v. 24b). The word "flesh" here indicates the earthiness of humanity. The word *'echad* means "one," "same," or "single."[72] The first man was intended to form a unique human relation with his wife. They were no longer two but became one. "What is being pinpointed is solidarity. The man by himself is not one flesh. The woman by herself is not one flesh."[73] The two beings formed a new entity by a singular covenant.

Fifth, the family was originally characterized by *relational purity*. "Both the man and his wife were naked, yet felt no shame" (v. 25). The holiness of prelapsarian man in his covenantal unity as husband and wife was displayed here. The statement disrupts human culture, for all human beings, except for those whose consciences have been seared by continual embrace of perversity, properly feel shame at nakedness. Luther believed that before the Fall, human beings

71. Simon Sebag Montefiore, *The World: A Family History of Humanity* (Knopf, 2023), xxxiii.

72. Herbert Wolf, "אֶחַד," in R. Laird Harris, Gleason L. Archer Jr., and Bruce K. Waltke, eds., *Theological Wordbook of the Old Testament* (Moody Press, 1999), 30.

73. Hamilton, *Genesis*, 121.

had their greatest glory in their nakedness, but sin made nakedness shameful.[74]

Sixth, much about prelapsarian humanity remained true of them even *after the Fall.* Adam continued to exercise teaching authority by giving his wife a proper name that could be confused with no other woman. "Adam named his wife, 'Eve,' because she was the mother of all the living" (Gen. 3:20). The Hebrew *chawwa*, "Eve," means "life-giver." Redolent of the Spirit of God as life-giver, the woman reflects this important work of God. While woman does not create life in her own power, she is the avenue God chose to create new lives. This, too, is in likeness to God the Trinity. The identity of humanity in the triune likeness of God as equal and distinct did not cease with the Fall, although it was henceforth marked by struggle.

Seventh and finally, we may affirm the *continuing relevance* of their relationship. The sacred identity of the human family continues to be important to humanity in general and the people of God in particular. In the New Testament, elements of Genesis 2:18–25 serve as major teaching points for both Jesus and Paul. The following passages consider the importance of pre-fallen humanity for our identity and for our relationships today and should be consulted: Matthew 19:5; Mark 10:7–8; 1 Corinthians 6:16; 11:2–16; Ephesians 5:31; and 1 Timothy 2:8–15. These very texts are often hotly debated in contemporary culture.[75]

Conclusion: Some Practical Results

Three practical conclusions are suggested by the prelapsarian discourse on man and woman: First, we may recognize divine analogies in humanity both by relation and by being. Second, we must identify personal and social evils as misappropriations. Third, we should pray and seek the grace for God to manifest his communicable attributes in us.

First, drawing from both the long Christian tradition and the more recent ruminations of Bonhoeffer, we may use the divine analogies both by relation and by being. In practice, *the analogy of relations* of the Trinity in mutuality and order shed light upon human relations, especially in marriage. A man and woman entering

74. Luther, *Lectures on Genesis*, 140.

75. Cf. *The Baptist Faith and Message*, Art. XVIII.

a marriage covenant possess a basic equality. But covenant partners must also recognize the ordered biological differences between them, and account for those differences. A man and a woman in a marriage today may work together to determine that division of labor which best fits their many gifts and skills. Similarly, we may draw upon *the analogy of being*. Through the reality of God revealed in his communicable attributes, we may learn something about his image in humanity. If God the Trinity is loving, holy, and righteous, so ought his image to be loving, holy, and righteous. Again, we must be careful never to impose our fallen anthropological schemes on divine theology but remain chaste with human speculations and schematizations for relations.

Second, *personal and social evils* may arise through missing, misapprehending, or misappropriating the doctrine of the image of God. Misogyny and racism may arise when failing to account for the equal possession by every human being of the divine image. The common image requires respect for the human dignity due every human being. It also requires attempts to ensure the flourishing of every human.[76]

Third and final, *we must exhibit evangelical love, righteousness, and holiness*. One may speak much about love, while another trumpets righteousness, but love and righteousness require equal emphasis. A third perfection which Christ requires of believers (Matt. 5:48) also deserves attention today. May John Wesley's emphasis on divine holiness and on our call to communion with him as Trinity be revived in this day of wickedness:

> One happiness shall ye propose to your souls, even an union with Him that made them, the having "fellowship with the Father and the Son," the being "joined to the Lord in one Spirit." One design ye are to pursue to the end of time—the enjoyment of God in time and in eternity. Desire other things, so far as they tend to this; love the creature, as it leads to the Creator.[77]

---

76. Rhyne Putman and Malcolm B. Yarnell III, "Anthropology: Reclaiming the Sacred Dignity of Every Human Being in the Dogma of Anthropology," in Steven A. McKinion, Christine E. Thornton, and Keith S. Whitfield, *Confessing Christ: An Invitation to Baptist Dogmatics* (B&H Academic, 2024), 133–67.

77. Wesley preached this key sermon on divine holiness to the University of Oxford at the church of St Mary's on January 1, 1733. *A Plain Account of Christian Perfection* (1777), in *The Works of John Wesley*, 3rd ed., vol. 11 (Baker, 2002), 368.

Study Questions

1. Describe the various views of the image of God in humanity offered by theologians.

2. Which one of the views of the image of God detailed above do you currently believe to be most in need of recovery?

3. How may we fail to appropriate properly the doctrine of the image of God?

Suggested Resources

- Dietrich Bonhoeffer, *Creation and Fall*
- Martin Buber, *I and Thou*
- John F. Kilner, *Dignity and Destiny*

CHAPTER EIGHT

Who Am I?

We have been examining three great existential questions about humanity. The theological question, "Who are we?" was answered with reference to the song of God in Genesis 1. And the relational question, "Who are you?" was answered with reference to Adam's ballad in Genesis 2. Both the theological question about humanity, our importance to God, and the relational question of humanity, our importance to one another, were answered in the last chapter.

Now, we must answer the singular self-reflective human question, "Who am I?" The poetry of Ecclesiastes 3 provides fundamental insights into the meaning of the human individual. Our personal reality, sadly, has been tragically complicated by the descent of human beings into sin. According to Genesis 3, humanity willfully embraced rebellion against God and refused to honor him as Lord. Due to the deep harm done to humanity by the Fall, theologians across the Christian traditions generally recognize "two different aspects" of human nature. John Paul II referred to them as our "created nature" and our "fallen nature."[1]

We may refer to these two basic truths about our individual selves with the terms *imagedness* and *sinfulness*. *Imagedness* reflects our creation according to the likeness of God; *sinfulness* confesses

1. John Paul II, *Theology of the Body* (Philokalia, 2008), 6.

our willful rejection of God's rule. These two basic aspects of human personhood must also be explored. In this chapter, we will consider the identity of the human individual. In the next chapter, we turn our attention to the effect of sin upon human beings.

You Are a Human Being

Ecclesiastes 3:1 repeats the Hebrew preacher's lament that life exists "under the sun" or "under heaven" (Hebrew *tachat shamaiym*). This prominent phrase, which appears twenty-nine times in Ecclesiastes and nowhere else in the Old Testament, describes the limitation of human abilities. *Qoheleth*, "the assembler" or "teacher of collected truth," is a royal skeptic. King Solomon seems to have applied this title to himself in his latter days, after returning to the orthodoxy of his youth. He was disappointed and damaged by all he had seen, heard, and done.[2]

In this final of his four biblical contributions, Solomon questioned the limits of the human ability to know God.[3] He found we cannot even know our selves adequately, neither our beginning nor our end (Eccles. 3:11; 11:5). Such exhaustive if realistic skepticism has a poignant modern ring to it. The Enlightenment philosopher, David Hume, expressed similar doubts about man's ability to discern ultimate reality.[4] Solomon's overarching message was that life under

---

2. The prologue (Eccles. 1:1) and epilogue (12:9–10) speak of the royal author, "the son of David," in the third person.

3. On Solomon's contributions to the Psalms, Proverbs, Song of Songs, and Ecclesiastes, and his status as a collector of wisdom, see D. R. Jackson, "Solomon," in Tremper Longman III and Peter Enns, eds., *Dictionary of the Old Testament Wisdom, Poetry and Writings* (IVP Academic, 2008), 733–37.

4. Unlike Solomon, David Hume appears to have remained unrepentant, making skepticism his religion. Perceived a "demolisher" of popular religion, Hume threw "a veil" over his own views. James A. Harris, *Hume: An Intellectual Biography* (Cambridge University Press, 2015), 442–56. Uncomfortable with the radical atheism of the French *philosophes*, he nevertheless disappointed even his friend, Adam Smith, with his views on religion. Dennis C. Rasmussen, *The Infidel and the Professor: David Hume, Adam Smith, and the Friendship that Shaped Modern Thought* (Princeton University Press, 2017), 124–25, 186–98. Enlightening anecdotes regarding Hume's religion include his encounter with a fishwife who rescued him from a bog between New Town and Old Town in Edinburgh only after he recited the Lord's Prayer, and James Boswell's unsuccessful effort to convert Hume on his deathbed. Rasmussen, *The Infidel and the Professor*, 152, 206. On Hume's epistemological skepticism, see

the sun is *habel*, "futile" or "meaningless" or "vain." If we are looking for an answer to the question, "Who am I?" perhaps we have come to the wrong place! However, the Holy Spirit inspired and preserved this skeptical book in the canon because, despite its doubts, this great piece of wisdom literature also provides, surprisingly enough, the most hopeful answer.

Skepticism and Hope

We might compare Solomon's skeptical song with Dietrich Bonhoeffer's skeptical poem, "Who Am I?" The German theologian wrote a self-revealing piece while in prison. He and his friends were under the thumb of Hitler and his brutal Nazi regime. Having suffered intimidation, threat, and torture, despair dripped from the German theologian's pen as he stared death in the face: "They mock me, these lonely questions of mine."[5] Like Solomon, Bonhoeffer came to recognize the limits of human knowledge, human life, and thus also human optimism.

But despite doubts and despair over the overwhelming futility of our embodied life in this present age, Bonhoeffer still trusted we can be made right and given hope by God. He reversed his own cynicism about life in the final words of his poem from prison with a cry of personal faith: "O God, I am thine!" In the end, the Christian martyr reaffirmed his faith in the eternal truth that his personal human identity was safe within the Lord, for he has final sovereignty.

> Who am I? This or the other?
>
> Am I this one today, and tomorrow another? Am I both at once?
>
> Before others a hypocrite, and in my own eyes a pitiful, whimpering weakling?

David Hume, *An Enquiry Concerning Human Understanding*, ed. Peter Millican (Oxford University Press, 2008). On his religious skepticism, see David Hume, *Principal Writings on Religion*, ed. J. C. A. Gaskin (Oxford University Press, 2008).

5. Dietrich Bonhoeffer, *Letters and Papers from Prison,* ed. John W. DeGruchy, transl. Isabel Best et al., Dietrich Bonhoeffer Works, vol. 5, (Fortress Press, 2010), 460.

> Or is what remains in me like a defeated army,
> fleeing in disarray from victory already won?
>
> Who am I? They mock me, these lonely questions of mine.
>
> Whoever I am, thou knowest me; O God, I am thine![6]

Solomon, the assembler or collector of wisdom, expressed the same hope, notwithstanding his overarching attitude of worldly skepticism.

The Divine Plan

Ecclesiastes 3 begins with a poem about providence. Rather than explaining the contents of the divine counsel, Solomon describes its perfection through humanity's vagaries.[7] Using "merism," a form of speech that delights in contrasts, he catalogued fourteen pairs of opposition. Taken singly, these contrasts might cause confusion and distress. Taken together, these disparities present cosmic history as a tapestry in which God has woven the caprice of human existence with holistic meaning. "Qoheleth poetically expresses the truth that the universe is ordered and well made. There is a time for everything, and God orders the times."[8] The song's juxtaposed disparities, collected in this way, imply wholeness.

While verses 1 through 8 reflect poetically on divine providence, the next few verses provide a commentary. The commentary begins with a question and an answer, "What gain has the worker from his toil? I have seen the business that God has given to the children of man to be busy with. He has made everything beautiful in its time." Herbert Butterfield argued that it is best for man not to fight what God is doing in history but to live into it. God will have his way. Persons and nations may either "cooperate with providence" in faith or fight against providence in futility, but God will

6. Bonhoeffer's poem began on a somewhat optimistic note, but soon descended into weary skepticism, anger, and fear. Bonhoeffer, *Letters and Papers from Prison*, 459–60.

7. Cf. Genesis 1:26–27.

8. Tremper Longman III, *The Book of Ecclesiastes*, New International Commentary on the Old Testament (Eerdmans, 1997), 132.

ultimately prevail.[9] The human being under duress must be careful not to struggle against God's will, for he has given each person a meaningful call to follow.

At this point, we come to the pivotal claim in the book of Ecclesiastes: "Also, he has put eternity into man's heart, yet so that he cannot find out what God has done from the beginning to the end" (3:11b ESV). "This verse is widely thought to be one of the hardest in the book to interpret."[10] However, the difficulty is not in the words themselves, for they are simple. "Indeed, the first part of the verse strikes the reader as one of the most beautiful and inspiring of the Bible." The difficulty for some interpreters arises from such an optimistic outlook being contained in a book marked by overwhelming pessimism.[11] However, if we interpret Solomon's poem in the way we interpreted Bonhoeffer's poem, then this one sentence transforms the entire book with its hope. God's plan will prevail despite our context's overwhelming vanity.

What exactly do commentators find too positive for Solomon, the skeptical teacher, to have uttered? Verse 11 says God "made everything appropriate in its time." The word translated "appropriate" here is *yapeh*, "beautiful." *Yapeh* resonates with *tob*, "good" or "beautiful," the term which dominated Genesis 1. "Ecclesiastes 3:11 describes everything in general as God's creation 'beautiful in its time.'"[12] The beauty that pours forth from God to permeate heaven and earth—this is what brings order out of chaos. The unbearable weight of God's glory ultimately supplants the wickedness of angels and men with the righteousness of God.

The Human Heart

The beauty of creation is not Solomon's only allusion to Genesis 1. Three more arise in Ecclesiastes 3: First, Moses said God "made" (Hebrew *'asa*) man in his image, and Solomon used the same term (Gen. 1:26; Eccles. 3:11). Second, Moses said God made man from the earth. Solomon concurred, saying humanity came from "dust"

9. Herbert Butterfield, *Christianity and History* (Scribner, 1950), 99, 106–7.

10. Longman, *The Book of Ecclesiastes*, 118.

11. Longman, *The Book of Ecclesiastes*, 119.

12. Paul R. Gilchrist, "יָפֶה," in R. Laird Harris, Gleason L. Archer Jr., and Bruce K. Waltke, eds., *Theological Wordbook of the Old Testament* (Moody Press, 1999), 392.

(cf. Gen 2:7; Eccles. 3:20). Third, "the placing of *'olam*, eternity, in human beings might be analogous to God endowing his human creatures with his image" (Gen 1:26–27; Eccles. 3:11).[13] If God inhabits eternity, which he does, then Solomon's claim that God has placed eternity in human hearts correlates closely with Moses's statement that God made humanity in his image.

Two Hebrew terms in verse 11 require definition. First, the word *'olam* at root means "concealed" or "vanishing point." Various meanings are thus possible. The most popular interpretations are "eternity" and "ignorance." Either may fit the message of Ecclesiastes. However, interpreters agree *'olam* most often indicates "eternity" in this book (e.g., Eccles. 1:4, 10; 2:16; 3:14; 9:6; cf. 12:14). The dominant usage must be preferred. Unfortunately, because modernist interpreters expect only negative assessments from the Assembler, they often opt for "ignorance" instead.[14] But the book's meaning is clarified by the majority translation.

The second Hebrew term requiring further definition is *leb/lebab*. While *leb* sometimes refers to the physical heart, most uses refer metaphorically to "the very center of the human life."[15] *Leb* can refer to the emotions, the intellectual faculty, the will, and the spiritual state. *Leb* is "a comprehensive term for the personality as a whole, its inner life, its character. It is the conscious and deliberate spiritual activity of the self-contained human ego."[16] "That which comes out of the heart is quite distinctively the property of the whole inner man, and therefore makes him, as a consciously acting ego, responsible for it."[17]

---

13. Longman, *The Book of Ecclesiastes*, 119.

14. Longman, *The Book of Ecclesiastes*, 120–21. Cf. Anthony Tomasino, "עוֹלָם," in Willem A. VanGemeren, ed., *New International Dictionary of Old Testament Theology and Exegesis*, vol. 3 (Zondervan, 1997), 345–51; Allan A. Macrae, "עלם," in Harris, Archer, and Waltke, eds., *Theological Wordbook of the Old Testament*, 672.

15. Moisés Silva, ed., *New International Dictionary of New Testament Theology and Exegesis*, vol. 2 (Zondervan, 2014), 624.

16. Walther Eichrodt, *Theology of the Old Testament*, vol. 2, transl. J. A. Baker (Westminster Press, 1967), 143.

17. Eichrodt, *Theology of the Old Testament*, 2:144. Cf. Andrew Bowling, "לֵבָב," in Harris, Archer, and Waltke, eds., *Theological Wordbook of the Old Testament*, 466. Garrett affirms this expansive meaning. James Leo Garrett Jr., *Systematic Theology: Biblical, Historical, and Evangelical*, vol. 1, 2nd ed. (BIBAL, 2000), 500. Only the Greek New Testament's *kardia* restricts emotions. Garrett, *Systematic Theology*, 1:504.

The Septuagint most often translated *leb/lebab* with the Greek *kardia*.[18] In the New Testament, according to Moisés Silva, the heart "denotes the center of intellectual and spiritual life." "The powers of the spirit, reason, and will, as well as the movements of the soul—the feelings, the passions, the instincts—have their seat in the heart. One may say that the heart stands for the individual ego: it is simply the person."[19]

The conscience, too, is enclosed within *kardia* (Rom. 2:15). God places a deep-seated desire for his eternal presence within every human being. The heart compels us to look toward our Creator and remember we are accountable to him (v. 16). In his *Confessions*, Augustine of Hippo famously recognized this critical desire was universal. "Man is one of your creatures, Lord, and his instinct is to praise you. . . . You made us for yourself, and our hearts find no peace until they rest in you."[20]

Among the many references to *kardia* in the New Testament, the book of Romans teaches that God as Trinity both initiates and integrates salvation through the transformation of the human heart. In Romans 8:27, God the Father examines the hearts of men. In Romans 10:6–10, the Word pierces the ear then the heart to bring saving faith in the Person and work of God the Son. In Romans 5:5, the Holy Spirit sheds the love of God abroad in human hearts. And in Romans 8:26–27, the Spirit moves the heart beyond its ignorance into knowing faith.

However, the final half of Ecclesiastes 3:11 throws the cold water of human limitation upon the warmer aspirations of the human heart. The central verse in the book of Ecclesiastes ends on a frustrating note: "But man cannot discover the work God has done from beginning to end" (HCSB). Eternity is placed in the human heart, but we cannot see it. Man cannot remember his origin, and he doesn't grasp his conclusion. Unless God reveals his eternal counsel, what Scripture calls the "mystery" of his will, we know neither the beginning or the end of the world, nor the beginning or the end of ourselves.

Solomon's wise recounting of our epistemological limits must be embraced. Human investigations of history and nature constantly

---

18. But also with *dianoia*, *psyche*, *phren*, and *nous*.

19. Silva, ed., *New International Dictionary of New Testament Theology and Exegesis*, 2:625.

20. Augustine, *Confessions*, transl. R. S. Pine-Coffin (Penguin, 1961), 21.

encounter the limits of certainty, no matter how much we discover. We inevitably descend into probability, then sheer ignorance and speculation, often with self-derived arrogance. A modern scholar of human history admitted as much in his greatest work: "The first rule of history is to realize how little we know."[21] We cannot see the past well, and we cannot see the distant past at all. We cannot see the immediate future whatsoever, much less the end of all things. "Historians are bad prophets."[22]

Natural philosophers inevitably manufacture all sorts of conflicting theories about the beginning and end of the world in their speculations: Do we live in an eternal world, or is it a dependent creation?[23] Was there an expansive explosion that started the universe?[24] Does the fact that matter is slowing, according to the second law of thermodynamics, imply a cataclysmic eschatology?[25] What constitutes our general knowledge of the cosmos? What can we naturally know of its Creator? Romans 1–2 says we can know some things about God and his creation through nature and conscience. But we may conclude from such only that there is a powerful, invisible God, and that he will judge. We cannot naturally know how to find him, nor how to become righteous in his sight.[26]

Solomon, the assembler of natural wisdom, saw our limits of knowledge under the sun and concluded from his studies that we should enjoy the gifts of God while we have them (Eccles. 3:12–13). But we must also remember God is sovereign and guides history according to his providential plan (v. 14). God will judge us based on whether we seek his glory and the welfare of his world (v. 15). Luther recognized these truths all too well. The great Reformer said our first parents "had a most perfect knowledge of God," thus they

---

21. Simon Sebag Montefiore, *The World: A Family History of Humanity* (Knopf, 2023), xxxix.

22. Montefiore, *The World*, xxxix.

23. Plato advocated the idea of a "world soul," later woven by Plotinus into a trinity of sorts. Anthony Kenney, *Ancient Philosophy*, vol. 1, A New History of Western Philosophy (Oxford University Press, 2004), 63, 314–16.

24. Pierre Tielhard de Chardin, *The Phenomenon of Man*, transl. Bernard Wall (Harper &Row, 1959), 46–50.

25. Yandall Woodfin, *With All Your Mind: A Christian Philosophy* (Abingdon, 1980), 199–200.

26. Malcolm B. Yarnell III, *God*, vol. 1, Theology for Every Person (B&H, 2024), 134–41.

were prompted to worship their Creator.[27] Alas, in the Fall, human reason was perverted. Knowledge of God was reduced to a sense of impending judgment.

Luther poked fun at the foolishness of natural philosophers. We cannot even know for sure who our parents are, except by trusting what others say. We are not now aware of our own births. Moreover, our self-awareness seems to end at death, and we don't know when that will overcome us. "For what I ask does a philosopher know about heaven and the world if he does not even know whence it came and whither it tends? Indeed, what do we know about ourselves?" Luther concluded, "How awful was the fall into original sin, through which we have lost this knowledge and have become incapable of seeing either the beginning or end of ourselves."[28]

In a more positive vein, Irenaeus said, "The glory of God is a living man; and the life of man consists in beholding God."[29] David Kelsey agrees. The weight of God's glory is pulling humanity toward himself, and he wants his glory expressed on earth through our bodies. But because of the impending judgment, we must learn to flourish here "on borrowed breath."[30] Mystics and Quakers often draw upon John 1:9 to argue that God placed a spark in the human heart to seek him. These ideas suggest God originally placed his eternal image in temporal man.

Human Personhood

At this point, we must address our personhood. The biblical terms for the human person are neither exclusively individualist nor partitive. Biblical persons are individuals, but in a corporate sense that excludes divisive isolation. The perfections of God, who is One and Three, are reflected in those he has created in his image. There are, therefore, four dimensions to human personhood: First, human personhood reflects divine personhood. Second, our personhood

---

27. Martin Luther, *Lectures on Genesis: Chapters 1–5*, transl. Jaroslav Pelikan, Luther's Works, vol. 1 (Concordia, 1958), 66.

28. Luther, *Lectures on Genesis*, 124.

29. Irenaeus, *Against Heresies*, 4.20.7, in Alexander Roberts and James Donaldson, eds., *The Apostolic Fathers, Justin Martyr, Irenaeus*, Ante-Nicene Fathers, vol. 1 (1885; reprint, Hendrickson, 1994), 490.

30. David H. Kelsey, *Eccentric Existence: A Theological Anthropology*, vol. 1 (Westminster John Knox Press, 2009), 1:309–22.

includes introspective movement. Third, our personhood is irreducibly corporate. And fourth, personhood must be conceived holistically. Since we previously defined the image and the likeness of humanity, and since we just discussed the second aspect, the introspective movement of the human heart,[31] we will focus on the first, third, and fourth meanings here.

Reflection of Divine Personhood

Personhood is an aspect of the image which God gave to humanity. From the perspective of Scripture, human personhood reflects divine personhood. Patristic theologians argued that the divine Trinity created humans as persons for the purpose of existing in communion with him. God is personal; therefore, humanity is, too. Our sense of personhood is derived from God's relation to us and our relations to one another as human beings. "The life of God is eternal because it is personal, that is to say, it is realized as an expression of free communion, as love. Life and love are identified in the person."[32]

Corporate Personality

Third, human personhood includes corporate personality. In both Testaments, a human being is not human alone but with others. This is true both in creation as portrayed in the Old Testament (Gen. 2:18) and in redemption according to the New Testament. In the last chapter, we noted the Hebrew term *basar*, "flesh," enclosed two human beings within one (v. 24). This idea appears elsewhere. *Nephesh*, often translated "soul" or "life" or "living being" (v. 7), may also "refer to a living person or persons in totality."[33] Based on such Old Testament phenomena, Henry Wheeler Robinson coined his famous phrase, "corporate personality."[34] Corporate personhood was so entrenched in the Hebrew mind that Ezekiel had to remind the Israelites that individuals were ultimately responsible before God (Ezek. 18:4).

---

31. See the section entitled, "The Human Heart," above.

32. John D. Zizioulas, *Being as Communion: Studies in Personhood and the Church* (St. Vladimir's Seminary Press, 1985), 49.

33. Garrett, *Systematic Theology*, 1:498.

34. Henry Wheeler Robinson, *Corporate Personality in Ancient Israel* (Fortress Press, 1964).

In the New Testament, *soma*, "body," could be used as "both a corporate and an individual term."[35] The same is true of *anthropos*, "human being" or "person."[36] Paul spoke of the new corporate humanity in Christ as "one new man" formed of many (Eph. 2:15). Elsewhere, Paul used a masculine form of "one" to describe the church not in terms of an abstract concept, an impersonal thing, but as a living reality: "You are all one in Christ Jesus" (Gal. 3:28). Corporate personhood derives from the "in Christ" formula frequently used by Paul, as well as from his Adam–Christ typology. Earle Ellis and Aaron Son argue that such Pauline references are best understood not as elusive metaphors but as real entities.[37]

Holistic Beings

Finally, Scripture treats individual persons as holistic beings. Individual human beings are not composed of parts, as if body and soul are somehow detachable. Upon reviewing the biblical terms for humanity, Garrett concluded, "The Hebrew mind was more given to thinking of human life in holistic ways, and thus the various terms applied to human beings were more like different windows through which humans could be viewed than like pieces of a pie which has been cut."[38] These Hebrew and New Testament understandings must be emphasized in response to "the huge influence of the dualism of body and mind or soul" in both ancient and modern philosophy.[39] Every human is an entire being, composed of "a rational soul and a body," as the Council of Chalcedon confessed of Christ's humanity.[40]

---

35. Anthony C. Thiselton, *Systematic Theology* (Eerdmans, 2015), 143.

36. *Anthropos* generally indicates humanity as opposed to God or animals, while *anar* indicates the male human being or a husband opposite the female. Moisés Silva, *New International Dictionary of New Testament Theology and Exegesis*, vol. 1 (Zondervan, 2014), 299–301, 302–8.

37. E. Earle Ellis, *Pauline Theology: Ministry and Society* (Eerdmans, 1989), 8–14; Sang-Won (Aaron) Son, *Corporate Elements in Pauline Anthropology: A Study of the Selected Terms, Idioms, and Concepts in the Light of Paul's Usage and Background* (Editrice Pontificio Istituto Biblico, 2001).

38. Garrett, *Systematic Theology*, 1:506.

39. Thiselton, *Systematic Theology*, 141; J. P. Moreland and William Lane Craig, *Philosophical Foundations for a Christian Worldview*, 2nd ed. (IVP Academic, 2017), 8, 597.

40. Chad Van Dixhoorn, *Creeds, Confessions, and Catechisms* (Crossway, 2022), 27.

Unfortunately, René Descartes, the great philosopher of modernity, introduced a radical distinction between the body and the mind.[41] As a result, for many theological liberals, salvation comes for disembodied souls.[42] Against this, we note the biblical terms translated "soul" (Hebrew *nephesh*; Greek *psyche*) also indicate "life." Life was given to humanity with the body at creation (Gen. 2:7), so must we likewise be raised bodily (1 Cor. 15:13–14). "The biblical tradition presupposes what we should truly call an integrated psychosomatic relation of mind and body."[43] The human person does not wear the body like a disposable suit.[44] The human person is created an embodied life and will be raised in Christ by the Spirit to a new embodied life.

In summary, from a biblical perspective, the human being is no less than personal by virtue of creation in the image of the divine Trinity, but also corporate as well as introspective and holistic. The human being was created a composite body with soul, intended for fellowship both with God and with his creation. He looks inward toward the self, outward toward human community, forward toward the resurrection,[45] and upward toward God.

Extrabiblical Views

The limits of biblical revelation may frustrate, since Scripture may not answer the questions which we pose. However, biblical revelation is sufficient to bring us new life and to help us live for Christ. Every biblical truth must be retained, including every biblical truth

---

41. Anthony Kenney, *The Rise of Modern Philosophy*, vol. 3, A New History of Western Philosophy (Oxford University Press, 2016), 36–37, 212–19.

42. Millard J. Erickson, *Christian Theology*, 2nd ed. (Baker, 1998), 541–42.

43. Thiselton, *Systematic Theology*, 141.

44. Erickson, *Christian Theology*, 1189.

45. According to Solomon, "All go to one place. All are from the dust, and to dust all return" (Eccles. 3:20 ESV). We received our bodies from the dust of the earth (Gen. 2:7), and we return there (Gen. 3:19). The certainty of natural death under the sun reminds human beings of our relationship to the animals. Like animals, we are bodies who die. The utter futility of death pursues us; death is our "fate" (Hebrew *miqreh*). We came into this world with bodily form, and we return that form to the world when we die (Eccles. 3:20). If you have ever sat with one who is dying, you know the futility of death. It can be unnerving. For those without God, it can bring despair. But those who have faith that they will share in the resurrection of Christ have hope.

about humanity. Biblical anthropology, however, is not the only view of humanity being taught.

For instance, various extrabiblical anthropologies have swayed many regarding the person's individual constitution. These views often lead their adherents toward hopelessness. First, some believe humanity is marked by chance. Denying the guidance of divine providence, they assert that history in general and human life in particular lack a truly meaningful narrative.[46]

Second, some have portrayed human lives as inescapably and downwardly determined. God, the gods, or nature predestine(s) each person for a role, class, or caste. Such views are often developed in empires, as a few seek control over others by sacralizing hierarchy.[47] Reduced to their functions or roles, persons become subject to misuse and abuse. But every civilization, marked by human failure, remains subject to providential judgment.[48]

Third, some believe man is purely or primarily a disembodied soul. Ancient pagan philosophers correctly perceived the soul in man. But they also believed the body was a problem. Matter was demeaned by Plato and deemed evil by Manichaeans and Gnostics. Immortality might be regained through bodily escape.[49] Through such influences, the bodily needs of humans can be neglected or abused. A resurgence of Gnosticism has been detected in modern society, requiring Christians again to defend the embodied aspect of human existence.[50]

Fourth, modern naturalists sometimes view humanity as merely or primarily a body. There is no qualitative difference between a human being and any other creature. Humans are primarily subject to biological evolution.[51] Under this naturalist view, life can lose the values and virtues fostered under a supernatural view.

---

46. Garrett, *Systematic Theology*, 1:384–85.

47. The examples found in Islam, Hinduism, and American chattel slavery are not unique. Brian Klaas, *Corruptible: Who Gets Power and How It Changes Us* (Scribner, 2021).

48. Reinhold Niebuhr, *Human Destiny*, vol. 2, The Nature and Destiny of Man (Scribner, 1964), 302–7.

49. Garrett, *Systematic Theology*, 1:507–8.

50. Gregg R. Allison, *Embodied: Living as Whole People in a Fractured World* (Baker, 2021), 15–20.

51. John P. Newport, *Life's Ultimate Questions: A Contemporary Philosophy of Religion* (Word, 1989), 136–39.

Fifth, other modernists treat humans mechanically. They may see human beings as complex, perhaps as even possessing souls, but they are still subject to manipulation by the physical and social sciences. Anthropologists can see human beings as determined by their political and economic contexts, even by personal psychology.[52] Under this view, moral checks on physical coercion become dispensable.

Sixth, there has been a reductionistic "turn to the human self" in the West. The human is depicted as "the picture of the self-conscious and self-reliant, self-transparent and all-responsible individual." According to Fergus Kerr, this peculiar view "Descartes and Kant between them imposed upon modern philosophy."[53] The "turn to the self" has led some moderns to believe they can redefine their personal identity at will, including their gender.[54] Restraints on the self can be replaced by an attitude redolent of ancient paganism.

Universal Human Dignity

The last error just mentioned must be distinguished from the Reformation-era recovery of the Christian doctrines of universal liberty of conscience and universal human dignity. The responsibility of every human being to God alone as their Lord depends upon Scripture's teachings that every conscience is directly accountable to God for its actions (Rom. 2:15–16), that Jesus Christ is the only Mediator between God and humanity (1 Tim. 2:5–6), that salvation comes through faith in Jesus as Lord (Rom. 10:9–10), and that hierarchical pretensions are panned by the Lord himself (Mark 9:33–37). The doctrine of human dignity depends upon the human person being made in the image of God, as discussed in previous chapters.

52. Marxism and Freudianism provide well-known examples, but reactions to these systems can receive their humanistic presumptions. Reinhold Niebuhr, *Human Nature*, vol. 1, The Nature and Destiny of Man (Scribner, 1964), 42–48. Cf. Patrick Wilcken, *Claude Lévi-Strauss: The Father of Modern Anthropology* (Penguin, 2010).

53. Fergus Kerr, "The Modern Philosophy of Self in Recent Theology," in Robert John Russell, et al., *Neuroscience and the Person: Scientific Perspectives on Divine Action* (Vatican Observatory, 1999).

54. Andrew T. Walker, *God and the Transgender Debate: What Does the Bible Actually Say about Gender Identity?* (Good Book, 2017), 19–27.

Historically, human dignity was honored and human flourishing advanced where liberty of conscience has been recognized.[55]

Famously, Martin Luther promoted both the sufficiency of Scripture and the priority of the conscience over the church at the Diet of Worms.[56] However, liberty of conscience was opposed by Royalists like Henry VIII, Puritans like John Cotton, and other persecutors in the early modern period, including Roman Catholics and many Protestants. In response, dissenting Christians like Roger Williams,[57] William Penn,[58] and Isaac Backus[59] advocated religious freedom and promoted human flourishing. In the twentieth century, George W. Truett,[60] T. B. Maston,[61] and Martin Luther King Jr.[62] built on this dissenting legacy to advance both religious liberty and racial integration.

Both the liberal doctrine of the autonomous self and the Christian doctrine of the dignified human person prioritize the individual human being. However, the latter arises from the theological exegesis of sacred Scripture, is informed by careful reception of natural theology, and is restrained by moral conviction grounded in Christian dogma. Dissenting Christians, therefore, confess "the sacredness of human personality." They have learned to advocate a high personal anthropology, "in that God created man in His own image, and in that Christ died for man; therefore, every person

---

55. Rhyne Putman and Malcolm B. Yarnell III, "Anthropology: Reclaiming the Sacred Dignity of Every Human Being in the Dogma of Anthropology," in Steven A. McKinion, Christine E. Thornton, and Keith S. Whitfield, *Confessing Christ: An Invitation to Baptist Dogmatics* (B&H Academic, 2024), 133–67.

56. Roland H. Bainton, *Here I Stand: A Life of Martin Luther* (Abingdon, 1978), 129–47.

57. Malcolm B. Yarnell III, "Roger Williams's Contribution to Religious Liberty and Baptists: A Reassessment," *Southwestern Journal of Theology* 67.1 (2024): 9–30.

58. Andrew R. Murphy, *William Penn: A Life* (Oxford University Press, 2018).

59. Jason G. Duesing, "Isaac Backus and Baptist History: Assessing a 'Pioneer Champion of Religious Liberty,'" *Southwestern Journal of Theology* 67.1 (2024): 31–48.

60. Malcolm B. Yarnell III, "The Gospel, Religious Liberty, and Social Duty: The Holistic Theology of George Washington Truett," *Southwestern Journal of Theology* 64.2 (2022): 69–84.

61. Paul J. Morrison, *Integration: Race, T. B. Maston, and Hope for the Desegregated Church* (Pickwick, 2022).

62. Leroy Fitts, *A History of Black Baptists* (Broadman Press, 1985), 283–89.

of every race possesses full dignity and is worthy of respect and Christian love."[63]

The Constitution of the Human Person

Placing the various cultural errors aside, while maintaining universal liberty of conscience and universal human dignity, we must now consider popular Christian approaches to the constitution of the individual human person. The human being's personal constitution may be classified according to one of four prominent Christian views: trichotomy, dichotomy, monism, and conditional unity.

Trichotomy

Trichotomy leans heavily upon 1 Thessalonians 5:23, finding in its threefold prayer for the believer's "body, soul, and spirit" a description of the human constitution.[64] Man is thereby deemed to be composed of three parts. Trichotomy was popularized by some early Greek church fathers, who were likely influenced by Plato.[65]

In the Thessalonian text, however, Paul was not describing the human constitution but asking God to sanctify believers in their whole lives. A similar noncontextual reading of Luke 10:27 might encourage an even more complex description of the human constitution: Could man have four parts? Does "strength" indicate the human body? When should one stop counting parts?

Louis Berkhof said trichotomy fell from favor after Apollinaris developed his Christological heresy from it.[66] Apollinaris taught that Jesus Christ had a human body and was indwelt by the divine Word but lacked a human soul or mind. Trichotomy's partitive personhood doubtlessly informed him. As discussed previously,

---

63. *The Baptist Faith and Message*, Art. III. Article XVI, on religious liberty, similarly begins with a high personal anthropology: "God alone is Lord of the conscience, and He has left it free from the doctrines and commandments of men which are contrary to His Word or not contained in it."

64. Other texts provide secondary if tenuous support: 1 Corinthians 2:14–3:4; 15:44; Hebrews 4:12. Hebrews 4:12 certainly treats the soul and the spirit as distinct but also as indivisible.

65. Plato said the human being was created with the parts of intelligence, soul, and body. Plato, *Timaeus and Criteas*, transl. Desmond Lee (Penguin, 1977), 42–43.

66. Louis Berkhof, *Systematic Theology*, 4th ed. (Eerdmans, 1941), 191–92.

Christ must assume the whole of the human nature to redeem it. Apollinarianism removes the possibility of full human redemption.

Dichotomy

Trichotomy historically gave way to a second position, dichotomy. Augustine helped this view become popular.[67] Scholars note that the Greek New Testament terms *psyche* ("soul" or "life") and *pneuma* ("spirit") are interchangeable when applied to the human being. And *soma* ("body") and *sarx* ("flesh") likewise function interchangeably. The soul or spirit is thereby distinguished from the body or flesh.[68] Human beings are constituted of both the material and the immaterial dimensions of existence. Dichotomy became the most accepted Christian view for centuries.

It will be remembered that ancient dualism treated matter as inherently flawed and the soul as detachable from the body. A similar radical dualism appeared after Descartes argued the mind can exist without the body. Many modern Westerners now view the body as basically an encumbrance. This form of dualism reached heights in popular American Christianity through the ghostly view of immortality taught by the liberal theologian Harry Emerson Fosdick. He replaced the New Testament hope for the resurrection of the body with the immortality of the disembodied soul.[69] At the popular level, many moderns treat the human body as something interchangeable, disposable, little more than a suit of old clothes.

Monism

The third position, monism, rejects both dichotomy and trichotomy. Returning to Scripture for a fresh understanding of what comprises the individual human being, contemporary Monists argue the human constitution has a sweeping unity. John A. T. Robinson opposed the radical dualism he said was a Hellenistic idea and offered the Hebrew anthropology of Wheeler Robinson as an

---

67. Roland Teske, "Augustine's Theory of Soul," in Eleonore Stump and Norman Kretzmann, eds., *The Cambridge Companion to Augustine* (Cambridge University Press, 2001), 116.

68. Compare Matthew 6:25 (*psyche*) with 1 Corinthians 5:3, 5 (*pneuma*), Acts 15:26 (*psyche*) with Luke 23:46 (*pneuma*), and John 12:27 (*psyche*) with John 13:21 (*pneuma*).

69. Erickson, *Christian Theology*, 542, 1181.

antidote.[70] He argued the human being should be seen as a radical unity without fail. The Old Testament has no word for "body": "[I] t never needed one so long as the body was the man." "The Hebrew idea of personality is an animated body, and not an incarnated soul."[71] Some Monists conclude the human being, body and soul, ceases existence at death.[72]

Conditional Unity

The fourth view, conditional unity, correlates the Dichotomist and Monist interpretations. It agrees with Monists that the human individual was created with substantial unity but affirms "the intermediate state." According to the older Augustinian tradition, the created unitary nature of humanity has been compromised by death. Human sin and the penalty of death introduce a temporary division between the body and the soul.[73] The "intermediate state" assumes the human soul continues to exist in some sense after bodily death. At the resurrection, all deceased human beings receive their body again.

Proponents of conditioned unity like Millard Erickson recall several New Testament texts that support their position.[74] In Luke 23:43, Jesus promised the thief he would enter paradise "today." In Luke 16:19–31, Jesus narrated an extraordinary historical event involving Lazarus, Abraham, and a rich man. Christ's use of personal names in this detailed narrative indicates the reality of "the intermediate state."[75] Christ described their continuing existence after physical death in two sections of the abode of the dead: Lazarus resided in "Abraham's bosom," while the rich man was separated by a great gulf. Jesus elsewhere encouraged people not to be afraid of those

70. Erickson, *Christian Theology*, 543–45.

71. Henry Wheeler Robinson, "Hebrew Psychology," in Arthur S. Peake, ed., *The People and the Book* (Oxford University Press, 1925), 362, 366.

72. E. Earle Ellis, "New Testament Teaching on Hell," in Christopher M. Date, Gregory G. Stump, and Joshua W. Anderson, eds., *Rethinking Hell: Readings in Evangelical Conditionalism* (Cascade, 2014), 128

73. Teske, "Augustine's Theory of Soul," 122.

74. Erickson, *Christian Theology*, 545–48, 554–57.

75. While classifying it as a parable, Jeremias says the text teaches "the intermediate state" of Hades, which is prior to Gehenna. Joachim Jeremias, *The Parables of Jesus*, transl. S. H. Hooke (SCM Press, 1955), 129.

who can kill the body, for they cannot touch the "soul" (Greek *psyche*, "life"). Instead, they should be afraid of the one who has power over both body and soul (Matt. 10:28).

In 2 Corinthians 5, Paul said believers currently groan "in this tent" while they await their future "heavenly dwelling" (vv. 2–4). A little later, he said that when we are "away from the body," we will be "with the Lord" (vv. 6–8). Elsewhere in his Corinthian correspondence, he described the final bodily resurrection as a fundamentally transformed personal existence that is victorious rather than woeful (1 Cor. 15:12–58). Building on Jesus's doctrine of the intermediate state, Paul taught a threefold progress in the Christian's personal humanity:

- In this age, we experience a difficult bodily existence.
- After personal physical death, Christians can expect a disembodied existence in the presence of God.
- At the Second Coming of Jesus Christ, we will be raised bodily.

John's description of the souls of the Christian martyrs who continued to exist, pray, and receive succor in the presence of God "under the altar" in the time between the first advent of Jesus Christ and his second advent (Rev. 6:9–11; cf. 19:11–21)—that is, between their personal deaths and their participation in the final resurrection—reinforces this Pauline pattern.

Summary

My own conclusion about the constitution of the human person connects with Augustine and Erickson. Personal human existence involves a threefold movement, proceeding from creation through the Fall to the resurrection:

The human person in creation: Each human person is created as a unity of body and soul (and spirit). Humans are more complex than a simple dichotomy, trichotomy, or monism on its own might allow. Each aspect of the human person's constituency is important; body and soul are required for personal integrity. We might say that God created the human to be an "embodied soul" or, conversely, a "soulish body."

The human person after the Fall: Sadly, the human constitution was compromised by sin and subjected to the penalty of death. The current state of humanity is challenged not only by personal sin but by corporate oppression from evils that appear in every human institution. The individual human's entire constitution requires redemption, for death is the penalty of sin.

The human person and the resurrection: We must affirm both the created soul that survives death and the resurrected body that Christ has wrought. There will be a temporary separation of body and soul between personal bodily death and the bodily resurrection of believers. And finally, both the created state and the final state present the individual human as a unity, an embodied soul or soulish body.

Conclusion: Take Your Humanity Seriously

Beginning in verse 16 of Ecclesiastes 3, Solomon recalled the coming judgment. On the one hand, he said, "God will judge" (v. 17). God will pronounce judgment on human beings, discerning between "the righteous and the wicked." And we have some natural knowledge of this impending judgment (v. 18). (Paul later taught that through the accusing or excusing movement of the human "conscience," our conduct of righteousness and wickedness is recorded for the divine court; Rom. 2:15–16.) On the other hand, however, Solomon said that human knowledge of when God's judgment will occur is beyond natural means. Solomon admitted he didn't know what happens to the "spirit" of a human person, much less of an animal (Eccles. 3:21–22).

The future certainty of divine judgment reminds us that we must take seriously the basic truths of human reality highlighted at the beginning of this chapter: We possess "imagedness," and we possess "sinfulness." Our bearing of the divine image lends human persons unparalleled importance among the creatures of God (Gen. 1:26–31). As Bonhoeffer learned through his own suffering, the proper answer to the question, "Who am I?" is, "I am yours, Lord."

God's promise to render judgment upon sinners further demonstrates the seriousness with which God takes the treatment of those whom he made in his personal image. If we damage the image that human beings carry, then God holds us accountable (Gen. 9:5–6).

We have been created in the image of God, and our imagedness of God means each human life retains great dignity.

Human beings, as individual persons and in community, were created for relationship with God. We were also created to serve him by ruling creation for his purposes. The dignity of bearing the divine image must not be diminished. Our persons, body and soul, are important to God, so we must respect every human being, body and soul. We should treat our own persons with care and appreciation, and we should treat other persons with the same care and appreciation. Humanity in its imagedness and in its sinfulness deserves to be taken seriously. Neither truth may be diminished. In the next chapter, we will examine the problem of sinfulness.

At this point, we bring our exploration of individual human personhood to an end. Ecclesiastes 3 reveals who human beings are, particularly as individuals. It exhilarates us by prompting our individual hearts to ponder eternity, but it frustrates by reminding us of our dying bodies and the impending judgment. Here are ten systematic conclusions about individual human persons derived from the theological interpretation of Ecclesiastes 3:

1. Humanity under the sun is subject to the vagaries of time, from the swells of life and waves of dangers, beginning in the moment of one's birth and continuing to one's temporal end in death (v. 2).
2. The best way to live under the sun in this age is to work at what God appoints us (v. 10) and enjoy what God gives us (vv. 12–13).
3. God makes everything "beautiful" or "appropriate" in its time (v. 11a). Divine providence brings meaning to our proximate realities, so it is foolish to fight against providence (v. 14) and wise to help humans flourish (v. 15).
4. Human beings are creatures bound to time and space. We are certainly embodied creatures, but God "also put eternity in their hearts" (v. 11b). We live under the sun, but God placed a powerful spiritual desire within us to draw us upward.
5. Humanity's innate desire for God cannot be satisfied through human effort (v. 11c). Our

earthly context severely limits our ability to discern truth, especially concerning that which is past and that which is to come.

6. The human creature is aware of and desires eternity but remains bound here. "Adam" is earthy from beginning to end (Gen. 2). We came from dust, and we return to dust (Eccles. 3:20). Humanity has a "heart" intended for God, yet a body like an animal intended for earthly existence (v. 19). The dual nature of humans as both earthy in body and eternal in heart is clearly affirmed. But this duality is not divisible. We were created embodied beings.
7. The human creature is morally evaluated by God as either "righteous" or "wicked" (v. 17). We know God will hold each one accountable. Solomon elsewhere affirmed that God made humans upright, but our hearts devise wicked plans (7:29).
8. Solomon considered the end of the child of Adam (3:21): Will the spirit go upward to God when it dies, or downward to the earth with the animals? According to his natural realism, this text affirms our lack of knowledge. It may refer obliquely to heaven and hell.[76]
9. Solomon concluded it is good for a human to enjoy what one can, here in this world. We are unable to enter eternity by our own power. Man's knowledge of that which he longs for is beyond natural grasp (3:22; cf. Eccles. 8).
10. Ecclesiastes by its place in the canon indicates that nature reveals truths about the Creator God and about his exalted creatures. But special revelation is required to know the beginning and the end of humanity (3:11c).

---

76. In the New Testament, the bodily resurrection is assured, so the human being must expect eternal presence with God or eternal consignment to the lake of fire (Matt. 25:31–46; Rev. 20:4–6, 11–15; 21:5–8).

Having considered the image of God in humanity as created, we must next consider humanity as fallen, but ultimately as redeemed and as resurrected.

Study Questions

1. What are the four aspects of human personhood? Which struck you as a new idea? Do you think it is biblically defensible?

2. Describe the four common Christian views of the human person's constitution. Which do you prefer, and why?

3. On what biblical basis might you defend the Christian teaching of liberty of conscience?

Suggested Resources

- Walther Eichrodt, *Theology of the Old Testament*
- Henry Wheeler Robinson, *Corporate Personality in Ancient Israel*
- John Zizioulas, *Being as Communion*

CHAPTER NINE

Where Are You?

After their rebellion against God, the first man and first woman hid from him in shame. They realized their evil action separated them morally from God. Moses said God called out to the man, "Where are you?" (Gen. 3:9). The omniscient Lord was not seeking information. Rather, God was spurring the man and the woman to consider their personal journey, as if saying, "Where were you once? Where are you now? Why are you hiding from my presence? Where will you go in the future?"

Martin Buber tells a story about a chief rabbi in Byelorussia being persecuted. The rabbi graciously spoke to his skeptical jailer about the question God first posed in Genesis 3. He asked the jailer if he believed the Scriptures are "eternal" and "that every era, every generation, and every man is included in them?" The jailer agreed. The rabbi continued, "Well then, in every era, God calls to every man, 'Where are you in your world?'"[1]

1. Martin Buber, *The Way of Man: According to the Teachings of Hasidism*, 2nd ed. (Routledge, 2020), 4. Buber, a Jewish philosopher and theologian, fled Nazi Germany to take up residence in the land which later became modern Israel. He authored some of the most helpful biblical anthropology available today and has been influential upon Jewish and Christian theologians. Buber argued that God doesn't want us to hide from him but to know him. God desires not an abstract but a direct relationship. We find our full humanity when we enter a personal relationship with God. Buber defined six steps in the journey into reality: Consider where you are in your journey;

This question, "Where are you?" must be faced individually by every person. It prompts us to consider our own journey. Once, human beings walked with God in the cool of the day. Now, we hide, "afraid" of God, because we feel exposed to judgment (Gen. 3:10). Originally, "nakedness" reflected innocence between human beings. But sin caused a "radical shift." Now, nakedness invariably indicates existential danger.[2]

Thankfully, God graciously reestablished dialogue with humanity to draw us back from our slide into futility and death. He began gently calling the first human beings to come back to the light. That same day, the Lord invited Adam and Eve to resume their journey toward life by offering the promise of redemption through the seed of Eve (Gen. 3:15). The problem of sin confronts us within and without, and God alone offers the solution.

Locating the Doctrine of Sin

Sin as a doctrine does not fit well, for evil is the contradiction of God's character and activity. The current discussion will grate against the reader accustomed to the beauty, logicality, and goodness of God. Sin is outrageously ugly, frustratingly illogical, and downright distasteful. Sin makes no sense. Moreover, every proposed theory about the nature and transmission of sin will strike most readers as offering an unsatisfactory solution in some important way. However, sin is attested in nature and in Scripture, so we must try our best to understand it, or at least deal with it in our system. Welcome to the bad news, but hold on, for the good news is coming.

Under which doctrine should we treat the problem of human sin, technically known as "hamartiology"? Sin might be treated under theology proper, the doctrine of God. After all, sin is a contradiction against God's very character and activity. David said, "Against you—you alone—I have sinned and done this evil in your sight. So you are right when you pass sentence; you are blameless when you judge" (Ps. 51:4).

---

hear God's personal call to you; resolve to act on his call; take responsibility for yourself; live for others; and live in the context where God has placed you now. Bernhard Ott, "Transforming the Habitus," *Mennonite Quarterly Review* 93 (2019): 204.

2. John Paul II, *Theology of the Body* (Philokalia, 2008), 23–24.

Sin might also be treated as an aspect of angelology, since the ancient serpent, Satan, tempted humanity to sin (Gen. 3:1–5; Rev. 20:2). It might also be treated under anthropology or accorded its own locus. The doctrine of sin might even be treated under soteriology, ministry, or society, for these arenas are deeply affected by sin. We shall treat sin after the doctrine of humanity, for sin is our responsibility.

Certain errors about sin should be avoided. For instance, some argue we are now born with original innocence, that is, without a sin nature. They deem the idea of a sinful nature fictional, even harmful. Others say the problem is communal, environmental, or cultural guilt. They dismiss personal guilt, blaming society instead. From an opposing perspective, others argue sin is entirely personal, not communal. They presume society does not effect individuals nor that private sins effect society. Finally, some minimize the consequences of sin or remain reluctant to speak of God's hatred for sin.[3]

Scriptural Terms for Sin

To set our discussion on the right track, let us survey some common biblical terms for sin. Psalm 51 provides an inventory of sin in its various permutations. The psalmist understands sin is reprehensible because it is directed first and foremost and finally against God.[4] "Against you—you alone—I have sinned and done this evil in your sight" (Ps. 51:4a). Two prominent biblical terms for sin, which may be translated as "impiety" and "missing the mark," provide us with a basic classification system for the remaining terms. The first set of biblical words emphasize the heart's rebellion against God. The second set indicates the creature's exhibitions of sin. We develop a more complete understanding of sin as this chapter proceeds.

3. Karl Menninger, *Whatever Became of Sin?* (Bantam, 1973).

4. Malcolm B. Yarnell III, *Who Is the Holy Spirit? Biblical Insights into His Divine Person* (B&H Academic, 2023), 43–47.

Personal Rebellion

First, "impiety," "irreligion," or "unrighteousness" is sin against God in worship. The Greek verb *asebeo* (literally "not to worship") indicates a failure to ascribe glory to the one true God. Similar Greek terms include *adikia* ("wrongdoing;" Col. 3:25) and *anomia* ("lawlessness;" Matt. 13:41; 23:28; 24:12). Other biblical terms which indicate sinfulness in worship include the Hebrew noun *ma'al*, typically translated as "unfaithful." It applies both to the relationship between God and his people and to the relationship between husband and wife (e.g., Lev. 6:2; Num. 5:12, 27). The Hebrew term *shiquts*, translated as "abomination" (Dan. 9:27; 11:31; 12:11), is particularly reprehensible to God. It indicates the attempt to place another person or thing in God's place, upon his altar. God brings great tribulation where the "abomination" appears (Greek *bdelygma*; Matt. 24:15). The Hebrew term *'awen*, "perversion," indicates a bending or twisting and is affiliated with "idolatry" (Hebrew *teraphim*; 1 Sam. 15:23b).[5]

Sinful Acts

Second, the most common term for "sin" means "missing the mark," indicating a voluntary and culpable activity.[6] The Hebrew term is *chata'ah* (Gen. 4:7) while the common Greek verbs and nouns are, respectively, *hamartano* and *hamartia*. The study of sin in theology is often entitled "hamartiology." Other biblical terms which indicate the creature's exhibition of sin include the Hebrew *'abar*. In Numbers 14:41–42, *'abar* is translated as "going against" (CSB) or "transgressing" (NASB). It indicates one is going beyond an established limit. Another Hebrew term, *'avel*, has been translated as "unjustly" (CSB) or "iniquity" (NASB1995). *'Avel* indicates deviation from a right course (e.g., Lev. 19:15). "Rebellion" is indicated by the Hebrew term *pesha'* (Isa. 1:2) and by a group of Greek terms, *apeitheia* ("disobedient"; Eph. 2:2), *aphistemi* ("turns away"; Heb. 3:12), and *apostasia* ("apostasy"; 2 Thess. 2:3).[7]

---

5. James Leo Garrett Jr., *Systematic Theology: Biblical, Historical, and Evangelical*, vol. 1, 2nd ed. (BIBAL Press, 2000), 527–28.

6. Garrett, *Systematic Theology*, 1:527.

7. Garrett, *Systematic Theology*, 1:528–29.

Original Sin

"Original sin" (Latin *originale peccatum*) is an important doctrine developed by Augustine of Hippo.[8] Later theologians came to distinguish between the point of origin of sin, the first human act of sin, and the inheritance of original sin by Adam's posterity. We must discuss not only the origination of sin, but also how original sin was transmitted to Adam's posterity as well as its impact upon them. Careful theological interpretation of Genesis 3 and Romans 5 will be important in this discussion. Original sin considers both the origination of sin and the initial sinful act by Adam and Eve.

The Origination of Sin

Where did sin come from in the first place? Sin was clearly not caused by God. God's actions are always "good" (Ps. 119:68), and the creation which God made was "good," indeed "very good" (Gen. 1:31). Man before the Fall was characterized by a goodness we might call "original goodness" or "original innocence."[9] If they originate anywhere then, sin and evil start from creation. According to James 1:13–15, God does not tempt us to do evil things. Instead, human beings are led astray by their "own evil desire." After we conceive the desire for evil within ourselves, our sinful acts and the punishment of death follow. According to 1 John 2:16, human beings are enticed by "lust of the flesh," "lust of the eyes," and "pride of life."

Three truths about the origination of sin must be retained: First, recall God's perfect goodness and reject the idea of divine evil or divine origination of evil. When God does send bad things into the world, it is his responsive judgment to the world. Second, retain the truth about creation's original goodness. Third, the world alone is responsible for its evil.

Working within these three doctrinal parameters, theologians have located the origin of sin within the moral agency of angels and human beings. Henri Blocher, the contemporary French Reformed theologian, argues that sin is not revealed as part of God's good

8. While Augustine considered the origination of sin, he used the term "original sin" for the condition of sin. William E. Mann, "Augustine on Evil and Original Sin," in Eleonore Stump and Norman Kretzmann, eds., *The Cambridge Companion to Augustine* (Cambridge University Press, 2001), 45–48.

9. John Paul II, *Theology of the Body*, 5–6.

creation. Sin is, for instance, rationally incoherent, incongruent with the divine logos. Blocher argues that we cannot even ascribe to God the creation of anything evil, even that God created in such a way that allowed for its possibility.[10]

The Initial Act of Sin

The first sin in human history is described in Genesis 3:1–6. It occurred during a theological conversation. Satan began a dialogue by questioning the veracity of the Word of God: "Did God really say?" (v. 1). The conversation then proceeded to pervert God's Word. We are not told how Eve came to a new claim, that she could not even "touch" the tree. Perhaps it was Adam's Pharisee-like addition. Perhaps it was Eve's invention, left uncorrected by Adam. Wherever this human law derived, it restricted human freedom in an unappealing and unnecessary way. It ascribed to God words for which we have no direct evidence he uttered: "or touch it" (Gen. 3:2–3; cf. 2:17).

The next twisting came with the serpent's call on the woman to disbelieve the Word of God. Having questioned God's Word, now he contradicted it: "No! You will certainly not die" (3:4). The serpent then subverted the Word of God. He cast doubt on God's goodness toward humanity. Although God created humanity in his image and likeness, the serpent said God didn't want humanity to be "like God" (v. 5). Man's grasping after "knowing good and evil," John Calvin said, is the attempt to make humanity more than it already is. They wanted to claim for themselves "the Divine glory, or equality with God." Against such grasping for glory, he argued, "the principal point of wisdom is a well-regulated sobriety in obedience to God."[11]

Satan promised the human beings they could be "like God" (v. 5). According to Deitrich Bonhoeffer, the serpent promised that direct disobedience toward God—eating of the tree of the knowledge of good and evil—would make "humankind similar to God in knowing-out-of-its-own-self about good and evil, in having no limit and acting-out-of-its-own-resources, in its aseity, in its being

10. Henri Blocher, *Original Sin: Illuminating the Riddle* (InterVarsity Press, 1997), 56–57.

11. John Calvin, *Commentaries on the First Book of Moses Called Genesis*, vol. 1, transl. John King (1843; reprint Baker, 1996), 151.

alone."[12] In other words, humanity was told it could become like God in his independence. Satan promised humanity self-sufficiency and limitlessness, a perversion of true human freedom. Rather than merely being made in the image of God, a being limited through its created likeness to God, humanity wanted to become God himself. Such self-centeredness is the root impulse in idolatry.

The internal temptation within Eve demonstrates an echo between the Old Testament record in Genesis 3:6 and the New Testament's record of human self-temptation in 1 John 2:16: The tree appealed to her flesh—she saw that it was "good for food." The tree also appealed to her eyes—it was "delightful to look at." Finally, it appealed to her mind—it seemed "desirable for obtaining wisdom." From her partialities, Eve moved to disobey God. She took some fruit of the tree and ate it, and she gave some to her husband, who also ate it. While Eve took the lead, Adam remained culpable. Some have argued Adam chose to sin so as not to leave Eve alone, but this takes us beyond the biblical text and perversely turns an act of sin into an act of love.[13]

The Transmission of Sin

We may now address the impact of original sin upon the descendants of Adam and Eve. While discussing the process of sin's transmission, we must keep in mind two distinct questions about our woeful inheritance: First, did humanity inherit a sinful nature from Adam? Second, do his offspring also inherit responsibility for Adam's personal guilt?

Two Pauline texts have proven extraordinarily critical in answering these questions. In Ephesians 2:3, the apostle wrote, "We too all previously lived among them in our fleshly desires, carrying out the inclinations of our flesh and thoughts, and we were by nature children under wrath as the others were also." All human beings, therefore, inherit a sin "nature" (Greek *physei*). This nature makes them ultimately subject to divine wrath as it issues forth in sinful activity.

12. Dietrich Bonhoeffer, *Creation and Fall: A Theological Exposition of Genesis 1–3*, ed., John W. DeGruchy, transl. Douglas Stephen Bax, Dietrich Bonhoeffer Works, vol. 3 (Fortress Press, 1997), 113.

13. Cf. John S. Hammett and Katie J. McCoy, *Humanity*, Theology for the People of God (B&H Academic, 2023), 320.

Harold Hoehner says the context makes it clear God's judgmental wrath comes upon the sinful actions of people.[14] Voluntary rebellion has personal consequences.[15] Revelation 20:13 similarly states that judgment is based on "works."

With the second passage, Romans 5:12, translations of the Greek have proven difficult. Following the Latin version of his day and responding to Pelagius, Augustine crafted his doctrine of original sin based on a partial mistranslation. The Greek conjunction, *eph ho*, should be translated as causal, "because." But Augustine translated *eph ho* with the Latin locative, *in quo*, "in whom" or "in him." This allowed the bishop to argue that all of Adam's descendants are guilty before God because of Adam's personal action.[16]

Greek New Testament	**Christian Standard Bible**
Διὰ τοῦτο ὥσπερ δι' ἑνὸς ἀνθρώπου ἡ ἁμαρτία εἰς τὸν κόσμον εἰσῆλθεν	Therefore, just as sin entered the world through one man,
καὶ διὰ τῆς ἁμαρτίας ὁ θάνατος,	and death through sin,
καὶ οὕτως εἰς πάντας ἀνθρώπους ὁ θάνατος διῆλθεν,	[also] in this way death spread to all people,
ἐφ' ᾧ πάντες ἥμαρτον·	because all sinned.

For the sake of clarity, it may be helpful to place the original Greek and a more literal English translation of Romans 5:12 next to one another. Four doctrines from the four simple clauses in the text, when properly translated, thereby become clear. These four doctrines are related to one another although not entirely integrated with one another: First, Adam introduced sin into the world. Second, sin brings death. Third, death extends to everyone. Fourth,

14. Harold W. Hoehner, Philip W. Comfort, and Peter H. Davids, *Ephesians, Philippians, Colossians, 1 and 2 Thessalonians, Philemon*, Cornerstone Biblical Commentary (Tyndale House, 2008), 48.

15. "We had rebelled, knowingly and voluntarily, against the loving authority of God and so had fallen under the dominion of Satan." John R. W. Stott, *God's New Society: The Message of Ephesians*, The Bible Speaks Today (InterVarsity Press, 1979), 75.

16. E.g., Augustine, *On Marriage and Concupiscence* 45, in Philip Schaff, ed., *Augustin: Anti-Pelagian Writings*, Nicene and Post-Nicene Fathers, First Series, vol. 5 (1887; reprint Hendrickson, 1995), 301.

universal death is due to universal personal participation in sin. The exact means of sin's transmission from Adam to his descendants is not enumerated in the first clause.

Augustine's theological exegesis, which redeployed traducianism against Pelagianism, shaped Western thoughts about the transmission of sin. After Augustine, because of his polemical needs and his peculiar translation, a critical question confronted subsequent interpreters: Are universal guilt and death due to Adam's personal sin, or are they due "to all having sinned in their personal lives"?[17] Richard Longenecker discovered four primary interpretative theories: Every human being sinned in Adam; all humanity was represented in Adam; Adam set a bad example; and depravity is inherited but guilt is not.[18]

After Augustine, the Western doctrine of sin's transmission settled historically into five primary traditions: Traducianism, Pelagianism, Federalism, Arminianism, and a common Baptist view.

Traducianism

This classical view began with Tertullian of Carthage, who said each human soul derived from Adam.[19] "Each generation, he claims, is an offshoot (*tradux*) of the previous one. Sin is hereditary, transmitting the qualities of the fallen Adam to all his descendants."[20] The Latin dictum *tradux animae tradux peccati* captures the main idea: "the root of the soul is the root of sin."

After seeing Pelagius argue Adam was merely a bad example, Augustine deepened traducianism with his natural headship theory: He located all human beings physically in Adam. The sin "in" Adam was thereby transmitted to subsequent generations through "concupiscence," the sexual act itself being deemed inherently sinful.

---

17. F. F. Bruce, *Romans: An Introduction and Commentary* (InterVarsity Press, 1985), 133.

18. Richard N. Longenecker, *The Epistle to the Romans: A Commentary on the Greek Text*, New International Greek New Testament Commentary (Eerdmans, 2016), 578.

19. "The soul which in the beginning was associated with Adam's body . . . proved to be the germ of the entire substance of the human soul and of that part of creation." Tertullian, *On the Soul* 9, in Alexander Roberts and James Donaldson, eds., *Latin Christianity: Its Founder, Tertullian*, Ante-Nicene Fathers, vol. 3 (1885; reprint Hendrickson, 1994), 189.

20. Anthony C. Thiselton, *The Thiselton Companion to Christian Theology* (Eerdmans, 2015), 774.

Born with Adam's original sin, therefore, everyone inherits also his guilt. In response, infants may be baptized to remove this sin.[21] Roman Catholics continue to teach traducianism, but all the various Western views developed from Augustine's natural headship theory vary in one degree or another.[22]

Pelagianism

According to a contemporary of Augustine, the British monk Pelagius, every human person is born free from any taint of corruption or guilt. Adam serves as a bad example. Whether a person adopts sin is entirely up to the individual exercise of the natural will, and this exercise occurs apart from grace. Determined to promote holiness, Pelagius argued that one may even conceivably live a life without sin. Augustine reacted harshly to Pelagius. Pelagianism was broadly deemed heretical both in the West and the East, primarily because it seemed to make Christ's incarnation unnecessary.[23]

Reformed Federalism

Reformed theologians typically received Augustine's system of nature and grace but recast the doctrine of transmission. The dominant Reformed position, the federal headship theory, or federalism, says God appointed Adam to be the representative head of all humans through a so-called "covenant of works." God originally gave Adam both "a command for guidance" and "a threat of punishment in case of transgression" (cf. Gen. 2:16–17). Reformed scholars found that these two stipulations reflect the rudiments of a covenant

---

21. Augustine, *On Marriage and Concupiscence*, 301; Augustine, *Enchiridion on Faith, Hope, and Love*, ed. Thomas S. Hibbs (Regnery, 1996), 32, 52–56.

22. Lutherans retained the Augustinian definition but without baptismal regeneration. "The punishment and penalty of original sin, which God has imposed upon the children of Adam and upon original sin, are death, eternal damnation, and also other bodily and spiritual, temporal and eternal miseries, and the tyranny and dominion of the devil, so that human nature is subject to the kingdom of the devil and has been surrendered to the power of the devil, and is held captive under his sway, who stupefies and leads astray many a great, learned man in the world by means of dreadful error, heresy, and other blindness, and otherwise rushes men into all sorts of crime." *The Formula of Concord: Solid Declaration*, Art. 1, in *The Book of Concord: The Confessions of the Evangelical Lutheran Church*, ed. Robert Kolb and Timothy J. Wengert, transl. Charles Arand et al. (Fortress Press, 2000), 534.

23. Garrett, *Systematic Theology*, 1:565, 569.

(cf. Hosea 6:7). Human beings are imputed both Adam's sin nature and his personal guilt due to his representative headship. For the purposes of salvation, an individual's covenant head may either be Adam or the second Adam, Jesus Christ (cf. 1 Cor. 15:45–49).[24]

According to the leading English Calvinistic creed, the Westminster Confession of Faith, every person receives Adam's "original corruption" and is compelled thereby to commit "actual transgressions." Human beings are judged to be guilty before God both for original sin and for personal transgressions.[25] Calvinistic theology goes on to teach that God graciously intervenes to save some human beings. Every person is eternally predestined to be under one federal head or the other. Herman Bavinck admitted the Reformed position can be "overly developed and treated too scholastically," but he still considered it the superior system.[26]

Reformed Arminianism

The movement which received its name from the early modern Dutch theologian Jacob Arminius developed in conversation with Reformed federalism. However, the two systems remain "incompatible" due to divergent doctrines of God and humanity.[27] Arminians emphasize divine love and human free will, while the Reformed emphasize divine sovereignty and individual predestination. Arminians agree that every human person is born with a sin nature and with guilt. However, prevenient grace removes the impediment to the human will. This allows a person to escape condemnation through faith. People are enabled by the grace that comes

---

24. Herman Bavinck, *God and Creation*, ed. John Bolt, transl. John Vriend, vol. 2, Reformed Dogmatics (Baker Academic, 2004), 564–65.

25. "Every sin, both original and actual, being a transgression of the righteous law of God, and contrary thereunto, doth, in its own nature, bring guilt upon the sinner, whereby he is bound over to the wrath of God, and curse of the law, and so made subject to death, with all miseries spiritual, temporal, and eternal." *The Westminster Confession of Faith* (1547), 6.6, in Philip Schaff and David S. Schaff, *The Evangelical Protestant Creeds*, vol. 3, The Creeds of Christendom, 6th ed. (1931; reprint Baker, 1993), 616.

26. Bavinck, *God and Creation*, 568. Bavinck rejected the Roman Catholic version of traducianism for being too optimistic about post-Fallen humanity and the Lutheran version for being too optimistic about pre-Fallen humanity. Bavinck, *God and Creation*, 571–76.

27. Roger E. Olson, *Arminian Theology: Myths and Realities* (IVP Academic, 2006), 62.

before personal salvation to respond to the gospel of Jesus Christ. Arminianism teaches a form of "evangelical synergism."[28]

Among the classical western options, Pelagianism remains the outlier, because it denies the existence of a sinful human nature. But the other three classical positions, although generally considered orthodox, seemed to go beyond Scripture with their various doctrines of original guilt, baptismal regeneration, imputed guilt, and prevenient grace. They each solved the riddle of original sin through one innovation or another. A fifth view, however, chose to retain original sin while rejecting original guilt.

A Common Baptist View

The leading Southern Baptist confession adopts a different approach to the four views outlined above. *The Baptist Faith and Message* asserts that while Adam and Eve "brought sin into the human race," and their descendants "inherit a nature and an environment inclined toward sin," condemnation is applied to those who are "capable of moral action" and "become transgressors."

> In the beginning man was innocent of sin and was endowed by his Creator with freedom of choice. By his free choice man sinned against God and brought sin into the human race. Through the temptation of Satan man transgressed the command of God, and fell from his original innocence; whereby his posterity inherit a nature and an environment inclined toward sin. Therefore, as soon as they are capable of moral action, they become transgressors and are under condemnation. Only the grace of God can bring man into His holy fellowship and enable man to fulfill the creative purpose of God.[29]

Adam Harwood of New Orleans Baptist Theological Seminary recently defended this common Baptist position. Through his exhaustive study of original sin in Scripture, he made three important

---

28. *The Five Arminian Articles* (1610), in Schaff and Schaff, *The Evangelical Protestant Creeds*, 545–49; Olson, *Arminian Theology*, 61–63.

29. *The Baptist Faith and Message*, Art. III. Cf. William L. Lumpkin and Bill J. Leonard, eds., *Baptist Confessions of Faith*, 2nd ed. (Judson Press, 2011), 412.

discoveries: First, "Paul's understanding of the circumstances of God's wrath combined with the context of Ephesians 2:3 favors the view that judgment comes as a result of sinful actions rather than a sinful nature." Second, "Because infants are unable to commit sinful actions, they are therefore not subject to God's judgment and wrath." Third, Psalm 51:5 supports the doctrine of a corrupted nature of "sinfulness" but not of an inherited "guilt."[30] In his historical studies, Harwood discovered that most Baptists believe human beings inherit Adam's sin nature. However, they denied humanity inherits Adam's guilt. Guilt remains personal and eternal judgment is applied personally. This view was variously affirmed by E. Y. Mullins, W. T. Conner, H. Herschel Hobbs, and Millard Erickson, among other Baptists.[31]

Personal Sin and Corporate Sin

With the issue of the origin and transmission of sin surveyed, we must now consider sin in its dual manifestation in human life. A proper definition of sin must necessarily include both the personal and the social dimensions of sin. On the one hand, we must address the priority of justice for personal sin. On the other hand, social sin is also judged.

Personal sin is affirmed in such texts as the refrain of Ezekiel 18: "The person who sins is the one who will die" (vv. 4b, 20a). The Israelites in Ezekiel's day sought to avoid personal guilt by appealing to the sins of their forefathers. In response, "Both Jeremiah and Ezekiel saw this as a pernicious doctrine, because it inevitably led to a spirit of fatalism and irresponsibility."[32] The prophets necessarily corrected this overly wrought corporate view of sin and guilt (cf. Num. 16:22; Deut. 24:16; 2 Chron. 25:4; Jer. 31:29). Conscience and Scripture, moreover, attest judgment is finally upon individual persons (Rom. 2:15–16; Rev. 22:12). Jesus likewise promised he

30. Adam Harwood, *The Spiritual Condition of Infants: A Biblical-Historical Survey and Systematic Proposal* (Wipf & Stock, 2011), 49.

31. Harwood, *The Spiritual Condition of Infants*, 144, 151. Cf. Adam Harwood, *Born Guilty? A Southern Baptist View of Original Sin* (Free Church Press, 2013).

32. John B. Taylor, *Ezekiel: An Introduction and Commentary*, Tyndale Old Testament Commentaries (InterVarsity Press, 1969), 146.

would separate true believers from the hypocrites based on their own personal actions (Matt. 25:31–46).

Social sin, or at least the detrimental impact of personal sin upon other people, is affirmed in such texts as Deuteronomy 5:9–10. "Do not bow in worship to [idols], and do not serve them, because I, the LORD your God, am a jealous God, bringing the consequences of the fathers' iniquity on the children to the third and fourth generations of those who hate me, but showing faithful love to a thousand generations of those who love me and keep my commands." God judges social sin but he limits that judgment and expands social blessing. Christ also seems to have recognized a form of social sin, promising judgment upon the "nations," but his judgment will be distributive rather than corporate (Matt. 25:32).

The impact of sin was not merely personal in the beginning. Sin resulted in three sets of broken relationships. Sin affected and continues to affect human relationships with God, with oneself, and with other people. First, in relation to God, sin brings the human person the spiritual experiences of "fear" (Gen. 3:10) and "adversity" (Deut. 30:15), and of being "guilty" before (Num. 5:8; cf. Matt. 5:21–22) and separated from God (Isa. 59:2).

Second, in relation to oneself, sin brings shame (Gen. 3:8; cf. 2:25), unrest (Prov. 22:8; Isa. 57:20–21; Matt. 6:25–33), moral corruption (Rom. 1:18–32), and physical decay unto death (1 Cor. 15:20–22; 2 Cor. 5:1–5).

Third, in relation to others, sin brings familial fracturing (Gen. 3:14–19), social turmoil (James 4:1–4), and universal suffering (Rom. 8:19–22). In modern Western cultures, our extreme individualism sometimes overlooks aspects of the social impact of sin, but the horrific ruination of every human culture and subculture is real and pervasive. No human community, whether a family, a religious community, or a nation, can decisively avoid the truth of its own depravity. Even the cosmos suffers from humanity's rebellion.

Defining Sin

There are three historical groups of Christian answers to the question of the definition of sin. We have grouped the following definitions according to various classical definitions of sin, to various doubtful definitions of sin, and to recent evangelical definitions of sin. A rounded definition should include both the personal and the social dimensions of sin.

Classic Definitions of Sin

Under various classical definitions of sin, we may consider, first, pride. The early church father, Augustine of Hippo, followed by neo-orthodox theologians like Reinhold Niebuhr, located the root of sin in what Niebuhr called "inordinate self-love," or pride.[33]

Second, drawing on a different idea in Augustine, Thomas Aquinas treated sin primarily as the privation of good. Evil itself "cannot be a nature," for everything that God creates is good.[34] Instead, evil as "the absence of good" was brought about by the willfulness of creatures. This approach preserves theology from ascribing evil to God as its author.[35]

Third, some distinguish between the sin nature and the actions of sinful persons who inherit that nature. Ulrich Zwingli, the first major Reformed theologian, promoted this distinction, arguing along similar lines to the common Baptist view outlined above.[36] However, as noted, the Reformed typically say the descendants of Adam are punished for their inherited sin nature as well as their personal acts.

Fourth comes the Reformed doctrine of "total depravity." John Calvin and the Reformed tradition generally have seen the whole human as perverted by sin. This does not mean that every human commits every sin, nor that we are incapable of outwardly good acts. However, before God, all human works are sinful by reason of our sinful motives.[37]

Fifth, Walter Rauschenbusch stressed the social aspects of sin. The structures of human society may oppress the weak and poor,

33. Reinhold Niebuhr, *Human Destiny*, vol. 2, The Nature and Destiny of Man (Scribner, 1964), 137.

34. Thomas Aquinas, *Compendium of Theology*, transl. Richard J. Regan (Oxford University Press, 2009), 91.

35. Augustine, *Enchiridion on Faith, Hope, and Love*, 10–12.

36. The Zwinglian and Baptist view avoids the problem of ascribing injustice to God and is commensurate with monergism at the same time. Oliver Crisp, "Sin," in Michael Allen and Scott Swain, eds., *Christian Dogmatics: Reformed Theology for the Catholic Church* (Baker Academic, 2016), 212–14.

37. Richard A. Muller, *Calvin and the Reformed Tradition: On the Work of Christ and the Order of Salvation* (Baker Academic, 2012), 51.

as with slavery. These structures encourage and reward personal sin. The influence of social and institutional sin is often difficult to detect, but it is nevertheless demonstrable.[38]

Sixth, as we saw with the transmission of sin, many distinguish between the communal inheritance of the sin nature and the guilt of the individual person. Baptists commonly argue original sin is the inheritance of a tendency to sin and that guilt is not incurred until the human person sins. This position often proceeds to assume some "age of accountability."[39]

Doubtful Definitions of Sin

Next, we must consider diverse doubtful definitions of sin. Leo Garrett evaluated five other definitions of sin and found them insufficient: Speaking to the personal dimension of sin, Reinhold Niebuhr defined it as the anxiety of finiteness. Sin is a dialectic between finitude and freedom. Niebuhr found the answer to be a change in attitude. Paul Tillich defined sin as existential estrangement. Sin is the personal act of turning away from the self and the world, and the answer is found in personal realization.

Speaking from the social side, Liberation Theology often treats sin as economic struggle, effectively negating personal sin to focus on social sin. The liberation theologian's answer may entail civil revolution. Harrison Sacket Elliott located sin in individualism and competitiveness. He said God and humanity are intended to cooperate. The problem is in our egoism. To focus on sin may be psychologically unhealthy; instead, change comes through education. F. R. Tennant tied sin to our animal nature. Sin, he said, comes with bodily nature, and the answer is evolution.[40]

Evangelical Definitions of Sin

Finally, we must consider various evangelical definitions of sin. Millard Erickson provided a Christological and anthropological definition of sin. Sin primarily concerns a person's unwillingness to believe in Jesus Christ (John 16:9). Sin is, moreover, any lack of

38. Recognizing the social dimensions of human sin does not mean the institutional solutions offered by proponents must be received. Walter Rauschenbusch, *A Theology for the Social Gospel* (Abingdon, 1987), 69–76.

39. Garrett, *Systematic Theology*, 1:581–82.

40. Garrett, *Systematic Theology*, 1:523–24, 541–44.

conformity, active or passive, to the moral law of God. This may be a matter of act or a matter of thought or of inner disposition.[41]

Leo Garrett offered a dirge of practical sins described in Scripture. Sin is a violation of the law of God, unfaithfulness to the covenant, and willful and prideful rebellion against God. Sin is idolatry or the worship of the creation instead of the Creator, unbelief or not trusting in the true God. Sin is selfishness, as well as sloth or apathy.[42]

We may add to these evangelical definitions by noting how sin is found in every aspect of human existence, using a threefold paradigm:[43]

1. To begin with, sin is *cosmic*. Paul warned, "See to it that no one takes you captive through philosophy and empty deception, according to the tradition of men, according to the elementary principles of the world, rather than according to Christ" (Col. 2:8 NASB1995).
2. In addition, sin is *communal*. "Now, behold, the cry of the sons of Israel has come to Me; furthermore, I have seen the oppression with which the Egyptians are oppressing them" (Exod. 3:9 NASB1995; cf. Acts 7:34).
3. But ultimately sin is *personal*. "All the nations will be gathered before Him; and He will separate them from one another, as the shepherd separates the sheep from the goats; and He will put the sheep on His right, and the goats on the left" (Matt. 25:32–33 NASB1995).

41. Erickson, *Christian Theology*, 596.

42. Garrett, *Systematic Theology*, 1:526–34.

43. This threefold division was first suggested to me by Baylor professor Malcolm Foley. Thiselton argued in a similar way that "the biblical traditions of sin" indicate "a human condition that has corporate, structural, and communal dimensions." "Many postmodern understandings of the human as corporately under bondage to forces of power beyond the control of the individual have more in common with biblical perspectives than the shallow liberal theological optimism that speaks only of the infinite value of an individual 'soul.'" Anthony C. Thiselton, *The Hermeneutics of Doctrine* (Eerdmans, 2007), 196.

The Severity of Sin

Scripture certainly speaks of differing severities of sin. However, even as we recognize the diverse levels of sin, we must remember that every sin remains worthy of eternal judgment. Sin is rooted in the human person through the heart's rebellion against God. One human sin never justifies another.

There are different severities of sin against the divine Persons: Jesus said, "Therefore, I tell you, people will be forgiven every sin and blasphemy, but the blasphemy against the Spirit will not be forgiven. Whoever speaks a word against the Son of Man, it will be forgiven him; but whoever speaks against the Holy Spirit, it will not be forgiven him, either in this age or in the one to come" (Matt. 12:31–32). The context of this passage indicates the sin against the Spirit involves knowledgeable and intentional blasphemy, ascribing to the devil the work of the Holy Spirit in Christ (v. 24).

There are also different severities of lack of repentance toward God: "Woe to you, Chorazin! Woe to you, Bethsaida! For if the miracles that were done in you had been done in Tyre and Sidon, they would have repented in sackcloth and ashes long ago. But I tell you, it will be more tolerable for Tyre and Sidon on the day of judgment than for you" (11:21–22). Jesus also warned that he will hold those to greater account who caused one of his "little ones" to stumble (18:5–7). Again, the severity of the sin depends on the willfulness of the sinner.

There are, finally, different severities for high-handed sins: "So Pilate said to him, 'Do you refuse to speak to me? Don't you know that I have the authority to release you and the authority to crucify you?' 'You would have no authority over me at all,' Jesus answered him, 'if it hadn't been given you from above. This is why the one who handed me over to you has the greater sin'" (John 19:10–11). The severity of sin again depends on knowledge and intention. The religious leaders knew what they were doing better than did the Roman governor.

Anthony Thiselton identified three increasing levels in the severity of sins. First, there is "straying," an almost, but not quite, accidental slipping into evil. Second comes "rebellion," a direct act of premeditated evil. Third, there is "wickedness" or "idolatry," the state of being evil. In this state, the idolatrous heart contains willful hatred toward God. "It is the most terrifying and deep-seated of the three groups of terms."[44]

From a pastoral perspective, it must also be noted that certain sins have greater impact upon the human person, corrupting body and soul. For instance, murder, the wrongful taking of a human life, presents an immediate and permanent problem to the one whose physical life has been taken. God imposes stern penalties upon those who murder or abuse a human being, for he treasures those whom he made in his image (Gen. 9:5–6; Prov. 14:31). Other sins also carry severe consequences: "Sexual immorality" harms our human bodies and offends his Holy Spirit (1 Cor. 6:18). The prophets repeatedly link human adultery, a man breaking his marriage covenant, to spiritual idolatry, a man breaking his covenant with God (e.g., Isa. 1:21; 50:1; Jer. 3:8; Ezek. 16:1–63; Hosea 4:12–14).

Systematic Summary

We may summarize the doctrine of sin according to seven theological loci. Sin can be systematized with the doctrines of God, creation, humanity, personal salvation, the church, society, and the end.

1. Sin does not derive from God. Sin offends God to the degree that eternal separation from God, death, is necessary for the sinner. God redeems humanity so that our sin need not necessarily condemn us as persons forever.
2. Sin impacted God's good creation such that no element of the world remains untouched. Creation was "subjected to futility" and is "groaning" under the weight of sin as it awaits humanity's final resurrection (Rom. 8:20–22).
3. Human beings are born with a nature and environment inclined toward sin. Every human transgresses, and we deserve judgment. The only hope for human beings to escape judgment is the grace of God.

44. Thiselton, *The Thiselton Companion*, 770.

4. Personal salvation from sin is offered to believers through the gift of faith in Christ alone (John 3:16). The critical sin of the unbeliever is his or her lack of faith in the One who created us and offers us salvation (John 3:18). Although believers are immediately justified, sanctification is a process (Rom. 7:14–25; 1 John 1:8). The life of true faith, authentic faith, includes abiding in Christ. Such abiding is manifested in the fruit of the life of faith (John 15:1–8).
5. Sin is present within the church, because humanity is fallen. There are false believers, and true believers continue to struggle against sin (Rom. 7:14–25). Churches must confront sin by recalling God's holy law. Churches must extend forgiveness through preaching the good news of Jesus Christ. Churches address gross sin within the church through formal discipline (Matt. 18:15–20; 1 Cor. 5:1–13) and receiving back the repentant (2 Cor. 2:5–11).
6. Both human persons and societies are perverted by sin.[45] The individual remains ultimately responsible for his or her own sins (Ezek. 18:20). At the final judgment, we must account for our works. National sins are manifested in history, as is often divine judgment through providence. The gospel brings personal and social change. Christians are responsible for personal sanctification and social flourishing. True faith is alive, not static.[46]

45. "Our fathers sinned, and are no more; and we bear their iniquities" (Lam. 5:7 ESV).

46. "You see that faith was active together with his works, and by works, faith was made complete" (James 2:22).

7. In the New Jerusalem, the reign of sin will cease.[47] Those who have a personal relation with the Triune God have a place there, but not those dominated by sin.[48]

Conclusion: Is It Well with Your Soul?

Despite our utter sinfulness and every reason to despair of ourselves, God calls us to receive the hope of our humanity in its reconstitution in his Son. Bonhoeffer wrote, "*Ecce homo*—behold God become human, the unfathomable mystery of the love of God for the world. God loves human beings. God loves the world."[49] God loves you, even though you and I are sinners, and he sent his Son to prove it by dying on the cross and arising from the dead. The question is whether we will be born again by the Holy Spirit (John 3:3–8), believing in Jesus as the only begotten Son of God (John 3:10–18) and repenting of our evil deeds (John 3:19–21).

Horatio G. Spafford found comfort amid the trials and tragedies of this world, when he remembered that Christ shed his blood to provide us with peace and hope. His own trial led him to write a hymn that has comforted countless thousands of believers who have struggled with sin, and its results of doubt and despair.[50] When the

---

47. "Then I heard a loud voice from the throne: Look, God's dwelling is with humanity, and he will live with them. They will be his peoples, and God himself will be with them and will be their God. He will wipe away every tear from their eyes. Death will be no more; grief, crying, and pain will be no more, because the previous things have passed away" (Rev. 21:3–4).

48. "Blessed are those who wash their robes, so that they may have the right to the tree of life and may enter the city by the gates. Outside are the dogs, the sorcerers, the sexually immoral, the murderers, the idolaters, and everyone who loves and practices falsehood" (Rev. 22:14–15).

49. Bonhoeffer continued: "Not an ideal human, but human beings as they are; not an ideal world, but the real world. What we find repulsive in their opposition to God, what we shrink back from with pain and hostility, namely, real human beings, the real world, this is for God the ground of unfathomable love. God establishes a most intimate unity with this. God becomes human, a real human being. While we exert ourselves to grow beyond our humanity, to leave the human behind us, God becomes human; and we must recognize that God wills that we be human, real human beings." Dietrich Bonhoeffer, *Ethics*, ed. Clifford J. Green, transl. Reinhard Krauss et al., Dietrich Bonhoeffer Works, vol. 6 (Fortress Press, 2005), 84.

50. Simon Sebag Montefiore, *Jerusalem: The Biography* (Weidenfeld & Nicolson, 2011), 365–66.

guilt and consequences of your very real sin assail you, remember Christ provided you hope through his sacrificial shedding of his own blood on the cross:

> When peace like a river, attendeth my way,
> When sorrows like sea billows roll;
> Whatever my lot, Thou hast taught me to say,
> It is well, it is well, with my soul.
>
> Tho' Satan should buffet, tho' trials should come,
> Let this blest assurance control,
> That Christ has regarded my helpless estate,
> And hath shed His own blood for my soul.
>
> My sin—oh, the bliss of this glorious tho't:
> My sin not in part, but the whole
> Is nailed to the cross and I bear it no more,
> Praise the Lord, praise the Lord, o my soul![51]

Study Questions

1. What are the differences between sin described as "impiety" and sin described as "missing the mark"?

2. Describe the five Western systems which deal with the transmission of sin. Which system do you prefer, and why?

3. On what biblical basis might you argue for the reality of social sin? On what biblical basis might you argue for the reality of personal sin?

51. Horatio G. Spafford, "It Is Well with My Soul," in *The Baptist Hymnal* (Convention Press, 1991), 410.

Suggested Resources

- Henri Blocher, *Original Sin*
- Adam Harwood, *Born Guilty?*
- Roger E. Olson, *Arminian Theology*

CHAPTER TEN

Who Will Save Us?

> Wretched man that I am! Who will set me free from the body of this death? Thanks be to God through Jesus Christ our Lord! (Rom. 7:24–25a NASB)

We began our discussion of the second Person of the divine Trinity by establishing the biblical basis of his being the Son of God the Father and that he became man. We then traced the early church's reception of the biblical revelation of his absolute deity and assumed humanity. Next, we explored the truth of the inseparable operations of the Trinity as applied to the entire divine work. Afterward, we reviewed God's works of creation, election, and providence. We also paid special attention to those creatures known as human beings. Humanity was created in the divine image, but we fell into sin and deserve death.

Now, we must address the work of God in saving us from sin and death. But who will save us? The simple answer is, of course, God, but we must remember to confess that the Trinity—God the Father and the Son and the Holy Spirit—is our Savior. The biblical evidence for Trinitarian salvation is extensive:

1. In the canon of the Old and New Testaments the title "Savior" is repeatedly assigned to

"God" (e.g., 2 Sam. 22:3; Ps. 42:5, 11; Isa. 45:21; Luke 1:47; 1 Tim. 1:1; Jude 1:25) and "Lord" (e.g., Ps. 140:7; Isa. 43:3, 11; Hosea 13:4).

2. In the New Testament, "Savior" is primarily applied to Christ Jesus (e.g., Acts 5:31; Eph. 5:23; Titus 1:4). He possesses the combined divine title, "God and Savior" (Titus. 2:13; 2 Pet. 1:1; cf. Jude 25), as well as "Lord and Savior" (2 Pet. 1:11; 2:20; 3:2, 18; cf. Luke 2:11; Phil. 3:20).
3. The Holy Spirit necessarily effects or applies our personal salvation (e.g., Matt. 3:11; John 3:3–8; 1 Cor. 12:3; Phil. 1:19; 2 Thess. 2:13; Titus 3:6; Rev. 22:17).

As with creation, election, and providence, the divine work of salvation, therefore, belongs inseparably to the three Persons as One. Our Savior is the one God, who is the Father and the Son and the Holy Spirit.[1] However, whereas God the Father was principal in creation and election, the divine economy of salvation centers in the Person of the Son. From the Father and by the Spirit, the eternal Son became the human being, Jesus, our promised Messiah.

In chapters 3 and 4 above, we established the essential, entire, and eternal deity of the Son, but a full portrait of the Son may not conclude with his divine nature. Orthodox Christology must proceed to consider God's work to save humanity, a work which required the incarnation of God the Son. The divine economy of salvation began with the eternal Word's assumption of human nature. The Word remained truly and personally divine but also became a human being, one Person with two natures. Human salvation is grounded in and thoroughly ensured by the incarnation of the second Person of the eternal Trinity.

A proper portrait of Christ must include his incarnation, which is also his work. Donald Baillie agrees:

---

1. John Stott found "three essentials to which evangelical people are determined to bear witness. They concern the gracious initiative of God the Father in revealing himself to us, in redeeming through Christ crucified, and in transforming us through the indwelling Spirit. For the evangelical faith is the trinitarian faith." John Stott, *Evangelical Truth: A Personal Plea for Unity, Integrity and Faithfulness* (Langham Global Library, 2013), 18.

> A true Christology will tell us not simply that God is *like* Christ, but that God was *in* Christ. Thus it will tell us not only about the *nature* of God, but about his *activity*, about what He has done, coming the whole way for our salvation in Jesus Christ; and there is no other way in which the Christian truth about God can be expressed.[2]

Through his human life, Christ perfects our humanity, opening the way for our salvation (Heb. 2:10). The incarnation of God in Christ constitutes the necessary presupposition for his provision of our salvation. However, the incarnation does not conclude his saving work, for his incarnation proceeds to his death, resurrection, ascension, heavenly reign, and his victorious return.

Paul summarized the Christian message of salvation in this way: "That is, in Christ, God was reconciling the world to himself, not counting their trespasses against them, and he has committed the message of reconciliation to us" (2 Cor. 5:19). A true portrait of Jesus Christ must, therefore, emphasize both his deity and his humanity as integral to his work as Savior.

The glorious message of Christ's redemption of us from our sins is so important that it is described in multiple ways in Scripture. We have space to survey only some expressions of his salvation of us in this chapter. Following the example of the classical creeds,[3] we may summarize the Christian message of salvation through a holistic description of Christ's eternal Person and redemptive work as follows.

Christ's Provision of Salvation
The Elect One: The gospel of our salvation begins in eternity with God's mysterious election to sum up all things in his beloved Son (Eph. 1:9–10).
Incarnation: The gospel of our salvation temporally begins with the eternally begotten Son of God becoming flesh, or assuming human nature, in the preacher named Jesus, the son of Mary (Matt. 1:21; Luke 1:34; John 1:14; Phil. 2:7).

2. Italics his. D. M. Baillie, *God Was in Christ: An Essay on Incarnation and Atonement*, 3rd ed. (Faber and Faber, 1961), 66–67.

3. See the descriptions of the gospel contained in the central Christological sections of the Nicene Creed, the Apostles' Creed, and the Athanasian Creed.

Death and Resurrection: Jesus recapitulated our humanity by perfecting it through his obedience and sufferings (Eph. 1:10; Heb. 2:9–18). Christ's death and resurrection constitute the core of the Christian gospel (1 Cor. 15:3–5). He died for our sins and arose for our justification (Rom. 4:25). Those who believe and confess his divine-human person and his gospel will be saved (Rom. 10:8–10).
Heavenly Session: Christ's saving work does not end in his death and resurrection but proceeds to his ascension, his eternal presentation of his once-for-all sacrifice, and his heavenly intercession (1 Tim. 3:16; Heb. 4:2, 14–16; 7:27; 9:12, 14; 10:14).
Eternal Lord: The gospel is consummated with his Second Coming, final judgment, and eternal reign over the kingdom of God on earth in the New Jerusalem, wherein the saints are included by union through the Holy Spirit with the eternal Christ to enjoy the beatific vision of God (Rom. 8:1–17; Rev. 19–22).

Table 1: Holistic Description of Christ's Person and Work as Savior

It should be little surprise that Christian dogma centers upon Christ's work as Savior. The offer of personal salvation made available in Christ constitutes the ultimate existential crisis for every human being (John 5:22; Col. 3:11). Because everything in the universe is centered in and ruled by Christ, so must theology be centered in and ruled by Christology. Karl Barth stated this truth abstractly: "An ecclesiastical dogmatic must, of course, be Christologically determined *as a whole and in all its parts*."[4] John Fawcett declared with passion: "There is nothing in our religion which hath either truth, reality or substance, but by virtue of its relation to Christ and what he has accomplished on earth on our behalf."[5]

In this chapter, we explore together Scripture's teaching that Jesus Christ is our Savior. Our Lord, in his Person and work, dominates our understanding of God's relation to the universe, including humanity, from the creation of all things through their redemption to their final consummation. Especially, however, the work of Christ is concerned with the gospel of our salvation. Scripture contains many descriptions of his saving work, some of which we review here.

Scripture describes the Savior as the Promise, the Messiah expected to redeem Israel. To become our Mediator, God the Word

4. Barth expressed his claim thus: "As surely as the revealed Word of God, attested by Holy Scripture and proclaimed by the Church, is its one and only criterion, and as surely as this revealed Word is identical with Jesus Christ." Karl Barth, *The Doctrine of the Word of God*, ed. G. W. Bromiley and T. F. Torrance, transl. G. T. Thomson and Harold Knight, Church Dogmatics I/2 (T&T Clark, 1956), 123.

5. John Fawcett, *Christ Precious to Those That Believe: A Practical Treatise on Faith and Love* (1799; reprint, Positive Action for Christ, 2005), 2.

had to become a Man. Jesus is, therefore, both "God and Savior." The apostles emphasized his saving work in their "proclamation." Finally, he and his work of redemption constitute the very essence of "the gospel," the good news which must be personally believed and confessed. Jesus Christ is truly our God, our Lord, and our Savior.[6]

Jesus Saves

The truth that Jesus saves us is conveyed in the New Testament through sundry soteriological titles applied to his Person, a variety of terms applied to his work, and diverse descriptions of the church's continuing communication that Jesus saves. Each title, term, and descriptor can stand on its own as significant, but when they are rehearsed together a crescendo of praise rises from within the heart for the One who saves us.

A summary review of a few soteriological titles, terms, and indicators of Christian proclamation suggests how important the divine work of redemption is in Scripture. The New Testament terms *word*, *truth*, and *faith*, as well as *teaching*, *testimony*, and *tradition*, among others, tell us Jesus is the One who saves. They also tell us something about how people are saved by God.

The Word

First, Jesus is "the Word" who saves. We previously rehearsed the ontological significance of this title applied to Christ.[7] Building on its early appearance in the Torah, the Hebrew term *dabar* was granted divine agency and personhood by the prophets (cf. Isa. 40:6–8; 55:8–11). The Greek nouns *logos* ("word") and *rhema* ("message") in the New Testament established this meaning beyond contestation. The title of Word, therefore, tells us that he participates in divine reality. It also tells us that he is our Savior.

His identity as Word describes the way he saves us. The Word, who is God in Christ (John 1:1, 14), powerfully engages the human heart, bringing conviction of sin (Heb. 4:12). The eternal Word also works personal salvation in those who hear, believe in, and confess

6. He is also our Prophet, our Priest, and our King. His threefold office is considered in the next chapter.

7. See above, chapter 3.

him as the risen Lord through his apostles' proclaimed Word about him (Rom. 10:8–10). The incarnate Word then continues to guide the believer into lifelong repentance through his written Word (2 Tim. 3:15). And those who reject the saving words proclaimed by believers reject the eternal Word of God himself (John 15:20).

The Truth

Second, Jesus is "the Truth" who saves. The New Testament word group for truth (Greek noun *aletheia*, adjective *alethes*) refers theologically to God the Trinity in his nature and work. First, God the Father possesses the perfection of being "true" (John 3:33; 8:26; 17:3). Second, the Son describes himself as "the truth" (14:6). Third, the Holy Spirit is ascribed the nature of "truth" (v. 17). God the Trinity is the perfection of truth; He is truth in essence.[8] The title of Truth, therefore, tells us that he participates in divine reality.

God's title of Truth also tells us that he is our Savior. Through his economy of salvation, God reveals the truth about himself. This saving revelation comes today in Scripture and through its proclamation. Scripture is sufficient for bringing "wisdom for salvation" and for completing the Christian life (2 Tim. 3:15–17); its truth "cannot be broken" (John 10:35). The church serves God as "the pillar and foundation of the truth" in the world by proclaiming the saving work of Jesus Christ in his incarnation, death, resurrection, and ascension (1 Tim. 3:15–16).

The New Testament testimony grounds truth in God's nature and reveals his redemptive truth through the saving message about Jesus Christ. That message is conveyed in the written Scriptures and through the church's witness. "God is truth by nature; Scripture is truth by grace."[9] Those who believe the church's proclamation of salvation in Christ are promised the gift of eternal life (John 19:35; 20:31).

The Faith

Third, faith in Jesus saves the true believer. The New Testament word group translated "faith" or "belief" (Greek *pistis*) indicates both

8. David S. Dockery and Malcolm B. Yarnell III, *Special Revelation and Scripture* (B&H Academic, 2024), 91–118.

9. Dockery and Yarnell, *Special Revelation and Scripture*, 92.

one's personal reception of the saving message of Jesus Christ and the propositional content of that saving message.[10] Encapsulating both senses, Luke says that "the faith," which came through "the word" proclaimed by the apostles, worked powerfully in the hearts of those who initially heard it, prompting "obedience" to God (Acts 6:7).

The zealous Pharisee named Saul once persecuted the Christian community (Acts 8:1–3). But when he subsequently heard from Christ directly on the road to Damascus he likewise embraced the faith (Acts 9:3–6; 22:6–21; 26:12–23). Afterward taking the name Paul, he was set apart to go and proclaim the faith, which he did boldly (Acts 13:2–3, 9–12; Gal. 1:23). Paul portrayed "the faith" as something into which Christians constantly move: "until we all reach unity in the faith . . . , growing into maturity with a stature measured by Christ's fullness" (Eph. 4:13). This indicates the truth of the faith, Christ in his "fullness," is far greater than the human mind can immediately grasp. The church is rooted in and built up from this faith (Col. 2:7).

The contents of "the faith," centered on "the resurrection," ought never be compromised (2 Tim. 2:18). Christians must be warned that their personal soundness requires unrivaled fidelity to the reality of "the faith" (Titus 1:13). Paul specifically identified "the faith" with "the gospel," "this gospel" about Christ, arguing it requires the church's steadfast grounding (Col. 1:23). The important biblical term "faith," therefore, tells us that Christ is our Savior. It also tells us how the salvation he worked for us can be personally appropriated.

The Teaching

In the New Testament, multiple word groups inform us about the communication of divine truth. The New Testament uses of the terms "teaching," "testimony," and "tradition" provide a paradigm for defining the church's communication of God's saving revelation. The instructive revelation about Christ originates with God and draws the apostles and the church into that communicative activity

---

10. Gerhard Kittel, Gerhard Friedrich, and Geoffrey William Bromiley, eds., *Theological Dictionary of the New Testament, Abridged in One Volume* (Eerdmans, 1985), 854.

as his instruments. The intended recipients of this communication are the people in the world.

The fourth exemplary term that indicates God is our Savior and how he saves us is "the teaching." The Old Testament promised the new covenant would be directly taught by God himself and by his Spirit (Jer. 31:33; Ezek. 36:27). This promise was fulfilled in the teaching ministry of the Son. The "teaching" (Greek noun *didache*), understood as a body of truth, was taught by Jesus Christ and focused on his person and work. "In the NT it refers to the whole *didáskein* of Jesus in Mt. 7:28 etc., i.e., his proclaiming God's will in both form and content."[11]

Jesus said his teaching is true because it originates with the Father (John 7:16–18). The teaching by Christ and about Christ is, moreover, the self-revelation of God (Gal. 1:12) and of the Holy Spirit (John 14:26). The saving message that Christ focused on in his teaching included the central gospel truths that he would suffer, that he would die, and that he would arise from death on the third day. However, the disciples did not immediately understand the meaning of Jesus's teaching about the way he would work our salvation (Mark 9:31). Later, when they finally understood and believed, they knew they were called to proclaim this truth to the world.[12]

The Testimony

Fifth, the apostles' testimony to Jesus saves those who believe and confess him as Lord. "Witness" or "testimony" (Greek noun *marturion*, verb *martureo*) in the New Testament centers upon God and Christ. General revelation witnesses about God to all people (Acts 14:17). However, as we discovered in the first volume of Theology for Every Person, the divine revelation that is available to every person through nature and conscience does not offer

11. "This is also the meaning in Jn. 7:16–17." Kittel, Friedrich, and Bromiley, eds., *Theological Dictionary of the New Testament, Abridged in One Volume*, 166.

12. "The post-apostolic fathers build on this sense, but in the main the NT stress is on God's teaching through Jesus and the apostles, with a consequent enhancing of the Christian sense of mission in its teaching ministry." Kittel, Friedrich, and Bromiley, eds., *Theological Dictionary of the New Testament, Abridged in One Volume*, 166.

knowledge about the way of salvation.[13] That is why the church was given the testimony about Christ to give to the world.

John the Baptist centered his witness or testimony on the Person of Jesus Christ (John 1:7). Christ told the apostles they would testify to rulers about him (Matt. 10:18). "Luke's usage in Lk. 24:48 and Acts embraces witness to facts concerning Jesus that are directly known. But this witness can be given only if the meaning of the facts is appreciated, so that the witness takes the form of believing, evangelistic confession."[14] Both Stephen and his former persecutor, Saul/Paul, were appointed witnesses of Christ (Acts 22:20; 26:16). Their testimony recalled his resurrection (Acts 4:33).

The Holy Spirit is given to new converts to testify to their salvation (Acts 15:8). In turn, Christians are sent to witness of Christ to all people (Acts 1:8; 22:15). Their lives confirm their witness to their conversion (1 Cor. 1:6), and God testifies to the truthfulness of his witnesses (Rom. 1:9; 2 Cor. 1:23; etc.). As Christians testify to the gospel of Jesus Christ today, the Holy Spirit provides an internal witness to their external testimony.

Jesus Christ himself is the "faithful" and "true witness" in perfection (Rev. 1:5; 3:14). Both the perfect testimony of God about Christ, a testimony that brings salvation, and the Christian's subordinate testimony are taught by the apostle John in his first epistle:

> If we accept human testimony, God's testimony is greater, because it is God's testimony that he has given about his Son. The one who believes in the Son of God has this testimony within himself. The one who does not believe God has made him a liar, because he has not believed in the testimony God has given about his Son. And this is the testimony: God has given us eternal life, and this life is in his Son. (1 John 5:9–11)

---

13. Malcolm B. Yarnell III, *God*, vol. 1, Theology for Every Person (B&H Publishing, 2024), 140, 164–65.

14. Kittel, Friedrich, and Bromiley, eds., *Theological Dictionary of the New Testament, Abridged in One Volume*, 567.

The Tradition

Sixth, the tradition of the gospel which came through the apostles also offers us knowledge about Christ and salvation. Jesus prayed not only for his disciples but "for those who believe in me through their word" (John 17:20). The words of Christ and about Christ are intended to be preserved and transmitted.

The New Testament Greek terms for "tradition," which literally mean "handing on" (noun *paradosis*, verb *paradidomi*), describe the communication of the saving truth about God in Christ.[15] Paul said that he handed over to the churches what he received from the Lord about the gospel of salvation and the Lord's Supper (1 Cor. 11:23; 15:3). Jude instructed the church to "contend for the faith that was delivered to the saints once for all" (Jude 3).

"Tradition," however, can carry a negative meaning. The traditions "of men" may directly contradict that which God intends to be passed on. Citing Isaiah 29:13, Jesus excoriated the religious teachers of the Israel of his day, the Pharisees and scribes, for "abandoning the command of God." Instead, "you hold on to human tradition" (Mark 7:6b–8). Jesus said the purveyors of false tradition are "hypocrites" (v. 6a).

The apostle Paul defended the purity of his understanding of the gospel of Jesus Christ as coming from the Lord himself rather than via human tradition (Gal. 1:12). He also warned against the fallen tendency to substitute human "philosophy" and "empty deceit" for true revelation. Believers should be "rooted" in, "built up" from, and "established" in Christ. The assured tradition is that which "you were taught" by the apostles of Christ (Col. 2:6–8).

Other Terms

Yet more terms describe the saving message about Jesus Christ. Paul passed to his auditors the "pattern" (Greek *typos*) of truth which frees from sin (Rom. 6:17). It is wise for believers to preserve that pattern (2 Tim. 1:13). Both Paul and John refer to the saving message of Jesus Christ as the saving "revelation" (Greek *apokolypsis*). This revelation was once a mystery but has now been disclosed (Rom. 16:25; Eph. 3:3; Rev. 1:1).

15. Malcolm B. Yarnell III, *The Formation of Christian Doctrine* (B&H Academic, 2007), 61–62, 128–38.

John uses a multiplicity of metaphors in his Gospel to describe Jesus as the Savior of those who believe in him. He is "the way" (Greek *hodos*), "the life" (Greek *zoe*), "the light" (Greek *phos*), and "the grace" (Greek *charis*) of God (John 1:4–5, 7–9, 14, 16–17; 14:6), as well as "the Messiah" (Greek *Christos*), "the Son of God" (Greek *huios tou theou*), "the King of Israel" (Greek *basileus tou Israel*), and "the Lamb" (Greek *amnos*) "who takes away the sins of the world" (John 1:25, 29, 36, 41).

Many books and articles have been written about these Christological terms, alongside many other descriptors of the Savior and his saving work. But we must now turn our attention to four prominent titles and terms which the Bible uses to describe the Person and work of the One who saves us: "the promise," "God and Savior," "the proclamation," and "the gospel."

The Promise

God the Trinity's Promise

The revelation of the "promise" of God came through the messianic proclamation of the Old Testament prophets.[16] God gave the first explicit messianic promise to Abraham through covenant (Gen. 12:1–3). "Thereafter Abraham rested his confidence in this divine power and lived to see the Lord's assurances implemented in what Paul, millennia later, was to call the 'covenants of the promise' (Eph. 2:12; cf. Gal. 3:6–17)."[17]

After Abraham, the other prophets reminded the Israelites to put their hope in a future messianic ruler whom they described both simply yet with increasing depth. The promise was later used in the apostles' primitive preaching to connect the Old Testament hope with its New Testament fulfillment. The promise considers the twofold coming of God, in the divine Persons of the Son and the Spirit.[18]

16. Abraham J. Heschel, *The Prophets* (HarperCollins, 2001), 236–37. While Heschel writes primarily from an anthropological perspective, he recognized the prophets had a "transcendent anticipation." Heschel, *The Prophets*, 622–24.

17. R. K. Harrison, "Promise," in *Evangelical Dictionary of Biblical Theology* (Baker Book House, 1996), 639.

18. Harrison, "Promise," 639.

"In the NT the Greek verbal and noun form of 'promise' occurs more than 40 times. With the exception of Acts 23:21 the reference is always to the promises of God to man."[19] Peter called on all people, beginning with those in Jerusalem, to trust in "the promise" of Jesus Christ. For God promised to redeem Israel and "all who are far off" through his Son (Acts 2:39).

Paul likewise grounded the hopeful gospel of Christ's death and resurrection in "the promise that was made to our ancestors" (Acts 13:32; cf. Acts 26:7; Rom. 4:13; etc.). Jesus likewise referred to the coming of the Holy Spirit as "the Father's promise" (Acts 1:4). The promise, in other words, comes from the Father through the Son in the Holy Spirit.[20] This promise was given to Israel but intended for everyone.

The Scriptural Progress of the Promise

We must note the progressive revelation of the promise in the biblical text. The biblical idea begins with the Hebrew term *dabar*. *Dabar* is the effective personal word of the Lord, acting to fulfill what he promised.[21] According to the Psalms, the promise is rooted in God's nature as both eternal (Ps. 105:8) and graceful (119:58). His promise can be trusted because he must fulfill it by virtue of his righteousness (Ps. 119:123; cf. Neh. 9:8; Num. 23:19) and will doubtlessly fulfill it by virtue of his perfect power (1 Kings 8:15, 24; 2 Chron. 6:4, 15). "The grass withers, the flowers fade, but the word [*dabar*] of our God remains forever" (Isa. 40:8).

The contents of God's promises were revealed in the context of a grace-bearing "covenant" (Hebrew *berith*; Greek *diatheke*), the progressive forms of which found their fulfillment in Jesus Christ.[22]

---

19. Barry J. Beitzel, "Promise," in Walter A. Elwell, ed., *Baker Encyclopedia of the Bible* (Baker Book House, 1988), 1766.

20. Beitzel, "Promise," 1768.

21. Francis Brown, Samuel Rolles Driver, and Charles Augustus Briggs, *Enhanced Brown-Driver-Briggs Hebrew and English Lexicon* (Oxford University Press, 1977), 182.

22. The covenant of saving grace must be distinguished from the covenant of preserving grace. The covenant with Noah concerned the Lord's provision of protection through human government (Gen. 9:1–7) and patience in universal judgment (Gen. 9:8–17). Cf. Samuel Renihan, *The Mystery of Christ: His Covenant and His Kingdom* (Founders Press, 2019), 78–84.

From beginning to end, the covenant promises in the canon expected and enclosed an expanding audience (Gen. 12:1–3):

- First, God never forgot but remembered "his holy promise to Abraham his servant" (Ps. 105:42).
- Second, because he has "spoken" it, God will uphold his promise to "the house of Israel and the house of Judah" (Jer. 33:14).
- Third, the promise is also intended to include "all who are far off, as many as the Lord our God will call" (Acts 2:39).

The promises of God are thus revealed progressively through the biblical canon. Among the prominent promises in the Old Testament are the *protoevangelium*, the promise to Abraham, and the promise to David, as well as the prophetic promises of an exalted child, a new covenant, the suffering Servant, and the triumphant Son of Man. These promises culminated with the coming of Jesus Christ in the New Testament.

The Initial Promise

The Protoevangelium: The first revealed hint about the divine promise came immediately after humanity's Fall into sin. The Lord told the Serpent: "I will put enmity Between you and the woman, And between your seed and her seed; He shall bruise you on the head, And you shall bruise him on the heel" (Gen. 3:15 NASB1995). The New Testament identifies the serpent with Satan (Rom 16:20; Rev 12:9; 20:2). The woman's "seed" is at war with the serpent's "seed."

Some speculate the seed of Satan refers to an evil race of men, but this interpretation removes the wicked from being "true humanity." "It seems more plausible to seek the seed of the serpent outside of the human race."[23] Whatever the exact meaning of the seed of Satan, this text is rightly identified as the *protoevangelium*, "the first glimmer of the gospel." It inaugurates the Bible's discussion about the seed of the woman. And the seed who redeems humanity,

---

23. Geerhardus Vos, *Biblical Theology: Old and New Testaments* (1948; reprint Banner of Truth, 2017), 4.

according to Paul, is the Christ. And Christ is the descendant of Abraham (Gal. 3:16; cf. Rom. 9:6).[24]

The Promise to Abraham: An explicit promise of redemption came to Abraham with the divine blessings given in the covenant described in Genesis 12. God called him to forsake his country, his people, and his father, and go to a new land. Yahweh repeatedly said, "I will bless," indicating an overarching movement of divine grace (Gen. 12:1–3). God sovereignly elected to bless Abraham and others through Abraham. The promise of election was not merely for Abraham. "The election of Abraham, and in the further development of things, of Israel, was meant as a particularistic means toward a universalistic end."[25] He received a threefold promise, the last portion offering blessing to all humanity.

The contents of the promise received more detail in subsequent encounters. In Genesis 15, God promised to bless Abraham's posterity, although he yet had none. Moses reported that in an act of reception with huge importance, "Abram believed the Lord, and he credited it to him as righteousness" (Gen. 15:6; cf. Ps. 106:31; Hab. 2:4; Rom. 4:3, 5, 9, 11, 22; Gal. 3:6; James 2:23). In chapter 17, God added an eternal dimension. "It is a permanent [*'olam*] covenant to be your God and the God of your offspring after you" (Gen. 17:7b). According to Thorlief Boman, "The Hebrew language knew no word that compassed more than *'olam*." It extended the reality of the promise beyond the progress of time into eternity.[26]

Despite his initial and repeated acts of faith, Abraham took time to learn to stop trying to fend for himself. The greatest test of whether Abraham truly believed in the promise was God's command that the old man sacrifice his son in Genesis 22. Abraham spoke prophetically, when he explained to Isaac, "God himself will

---

24. Derek Kidner, *Genesis: Introduction and Commentary*, Tyndale Old Testament Commentary (InterVarsity Press, 1967), 70. Geerhardus Vos described it as "the first redemptive special revelation." Vos, *Biblical Theology*, 41.

25. Vos, *Biblical Theology*, 77.

26. Thorlief Boman, *Hebrew Thought Compared to Greek*, transl. Jules L. Moreau (Norton, 1970), 153. "In the term *'olam* is contained a designation of time extending so far that it is lost to our sight and comprehension in darkness and invisibility." "When *'olam* refers to the past, it can mean eternity. . . ." "Used of the future, *'olam* can mean boundless time to come." Boman, *Hebrew Thought Compared to Greek*, 151. "The expression *me'olam 'adh 'olam*, from eternity to eternity, demonstrates that the endlessness of time stretches backward as well as forward (Pss. 90.2; 103.17; Jer. 7.7; 25.5)." Boman, *Hebrew Thought Compared to Greek*, 153.

provide the lamb for the burnt offering, my son" (v. 8). The promise must be sealed with a sacrifice, a sacrifice only God himself can provide.

The Promise to David

The promise of redemption came next to David. In 2 Samuel 7, the Lord called David, saying he would remain present and protect him (vv. 8–9a). He promised, "I will make a great name for you," "designate a place for my people Israel and plant them," and "give you rest" (vv. 9b–11a). Moreover, the Lord said he would "make a house for you," "raise up after you your descendent, who will come from your body," and "establish his kingdom" (vv. 11b–12). David's descendent "will build a house for my name" (v. 13a).

Concerning David's descendent, the Lord promised to "establish his kingdom forever [*'ōlam*]" (v. 13b, 16). The eternal nature of the promised reign is astonishing enough, but God then promised David's bodily son a filial relationship with God, too. "I will be his father, and he will be my son" (v. 14a). The Lord said David's son, who will also be God's Son, would be disciplined yet remain beloved. "When he does wrong, I will discipline him with a rod of men and blows from mortals" (v. 14b). "But my faithful love will never leave him as it did when I removed it from Saul, whom I removed from before you" (v. 15). This foreshadowed the vicarious atonement of the righteous Christ for the sins of the people.

The Royal Psalms: The eternal, filial, and atoning promise regarding David's descendent was given further detail in the royal psalms. These poems were initially written for the king's coronation and other life events. "They became part of the seedbed of messianic hope—Israel's hope that one day the Lord would send the ideal Davidic king, the Messiah."[27] They provide intimate details of the life, death, and resurrection of the one future king, the Messiah. We must review four royal psalms, although other Messianic psalms like Psalms 45 and 69 require consideration.

Psalm 2 put evil rulers on one side, and the "Lord and his Anointed [Hebrew *masiah*]" on the other (v. 2). The Lord says he "installed my king" in Jerusalem (v. 6). The Lord said to the

27. Nancy deClaissé-Walford, Rolf A. Jacobson, and Beth LaNeel Tanner, *The Book of Psalms*, New International Commentary on the Old Testament (Eerdmans, 2014), 20–21.

Messianic Son of David, "You are my Son; today I have become your Father" (v. 7), then granted him rule over all nations (vv. 8–9). Rulers are called to serve him (vv. 10–11), and rebels are called to "pay homage to the Son or he will be angry and you will perish in your rebellion" (v. 12). The apostles applied Psalm 2:7 to Jesus repeatedly (Acts 13:33; Heb. 1:5; 5:5).[28]

Charles Haddon Spurgeon named Psalm 22 the "psalm of the cross," believing Christ cited it word for word upon his cross.[29] The human Messiah suffers and dies in this psalm. Danny Akin said his suffering involved "spiritual separation (22:1–2), verbal scorn (22:7–8), personal solitude (22:9–11), bodily suffering (22:12–16), and personal shame (22:17–18)."[30] His apostles recognized the details about Christ's suffering were direct prophecies.[31] Despite his trauma, in the end, the Messiah did not fear even death. He cried out to be rescued (vv. 19–20), then exclaimed in joyful triumph, "You answered me!" (v. 21b).

Spurgeon said the Holy Spirit interpreted Psalm 16 for us. For instance, "In the ninth and tenth verses, like the apostles on the mount, we can see 'no man but Jesus only.'"[32] This psalm was quoted by Peter in his inaugural sermon to verify the resurrection of the Messiah (Acts 2:25–28). Psalm 16:9–11 foretold his resurrection: "Therefore my heart is glad and my whole being rejoices; my body also rests securely. For you will not abandon me to Sheol; you will not allow your faithful one to see decay. You reveal the path of life to me; in your presence is abundant joy; at your right hand are eternal pleasures." Paul likewise said the psalm was fulfilled in Jesus (Acts 13:35).

28. Meditation on the last verse led Andrew Fuller to reject the hyper-Calvinist teaching that only the elect are called to repentance. Fuller recognized that every human being has a duty faith to "kiss the Son," thus launching the modern mission movement. Andrew Fuller, *The Gospel Worthy of All Acceptation* (1786), in Joseph Belcher, ed., *The Complete Works of the Rev. Andrew Fuller*, vol. 2 (Sprinkle, 1988), 328–32.

29. C. H. Spurgeon, *The Treasury of David*, 3 vols. (Hendrickson, [n.d.]), 1:324.

30. Daniel L. Akin, "The Person of Christ," in Daniel L. Akin, Bruce Riley Ashford, and Kenneth Keathley, eds., *A Theology for the Church*, rev. ed. (B&H Academic, 2014), 395.

31. Compare Psalm 22:7–8 with Mark 15:29ff; Psalm 22:16 with John 20:25; Psalm 22:28 with Matthew 27:35.

32. Spurgeon, *The Treasury of David*, 1:192.

Psalm 110 was cited most often in the New Testament. Jesus Christ asked the Jewish leaders to interpret it, but they were unable. Jesus provided the key: "David calls him 'Lord.' How, then, can [the Christ] be his son?" (Luke 20:44). The Lord's hermeneutic remained "enigmatic" to his initial auditors. Enlightened understanding came "only with Jesus' resurrection and with the disciples' faith in the risen Jesus."[33] Verse 1 of Psalm 110 requires Trinitarian Christological exegesis, for "the LORD," who is God, says to "my Lord," who is the Messiah: "Sit at my right hand until I make your enemies your footstool." Verse 4 grants this king an eternal priesthood, too. All anointed offices, therefore, end in the Messiah. The author of Hebrews found this significant for Christ's superior priesthood (Heb. 5:6; 7:15, 21). We find it significant for his deity.

David was promised that his descendent would be not only his son but the Son of God, and that this Promised One would reign without end. The royal psalms prophesy regarding the grant of universal dominion to the Messiah (Ps. 2), the death and the resurrection of the Messiah (Pss. 22; 16; cf. 69), and the personal divine reality of the Messiah (Ps. 110; cf. 45).

The Promise Through the Prophets

Various promises about the Messiah proclaimed by the Old Testament prophets point toward the Person and work of Jesus. These include, among other prophecies, that the Messiah will be an exalted child, bring a new covenant, suffer as a servant, and ascend in triumph.

The Promise of an Exalted Child: Two prophecies about the Messiah as a child were granted to Isaiah. The first was, "Therefore the Lord himself will give you a sign. Behold, the virgin shall conceive and bear a son, and shall call his name Immanuel" (Isa. 7:14 ESV). Much ink in the modern period was spilled over the Hebrew term *almah* for "virgin." Because a different Hebrew term, *betulah*, more clearly described a virgin, critical scholars biased against a supernatural interpretation argued it meant merely a young woman. But the Septuagint translated *almah* with the Greek *parthenos*,

33. David W. Pao and Eckhard J. Schnabel, "Luke," in G. K. Beale and D. A. Carson, eds., *Commentary on the New Testament Use of the Old Testament* (Baker Academic, 2007), 373.

which clearly specifies a virgin.[34] The child of Isaiah 7 receives a name suggesting he is more than merely human: "Immanuel" means "God with us." Matthew 1:23 applied this title to Jesus, indicating the presence of God in the presence of the child.

Isaiah 9 affirmed the Messiah would come as a child. Moreover, he will rule by divine right. The literal ascription of deity, eternality, authority, and fatherhood to the Messiah through his divine titles can only be explained through the full sharing of the Son with the Father in the divine nature. According to John, therefore, the Son is one with his Father (John 10:30; 16:15):

> For a child will be born for us, a son will be given to us, and the government will be on his shoulders. He will be named Wonderful Counselor, Mighty God, Eternal Father, Prince of Peace. The dominion will be vast, and its prosperity will never end. He will reign on the throne of David and over his kingdom, to establish and sustain it with justice and righteousness from now on and forever. The zeal of the LORD of Armies will accomplish this. (Isa. 9:6–7)

The Promise of a New Covenant: Next, the prophets turned their attention to the promise of a new covenant. Both Jeremiah and Ezekiel, rightly disappointed with Israel's constant and continuing failure to keep the old covenant, were granted promises that the Lord would bring in a new covenant. Jeremiah prophesied the new covenant would create an intimate relationship between God and the redeemed person, such that fidelity would become primary and human teaching secondary (Jer. 31:31–34a). Ezekiel prophesied the people will receive new hearts in the new covenant by a unique work of the Spirit of God (Ezek. 36:26–27). Ezekiel also prophesied the new covenant would endure, ensuring God's permanent presence (Ezek. 37:26–27).

The Promise of the Suffering Servant: The sixth promise we should note concerns the suffering of the Servant of God. Isaiah 52:13–53:12 is the last and the greatest of the servant songs. It

---

34. Some evangelical scholars affirm a double fulfillment: The child of Isaiah is born of a young woman, while the Messiah of Isaiah 9 will be born of a virgin. Craig L. Blomberg, "Matthew," in Beale and Carson, eds., *Commentary on the New Testament Use of the Old Testament*, 5.

indicates the humiliation of the Servant, his vicarious suffering for others, and his final triumph granted by God.[35]

The Promise of the Triumphant Son of Man: Finally, Daniel 7 describes the final triumph of the promised Messiah. It was cited numerous times in the New Testament as a self-reference by Jesus Christ (Matt. 16:27–28; 26:64; Mark 13:26; 14:62; Luke 21:27) and as an apostolic affirmation applied to Jesus (Acts 7:56; Rev. 1:6; 14:14).

Daniel 7:9–10 sets the scene for the full meaning of this son's triumph. "The Ancient of Days" refers to the eternal God on his glorious throne:

> As I kept watching, thrones were set in place, and the Ancient of Days took his seat. His clothing was white like snow, and the hair of his head like whitest wool. His throne was flaming fire; its wheels were blazing fire. A river of fire was flowing, coming out from his presence. Thousands upon thousands served him; ten thousand times ten thousand stood before him. The court was convened, and the books were opened.

After this, the "son of man" approached the Lord. Daniel's vision resumes a little later (vv. 13–14):

> I continued watching in the night visions, and suddenly one like a son of man was coming with the clouds of heaven. He approached the Ancient of Days and was escorted before him. He was given dominion and glory and a kingdom, so that those of every people, nation, and language should serve him. His dominion is an everlasting dominion that will not pass away, and his kingdom is one that will not be destroyed.

The One who approached the throne in Daniel 7 has the attributes of both humanity and deity. His humanity is emphasized by the term, "Son of Man." But this man is granted eternal rule and participates directly in the divine throne. Jesus, whose "favorite

35. We shall consider this passage in chapter 12.

self-designation" was "Son of Man,"[36] angered the High Priest by asserting that he would come "on the clouds of heaven." He thereby revealed that he is the promised divine-human Christ (Matt. 26:64).[37]

If taken individually and apart from the canon, these diverse prophetic promises are difficult to reconcile. Taken together and interpreted in the light of the New Testament, these prophecies of an exalted child, a new covenant, a suffering servant, and a triumphal son of man point to the One who is eternal God and messianic man, the One who died, arose, and ascended.

The Promise in the New Testament

The Greek noun *epangellion* indicates a promise guaranteed by an oath (cf. Acts 23:21). The verb *epangellomai*, in the middle voice, indicated the promise to man is fulfilled by virtue of God's own character.[38] The promise also precedes and encloses the law. According to Paul, the promise came first by centuries (Gal. 3:17). The promise, not the law, guaranteed God's people would receive an inheritance (v. 18). God's promise to the community of faith regarding Abraham's "seed" (Greek plural *spermasin*) focuses not on the community but on the Messiah promised to save the community. Christ is the "seed" (Greek singular *spermatid*; vv. 16, 29).

The New Testament repeatedly subordinates the law to Christ and refers salvation to faith in Christ. The only way a human being may appropriate the blessings of the promise is "on the basis of faith in Jesus Christ" (Gal. 3:22). All of God's promises find their agreement in Christ (2 Cor. 1:20). Christ is the Promise himself. That God requires faith guarantees salvation is by "grace" (Rom. 4:16). Faith alone is the determinant for becoming "coheirs of the same promise" (Heb. 11:9).

While the promise came through the seed of Abraham, its reception was never determined by genealogy. "That is, it is not the children by physical descent who are God's children, but the children of the promise are considered to be the offspring" (Rom. 9:8).

---

36. D. L. Bock, "Son of Man," in Joel B. Green, Jeannine K. Brown, and Nicholas Perrin, eds., *Dictionary of Jesus and the Gospels*, 2nd ed. (IVP Academic, 2013), 894.

37. Blomberg, "Matthew," 93–95.

38. Moisés Silva, *New International Dictionary of New Testament Theology and Exegesis*, 2nd ed., 5 vols. (Zondervan, 2014), 2:230–36.

The true "seed of Abraham" are those who have faith in Christ, those who "belong to Christ" (Gal. 3:29).

The promise comes through various instrumental covenants, specifically the covenant with Abraham, but also the covenant with David. However, the promise is finally located in "the new covenant" (Jer. 31:31–34; 33:14), fulfilled in Jesus Christ (Rom. 9). Christ memorialized his fulfillment of "the new covenant in my blood" through instituting the Supper for his church's observance (Luke 22:20; 1 Cor. 11:25).

The promise included the greatest gift of all. This gift is not the land as the means of life, nor the genealogy as the instrument for beginning life. Conception and land are real and necessary gifts for the generation and maintenance of human bodies and souls. However, the greatest gift is God himself. God regenerates and indwells his people in his Spirit, recreating us with new life (Hag. 2:5; 2 Cor. 3:6).

Peter said that false prophets may "promise freedom," but they are "slaves of corruption" (2 Pet. 2:19). God's people, created by his word of promise, must respond now in heartfelt obedience and worshipful praise.[39] Regarding the future, Peter said the Lord has not delayed his promise, but is "patient with you, not wanting any to perish but all to come to repentance" (2 Pet. 3:9). Our ultimate hope is "based on his promise," so "we wait for new heavens and a new earth, where righteousness dwells" (v. 13). God's goal is life with him, the blessed vision of the eternal Trinity.[40]

Finally, regarding the future fulfillment of the Messianic promise, note the names and actions ascribed to Jesus in John's Apocalypse. The Lamb, the eternal Son, crucified as a man but now risen, resides on the divine throne. As promised, he rules with the Father, is worshiped with the Father, and will be the final judge. With the Father and the Spirit, the promised Son makes three speeches in the end (cf. Rev. 1:12–20; 5:1–14; 7:17; 19:11–16; 21:22–23; 22:7, 12–16, 20.)

---

39. The Psalms teach believers to express their utter dependence upon and continual need for his promise (Ps. 119:50, 58, 123, 133, 148, 162, 170, 172).

40. "And this is the promise that he himself made to us: eternal life" (1 John 2:25).

God and Man

Hans Conzelmann argued in his commentary on Luke that Christ was regarded as "the middle of time."[41] Oscar Cullmann came to a similar position from his reading of John. When Christians speak of "a mid-point of time," we mean "the centre and climax which gives history a meaning." Cullmann argued Christ is not merely the temporal center but the meaningful climax. Christ orients the narrative of divine action and encompasses reality. "All revelation, all God's acting is disclosed from this mid-point. If the subject of this action at the decisive climax in history is the incarnate Lord, Jesus of Nazareth, if in him God has revealed his inmost essence, his *doxa* (John 1:14), then *he* must be the vehicle of all God's acting in relation to the world."[42]

To say that Christ Jesus is the center of history prompts us to recognize that several ontological claims derive from Scripture's narrative of redemption history: Jesus Christ is God the Son, begotten of the Father, in eternal undiminished communion with the Father and the Spirit. He is the revelation of God and "the link between the Old Testament and the New."[43] He brought into temporal reality the eternal promise of redemption and thus occupies the center of history, between creation and consummation. He is also the climax who brings meaning to all creation, because he is Lord over history and entered history to redeem it. As we saw in chapter 6, while Christ enters and thereby centers history, he also begins it and ends it.

The Double Hermeneutic

Jesus Christ himself is the ultimate Promise of God for us. But who is Jesus Christ, and what is he doing? Scripture provides a plenitude of witness to Christ in his Person and work. How do we wrap our minds around the greatest person and greatest actions in human history? Though difficult, it becomes possible only in worship. As we approach the Person of Jesus Christ, we must remember

41. Hans Conzelmann, *The Theology of St. Luke* (Fortress Press, 1982). The book's German title was *Die Mitte Der Zeit.*

42. Oscar Cullmann, *Salvation in History* (Harper and Row, 1967), 270.

43. Sidney Greidanus, *Preaching Christ from the Old Testament: A Contemporary Hermeneutical Method* (Eerdmans, 1999), 49.

the Bible reveals both his humanity and his deity. Orthodox scholars have thus learned to use a "double hermeneutic" or "personal exegesis," for this method alone makes sense of Scripture's manifold witness to Christ as Savior.

Paul revealed the twofold identity of the Promise in the most significant statement of his first pastoral epistle, bringing together his Person with his work: "There is one God, and one mediator between God and men, the man Christ Jesus; Who gave himself a ransom for all" (1 Tim. 2:5–6a KJV). "Here, then, is the double uniqueness of Jesus Christ, which qualifies him to be the only mediator. First there is the uniqueness of his divine–human person, and secondly the uniqueness of his substitutionary, redeeming death."[44] In Christ alone could God and men be reconciled, for he alone is God and man, and by his vicarious death alone are we reconciled.

You may remember that Athanasius of Alexandria was the greatest defender of Christian orthodoxy against the deception of the greatest heresy, Arianism.[45] Athanasius found it was beneficial to define the *skopos*, "scope" or "theme," of the biblical narrative. By this, he meant the double hermeneutic. Athanasius simultaneously affirmed the unity of Jesus Christ, God the Word, yet maintained the distinction of his two natures.[46]

This dually directed hermeneutic has its roots in the Old Testament promises. Anthony Thiselton identified "two different streams of hope" among the Jews. The "prophetic" stream hoped for a human Messiah endowed with the Spirit to save the people. The "apocalyptic" stream hoped God himself would intervene directly in history. Both streams of hope—for God to save his people and for a man to bring that salvation—were fulfilled in Jesus Christ.[47]

Having surveyed the promise of the Savior in the Old Testament, the fulfillment of that promise in the person of Jesus Christ in the New Testament, and the Christological implications of

---

44. John R. W. Stott, *Guard the Truth: The Message of 1 Timothy & Titus*, The Bible Speaks Today (InterVarsity Press, 1996), 71.

45. See chapter 4 above.

46. "You must understand, therefore, that when writers on this sacred theme speak of Him as eating and drinking and being born, they mean that the body, as a body, was born and sustained with the food proper to its nature; while God the Word, who was united with it, was at the same time ordering the universe and revealing Himself, through His bodily acts as not man only but God." Athanasius, *On the Incarnation* (St. Vladimir's Seminary Press, 2012), 46.

47. Anthony C. Thiselton, *Systematic Theology* (Eerdmans, 2020), 232–36.

his fulfillment of the divine promise, let us consider other important biblical teachings which assure us that Jesus saves.

God and Savior

The exalted titles *Soter* (Greek "Savior") and *Theos* (Greek "God") were well known in the ancient world. Among the Greeks, rescuers like Hercules and healers like Asclepius received the designation of *Soter*.[48] Adopting the pagan traditions of the royal cult from the Egyptians, Persians, and Greeks, the Romans named their emperors, "Savior God" (Greek, *Soter Theos*).[49] Rome periodically demanded everyone offer sacrifices in the imperial cult.

However, in the Greek translation of the Old Testament, *Soter* was reserved for the *Theos* of Israel.[50] When earthly preservation came to Israel, "Yahweh himself was the ultimate source of these deliverances."[51] Isaiah said, "there is no other God" than "God of Israel, Savior" (Isa. 45:14–15). He alone creates and provides "everlasting salvation" (vv. 17–18). The Lord says, "There is no other God but me, a righteous God and Savior" (v. 21). Zechariah said the coming Messianic king alone "has salvation" (Zech. 9:9 ESV).[52]

In the Synoptic Gospels, Luke's infancy narrative ascribes the title and the work of salvation equally to God and to Jesus (Luke 1:47, 69, 71, 77; cf. 2:30). An angel then announced Christ's identity through his major titles, "Today in the city of David a Savior was born for you, who is the Messiah, the Lord" (2:11). The angelic proclamation revealed both his deity ("Lord," "Savior") and his humanity ("Messiah," "born for you"). Echoing the Old Testament, the human name, "Jesus," was given to him, "because he will save his people

48. On the pagan heavenly hierarchies in which these heroes were located, see Michael F. Bird, *Jesus Among the Gods: Early Christology in the Graeco-Roman World* (Baylor University Press, 2022), 13–16. On Asclepius, see Catherine Nixey, *Heresy: Jesus Christ and the Other Sons of God* (London: Picador, 2024), 42–43.

49. A. T. Robertson, *Word Pictures in the New Testament*, 5 vols. (Broadman, 1931), 4:560.

50. Except for the rare assignment to a divine agent.

51. Moisés Silva, *New International Dictionary of New Testament Theology and Exegesis*, 2nd ed., 5 vols. (Zondervan, 2014), 4:425.

52. The names Joshua and Isaiah meant, "Yahweh is salvation," while Hoshea means, "Yahweh has saved." Silva, *New International Dictionary of New Testament Theology and Exegesis*, 4:424.

from their sins" (Matt. 1:21).[53] The Synoptic Gospels indicate the divine salvation wrought by Jesus encompasses both physical healing and preservation from death (e.g., Matt. 8:25; Mark 10:52).

Early in his ministry, the apostle Peter assigned eternal saving authority exclusively to Christ, thereby making "an absolute and universal claim for the Christian message of salvation."[54] In his second epistle, Peter repeatedly granted Jesus the titles, *Kyrios* ("Lord") and *Soter*, thereby reaffirming Christ's absolute divine authority and work of divine salvation (2 Pet. 1:11; 2:20; 3:2, 18). Peter also gave Christ the ontological title, *Theos* ("God;" 2 Pet. 1:1). Peter's reference to the church's location in "Babylon" alluded to and condemned the Roman emperor's pretensions (1 Pet. 5:13).

The apostle Paul ascribed the title *Soter* numerous times to God (1 Tim. 1:1; 2:3; 4:10; Titus 1:3; 2:10; 3:4). God the Father offers universal salvation in the gospel of Jesus Christ. He is "God our Savior, who wants everyone to be saved and to come to the knowledge of the truth" in Christ (1 Tim. 2:3b–4). Like Peter, Paul also applied the exclusively divine title of *Soter* to the Son of God, Jesus Christ (Phil. 3:20; Eph. 5:23; 2 Tim. 1:10; Titus 1:4; 2:13; 3:6).

In the book of Hebrews, the work of saving the people of God is ascribed to Christ. As the eternal High Priest, he is "the source of eternal salvation for all who obey him" (Heb. 5:9). He is "able to save completely those who come to God through him" (7:25; cf. 2:10). He will "bring salvation to those who are waiting for him" (9:28).

The New Testament applied the title of *Soter* only to God and to Christ. When Rome began persecuting believers who would not receive the emperor's "gospel" or offer sacrifices to him, Christians suffered horribly. The three angels of Revelation 14 delivered three messages to these early believers in their intense peril: The empire's false gospel faces temporal judgment, while Christ offers "the eternal gospel." "Babylon," an alias for Rome, will be destroyed. And God will judge those who heed the propaganda of the false prophet and worship the beast (Rev. 14:6–12).[55] The true Savior, who brings his followers through every earthly danger, therefore, deserves our eternal praise (7:10; 12:10; 19:1).

---

53. This virgin-born child was also given the title *Immanuel* ("God is with us"), with its divine and human allusions (Matt. 1:23; cf. Isa. 7:14).

54. Acts 4:12. Silva, *New International Dictionary of New Testament Theology and Exegesis*, 4:430.

55. Bird, *Jesus Among the Gods*, 17–21, 54–59; Nixey, *Heresy*, 226–27.

The church has called sinners to turn to the Lord Jesus Christ in faith by confessing he alone is *Soter Theos*. Christ is our willing Savior, just as he is our only God. Based on Christ's saving work, the greatest Baptist preacher of the early twentieth century, George W. Truett, asked, "If Jesus is God, what are you going to do with him? What are you going to do with Him?" He then provided the answer for the hungry soul who seeks spiritual nourishment. "Accept Him, friend, as your Saviour and the Redeemer of your lost soul! Accept him now and confess him in this host of His friends." The person who will confess Christ as God and Savior receives communion with the Master. "God help you to accept and confess Christ now."[56]

The Proclamation

The Greek term *kerygma* simply means, "proclamation" or "preaching."[57] In its full theological sense, the New Testament *kerygma* indicates, "the apostolic proclamation of salvation through Jesus Christ." This theological meaning derives from its contextual uses as an analysis of the relevant passages will show. The relevant word group derives from the noun *kerux*, "herald," which is Indo-European at root. Among the ancient Greek city states, a herald was sent out with a message from a political authority. The herald possessed certain characteristics, including that he operated under a higher authority rather than under his own authority. He was a mere conveyor of a message and possessed no power to negotiate the content of that message. His very act of proclamation made his message immediately valid to the hearer. Finally, the herald was distinguished over against a mere messenger in that his message was "binding, commanding, and settling."[58]

In the Septuagint, the verb *kerusso*, "to call" or "to proclaim," was used in one of four ways. The proclamation might launch a religious festival or constitute a military call to arms. It could also be a prophetic announcement of either judgment on the one hand or of

56. George W. Truett, *Who Is Jesus?*, ed. Powhatan W. James (Eerdmans, 1952), 23.

57. Silva, *New International Dictionary of New Testament Theology and Exegesis*, 2:674.

58. Silva, *New International Dictionary of New Testament Theology and Exegesis*, 2:675.

liberty to captives on the other hand. In their reviews of the biblical concept, various scholars focused on different aspects of the New Testament use. Some emphasized the propositional content of the proclamation; others dwelt on the personal encounter of faith that preaching engendered.

C. H. Dodd famously emphasized the propositional content of the apostolic preaching,[59] while Rudolf Bultmann dwelt upon the listener's personal experience or existential encounter with God through the proclamation of Christ, which confronts the listener and demands a decision immediately.[60] Dodd pointed to the facts of the apostles' proclamation; Bultmann warned against abstractions and called for personal response. The latter wrote, "Faith can be only the affirmation of God's action upon us, the answer to his Word directed to us."[61] In response, many evangelicals concluded the apostolic proclamation contains both personal and propositional aspects.[62]

In the New Testament, the descriptive noun *kerux*, "herald," is used three times; the active noun *kerygma*, nine times. However, the verb *kerusso* is used sixty-one times. The verb is most often completed with *evangelion*, "gospel," as the object, but "Christ" and "kingdom" also served as the object. The word group is used most often by Paul and the Synoptic evangelists. As in secular usage, the act and content of the proclamation surpass the herald in importance.[63]

The apostle Paul affirmed both the personal activity and the propositional content of the term. In 1 Corinthians 15, Paul outlined the propositional content of the apostolic proclamation, centering on Christ's death and burial, followed by his resurrection and appearances (vv. 3–11). In Galatians 1, he emphasized personal reception of the gospel: "I did not receive it from a human source . . . , but it came by a revelation of Jesus Christ" (v. 12). Christ in turn called Paul, "so that I could preach him among the Gentiles" (v. 16). The proclamation of the propositional content of the gospel

59. C. H. Dodd, *The Apostolic Preaching and Its Developments: Three Lectures with an Appendix on Eschatology and History*, rev. ed. (Hodder and Stoughton, 1963).

60. Rudolf Bultmann, *Jesus and the Word*, transl. Louise Pettibone Smith and Erminie Huntress Lantero (Scribner, 1958), 28–33.

61. Rudolf Bultmann, *Faith and Understanding I*, ed. Robert W. Funk, transl. Louise Pettibone Smith (Harper & Row, 1969), 63.

62. Dockery and Yarnell, *Special Revelation and Scripture*, 30–35.

63. Silva, *New International Dictionary of New Testament Theology and Exegesis*, 2:676–77.

prompted personal faith then further gospel proclamation—the personal and the propositional are mutually reinforcing.

A threefold pattern characterizes Paul's use of the *kerygma*. First, he sometimes emphasized the propositional content of the gospel being proclaimed (Rom. 1:1–4; 1 Tim. 2:5–7; 2 Tim. 4:1). Second, he could highlight how proclamation engendered personal reception (1 Tim. 3:16; 2 Tim. 4:2). Third, Paul intertwined the content of the gospel with its existential engagement: "This is the message of faith that we proclaim: If you confess with your mouth, "Jesus is Lord," and believe in your heart that God raised him from the dead, you will be saved. One believes with the heart, resulting in righteousness, and one confesses with the mouth, resulting in salvation" (Rom. 10:8b–10).

In Acts 2:14–39, Luke provided an account of the first kerygmatic proclamation, which was delivered by the apostle Peter. Peter began by noting God's current work in their midst (vv. 14–15). He then proclaimed the good news about Jesus through a Trinitarian exegesis of the Old Testament promises regarding Christ. First, the Holy Spirit verified Jesus is the Messiah by making prophecy promiscuous (Joel 2:28–32; Acts 2:16–21). Second, the messianic prophecies of David were fulfilled in Jesus's resurrection from the dead, in his exaltation to the right hand of the Father, and in his giving the Spirit (Ps. 16:8–11; Acts 2:22–33). Third, Jesus has been declared Lord by the Father's own oral proclamation (Ps. 110:1; Acts 2:34–36). Peter's inaugural proclamation of the gospel ended with a personal invitation to his audience to repent of sin and receive both forgiveness in the name of Jesus and the baptism of the Spirit (Acts 2:37–39).

In his own systematic exegesis, C. H. Dodd summarized the content of Peter's kerygmatic proclamation with a six-part statement. Dodd then offered a sevenfold summary of the content of Paul's kerygmatic proclamation. While the two apostles proclaimed the gospel with distinct styles, they shared a common understanding. Peter preferred a holistic presentation that centered on the death and resurrection of Jesus Christ, while Paul accentuated his death and resurrection. According to Dodd, their preaching was "identical in purport" with that of Jesus.[64] The table below collates Dodd's findings.

64. Dodd, *The Apostolic Preaching and Its Developments*, 24.

The Kerygma of Peter	The Kerygma of Paul
The age of fulfillment has dawned . . . This has taken place through the ministry, death, and resurrection of Jesus . . . By virtue of the resurrection, Jesus has been exalted at the right hand of God . . . The Holy Spirit in the church is the sign of Christ's present power and glory . . . The Messianic Age will shortly reach its consummation in the return of Christ . . . Finally, the kerygma always closes with an appeal for repentance, the offer of forgiveness and of the Holy Spirit, and the promise of "salvation," that is, of "the life of the Age to Come," to those who enter the elect community.[65]	The prophecies are fulfilled, and the new age is inaugurated by the coming of Christ. He was born of the seed of David. He died according to the Scripture, to deliver us out of the present evil age. He was buried. He rose on the third day according to the Scriptures. He is exalted at the right hand of God, as Son of God and Lord of quick [the living] and dead. He will come again as Judge and Saviour of men.[66]

Table 2: The Proclamation of the Apostles

The Gospel

We may now review select New Testament passages concerning the *evangelion*, "gospel" or "good news," of Jesus Christ. The propositional definition, proclamation, and personal reception of the gospel mirror our discoveries of the *kerygma*. First, however, some recent theological conversations demonstrate why we must recall the meaning of the gospel.

65. Dodd, *The Apostolic Preaching and Its Developments*, 21–23.
66. Dodd, *The Apostolic Preaching and Its Developments*, 17.

Contemporary Debates

Many cite the "gospel," although some ideas they attach to it seem tangential. Biblical, systematic, and pastoral theologians regularly affirm the centrality of the gospel,[67] but controversy can erupt. Biblical theologians like Matthew Bates and Scot McKnight have expressed concern about contemporary "superficiality."[68] They criticized some systematic theologians, detecting a shift in the discussion from the biblically oriented gospel of "the Kingdom of God" to an historically orientated "justification by faith." Bates and McKnight correctly remind us that *evangelion* includes vital faith in the King of the Kingdom, Jesus Christ.[69] However, we should also affirm that gospel allegiance begins with justifying faith.[70]

Justification and sanctification issue from the gospel, but personal justification necessarily precedes the good works that evince personal sanctification. However, it also remains true that unrepentant sinfulness may contradict external claims to personal justification. Moreover, the good works of faithful Christians may vary contextually according to diverse personal convictions and the multitude of social needs. Finally, it must not be forgotten that the one good work required of all evangelical Christians is evangelism.[71] Personal sharing of the gospel should remain a constant concern even while we engage in good works.[72]

---

67. E.g., Michael F. Bird, *What Christians Ought to Believe: An Introduction to Christian Doctrine through the Apostles' Creed* (Zondervan, 2016); J. D. Greear, *Gospel: Recovering the Power that Made Christianity Revolutionary* (B&H, 2011); Malcolm Yarnell, "The Gospel of Jesus Christ," Southwestern Seminary Chapel Video Recording, April 2013, https://swbts.edu/news/podcast/dr-malcolm-yarnell-the-gospel-of-jesus-christ-2/.

68. Scot McKnight, "Foreword," in Matthew W. Bates, *Salvation by Allegiance Alone: Rethinking Faith, Works, and the Gospel of Jesus the King* (Baker Academic, 2017), xii.

69. Bates, *Salvation by Allegiance Alone;* idem, *The Gospel Precisely: Surprisingly Good News about Jesus Christ the King* (Renew, 2021).

70. Malcolm B. Yarnell III, "Christian Justification: A Reformation Baptist View," *Criswell Theological Review,* new series, 2.2 (2005): 82–83.

71. Stott correlated the evangel and evangelism with evangelicalism: "In seeking to define what it means to be evangelical it is inevitable that we begin with the gospel. For both our theology (evangelicalism) and our activity (evangelism) derive their meaning and their importance from the good news (the evangel)." Stott, *Evangelical Truth,* 11.

72. Malcolm B. Yarnell III, "The Social Theology and Political Theology of James Leo Garrett Jr.," *Southwestern Journal of Theology* 65.1 (2022): 61–78.

Greek Terms

The Greek noun *evangelion* may be translated as "good news" or, in archaic English, "gospel." The noun and its cognates were rare in classical Greek but became more popular during the era of the early church. Among pagans, *evangelion* indicated a proclamation of good news about the emperor. Prominent in the Psalms and Isaiah in the Septuagint, the verb *evangelizo*, "to bring news" or "to announce," was identified with the proclamation of Yahweh's victory over the world. Among the rabbis, the term designated the Messiah or his forerunner.[73]

The word group became very common in the New Testament. The noun *evangelion* could serve as the object of either of the verbs *evangelizo* or *kerusso*. The verb dominated the writings of Luke, while Matthew and Mark preferred the noun. Paul used both the noun and the verb, while John used neither but preferred *martureo*, "witness." Peter and Paul treated *evangelion* as both settled yet dynamic. "Its message of Jesus Christ—risen from the dead and descended from David—is not limited to a single, past event, but is experienced as a word charged with power in the present so that it cannot be fettered by human chains."[74]

Significant Gospel Texts

Mark places the "gospel" of Jesus Christ front and center in his own "Gospel." "Now after John had been taken into custody, Jesus came into Galilee, preaching the gospel of God, and saying, 'The time is fulfilled, and the kingdom of God is at hand; repent and believe in the gospel'" (Mark 1:14–15 NASB1995; cf. Matt. 12:28). From this seminal dominical text, we see the gospel was not merely proclaimed by Jesus but personally appeared in Jesus. The gospel was promised in the Old Testament, was concerned with God's rule, and must be proclaimed. The gospel's impact is both certain and imminent but requires repentance and faith.

In perhaps his earliest epistle, Paul confronted preachers who were perverting the gospel of Jesus Christ. "I am amazed that you

73. Silva, *New International Dictionary of New Testament Theology and Exegesis*, 2:306–308.

74. Silva, *New International Dictionary of New Testament Theology and Exegesis*, 2:311.

are so quickly deserting Him who called you by the grace of Christ, for a different gospel; which is really not another; only there are some who are disturbing you and want to distort the gospel of Christ" (Gal. 1:6–7 NASB1995). He argued that believers should be careful to present the gospel just as it had been delivered to them by the apostles. Being a divine gift, human doctrines or works must not be added to it (v. 10). The apostle deemed those who "distort" the gospel "accursed" or "anathematized" (vv. 8–9 NASB1995).

Later, opening his magisterial epistle to the Romans, the apostle declared he was called and set apart for "the gospel of God" (Rom. 1:1). He then provided a list of his gospel's characteristics: It was promised beforehand in the Hebrew Bible. It is focused upon the Son of God (vv. 2–3), who is, on the one hand, the Son of David "according to the flesh." On the other hand, he was "declared" the Son of God in power "according to the Spirit of holiness" (vv. 3–4). Christ's resurrection from the dead verified his gospel and that he is "our Lord" (v. 4 ESV). The church has been called to take the grace of this gospel to "all the nations" (v. 5 ESV).

In his thesis statement for Romans, Paul showed the gospel must not only be propositionally conceived but personally received. Human personal reception involves both the mind and the will. Gospel proclamation is a matter of both "obligation" and passion for the apostle. It was certainly not a cause for shame (vv. 14–15). The gospel "is the power of God for salvation" to those who believe it (v. 16), and in it the righteousness of God is revealed "from faith to faith" (v. 17). The last phrase likely indicates the Word in which the preacher has faith is revealed through proclamation so that it might become the faith of the hearer (cf. Rom. 10:9–10).[75] The gospel, when received in faith, brings justification and life (Rom. 1:17).

Later in the same epistle, Paul made it clear that while the gospel must be received by human faith, its active agent is always God. When the gospel is preached, the Word of God engages the hearer, coming "near" the heart and the tongue (Rom. 10:8–9). For salvation to occur, the gospel must be both believed and confessed. Confessing to God the primal truth of salvation occurs in the human heart as

75. Cranfield lists twelve positions taken by interpreters and opts for the meaning of *sola fide*, "by faith alone." The majority interpretation seems to be "from the faith of God proceeding to the faith of man believing." C. E. B. Cranfield, *A Critical and Exegetical Commentary on the Epistle to the Romans*, vol. 1, International Critical Commentary (T&T Clark, 1975), 99–100; 99n.

well as through the human tongue (v. 10). True confession cannot be voiced apart from the dynamic activity of both the divine Word (Rom. 10:17) and the divine Holy Spirit (1 Cor. 12:3).

In 1 Corinthians 15, Paul provided a contextual frame and propositional structure for the gospel, achieving clarity in definition. The gospel was prophesied in Scripture (v. 3). It was delivered to Paul, then received by him. He then delivered it to others, requiring from them deep belief for salvation (vv. 1–2, 9). The gospel is composed of two major facts: Christ died for our sins, and Christ rose from death (vv. 3–4). The burial of Christ verified his death, while his multiple appearances verified his resurrection (vv. 3, 5–8). Finally, as a divine gift, the believer receives both faith and standing with God through the gospel (vv. 2, 10).

As a general New Testament rule, the *evangelion* which must be believed and confessed concerns both the personal identity of Christ and the redemptive work of Christ. One must voice the saving confession that "Jesus is Lord" (Rom. 10:9–10; 1 Cor. 12:3). This entails faith in the hypostatic union—that the eternal Son became a human being, and that this man remains the Lord God. Confessing that the Person of Jesus Christ is God come in the flesh is the fundamental saving confession (Matt. 16:17–19). If one is going to say truly that "Jesus is Lord," this also means he must become one's personal master. "Lord" is not merely a divine title; it is likewise an eternal divine claim upon absolute human fidelity (Luke 6:46–49).

Moreover, not only must the believer confess faith in the one Person of the Son, who is truly divine in nature and truly human in nature. The true believer must also confess faith in the death and the resurrection of the Son (Rom. 10:10). That God raised Jesus from the dead may not be entirely understood by the new hearer of the gospel, but this startling and transformative claim must be personally believed (cf. Matt. 16:21–23). If the gospel of Jesus Christ is heard, believed, and confessed, salvation exists (Rom. 10:13, 17). This gospel includes affirmation of Christ as truly divine and truly human and of Christ as having died and arisen from death. If the gospel is not believed, only judgment can be expected (vv. 20–21).

We have focused upon the personal and the historical dimensions of the gospel. As mentioned above, the apostle John added a significant detail. In Revelation 14:6–7, the gospel is said to be "eternal" (Greek *aionion*). As such, it participates in the reality of God. It may be proclaimed by angels as well as by men, and it must be proclaimed to all the nations. This eternal gospel calls human beings to fear God and remain intent upon his glory. The gospel is eternal, moreover, because it includes a reminder of the coming judgment, which has permanent consequences. As eternal, the gospel must end in the worship of God, who is himself eternal.

Conclusion: A Systematic Summary of the Gospel

Martin Luther, who studied the gospel intensively, said the church's primary responsibility is spreading the gospel through proclamation. The gospel "is not in truth that which is written in books and set down in letters, but rather a spoken message and living word, and a voice which sounds out into the world and is publicly proclaimed, that it may be heard everywhere."[76] While I agree with Luther's warning against mere academic discourse and heartily affirm his stress on oral preaching, we may also communicate the gospel in writing. The apostles and Luther himself disseminated the good news in both ways.

Following the detailed survey of Scripture just made, I believe the New Testament doctrine of the good news of our Savior should be summarized as follows:

1. The gospel includes the truth about both Christ's person and his work: Jesus is the Lord God incarnate, the promised Messiah who brings God's Kingdom.
2. For our salvation, Jesus died on the cross and was buried.
3. For our justification, he arose from the dead and was seen by many. By his life, death, and resurrection, Jesus recapitulated humanity itself.
4. Jesus Christ ascended to the right hand of the Father, where he now intercedes for his

76. Martin Luther, *Weimarer Ausgabe*, 12:259, cited in U. Becker, "Gospel, Evangelize, Evangelist," in Colin Brown, ed., *The New International Dictionary of New Testament Theology*, vol. 2 (Zondervan, 1976), 114.

followers and will soon return to judge the living and the dead.

5. The church must call upon all human beings to respond in repentance toward and faith in the man Christ Jesus as the one Lord God if they would be saved.
6. Saving faith, which comes through the verbal proclamation of the Word and by the internal grace of the Holy Spirit, requires both faith and confession.
7. The gospel was so prominent in the preaching of the Lord and his apostles, and its eternal consequences are so critical, that we can only conclude every Christian proclamation must highlight the gospel.

Who will save us from these bodies of death? As we noted at the beginning, the apostle Paul said salvation comes through nobody other than "Jesus Christ our Lord" (Rom. 7:24–25). The apostle Peter agreed: "And there is salvation in no one else; for there is no other name under heaven that has been given among men by which we must be saved" (Acts 4:12 NASB1995). The apostle John completed the apostolic chorus by reciting the words of Jesus Christ, who said, "I am the way, and the truth, and the life; no one comes to the Father but through Me" (John 14:6 NASB1995).

Our only Savior is God in Christ, the eternal Word. Jesus is the Son of God who became the promised Son of David through his incarnation so that he could save those who trust in his gospel and confess him as Lord. In the next chapter, we shall have more to say about the entire economy of Jesus Christ, whose work centered in his atoning death and justifying resurrection.

Study Questions

1. How would you describe in a holistic way Christ's Person and work as our Savior?

2. How would you summarize a whole-Bible view of God's promise? Describe the historical progress of his revelation of the promise.

3. What do you believe are the necessary components in a biblical definition of the gospel of Jesus Christ and its apostolic proclamation?

Suggested Resources

- C. H. Dodd, *The Apostolic Preaching and Its Developments*
- John Fawcett, *Christ Precious to Those That Believe*
- John Stott, *Evangelical Truth*

CHAPTER ELEVEN

What Is the Work of the Word?

◆ ◆

God in the incarnate Lord Jesus Christ acts to save us from the consequences of our sin. By his Spirit he brings those who believe in his resurrection and confess him as Lord into a right relationship with him. This was the burden of the last lecture. But exactly how did Jesus work our salvation, especially when he was on the cross? Although his death and resurrection constitute the key act in the Christian faith, what are his other works? If he is truly divine and truly human, does he continue to act as God even after he became man? This chapter examines the work of the Word to answer such questions.

To understand the work of the incarnate Lord in its fullness, we must consider four major truths: First, we must examine the truth that the one Christ continues to act as God even as he became man. Second, we must consider the work of Christ as the One Mediator according to his threefold office of Prophet, Priest, and King. Third, because it constitutes the critical center of the Bible's message about God's work to grant us salvation, we must examine what Scripture says about the atoning work of Christ upon the cross. Fourth, we must consider how Christ saves us in his resurrection, ascension, heavenly session, return, judgment, and eternal reign. The first two questions are explored in this chapter, while the remaining chapters of this book focus on the other truths about the work of Christ.

The Word Acts as God and as Man

Orthodox Christians believe that Christ is truly divine and truly human, indeed the perfect Man. He is one Person, who carries the names of "Jesus" and "Messiah" in his humanity and the name "the Son of the living God" in his deity. These profound truths were revealed by the Father to the apostle Peter. Peter was truly "blessed" to be the first human being to voice the primal Christian confession (Matt. 16:13, 16–17). The one Person, Jesus Christ, is God and Man.

Not only is the one Person, Jesus Christ, truly God and truly Man. He acts from both his divine nature and his human nature. Indeed, he is the only Person in existence who can act in both ways, for he is the only divine Person who assumed human nature. The actions of the one Christ, therefore, stem from his eternal deity and from his assumed humanity. Indeed, his work as the Mediator of salvation depends upon his ability to act both as God and as man: Being God, Christ is the giver of life (John 1:4; 5:21, 26); being Man, he suffered death to bring us life (Isa. 53:5; 1 Pet. 2:24). He has two natures, and each nature is active in and through his Person.

Even as Christ acts from both natures, his deeds remain the work of one Person. The one Person Jesus Christ acts as God and acts as man. The term *theandric* [Greek "divine–human"] has been used to describe the work of the incarnate Word as a work both divine and human.[1] Thomas Aquinas provided an example of how the created humanity of Christ became the instrument by which the eternal Word performs our human salvation. "For example, touching a leper was an action of his humanity, but it came from the power

1. "By virtue of being God-made-man he accomplished something new in our midst—the activity of the God–man." Fourth Letter of Dionysius to Gaius, translated in David Coffey, "The Theandric Nature of Christ," *Theological Studies* 60 (1999): 407. John of Damascus interpreted Dionysius in a twofold sense: "The theandric activity therefore means this: that when God was made man, that is to say, when he became a human being, his human activity was divine, that is to say, was deified and was not without a share in his divine activity, and his divine activity was not without a share in his human activity, but each is contemplated along with the other." John of Damascus, *On the Orthodox Faith: A New Translation of An Exact Exposition of the Orthodox Faith*, ed. Norman Russell (St. Vladimir's Seminary Press, 2022), 217.

of his divinity that the touch cured the leper of leprosy. And all his human actions and sufferings were in this way salutary by the power of his divinity."[2]

As we turn our attention to the work of Christ, let us recall first that Christ is God and thus acts as God. Second, we will consider his assumption of human nature in the incarnation. Third, we will look at his activity as man, for he is truly human and acts in human ways. Fourth, we must recognize that all his actions are the work of one Person. This last point requires us to address the communion of his divine attributes and his human attributes in his one Person.

Christ Is God and Acts as God

The "formative" confession of the English Baptists properly affirmed the true deity of the second Person of the divine Trinity.[3] First, they confessed the unity of God, saying the three Persons are "every one of them one and the same God, and therefore not divided." Second, they confessed the eternal relations of origin, saying the Persons are "distinguished from one another by their several properties; the Father being from himself, the Sonne of the Father from everlasting, the holy Spirit proceeding from the Father and the Sonne."[4]

Christ acts as God because he participates in all the inseparable operations of God the Trinity. The English Baptists, therefore, confessed the Son of God "made the world" in the beginning, with the Father and with the Spirit.[5] Second, the Son "upholds and governes all the workes hee hath made."[6] In other words, the Son of God, who is truly God in his eternal possession of every divine attribute,[7] participates in every divine work. Jesus Christ is the Creator, Sustainer, and Lord of all, for he is truly one God with the Father and the Spirit.

2. Thomas Aquinas, *Compendium of Theology*, transl. Richard J. Regan (Oxford University Press, 2009), 164.

3. This confession, the *First London Confession* of 1644, was drawn up by seven churches which later became known as Particular Baptists. William L. Lumpkin and Bill J. Leonard, eds., *Baptist Confessions of Faith*, 2nd rev. ed. (Judson Press, 2011), 140.

4. *First London Confession*, art. II.

5. *First London Confession*, art. IX.

6. *First London Confession*, art. IX.

7. *First London Confession*, arts. I-II.

It is rash to believe in anything other than the true and full deity of the Son. The Son's deity entails his unqualified possession of all the divine attributes, including aseity, immutability, and eternality, as well as all his unqualified exercise of divine sovereignty, which includes his Lordship over every power and authority. The Christological formula adopted at the fourth ecumenical council, and received by theologians in most Christian communions, states this truth elegantly: "at no point was the difference between the natures taken away through the union, but rather the property of both natures is preserved and comes together into a single person and single subsistent being."[8]

From creation through preservation to the incarnation through the final consummation, Christ participates entirely in every divine act by virtue of his personal possession of the divine nature. Speaking to his divine nature, Paul affirmed the "fullness" of Christ's deity, and that his divine fullness dwelt in him "bodily" (Col. 2:9). John the apostle confessed the human Jesus alone received the Holy Spirit completely (John 3:34). Speaking to his divine acts, John the Baptist confessed Christ both gives the Holy Spirit and exercises final judgment (Matt. 3:11–12). These are actions which only one who is truly or fully the sovereign God may do.[9] Christ acts as God, because he is God.

Reinforcing this claim, the New Testament theologian Leon Morris noted Paul assigned "functions indifferently to God and to Christ." That which God the Father does, so does God the Son:

> Thus, he refers to the kingdom of God and the kingdom of Christ; it is the kingdom of both in Ephesians 5:5. The day of God in the Old Testament becomes 'the day of our Lord Jesus Christ.' He speaks of the grace of God and the grace of Christ, 'the gospel of God' and 'the gospel of Christ,' 'the church of God' and 'the churches of Christ,' 'the Spirit of God' and 'the Spirit of Christ,' the peace of God and the peace of Christ,

---

8. Council of Chalcedon, in Norman P. Tanner, ed., *Decrees of the Ecumenical Councils*, 2 vols. (Sheed and Ward, 1990), 1:*86.

9. The modifier "true" or "truly" includes the concept of fullness, but "full" or "fully" helpfully preempts Kenoticism, the gross modern error which quantifies then reduces the deity of Christ. "He is the One Mediator, fully God, fully man." *The Baptist Faith and Message*, art. II.B. See chapter 12 below.

> the judgment seat of God and the judgment seat of Christ.[10]

One major implication of his deity is that Christ remained truly God when he became truly man. Christ remained and acted as God, even upon the cross and in the tomb. Christ is the eternal Word come in flesh. The Word did not lose his divine nature, nor suspend his divine attributes, nor cease acting as God, even as he assumed our human nature. The greatest paradox of all is the *mysterium Christi*, "the mystery of Christ." This mystery, which may never be comprehended in its nature, confesses that the One who is God also became a man, and that he remains God as he does so.[11] Those seeking to make sense of the mystery of Christ are sometimes tempted to reduce the reality or operations of his deity. Alas, limiting Christ's divine will, divine authority, or divine activity constitutes a major error.

Christ said God's acts are his acts. "Truly, truly, I say to you, the Son can do nothing of Himself, unless it is something He sees the Father doing; for whatever the Father does, these things the Son also does in like manner" (John 5:19 NASB1995). John Chrysostom understood this is "the assertion of One declaring an Equality and entire agreement."[12] The adverb *homoios*, "likewise" or "in the same way," makes the acts of the Father and the Son coextensive. Jesus went on to say that his divine acts include revelation, resurrection, and judgment (vv. 20–22, 25–26). Moreover, anyone who does not honor the work of Christ as divine neither truly believes in God nor has eternal life (vv. 23–24).

After reviewing the declarations of Jesus regarding himself, Donald Baillie concluded, "Though it is a real man that is speaking, they are not human claims at all; they do not claim anything for the human achievement, but ascribe it all to God."[13]

---

10. "Sin is normally sin against God, but it is also sin against Christ." "Paul looks for God to be all in all as Christ is all in all." Leon Morris, *New Testament Theology* (Zondervan, 1986), 46–47.

11. D. M. Baillie, *God Was in Christ: An Essay on Incarnation and Atonement* (Faber and Faber, 1961), 106.

12. John Chrysostom, *Homily* 38, in Philip Schaff, ed., *Saint Chrysostom: Homilies on the Gospel of St. John and Epistle to the Hebrews*, Nicene and Post-Nicene Fathers, 1st Series, vol. 14 (1889; reprint, Hendrickson, 1994), 134.

13. Baillie, *God Was in Christ*, 127.

The Incarnation of Christ

The incarnation is a divine act worked by the eternal Word (John 1:14; Phil. 2:7) with the Father (John 6:57; Gal. 4:4) and the Spirit (Matt. 1:20; Luke 1:35). In becoming flesh, the eternal Word took mankind to his Person without changing his divine nature or destroying his human nature. The Lord truly became flesh, suffered, died, arose, and ascended to glory. The Lord did these things as a man, of course, for they are human actions. However, even while experiencing human changes, there was no alteration in his deity. It is a major error to teach anything other than the eternal Word's entire possession and exercise of his divine nature without cessation.

It is also a major error to teach anything other than his continual exercise of his human nature after the Incarnation. The choice of the word, "after," in that last sentence is important, for while his deity is eternal, his assumption of humanity has a starting point in time.[14] His humanity and his reign as the human Christ have no end either, for his humanity is united to his eternal Person. We must be careful to limit neither his personal unity nor his eternal deity by his work of assuming humanity to his Person; nor may we undermine his true humanity.

According to the apostles, Christ is the eternal Word of God who created the world (John 1:1–3; Col. 1:15–17; Heb. 1:2, 10) and "became flesh" in that world (John 1:14). The Son, who is one with God, did this by "assuming the form of a servant, taking on the likeness of humanity." This happened at a particular point in the created order, specifically, "when he had come as a man" (Phil. 2:7). Scripture thus reveals the incarnation is a divine act whereby the Son "assumes" and "takes" human nature. The eternal Son of God entered his own creation at a particular time and as a particular human creature: "When the time came to completion, God sent his Son, born of a woman, born under the law" (Gal. 4:4).

The Incarnation is, moreover, manifestly a work of God the Trinity. The Father "sent his Son" (Gal. 4:4). Apart from any human sexual relationship, the Holy Spirit "conceived" the body of Christ

---

14. The Incarnation has both eternal and economic aspects, according to the patristic interpretation of Proverbs 8:22. Athanasius, *Against the Arians* 2.20, in Philip Schaff and Henry Wace, eds., *Athanasius: Select Works,* Nicene and Post-Nicene Fathers, 2nd Series, vol. 4 (1892; reprint Hendrickson, 1994), 376.

in his mother, Mary (Matt. 1:18, 20, 25). Through his incarnation, the Word of God fulfilled the prophecy he earlier gave to Isaiah. Jesus was named "Immanuel," which means "God is with us" (Isa. 7:14; Matt. 1:23). The incarnation of Jesus Christ was a divine act by which the nature of humanity was united with the Person of the divine Son, such that the Son became truly a human person while remaining truly a divine person.

The Incarnation is the initial act in the divine plan "to bring everything together in Christ, both things in heaven and things on earth in him" (Eph. 1:10). This plan is then worked by Christ through his death, resurrection, ascension, heavenly session, return, final judgment, and eternal reign. Paul repeatedly uses the locative—"in Christ," "in him," "in the Beloved"—and locates the progress of the universe "through" and "in" his Person.[15] Coming in the context of his Trinitarian hymn, Paul's claim has led theologians in the broadly Reformed tradition to affirm "the new Covenant" is "the everlasting Covenant of grace between God and Man."[16] God elected to bring salvation to "his creature man," but only by doing so "in Christ."[17]

The Greek patristic doctrines of *enhypostasis*, "in the person," and *communicatio idiomatum*, "the communion of properties,"[18] help to explain the truth of the Incarnation. Leontius of Byzantium, a theologian active in the early sixth century, coined the term *enhypostasis* to explain that Christ united our human nature with its properties to his divine person.[19] A second Leontius soon after used the same term to develop orthodox Christology. Leontius of Jerusalem carefully distinguished person from nature and maintained the integrity of both the divine nature and the human nature. He argued that the eternal Word's personal union of deity and humanity allowed God to lift mankind to himself.[20]

Leontius of Jerusalem's Christology informed the Second Council of Constantinople (553). Defenders of orthodoxy at this council, the fifth ecumenical council, used the Leontine idea to integrate the unity of Christ advocated at the Council of Ephesus (431)

---

15. Malcolm B. Yarnell III, *God the Trinity: Biblical Portraits* (B&H Academic, 2016), 182–91.

16. *First London Confession*, art. X.

17. *First London Confession*, art. III.

18. On *communicatio idiomatum*, see below.

19. John Meyendorff, *Christ in Eastern Christian Thought* (St Vladimir's Seminary Press, 1975), 61–68.

20. Meyendorff, *Christ in Eastern Christian Thought*, 73–79.

with the two natures Christology advocated at Chalcedon (451). The churches in 553, "preferring the Bible to Hellenism," confessed the two natures united in one Person.[21] Christ's human nature was made personal by the eternal Logos taking our nature to himself in the incarnation. Neither Christ's personal unity nor his divine nature were disturbed by the Incarnation; rather, his powerful deity preserved his humanity.[22]

The *First London Confession* reaffirmed these same truths, treating Christ's Incarnation after his divine work of Creation, and preserving his personal union while distinguishing his two natures.[23] The great eighteenth-century Baptist theologian John Gill likewise addressed the nature of the personal union of God and man in Christ. He made five statements which summarize the orthodox grammar of the Incarnation of God as man in contemporary language:

> 1. Christ only assumed the human nature to his divine Person; but both natures, human and divine, are united in his Person.
> 2. This union is hypostatical, or personal. . . . This is not a union of two persons, but of two natures in one person.
> 3. This is a union of natures; but not a communication of one nature to another. The properties of each nature remain distinct.
> 4. This union lies in a communication of, or rather in making the personality of the Word, common to the human nature.
> 5. This union is indissoluble: though death dissolved the union between the body and soul of Christ, it did not, and could not dissolve the union between the human nature and person of Christ; wherefore, in consequence of this union, he raised up the temple of his body,

21. Meyendorff, *Christ in Eastern Christian Thought*, 60.

22. Cf. Basil Studer, *Trinity and Incarnation: The Faith of the Early Church*, ed. Andrew Louth, transl. Matthias Westerhoff (Liturgical Press, 2002), 226–27. On these three councils, see chapter 4 above.

23. *First London Confession*, art. IX.

> when destroyed, the third day, and thereby declared himself to be the Son of God.[24]

Gill's summary of the truth about Christ's personal union of two natures can help modern Christians recover the truth about the reality of Jesus Christ. Gill understood that if we do not properly teach who Christ is, then we risk leading people astray. The act of idolatry, which entails worshiping a God who is different from the One who reveals himself in Scripture, brings divine judgment. Gill, therefore, recalled the patristic, medieval, and Reformation consensus about Christ's personal union.

Jesus Christ is the eternal Word who became flesh. He thereby assumed our human nature to his divine Person. His unity of Person includes both his divine nature and his human nature. His two natures retain their integrity and distinction when united to his Person. Christ is thus one Person, who became and remains forever afterward truly human, just as he is eternally and immutably the one true God. Because Christ is divine, he could and did embrace our humanity and overcome death for us. Christ's personal union of deity and humanity constitutes the basis of our salvation.

Christ Is Human and Acts as a Man

The book of Hebrews emphasizes the full humanity of Jesus Christ. After building the case for the deity of Christ in chapter 1, the author addressed his humanity. Hebrews 2 demonstrates the humanity of Christ in the divine economy of salvation with prophecies from the Old Testament. The Son became man to subject the world to God:

> For he has not subjected to angels the world to come that we are talking about. But someone somewhere has testified: "What is man that you remember him, or the son of man that you care

24. Style adjusted for contemporary readers. John Gill, *A Body of Doctrinal Divinity; Or A System of Evangelical Truths, Deduced from the Sacred Scriptures* (London, 1839), 385–86. On the history of the terms *enhypostasis*, which says the humanity of Christ exists in his eternal Person, and *anhypostasis*, which says there is no humanity apart from this hypostatic union, see U. M. Lang, "Anhypostasis-Enhypostasis: Church Fathers, Protestant Orthodoxy, and Karl Barth," *Journal of Theological Studies* 49 (1998): 630–57.

> for him? You made him lower than the angels for a short time; you crowned him with glory and honor and subjected everything under his feet." For in subjecting everything to him, he left nothing that is not subject to him. As it is, we do not yet see everything subjected to him. (Heb. 2:5–8a; cf. Ps 8:4–6)

Christ's resubmission of the world to God is now in progress, but first, it required his incarnation. Second, it necessarily involved his obedient embrace of death. He perfected humanity both through his active exercise of the divine work of redemption and through his reception of our punishment as a human being. Third, he returned to the manifestation of his divine glory and will bring redeemed humanity with him:

> But we do see Jesus—made lower than the angels for a short time so that by God's grace he might taste death for everyone—crowned with glory and honor because he suffered death. For in bringing many sons and daughters to glory, it was entirely appropriate that God—for whom and through whom all things exist—should make the pioneer of their salvation perfect through sufferings. (Heb. 2:9–10)

Christ had to become a human being, because only a person who truly participates in the flesh and blood of human nature can redeem our humanity. His assumption of human nature enabled him to destroy the devil and death and to free humanity, which was previously held captive by the fear of death: "Now since the children have flesh and blood in common, Jesus also shared in these, so that through his death he might destroy the one holding the power of death—that is, the devil—and free those who were held in slavery all their lives by the fear of death" (Heb. 2:14–15).

Due to the assumption of human nature by the Son of God, the creation order was overturned, and humanity was exalted above the angels. Because he was tempted as a man, he could atone for the sins of humanity. And because he remained faithful to God in his humanity, he can help us remain faithful to God as our empathetic high priest: "Therefore, he had to be like his brothers and sisters in every way, so that he could become a merciful and faithful high priest in matters pertaining to God, to make atonement for the sins of the people. For since he himself has suffered when he was tempted, he is able to help those who are tempted" (vv. 17–18).

Biblical exegetes have long concluded that Scripture teaches Christ became truly human. He acted and still acts as a human being. Take, for instance, the testimony of Martin Luther, who preached often about the humanity of Jesus. In his first Christmas sermon, he affirmed, "Jesus was a natural man in every respect just as we, the only difference being in his relation to sin and grace, he being without a sinful nature."[25] "He ate, drank, slept, and waked; was weary, sad, joyous; wept, laughed; was hungry, thirsty, cold; sweated, talked, worked, prayed."[26] Soon after, Luther warned, "For whoever will disregard the life and sojourn of Christ upon earth, and will wish to find him in some other way, as he now sits in heaven, will always fail. He must look for him as he was and as he sojourned on earth and he will then find life."[27]

In 1610, the first Baptists similarly confessed Christ's incarnation was the prelude to his life, death, resurrection, and triumph. "Jesus Christ, as pertaining to the flesh, was conceived by the Holy Spirit in the womb of the Virgin Mary, afterward was born, circumcised, baptized, tempted; also that he hungered, thirsted, ate, drank, increased both in stature and in knowledge; he was wearied, he slept, at last was crucified, dead, buried, he rose again, ascended into heaven; and to himself as only King, Priest, and Prophet of the church, all power both in heaven and earth was given."[28]

Robert Shank concluded Christ's assumption of humanity was necessary to accomplish our atonement. "It was as man that Jesus accomplished the atonement. 'Since by man came death,' wrote Paul to the Corinthians, 'by man came also the resurrection of the dead' (1 Cor. 15:21). Since by man came the Fall, by Man came also the Reconciliation."[29] Jesus experienced fully the temptations common

---

25. Martin Luther, *Sermons on Gospel Texts for Advent, Christmas, and Epiphany*, transl. John Nicholas Lenker et al., Sermons of Martin Luther, vol. 1 (reprint, Baker, 1989), 140.

26. Cited in James Leo Garrett Jr., *Systematic Theology: Biblical, Historical, and Evangelical*, vol. 1, 2nd ed. (BIBAL Press, 2000), 612.

27. Luther, *Sermons on Gospel Texts for Advent, Christmas, and Epiphany*, 189.

28. *Short Confession of Faith*, art. 7, in Lumpkin and Leonard, eds., *Baptist Confessions of Faith*, 94.

29. Robert Shank, *Elect in the Son: A Study of the Doctrine of Election* (Bethany House, 1989), 63.

to humanity and overcame them. He thereby perfected our humanity by submitting his own body to the will of God. The Incarnation was the prelude to his obedient human life, propitiatory human death, and life-giving resurrection. "Fully perfected, He became through His sacrificial death the author of eternal salvation to all who obey Him (Heb. 5:9)."[30]

We shall return to Christ's human work in his threefold office, but first, we must consider the problem of relating his divine acts and his human acts to his Person. The divine Son acts through his humanity to redeem humanity and restore his kingdom over creation. The human body of Christ served as the avenue of his divine movement, yet he remained truly human in his activity. The divine Son is not diminished by his humble assumption of humanity; rather, he reveals himself as mysterious and sovereign Lord through his humility and exaltation.

The One Christ Acts as God and as Man

Maintaining simultaneously both sets of truths—that Christ is truly God and acts as God, and that Christ is truly human and acts as a man—may be difficult for our minds, but both must be continuously affirmed. Leo's "Tome," received by the Council of Chalcedon as a universal statement of Christological orthodoxy, states these truths succinctly: "As God is not changed by showing mercy, neither is humanity devoured by the dignity received. The activity of each form is what is proper to it in communion with the other: that is, the Word performs what belongs to the Word, and the flesh accomplishes what belongs to the flesh."[31]

On the one hand, Scripture treats Christ as God, who acts in his humanity. As God, he humbles himself to take the nature of man to his Person (Phil. 2:6–7), as man he is exalted and given "the name that is above every name" (Phil. 2:9). As God he is "Lord of all" (Acts 10:36; Rom. 10:12), as man all authority was given into his

30. "Jesus came to the cross [having] met every temptation common to man—and temptations beyond those of all other men—with unwavering commitment to righteousness (Heb 1:9), striving mightily against sin (12:4) and learning obedience to the Father's will through the things He suffered (5:8)." Shank, *Elect in the Son*, 69.

31. Letter of Pope Leo to Flavian, in Tanner, ed., *The Decrees of the Ecumenical Councils*, 1:*79. "Christ is the fountain of life, as God, and not as man; but He died as man, and not as God." Thomas Aquinas, *Summa Theologica*, vol. 4, transl. Fathers of the English Dominican Province (Christian Classics, 1981), 2287.

"hands" (John 13:3). As God he is "Spirit" and "life" (2 Cor. 3:17–18; John 1:4), as God in man his very "words" are "Spirit" and give "life" (John 6:63). As God he speaks to the consciences of all men (Rom. 2:14–16), as the man who is God his very "blood" may cleanse those same consciences (Heb. 9:14).

On the other hand, Scripture treats Christ as man, who receives every divine privilege, for he is the eternal God: As man he receives authority over everything everywhere (Matt. 28:18), as God he always already possesses full divine authority. He is "King of Kings and Lord of Lords" (Rev. 19:16). As man Christ received glory when he ascended to the Father (John 17:5; Phil. 2:10), as God he always already possesses this glory with the Father (John 6:62; 17:5). As man Christ has been exalted above every name (Eph. 1:20–21), as God he always already possesses perfect "equality with God" (Phil. 2:6). As the perfect man he is crowned with all "glory and honor" (Heb. 2:7, 9), as God he receives this "worship" from his own creatures (Heb. 1:6).

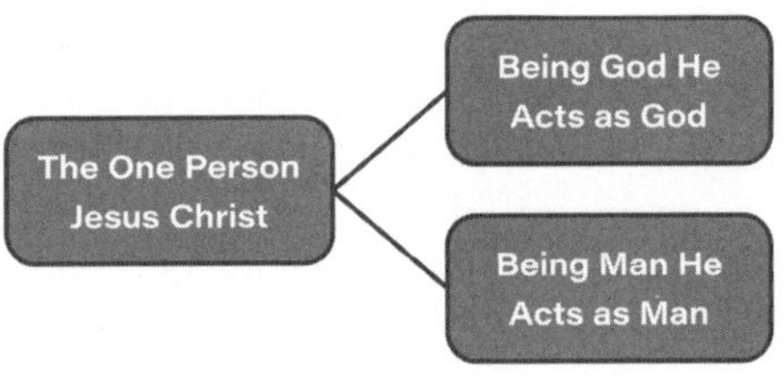

Figure 9: The Actions of Jesus Christ

You will remember that proponents of ancient Nestorianism compromised the unity of the person of the Son by diminishing his deity. They denied Mary could carry his deity along with his humanity in her womb.[32] More recently, modern Kenotic theologians have said the Son either laid aside or failed to exercise his deity in his incarnation.[33] Ancient Nestorians and modern Kenoticists compromise the two natures of his one Person, thus robbing the atonement of mediatorial power.

32. See chapter 4 above.

33. See chapter 13 below.

Gregory of Nazianzus, in the third of his five great theological orations, addressed the Person and work of the Son. His theological exegesis of the biblical canon provides a more faithful description of Jesus Christ. Gregory deployed the double hermeneutic in a sublime litany to Christ. He described Christ's actions as the dialectical activity of One who is human yet divine. Christ truly became a man, even as he remains eternally the one true God:

> As man he was baptized, but he absolved sins as God. As man he was put to the test, but as God he came through victorious. He hungered, yet he fed thousands. He thirsted, yet he exclaimed, "Whosoever thirsts, let him come to me and drink."
>
> He was tired, yet he is the "rest" of the weary and burdened. He was overcome by heavy sleep, yet he goes lightly over the sea, rebukes winds, and rescues Peter from drowning. He paid his tax, yet he used a fish to do it; indeed, he is emperor over those who demand the tax. He is stoned, yet not hit.
>
> He prays, yet he hears prayer. He weeps, yet he puts an end to weeping. He asks where Lazarus is laid—he was man; yet he raises Lazarus—he was God.
>
> He is sold, and cheap was the price—thirty pieces of silver; yet he buys back the world at the mighty cost of his own blood. A sheep, he is led to the slaughter, yet he shepherds Israel and now the whole world, too. A lamb, he is dumb; yet he is the "Word."
>
> He is weakened and wounded, yet he cures every disease, every weakness. He is brought up to the tree and nailed to it, yet by the tree of life he restores us. He is given vinegar to drink, gall to eat, but he is the one who turned water into wine, who took away the bitterness, who is all sweetness and desire.
>
> He surrenders his life, yet he has power to take it up again. Yes, the veil is rent, for things of heaven are being revealed, rocks split, and dead

> men have an earlier awakening. He dies, but he vivifies. And by death he destroys death.
>
> He is buried, yet he rises again. He goes down to Hades, yet he leads souls up and ascends to heaven. And he will come to judge the living and the dead.[34]

Christ is God who became Man, and he continues to be God in his strength even as he became man in humility. The Son's condescension did not diminish his deity, nor did his incarnation compromise his Person. Rather, Christ perfected our humanity. He who is forever rich in deity assumed humanity to take our poverty, so that we might become rich in him (2 Cor. 8:9). Christ never laid aside any aspect of his deity in the incarnation, for he is "the same yesterday, today, and forever" (Heb. 13:8). Simply immutable, the Word lost none of his perfections by nature; rather, Christ offered us the right to share in his communicable perfections by grace.

The Communication of Attributes in One Person

Jesus Christ acts both according to his deity and according to his humanity, yet he acts not as two persons but One. He who is both God and man acts as God and acts as man, without diminishing his unity. Seeking to explain the biblical phenomena behind this truth, theologians have affirmed *communicatio idiomatum*, the "interchange of properties" or "communication of attributes." Expressed by Cyril of Alexandria and defended at the fifth ecumenical council, this doctrine holds "that while the human and Divine natures in Christ were separate, the attributes of the one may be predicated of the other in view of their union in the one Person of the Saviour."[35]

The location of his twofold working in his one Person allows Scripture to ascribe human acts to his Person under the name of his deity, even as it allows the ascription of worship to his one Person under the name of his humanity. The divine and human natures retain their necessary integrity in his perfect Person, even as his one

---

34. Edited for style. Gregory of Nazianzus, Oration 29.20, in *On God and Christ: The Five Theological Orations and Two Letters to Cledonius*, transl. Lionel Wickham and Frederick Williams (St. Vladimir's Seminary Press, 2002), 87–88.

35. F. L. Cross and E. A. Livingstone, *The Oxford Dictionary of the Christian Church*, 2nd ed. (Oxford University Press, 1993), 321–22; Meyendorff, *Christ in Eastern Christian Thought*, 66–67, 84–86. Cf. Aquinas, *Compendium of Theology*, 162.

Person both acts and receives according to the propriety of his two natures. Martin Luther explains:

> In brief, whatever this Person, Christ, says and does, is said and done by both, true God and true man, so that all His words and works must always be attributed to the whole Person and are not divided, as though He were not true God or not true man. But this must be done in such a way as to identify and recognize each nature properly.[36]

Some biblical texts describe a human action with his divine name. As the Son of God, "the Lord" and "God" himself, he "breathed" the Holy Spirit upon the disciples through his bodily breath (John 20:22). This truly divine Person reconciles us by his human "death" (Rom. 5:10) and cleanses us from sin by his human "blood" (1 John 1:7; cf. Acts 20:28). As the human Christ, he was crucified by "the rulers of this world," but this man was also already and always "the Lord of glory" (1 Cor. 2:8 ASV).

Other texts ascribe a divine attribute or action to his human name. As a man, "Jesus Christ" nevertheless possesses the divine attribute of immutability, being "the same yesterday, today, and forever" (Heb. 13:8). As a man, "the Lamb," was "slain," but he has the divine right to stand "in the midst of" the throne ruling creation. He was the only human "found worthy" to take the scroll containing the divine decree from his Father's hand. As the Lamb, he sends the Holy Spirit with omnipotence and omniscience "into all the earth" from and through his own crucified and resurrected human body. Together with his Father and his Spirit, the Person of the Lamb rightly receives eternal worship as God from all the creatures of heaven (Rev. 5:5–14).

A Summary Statement of Christ's Divine–Human Work

The concurrence of both divine and human activity in the one Christ requires us to maintain multiple truths simultaneously and without distortion. It may be helpful here to summarize the import of the doctrine of Christ's work as it has been developed in

36. Martin Luther, *Sermons on the Gospel of St. John, Chapters 14–16*, ed. Jaroslav Pelikan and Daniel L. Poellot, Luther's Works, vol. 38 (Concordia, 1961), 254.

a theandric way. Such a doctrine of the work of Christ respects the truths of his hypostatic union of two natures, his taking of humanity to his divine Person, and the communication of his divine and human properties in his Person. Seven truths come to mind:

1. The Logos was, is, and remains forever eternally one Person.
2. He retains his divine nature, which cannot receive addition or suffer subtraction, for he is immutable. If you distort his deity in any way, you reject divine immutability, erase the Creator–creature divide, and compromise the integrity of his divine nature and its properties.
3. The eternal Logos assumed human nature, becoming a true human being, both body and soul, so that he could redeem and restore humanity.
4. Upon assuming his humanity, his personhood remains. Neither his eternal divine nature, nor his humanity are compromised, commingled, or separated.
5. He acts in divine ways without dividing his unitary person, without violating the integrity of his divine nature, and without distorting or losing properties.
6. When the eternal Word of God became a human being with a whole human nature, body and soul, the human nature with its properties was maintained by God. He thus acts in human ways.
7. When the Son acts in divine ways after the Incarnation, the integrity of his human nature is not violated.

Christ retains both divine attributes and human attributes in his one Person, for he has both the divine nature and the human nature. This union distorts neither the unity of his Person, nor the integrity of his deity, nor the integrity of his humanity. Metaphors may help us understand aspects of the great mystery of his work, but they can never fully explain him. Early, medieval, and evangelical theologians used several similes to illustrate the two natures acting in the one Person: The unity of light in the body of the sun, a mass receiving light and heat without loss, and the human unity of body and soul.[37]

Why Does He Act as Both God and Man?

The last great Lutheran theologian of the Reformation, Martin Chemnitz, said the hypostatic union of the two natures in Christ laid "the foundation for all our comfort."[38] His logic for this vital claim derives from our incapability to save ourselves and from God's merciful character. If we are to be reconciled with God, God himself must overcome the natural and sinful division which separates humanity from God. Sadly, "our wretched human nature because of sin has been torn away and alienated from God, who is life itself."[39] The breach in our relationship with God could be overcome only and uniquely and eternally through the person and work of the One who is Son of God yet also Son of Man.

Chemnitz described our upward progress into a saving relationship with God as being enabled only through the eternal Son's humble assumption of humanity. To accomplish our salvation, "His physical body, which is of the same substance with us, is most intimately joined and united with the divine nature in the person of the Son of God because of the hypostatic union." "In this way" Christ was able to effect "the restitution and reparation" of our human nature. He both justifies us legally and perfects our humanity ontologically. "In turn," we are "made participants of the divine nature in Christ." It is only through our humanity's union with Christ in his divine–human Person that we have fellowship with God. Through Christ alone do we "receive fellowship with the Father, the Son, and the Holy Ghost."[40]

From an ontological perspective, Christ's unity with God by nature and Christ's unity with humanity by nature enables human beings to be reunited with God by grace. From an economic

37. Cf. Martin Chemnitz, *The Two Natures of Christ*, transl. J. A. O. Preus, Chemnitz's Works, vol. 6 (Concordia, 1971), 87–102; Meyendorff, *Christ in Eastern Christian Thought*, 82.

38. Chemnitz, *The Two Natures of Christ*, 41.

39. Chemnitz, *The Two Natures of Christ*, 41.

40. Chemnitz, *The Two Natures of Christ*, 41.

perspective, only the one person, Jesus Christ, who possesses both natures, may effectively work reconciliation between God and man. Paul leads us to this truth with his Christological summation of the Shema: "For there is one God and one mediator between God and mankind, the man Christ Jesus, who gave himself as a ransom for all, a testimony at the proper time" (1 Tim. 2:5–6; cf. Deut. 6:4). This truth may be stated in a twofold manner.

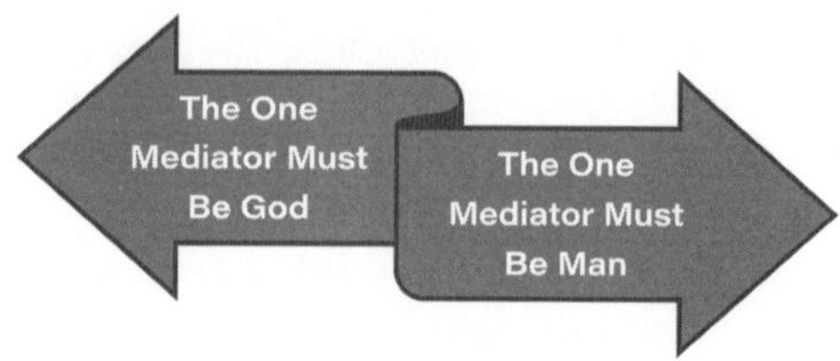

Figure 10: Christ the One Mediator

Only one Person is capable of saving humanity. He must be God, and he must be man. First, from the standpoint of God, he must be divine to reconcile us with God, for only one who is God may offer forgiveness. Second, from the standpoint of humanity, he must be human to atone for our sin, for only man can merit and receive forgiveness of sins. As God, he offers the grace of salvation; as man, he earns forgiveness from God by actively obeying the will of God and passively receiving the punishments for our sins.[41] The Second Person of the Trinity alone can reconcile God with man, for only he is, as the *Chalcedonian Definition* says, "the same perfect in divinity and perfect in humanity, the same truly God and truly man."[42]

41. Chemnitz gave seven reasons, or "sweet consolations," why only God the Son could become human to save us. His reasoning drew from both Scripture and the theological exegesis of the early church fathers: Only our "Creator" could become our "Re-Creator" (Col. 1:17–18). Only the One who is "life" itself could restore life to us (John 1:4; 1 John 1:1–2). Only the Son of God by nature could make us sons of God by grace (John 1:12). Only the One who is the "very image" of God could restore our lost or damaged image (Heb. 1:3 ASV; cf. Gen. 1:26). Only the One who is "full of grace" could bring us the "grace upon grace" we require (John 1:14, 16). Only "the middle person of the Trinity" could be "the Mediator" between God and fallen humanity. Only the Logos could reveal God. Chemnitz, *The Two Natures of Christ*, 44–46.

42. The *Chalcedonian Definition*, in Tanner, ed., *The Decrees of the Ecumenical Councils*, 1:*86.

Such truths about Christ in his Person and work were settled by the Council of Chalcedon in 451, but its definition received challenges requiring clarification.[43] After the dust settled, few detractors from Chalcedonian Christology remained. But after the Enlightenment, opposition to orthodox Christology intensified. Craig Blaising found that modern challenges to Chalcedon originated within the modern worldview.[44] Carl Henry reviewed twentieth-century scholars who objected to Chalcedon, finding their opposition derived from modernist divisions between ontology and function, and history and revelation, or from process philosophy.[45] Henry listed fourteen prominent evangelicals who joined with Roman Catholic and Eastern Orthodox theologians in explicitly defending Chalcedon, from B. B. Warfield to Gerald Bray to Henri Blocher. Henry aligned with the orthodox but his contribution to the project was incomplete.[46]

A Debate Among Evangelicals

From these profound truths that the early theologians discovered from Scripture about the Person and work of Jesus Christ, the widely recognized orthodox doctrine of *communicatio idiomatum* was developed. *Communicatio idiomatum*, or "communication of properties," states that although the human and divine natures in Christ are separate, the unique properties of each nature are predicated of the one Person of the Savior.[47] This explains, for instance, how "God" can be said to shed his "blood" (Acts 20:28) and how "the Lord of glory" was "crucified" (1 Cor. 2:8).

---

43. See chapter 4 above.

44. Craig Blaising, "Chalcedon and Christology: A 1530th Anniversary," *Bibliotheca Sacra* 138 [552] (1981): 328–29.

45. Carl F. H. Henry, *The Identity of Jesus of Nazareth* (Broadman Press, 1992), 90–95, 97–102. Cf. Carl F. H. Henry, "New Dimensions in Christology," in David S. Dockery, *New Dimensions in Evangelical Thought: Essays in Honor of Millard J. Erickson* (InterVarsity Press, 1998), 299–316.

46. Henry, *The Identity of Jesus of Nazareth*, 95–97. Henry hoped for a renaissance of Trinitarian "theocentricity" and orthodox "christocentricity." He noted his own teacher, Gordon Clark, was unable to complete his Christology. Alas, Henry's last major project also remained incomplete, even as he provided the outline for a recovery of Christological and theological orthodoxy. Henry, *The Identity of Jesus of Nazareth*, 110–11, 127.

47. Louis Berkhof, *Systematic Theology*, 4th ed. (Eerdmans, 1941), 324.

Drawing on this commonly accepted definition from the patristic era, some Reformation theologians went further and said his attributes are shared not just with Christ's Person but between his natures. The communication of properties allowed Lutherans generally to affirm the special presence of the physical body of Jesus Christ in the Lord's Supper. Chemnitz subtly defended this position, while still affirming Christ's body ordinarily resides in glory.[48] However, a radical Lutheran party, led by Johannes Brenz, argued that Christ's human body became ubiquitous. The official Lutheran formulary omitted the radical view.[49]

Representing Reformed theologians, Peter Martyr Vermigli disagreed strongly with the radical Lutherans. Vermigli argued the properties or attributes of the two natures of Jesus Christ are confined to each respective nature. Christ's body is, therefore, restricted to its locality in heaven. In a doctrine nicknamed the *extra Calvinisticum*, Vermigli asserted the two natures do not "extend as far as the other." In other words, the human nature is not made ubiquitous by the divine nature.[50] Sadly, mutual recriminations flew between earnest evangelicals.[51]

As noted in the first volume, distinguishing orthodoxy from heresy is necessary, but so is distinguishing error from heresy. Even as we must zealously protect the honor of God the Trinity and of Jesus Christ, we must also be aware that some matters may not constitute heresy but error. Theological conversation and discrimination call for grace as well as discernment. Among believers who maintain Trinitarian and Christological orthodoxy according to the biblically sound exegetical discoveries of the early centuries, we must exercise grace.[52] More importantly, we must proclaim the central work of God in Christ.

---

48. Chemnitz, *The Two Natures of Christ*, 430–34.

49. John Patrick Donnelly, "Introduction," in Peter Martyr Vermigli, *Dialogue on the Two Natures of Christ*, The Peter Martyr Library, vol. 2 (Sixteenth Century Essays and Studies, 1995), xv.

50. Vermigli, *Dialogue on the Two Natures of Christ*, 31.

51. Drawing on early church heresy, some Lutherans accused the Reformed of Nestorianism. In turn, some Reformed theologians accused Lutherans of Eutychianism. Justo L. González, *A History of Christian Thought*, rev. ed., 3 vols. (Abingdon Press, 1987), 3:128–30.

52. On the one hand, Jesus Christ warned his disciples to be prepared to battle against the thieves who would lead astray his sheep. The greatest thief, of course, is the devil (John 10:1–13). On the other hand, orthodox Christians may commune

The One Mediator

The saving work of Jesus Christ is encapsulated in his title of Mediator. Three truths about his work as Mediator require our consideration now. First, to perform this mediating work, Christ underwent humiliation, followed by his exaltation. Second, a definition of Christ's office of mediation is required. Third, the roles in the office of Christ as Mediator may be distinguished according to his threefold anointing as our Great Prophet, High Priest, and King of Kings.

Humiliation and Exaltation

The autodidact John Gill, a most capable systematic theologian, first treated the work of Christ under the rubric of his Incarnation. This led him to distinguish Christ's states. Gill's twofold division of the work of Christ into two states derived from his careful reading of the hymn in Philippians 2. The apostle Paul divided Christ's economy into two movements: humiliation (vv. 6–8) and exaltation (vv. 9–11).

The activities of Christ *in his state of humiliation* include his incarnation, the stages of his human growth, his baptism, and his temptations. These were followed by his suffering persecutions, his earthly poverty, and his voluntary obedience to God's will. The humiliation of Christ reached its critical stage in his passion, his death upon the cross, and his burial.[53] As important as his humiliation is for our redemption, so is Christ's exaltation necessary.

The activities of Christ *in his state of exaltation* began with his resurrection from death. They continued with his ascension to heaven and his current session at the right hand of the Father, from where he rules generally and intercedes for his own people. His exaltation continues with his future return, known as his "second coming to judgment."[54] Paul prophesied that at that time, "every knee will bow" and "every tongue will confess that Jesus Christ is Lord, to the

---

with Christ in different flocks. "But I have other sheep that are not from this sheep pen; I must bring them also, and they will listen to my voice" (John 10:16a). Vermigli forgave Brenz on his deathbed, though he still doubted Brenz's doctrine of heaven. Donnelly, "Introduction," xix.

53. Gill, *A Body of Doctrinal Divinity*, 390–410.

54. Gill, *A Body of Doctrinal Divinity*, 410–23.

glory of God the Father" (Phil. 2:10–11). His triumphant exaltation is so complete that "his kingdom will have no end" (Luke 1:33).

The Mediatorial Office of Christ Alone

In the seventeenth century, the Particular Baptists confessed, "Touching his Office, Jesus Christ onely is made the Mediator of the new Covenant, even the everlasting Covenant of grace between God and Man, to be perfectly and full the Prophet, Priest and King of the Church of God for evermore."[55] In the eighteenth century, Gill followed his forefathers in uniting the diverse works of Christ under his office of mediation: "His office in general is that of Mediator, which is but one." But "the branches" of his one office are "threefold, his prophetic, priestly, and kingly offices; all which are included in his name, Messiah, or Christ, the anointed."[56]

These orthodox if nonconformist Christians were led to their view by the general teachings of Scripture voiced in the most significant statement of Paul's first letter to Timothy. Paul's engrossing claim, cited above, is worth repeating: "For there is one God, and one mediator also between God and men, the man Christ Jesus, who gave Himself as a ransom for all, the testimony given at the proper time" (1 Tim. 2:5–6 NASB1995). Christ is both our divine Lord and our divine–human Mediator. His titles of "Master of all and mediator for all are inseparable, though distinguishable."[57]

The London Baptist theologians discovered Christ's office had been determined by his eternal will as God, but it was to be performed "in respect of his Manhood."[58] The significance of this bidirectional claim ought not be understated. It is with respect to his deity that Christ decides to save humanity, but it is with respect to his humanity that Christ obeys, suffers, and dies in his humiliation. As a man empowered by God, he then ascends to glory, intercedes for believers, and subjects all things to God. Those who would place either obedience, suffering, or submission upon the perfect deity of Christ, rather than upon his humanity exceed the bounds of orthodoxy.

---

55. *First London Confession*, art. X.

56. Gill, *A Body of Doctrinal Divinity*, 424.

57. Robert W. Yarbrough, *The Letters to Timothy and Titus*, Pillar New Testament Commentary (Eerdmans, 2018), 154.

58. *First London Confession*, art. XI.

In his call to this office, Christ was chosen, foreordained, and sent by God the Father. His central work to fulfill his call was to die on the cross and to arise from the dead, first atoning for man's sin then displaying his own eternal glory. The cross was necessary "that Christ should make a sacrifice for sinne, that hee shall see his seed, and prolong his dayes."[59] His office of mediation, which is the gospel that saves believers, "is so proper to Christ, as neither in the whole, nor in any part thereof, it may be transferred from him to any other."[60]

Jesus Christ is the one and only Mediator, truly God and truly man, and his office is threefold.

Christ's Threefold Office

Christ's singular mediation is performed via his threefold office. He works in three ways for three reasons: First, human beings operate with ignorance, and only Christ as the greatest prophet provides the knowledge we need. Second, human beings are alienated from God, and only Christ as the perfect priest can reconcile them to God. Third, the total inability of humanity to return to God requires the assistance of one who as true king possesses perfect divine power.[61]

Under the threefold office of Christ may be subsumed all of Christ's mediatorial work. While considering these offices, we must remember the one Christ performs these works. He performs them as the One who is both God and man and thus acts as both God and man. However, his natures and his works must be distinguished, even as the hypostatic union requires us to see them as the actions of his one Person. The office of Christ as Mediator is primarily an expression of his human work, but it is performed with eternal power.

The Old Testament highlighted the three roles of prophet, priest, and king by anointing their occupants to signify their consecration or setting apart to do their important work.[62] The Old Testament foretold, and the New Testament verified that each role was completed in the Messiah (Hebrew *Mashiach*; Aramaic *Mashiha*)

---

59. *First London Confession*, art. XII.

60. *First London Confession*, art. XIII.

61. *First London Confession*, art. XIV.

62. Objects were sometimes anointed, too. Gerhard Kittel, Gerhard Friedrich, and Geoffrey William Bromiley, *Theological Dictionary of the New Testament, Abridged in One Volume* (Eerdmans, 1985), 1322–23.

or Christ (Greek *Christos*). Messiah or Christ means "the Anointed One." Christ is the expected prophet, who would be greater than Moses (Deut. 18:14–22; Mark 9:2–13; etc.).[63] He is the expected priest, superior according to the order of Melchizedek (Ps. 110; Heb. 8:1–6; etc.).[64] He is the expected king, son of David and Son of God (2 Sam. 7:5–6; Matt. 21:1–11; etc.).[65] Jesus Christ, the incarnate Son of God, is "the one savior of the world: our everlasting prophet, priest, and king."[66]

First, in his role of *prophet*, Christ speaks the Word which reveals the will and way of the Lord. God is otherwise unknown to us. As the divine Son he is "wisdom" itself (1 Cor. 1:24), and as the human Christ "in him are hidden all the treasures of wisdom and knowledge" (Col. 2:3). He reveals "perfectly" the will of God. Various titles describe his role in revelation, including "prophet," "teacher," "apostle," and "messenger."[67] As God he understands perfectly the will of God, and as man he can and does reveal God's will "in his own person to man."[68]

Second, in his role of *priest*, he reconciles rebellious humanity with the offended God. Exalting the superiority of the priesthood of Christ vis-à-vis creation and the Old Testament cultus drives the book of Hebrews. In the priesthood of Christ, "a radical break with the ancient order occurs."[69] Regarding the creation order, Christ is superior in his deity, over the angels, and in his humanity. Regarding the Temple cult, Christ is superior in his covenant, priesthood, and sacrifice. Hebrews teaches Christ was consecrated to his superior priesthood according to the order of Melchizedek (Heb. 7:1–18).

---

63. Elizabeth W. Mburu and Michael S. Horton, "Introduction: Christ as Prophet," in Horton, Mburu, and Justin S. Holcomb, eds., *Prophet, Priest, and King: Christology in Global Perspective* (Zondervan Academic, 2025), 3–20.

64. Mburu and Horton, "Introduction: Christ as Priest," in Horton, Mburu, and Holcomb, eds., *Prophet, Priest, and King: Christology in Global Perspective (*Zondervan Academic, 2025), 81–92.

65. Mburu and Horton, "Introduction: Christ as King," in Horton, Mburu, and Holcomb, eds., *Prophet, Priest, and Kin: Christology in Global Perspective* (Zondervan Academic, 2025), 169–81.

66. Horton, Mburu, and Holcomb, "Conclusion," in Horton, Mburu, and Holcomb, eds., *Prophet, Priest, and King: Christology in Global Perspective* (Zondervan Academic, 2025), 255.

67. *First London Confession*, art. XV.

68. *First London Confession*, art. XVI.

69. Kittel, Friedrich, and Bromiley, *Theological Dictionary of the New Testament*, 360.

Through the blood of his cross, Christ offered himself as a "once for all sacrifice" with eternal effect (Heb. 9:24–10:14). By presenting himself to the eternal Father, Christ opened the way for other human beings to come boldly into the presence of God through his humanity (Heb. 4:14–16).

Emphasizing the theology of Hebrews, the London theologians provided more detail about his priesthood than his other two offices. They taught that "he was Priest, according to both natures." "He was a sacrifice most properly according to his human nature." Thus, Scripture speaks of his body and his blood as a sacrifice. However, "the chiefe force whereby his sacrifice was made effectuall, did depend upon his divine nature." He is not only the priest with the perfect sacrifice; he is also the perfect altar upon which the sacrifice was offered. The altar refers to his eternal Person, for he himself bears the sacrifice.[70]

Third, in his role of *king*, Christ ascended to the right hand of the Father and reigns over his people and over all creation. He has all power in heaven and on earth. On the one hand, he is "communicating and applying the benefits" of his Person and work to his own people. He strengthens them in the battle against the evil one. He also gives them the Holy Spirit.[71] On the other hand, he also has all power over every other creature in the world. He providentially guides even the evil ones to accomplish his will now.

One day, Jesus Christ shall fully perfect his kingdom, having brought all authorities to submit to himself. His goal is "that the glory of the Father may be full and perfectly manifested in his Sonne, and the glory of the Father and the Sonne in all his members."[72] As the human "Lamb" and "King of Kings," he works through both sacrifice and scepter to bring all authorities to submit to himself (Rev. 17:14; 19:14); and as the divine Sovereign ruling from the eternal throne, he exercises all authority and power forever and ever (Rev. 5:6–7, 13; 7:17; 22:1, 3).

70. *First London Confession*, art. XVIII.

71. *First London Confession*, art. XIX.

72. *First London Confession*, art. XX.

Conclusion

In this chapter, we explored the contours of a biblical and orthodox doctrine of the work of Christ as eternal God and creaturely man. We also highlighted his three roles as the one and only Mediator between God and humanity. In the next chapter, we must address the central work of Christ on the cross. The cross requires its own treatment, for Paul becomes our example when he writes under the inspiration of the Holy Spirit, "I decided to know nothing among you except Jesus Christ and him crucified" (1 Cor. 2:2).

Study Questions

1. If Jesus Christ is truly God, how does he act as God? Was there any limitation placed on his deity by his incarnation?

2. Define the terms *theandric*, *enhypostasis*, and *communicatio idiomatum*.

3. Why is Jesus Christ the only possible Mediator between God and man?

Suggested Resources

- D. M. Baillie, *God Was in Christ*
- Martin Chemnitz, *The Two Natures of Christ*
- John Gill, *A Body of Doctrinal Divinity*

CHAPTER TWELVE

Why the Cross?

◆ ◆

WHENEVER I TEACH THE SUBJECT of this chapter in the classroom, you can hear a pin drop as minds become active, and hearts are overwhelmed. The charged atmosphere has something to do with the professor, for I cannot help but surrender any air of academic objectivity. This is simply because I love that man, the man who died for me, with every fiber of my being. My teaching, which can transition into preaching, rises quickly toward and stays in the latter mode. But mostly, the students are enraptured, because as true believers they naturally sense that their entire being and every hope are utterly dependent upon what Jesus Christ did on his cross.

At times, the presence of the Holy Spirit has been so strong in the classroom that some students have sat there quietly and wept. Others linger after class and refuse to let their exhausted professor leave until they are certain they have truly grasped the basic insights of what they just heard. Most hearers simply cannot shake the absolute importance of what Jesus did on the hill called Golgotha, "the Skull," two millennia ago. Some ministerial students have even confessed they did not gain assurance of salvation until this lecture portrayed God their Savior shedding his own precious blood for their despicable sins. Others have written poems and composed songs. May the Lord touch your heart, too.

As we saw in chapter 10, the gospel of Jesus Christ centers on both his death and his resurrection. On the one hand, it is in Christ's office of priestly mediation through sacrifice that we must locate the central activity of his work for our redemption. On the other hand, we must also remember the victory of Christ is accomplished in his resurrection and demonstrates itself in our transformed lives. This chapter dwells upon Scripture's teaching of the cross. We will consider various theories of his atonement for us, and we will offer a holistic biblical view.

The ultimate power and mystery of the Christian religion resides in the atonement worked by Jesus Christ. There will always be something about Christ's cross and empty tomb that lies beyond our ability to comprehend. Scripture uses a rich multiplicity of analogies, metaphors, and similes to describe the profound truth of the atonement, which he works according to his divine–human Person. Although theologians may try to provide a complete definition, it should come as no surprise that no single theory of atonement suffices to describe Christ's central work of providing our salvation.

With that humbling reminder, we begin with a tentative definition of atonement. Next, we review the Old Testament teachings about the atonement, then the New Testament teachings. After our biblical review, we will consider the diverse interpretations of the atonement offered by Christians throughout the history of the church. Finally, we will offer a thicker description of the atonement that places the vicarious nature of Christ's atonement for our sins at the center of the whole event of the cross.

Defining the Atonement

In 1526, William Tyndale popularized the English term *atonement* through his translation of the Greek noun *katallage*.[1] *Katallage* indicated "the reestablishment of an interrupted or broken relationship" and is often translated "reconciliation."[2] The related Greek verb *hilaskomai* means "propitiate" or "conciliate."[3] Tyndale may

1. Tyndale also spelled it as "attonment" and "atonment." *The New Testament 1526*, transl. William Tyndale, ed. W.R. Cooper (British Library, 2000), 328, 384. According to the Oxford English Dictionary, the term first appears in the thirteenth century and becomes common by the seventeenth.

2. William Arndt, Frederick W. Danker, Walter Bauer, et al., *A Greek-English Lexicon of the New Testament and Other Early Christian Literature* (University of Chicago Press, 2000), 521.

3. Arndt, Danker, Bauer, et al., *A Greek-English Lexicon of the New Testament*, 473.

have chosen the term, because it pictures two warring parties being brought together as one, literally bringing "at-one-ment." According to Tyndale's contemporary, William Marshall, the sinner who has been reconciled to God does "make an onement with God."[4]

A biblical description of the atonement was provided by the apostle Paul in 2 Corinthians 5:18–21:

> Everything is from God, who has reconciled [*katallaxantos*] us to himself through Christ and has given us the ministry of reconciliation [*katallage*]. That is, in Christ, God was reconciling [*katallasso*] the world to himself, not counting their trespasses against them, and he has committed the message of reconciliation [*katallages*] to us.
>
> Therefore, we are ambassadors for Christ, since God is making his appeal through us. We plead on Christ's behalf, "Be reconciled [*katallagate*] to God." He made the one who did not know sin to be sin for us, so that in him we might become the righteousness of God.

A Preliminary Description

Building on the truths about the divine–human work of Christ which we discovered in the last chapter, we can detect seven aspects of the atonement in Paul's precise description of Christ's central work in 2 Corinthians 5:

1. The atonement is a gracious act which originates "from" God the Trinity.
2. The atonement operates "in" and "through" the Person of Jesus Christ. The inseparable work of the Trinity for reconciling man with God is centered in the second Person, who is God become man.
3. Christ removes the debt for our "trespasses" against God. The atonement uses a juridical metaphor, for the debt "counting against"

4. Erasmus of Rotterdam, *A Playne and Godly Exposition or Declaration of the Commune Crede*, transl. William Marshall (London, 1534), 158.

humanity is removed. It also uses a commercial metaphor, an exchange of "sin" and "righteousness."

4. Christ's work of atonement ends in "reconciliation," the restoring to mankind of a right relationship with God. As a divine work, the atonement has an objective dimension, for Christ altered the way God relates to humanity.
5. A subjective dimension of the atonement also exists, for the atonement affects "us" through Christ's assumption and transformation of humanity.
6. The people of God have "the ministry" of proclaiming the atonement.
7. God wants "the world" to hear the message of the atonement which will result in his eternal reign.

It may be helpful to develop this preliminary description derived from Paul with other relevant teachings from Scripture. First, the Trinitarian origin of the atonement is seen in the incarnate One who now resides at the right hand of God the Father (Dan. 7:13–14), and in the Holy Spirit who changes our hearts to receive God's law (Ezek. 34:26–27). God the Trinity graciously performs the atonement. He planned the new covenant which enables the atonement in Christ, who offered himself for our complete forgiveness (Heb. 10:10).

Second, the Person of Christ alone participates in eternity and creation. Therefore, he alone can serve as the Mediator between the infinite and immutable God and his finite and failing human creatures. He is the one Person who has two natures. He is Jesus, the man whose divine nature was revealed when he sat down at the right hand of God (Ps. 110:1; Dan. 7:13; Mark 14:62; Heb. 10:12). By his hypostatic union, Christ brought humanity to the divine throne itself. The final chapters of this book tease out the importance of this truth at length.

Third and fourth, Christ works the atonement in two ways, from his deity and in his humanity. As the second Person of the divine Trinity, he acts objectively to atone humanity. As a man, he subjectively and perfectly acts on our behalf. Hebrews 10 reinforces the Trinitarian and Christological aspects taught in 2 Corinthians 5. Hebrews follows the movement of the human Christ from his atoning death on earth to his triumphal occupancy of the heavenly throne: "But this man, after offering one sacrifice for sins forever, sat down at the right hand of God. He is now waiting until his enemies are made his footstool. For by one offering he has perfected forever those who are sanctified" (Heb. 10:12–14).

Fifth, God effects various transformations through the atonement. According to Hebrews 10, these changes are worked by Christ via his threefold human office of mediation: As Priest, Christ offered the "one sacrifice" (v. 12), thereby perfecting his followers. As Prophet, Christ "the Lord says" (v. 16). He thereby impresses his law on the hearts and minds of his people by his Spirit (Jer. 31:33–34; Heb. 10:16–17). And as King, Christ's "enemies are made his footstool" (Heb. 10:13). God subjects his angelic and human enemies to Jesus in history and thus to himself forever. Those who benefit from the atonement are reconciled from sin by Christ the Mediator.

Christ's reconciliation of human persons proceeds historically through covenant. From Genesis to Revelation, the biblical canon reveals the historical progress of his gracious promise: Immediately after their Fall, humanity was promised deliverance from the dominion of the serpent (Gen. 3:15). Abraham was then conveyed the promise of blessing for himself, his offspring, and the world (12:1–3). Sadly, his physical descendants broke the old covenant repeatedly, demonstrating only God could fulfill it for humanity. God promised our Savior would come through Isaac, then Jacob, David, and the remnant (Gen. 21:22; 25:23; 2 Sam. 7:11–16; Isa. 1:9; 8:14; 10:22–23; 28:22; Hosea 1:10; 2:23; Rom. 1:1–4; 9:5–33). God's covenantal promise of personal transformation (Ezek. 36:24–30; Jer. 31:31–34) was fulfilled in Christ's establishment of the new covenant by his blood atonement (Matt. 26:28; Heb. 9:15).

Finally, God is now sanctifying the redeemed by his Holy Spirit in Christ (Gal. 5:4–5, 16–26; Heb. 1:10–11; 2:10). His promise of personal reconciliation with God is to be proclaimed to everyone in the world by his church (2 Cor. 5:18–19). The gospel of Jesus Christ, which centers on Christ's death and resurrection, presents every human being with the decision either to be justified by grace through faith in Christ or to be condemned eternally (John 3:18–19; Rom. 5:17–21; Jude 4; Rev. 22:14–15). Christ will completely reconcile all things to himself as the eternal Priest–King in his new creation, over which he forever reigns as the God–Man (Eph. 1:20–23; 1 Cor. 15:20–28; Heb. 2:5–18; Rev. 21:1–5).

Diverse Evangelical Definitions

Augustus Hopkins Strong located the atonement under the rubric of Christ's priesthood rather than in the entire scope of his threefold office of Mediator. His logic was that Scripture emphasizes the sacrifice of Christ on the cross, and sacrifices are offered by priests. However, Strong also affirmed the moral, legal, and commercial metaphors in the biblical witness to the atonement. "The Scriptures teach that Christ obeyed and suffered in our stead, to satisfy an immanent demand of the divine holiness, and thus remove an obstacle to the divine mind to the pardon and restoration of the guilty."[5] Nevertheless, he concluded "the prevailing language is that of sacrifice."[6]

By way of contrast, James Leo Garrett Jr. provided a more wholistic definition of the atonement, saying it consists of

> the death–resurrection of the Lord Jesus, the twofold event which comprises the saving work of the eternal and incarnate Messianic Son of God, in its nature an historical act of eternal consequence—the penal substitutionary and propitiatory sacrifice which is both consistent with God's righteousness and expressive of God's love and demonstrates God's triumph over sin, death, and Satan, by means of which repentant, believing sinners are drawn through the forgiveness of sins to reconciliation with God and enter into the fellowship with Christ's death-resurrection, marked by the new life of cross-bearing and following in His steps in the new community of the forgiven.[7]

Whether one follows the restrictive location of the atonement by Strong, the broader definition given by Garrett, or my preliminary

5. Augustus Hopkins Strong, *Systematic Theology: A Compendium Designed for the Use of Theological Students* (Fleming H. Revell, 1907), 713.

6. Strong, *Systematic Theology*, 721.

7. James Leo Garrett Jr., *Systematic Theology: Biblical, Historical, and Evangelical*, vol. 2, 2nd ed. (BIBAL Press, 2001), 58.

description, two truths remain undeniable. First, the atonement has a rich depth with multiple dimensions which stretch our minds to their utter limits even as it addresses our hearts intimately. Second, the atonement is a world-transforming, human-reconciling, and ultimately indispensable doctrine in Christian theology.

The Atonement in the Old Testament

Four terms used in the Old Testament specify the context for understanding God's promise of atonement: covenant, ransom, redeemer, and blood. These terms help us understand the development of the atonement in the Messianic prophecies. The Old Testament terminology coalesced in the person and work of the Servant, the Messiah Priest–King. Isaiah revealed he would be both humiliated and exalted. The mystery of the Christological work of atonement was clearly prophesied in the Old Testament period, but human recognition of the revelation of the One who personally makes the atonement awaited the New Testament era.

Covenant

Covenant is the first prominent term in the Old Testament theology of atonement: Jeremy Treat offers three reasons why the doctrine of atonement takes a covenantal shape. First, "Covenant is indispensable for the context of atonement."[8] Covenantal relations provide the narrative within which the atonement overcomes the separation between God and humanity. Second, Christ's death is a "covenant sacrifice," whereby he "bears the covenant curses" of the old covenant and "ratifies the new covenant."[9] Third, covenant theology comprehends and correlates the diverse canonical witness to the atonement.[10]

Thomas F. Torrance began the second volume of his monumental Christology with covenant. He argued the promise of salvation contained in the old covenant was not performed by Israel but "fulfilled in Jesus Christ." The Hebrew term *berith* (Hebrew "covenant")

---

8. Jeremy R. Treat, "Covenant," in Adam J. Johnson, ed., *T&T Clark Companion to Atonement* (T&T Clark, 2017), 431–32.

9. Treat, "Covenant," 433–34.

10. Treat, "Covenant," 434–35.

derives from *barah*, "cut," indicating covenant requires sacrifice. *Barah* also means "eat," for covenant is manifested in a meal. The Hebrew term is affiliated with the Akkadian *baru*, "chain" or "bind," indicating entrance into a covenant begins with an oath to fulfill its terms.[11]

Two key statements by Jesus Christ show that he believed he fulfilled the Old Testament promise of atonement with God in his new covenant.[12] First, Jesus corrected his disciples' efforts to institute carnal hierarchy. He rebuked the world's tyrannies and forbade his disciples from instituting such systems. "Just as the Son of Man did not come to be served, but to serve, and to give his life as a ransom for many" (Matt. 20:28). The way of the Messiah is service through sacrifice, as he soon demonstrated.

Second, at the Last Supper, Jesus explained the reason for his approaching sacrifice by crucifixion. While celebrating a covenantal meal with his disciples, he recalled the founding of the old covenant when the wrath of God passed over the people. The Lord then pointed to the new covenant he was establishing in his cross: "For this is my blood of the covenant, which is poured out for many for the forgiveness of sins" (Matt. 26:28; cf. Exod. 12:1–32).

Ransom

Ransom is the second prominent term in the atonement: Two Hebrew word groups were translated into Greek as *lutrousthai* and *lutron*, "redeem" or "ransom." The Hebrew word group which includes *padah* focused on the hope for Israel's redemption from spiritual and physical bondage and into a restored relationship with God. God's redemption of Israel would take them "out of divine judgment and alien oppression into the liberty of the kingdom of God," and "through expiation from guilt and the power of sin and darkness."[13] In short, ransom is "redemption from the power of sin."[14]

The Hebrew word group which includes *kopher* and *kipper* focuses on the "actual wiping out of guilt, and so of effecting

11. Thomas F. Torrance, *Atonement: The Person and Work of Christ*, ed. Robert T. Walker (IVP Academic, 2009), 7–17.

12. Torrance, *Atonement*, 5–7.

13. Torrance, *Atonement*, 29–30.

14. Torrance, *Atonement*, 33.

propitiation between God and man."[15] Only God can work propitiation, and propitiation requires the shedding of blood. Leviticus 17:11 reveals that blood is the key to life, and that its vicarious covenantal shedding can restore life to sinful humanity: "For the life of a creature is in the blood, and I have appointed it to you to make atonement on the altar for your lives, since it is the lifeblood that makes atonement."

Torrance found two results came from ransom: First, "the removal of an objective obstacle between God and man." Second, "the restoration of communion between God and his people."[16] Torrance argued the effectiveness of ransom is not due to the cultic use of blood but to the divine covenant. The power behind the divine work of atonement derives from nowhere but God's self.[17]

We must be wary of the modern West's misplaced bias against blood atonement,[18] but Torrance's point is well taken: The power of the atonement resides not in liturgical representation of the atonement, whether the liturgy belongs to Israel or the church. The power of atonement, moreover, resides not in a theory of atonement but in the gracious working of God himself. We must distinguish divine movement from our human acts and descriptions.

Redeemer/Redemption

Redeemer introduces us to the third prominent set of Hebrew terms: The Old Testament doctrine of atonement depends on the Hebrew verb *gaal* and the noun *goel*. A *goel* was a powerful kinsman who could stand in the place of a person in distress and rescue him or her from slavery.[19] The role of David's ancestor, Boaz, in serving as kinsman–redeemer to Naomi is well known (Ruth 2:20). Boaz bought back Naomi's ancestral land, restoring a means of livelihood to her and Ruth.

Yet more significant—from the perspective of theology proper and the divine power which alone can work eternal atonement—is

15. Torrance, *Atonement*, 33.

16. Torrance, *Atonement*, 35.

17. Torrance, *Atonement*, 38.

18. Around 1800, Western society began to look down on the need for blood atonement. Cultural elites rejected retributive punishment, advocated the moral inviolability of persons, and doubted all humans are sinners. Stephen Holmes, "Penal Substitution," in Johnson, ed., *T&T Clark Companion to Atonement*, 308–10.

19. Torrance, *Atonement*, 44–45.

that God himself is humanity's Kinsman–Redeemer. The Lord is the Redeemer of his people, and he saves us through his work of redemption. Isaiah declares, "You, Lord, are our Father; your name is Our Redeemer [*goel*] from Ancient Times" (Isa. 63:16b). The psalmist uses the verb, "Remember your congregation, which you purchased long ago and redeemed [*gaal*] as the tribe for your own possession" (Ps. 74:2a).

Jesus Christ completed the role of Kinsman–Redeemer which was typified in the line of David and ascribed directly to the Lord God. The Messiah completed the role of *Goel* through his incarnation as our kin in flesh, the husbandly "Savior of the body," which is his bride, the church (Eph. 5:23). He is our "advocate" before the Father (1 John 2:1), and through his Spirit, he seals us for "the day of redemption," thereby guaranteeing our inheritance in him (Eph. 4:30).

Blood

Blood is the fourth significant Old Testament atonement term: The Hebrew word *dam* appears some 360 times in the Old Testament, typically indicating blood shed through human violence or blood shed for divine sacrifice. Scripture provides laws regarding blood, especially human blood: In general, blood is paired with "life" (*nephesh*; Gen. 9:4; Lev. 17:11, 14; Deut. 12:23). Life is in the blood, and all human life shares in the one blood of Adam (Acts 17:26, Western text; cf. Heb. 2:14).[20]

Human blood is very precious to God, so God holds man accountable for spilling innocent blood (Gen. 4:10–11; Deut. 21:9; Rev. 19:2). Human sin requires the payment of our blood. The CSB translates Ezekiel 18:13b as "His death will be his own fault." But a more literal translation is, "His blood will be on him." A proper blood sacrifice may make atonement for the human soul (Lev. 17:11). Indeed, there is no forgiveness of sin without shedding of blood (Heb. 9:22). God uses blood to establish covenantal relationship (Exod. 24:8).

In principle, human salvation comes by the means of blood. The blood of a pure sacrifice sanctifies both a holy people and the things used in right worship (Lev. 8:15; 14:25, 52; 16:19). God propitiated

20. One important ethical truth derived from this fact is that racism and ethnocentrism become reprehensible.

his wrath against human sin through proper sacrifice (Exod. 12:13). However, his righteous burning anger against sin is not propitiated by just any blood. Cultic worship according to form has little effect: "'What are all your sacrifices to me?' asks the Lord. 'I have had enough of burnt offerings and rams and the fat of well-fed cattle; I have no desire for the blood of bulls, lambs, or male goats'" (Isa. 1:11). One alone may truly atone for sin.

The Torah contains numerous laws regarding the various sacrifices Israel was expected to offer. The Mosaic book of Leviticus has a particularly large number of references. According to Richard Averbeck, "The NT employment of OT sacrificial concepts and practices binds the two Testaments together in ways that are important for understanding Jesus Christ, what he has done for us, and what this means for living the Christian life well."[21]

In the New Testament, Hebrews 10 develops the typology of sacrifice programmatically, noting the Levitical sacrifices required continual repetition (Heb. 10:11) yet were unable "to take away sins" (vv. 1–4). By contrast, the sacrifice of Jesus is eternally sufficient, "for by one offering he has perfected forever those who are sanctified" (v. 14). The New Testament repeatedly says Jesus fulfills the meaning of sacrifice. He is "our Passover sacrifice," "our burnt and peace offering," "our sin offering," and "our guilt offering." The Messiah as guilt offering was emphasized in the atonement theology of the Servant songs in Isaiah.[22]

Servant Messiah

In modern references to the doctrine of the atonement in the Old Testament, by far the most cited passage is the final Servant song of Isaiah.[23] Daniel Block said the Servant refers not to Israel, as Jewish interpreters contend, but "to a royal Davidic figure."[24] For the first time in Scripture, God has explicitly "linked the Messiah to a way of dealing with sin that yields atonement and forgiveness."[25]

21. Richard E. Averbeck, "Sacrifices and Offerings," in G. K. Beale et al., *Dictionary of the New Testament Use of the Old Testament* (Baker Academic, 2023), 727.

22. Averbeck, "Sacrifices and Offerings," 727–31.

23. The closest rival is Leviticus 16–17. See Johnson, ed., *T&T Clark Companion to Atonement*, 831–36.

24. Daniel I. Block, *Covenant: The Framework of God's Grand Plan of Redemption* (Baker Academic, 2021), 340.

25. Block, *Covenant*, 342.

The messianic "Servant," according to Isaiah 52:13–53:12, will suffer for his people's sins then be exalted for his people's justification.[26]

In the New Testament, both Christ and the apostles repeatedly cite this song, explicitly identifying the Servant with Jesus the Messiah and with his suffering on the cross (Matt. 8:14–17; Mark 10:45; Luke 22:35–38; John 12:38; Acts 8:30–35; Rom. 10:16; 15:21; 1 Pet. 2:19–25). "Beyond such actual quotations, the picture of Yahweh's servant in Isaiah 42:1–4 and Isaiah 52:13–53:12 is of more pervasive influence in the NT, especially in connection with an understanding of Jesus' death."[27] Even critical scholars correlate Jesus with the Servant.[28]

The immediate context of the final Servant song of Isaiah emphasizes the sinfulness of God's people and their need to trust in God's promise of salvation, which he works by the great power of his "arm."[29] Treat says the song portrays salvation "by a servant-king" and "for a kingdom of servants."[30] It is comprised of five stanzas, the first and last sung by God, the others by his people. John Oswalt highlights the air of astonishment, for God saves his people in an unexpected way: "The power of God's arm is not the power to crush the enemy (sin), but the power, when the enemy has crushed the Servant, to give back love and mercy."[31]

In the first stanza (Isa. 52:13–15) God reveals he and his Servant eternally planned the atonement and will accomplish it (v. 13). Atonement is entirely an act of divine grace from conception to fulfillment. God's plan includes the exaltation of his Servant (v. 13) but only through his humiliation (v. 14). The unfolding of God's plan will shock the world's rulers into silence (v. 15). Details about the Servant's humiliation are foretold in the next three stanzas

---

26. The first through third Servant songs may refer corporately to the people of God (Isa. 42:1–9; 49:1–6; 50:4–9), but the fourth Servant song doubtlessly concerns an individual who acts vicariously on behalf of the whole people of God. The first song says the Servant will restore justice to Israel and extend it to all nations.

27. J. Goldingay, "Servant of Yahweh," in Mark J. Boda and J. Gordon McGonville, eds., *Dictionary of the Old Testament Prophets* (IVP Academic, 2012), 703.

28. Christoph Barth, *God with Us: A Theological Introduction to the Old Testament*, ed. Geoffrey W. Bromiley (Eerdmans, 1991), 343.

29. John N. Oswalt, *The Book of Isaiah: Chapters 40–66*, New International Commentary on the Old Testament (Eerdmans, 1998), 375–76.

30. Jeremy R. Treat, *The Crucified King: Atonement and Kingdom in Biblical and Systematic Theology* (Zondervan, 2014), 85.

31. Oswalt, *The Book of Isaiah*, 376–77.

(53:1–3, 4–6, 7–9), while his exaltation is prophesied in the final stanza (vv. 10–12).[32]

The second stanza (Isa. 53:1–3) begins by noting the atonement wrought by God and his Servant is hidden from humanity (v. 1). The immediate incomprehension of the first disciples of Christ regarding his cross was thus expected.[33] The song uses the prophetic present tense to reveal the future suffering and death of the Servant (vv. 1–10a), switching to the future tense to reveal his ultimate exaltation (vv. 10b–12). From our perspective, the Servant's human "form" will lack any natural luster and be horribly maimed. He will be so "despised" that some will chose to ignore him while others vehemently reject him (vv. 2–3).

But according to the third stanza (Isa. 53:4–6) many will admit their initial response to the humbled Christ was wrong. People typically think that losers deserved their humiliation, yet God's people discern the substitutionary aspect of the Servant's suffering. We initially thought he was "struck down by God" (v. 4), but the truth is quite different. The contrasts in this stanza startle the reader: He was "afflicted," "pierced," and "crushed," because of "our rebellion," "iniquities," and "punishment" (vv. 4–5). He was not afflicted due to his sins, but to ours! We are sinners and entirely so (v. 6).

The divine plan of atonement worked by the Servant thus involves a two-way interchange. On the one hand, "the Lord has punished him for the iniquities of us all" (v. 6). On the other hand, "we are healed by his wounds" (v. 5). Martin Luther spoke of the atonement as a "wonderful exchange." By his work of "substitution," Christ our Servant and Lord "achieves that satisfaction which men were not able to produce for themselves."[34] Christ is "suffering in the place of those who should be suffering," and he suffers "by his

---

32. Paul's Christological hymn of humiliation and exaltation allusively echoes Isaiah's song (Phil. 2:4–11). Daniel J. Treier, *Lord Jesus Christ*, New Studies in Dogmatics (Zondervan Academic, 2023), 193–94; Moisés Silva, "Philippians," in G. K. Beale and D. A. Carson, eds., *Commentary on the New Testament Use of the Old Testament* (Baker Academic, 2007), 837.

33. On the revelation of "the messianic secret" by Jesus and the initial ignorance of the disciples, see William L. Lane, *The Gospel According to Mark: The English Text with Introduction, Exposition, and Texts*, New International Commentary on the Old Testament (Eerdmans, 1974), 292–308.

34. Paul Althaus, *The Theology of Martin Luther*, transl. Robert C. Schultz (Fortress Press, 1966), 202–3.

voluntary submission."[35] We are unable to merit forgiveness, so the Servant does everything for us. "In short, the suffering of the servant provides a substitutionary atonement for 'the many,' removing sins as well as its consequences and restoring a right relationship with God."[36]

In the fourth stanza (Isa. 53:7–9), God continues prophesying through the song he wrote for the lips of his people. They will praise his Servant for suffering death vicariously. Indeed, more than seven hundred years before his cross and death, Isaiah was told that Christ would be "silent" and "like a lamb," not defending himself before those who would kill him (Isa. 53:7; cf. Matt. 27:29–30; Mark 15:3; Luke 23:11–12; 1 Pet. 2:23). The Servant's death is described with the vivid verbs "taken away," "cut off," and "struck" (Isa. 53:8).

The song proclaims again that death did not properly belong to the Servant, but to us. He died "because of my people's rebellion" as well as our "oppression and judgment" (v. 8). And again, specific events about Christ's own vicarious death are foretold. "He was assigned a grave with the wicked, but he was with a rich man at his death" (Isa. 53:9; cf. Matt. 27:57–60; Mark 15:42–46; Luke 23:50–55; John 19:38–42). The Servant received honor even in death because of his true innocence. He knew no sin whatsoever (Isa. 53:10; cf. 2 Cor. 5:21; 1 Pet. 2:22).

The fifth stanza delivers yet another shock to natural men. The disciples of Jesus did not begin comprehending the transformative truth of Christ's death until after they witnessed with their own eyes and ears (and hands and fingers) that he had come back to life![37] But in his own voice, God repeatedly promised the Servant would live: "He will see his seed, he will prolong his days," "He will see light and be satisfied," and "I will give him the many as a portion and he will receive the mighty as spoil" (Isa. 53:10–12). God's promises include not only the resurrection of the Servant, but also his triumphal entry and eternal reign as Messianic King!

The Servant's substitutionary atonement is summarized in the final stanza. God says he was "pleased to crush him severely" so that he could "make him a guilt offering" to "carry their iniquities" (vv. 10–11). But how is the Servant's final exaltation in his resurrection, his triumphal ascent, and his eternal reign related to

35. Oswalt, *The Book of Isaiah*, 394.

36. Treat, *The Crucified King*, 82.

37. John 20:24–29

the atonement? God prophesied that his Servant, the Lamb, our Christ—he "will justify the many" (v. 11).[38] The song brings hope to sinners every time it is sung to those with ears to hear, for it declares that the children of the Servant will accompany him into his eternal kingdom.[39]

The substitutionary atonement worked by the Servant lays the ground for the justification of sinners by faith. It also leads to the establishment of the divine Kingdom through the Servant's resurrection, triumphal entry, and eternal reign as Messianic Priest–King. The Servant provides atonement for our participation in his eternal Kingdom via personal justification. This is God's provision of atonement! This is the gospel of Christ! This is our hope for salvation!

The Atonement in the New Testament

Having carefully heard the first Christian testament, we must turn our attention to the atonement in the next. First, we will see that the New Testament locates the fulfillment of the covenantal promise of the Old Testament in the incarnate Son of God. Second, we will survey prominent terms for the atonement in the New Testament. Third, we must pay particular attention to the blood of Jesus. Fourth, we will explore why the atonement is significant in New Testament theology. Finally, we will summarize the New Testament doctrine.

The Promise Is Fulfilled in Christ

The New Testament's extensive theological exegesis of the Old Testament focuses on the ancient promise of atonement. For the Christian exegete, references to sacrifice in Leviticus and the priestly portions of the Old Testament must be read through the New Testament. While Christological exegesis of the Hebrew Scriptures is broadly assumed by the apostles, it is emphasized by the book of Hebrews.

In Mark 14:21, Christ prophesied his crucifixion from the Old Testament. In Luke 24:25–27, he verified his crucifixion from it. Likewise, many of Christ's final testamentary words were previously prophesied. The well-known sayings of, and direct references

38. Oswalt, *The Book of Isaiah*, 404–7.

39. Oswalt, *The Book of Isaiah*, 395, 402.

to Christ on the cross include Psalms 22:1 (cf. Matt. 27:46), 31:5 (cf. Luke 23:46), and 69:21 (cf. John 19:28–30). In Luke 22:37, Jesus claimed he is the Servant prophesied in Isaiah 53:12: ""For I tell you that this which is written must be fulfilled in Me, 'And He was numbered with transgressors'; for that which refers to Me has its fulfillment." If Isaiah 52:13–53:12, the last and greatest of the suffering Servant songs is taken as messianic prophecy, as Jesus and the apostles certainly asserted, then the Servant song foretells both the humiliation and the exaltation of Jesus.

The book of Hebrews presents the Old Testament cult of sacrifice as a type fulfilled in the cross of Christ. Hebrews 7:20–8:6 and 9:1–10:18 provide a paradigm for distinguishing between the "heavenly" above (Heb. 8:5) and the "earthly" below (9:1). Christ's "once-for-all" (7:27; 9:12) work of sacrifice is far "superior" (8:6). Christ's heavenly covenant, temple, and priesthood, which center on his once-for-all sacrifice on the cross, are the perfect, true, and eternal "reality itself" (10:1). The Old Testament's earthly covenant, temple, priesthood, and sacrifices are merely "copies" (8:5; 9:23), which "shadow" (8:5; 10:1) and "model" (9:24), but they "can never perfect" (10:1; cf. 7:19; 9:9). Christ alone can and Christ alone does "perfect" our humanity (2:10; cf. 5:9; 10:14; 12:2).

Prominent New Testament Terms

As used in the New Testament several Greek terms help shape the Christian theology of the atonement. These include terms which point to Christ as the Person who fulfills the Old Testament promises of atonement. Jesus is *mesitas*, "mediator" (1 Tim. 2:5; Heb. 12:24) and *hiereus* and *archiereus*, "priest" and "high priest" (Heb. 4:14–15). His activity upon the cross is described as a *thusia*, "sacrifice" (Eph. 5:2; Heb. 9:26; 10:12; 11:4; cf. 1 Cor. 5:7), and as a *prosphora*, "offering" (Eph. 5:2; Heb. 10:10, 14).

Yet other terms describe the product or result of his atoning work, including *lutron* and *antilutron*, which mean "ransom" or "redeem" (Matt. 20:28; Mark 10:45; 1 Tim. 2:6), and *katallage* and *diallassomai*, which may be translated as "reconciliation" or "to be reconciled with" (Matt. 5:23; Rom. 11:15; 2 Cor. 5:18–20). Certain prepositions strongly suggest Christ's atonement was a work of substitution. They indicate he acted on behalf of or in the stead of others. *Anti*, one preposition of substitution, can be translated as "for," "instead of," or "in place of" (Matt. 20:28; Mark 10:45). *Huper*, a second preposition of substitution, means "instead of" or "on behalf of" (1 Tim. 2:6). Both prepositions are applied to the cross of Christ.

Historically, one Greek word group occasioned some controversy. *Hilasmos*, *hilasterion*, and *hilaskomai* are best translated "propitiation" or "make propitiation" (Rom. 3:25; Heb. 2:17; 1 John 2:2; 4:10). But C. H. Dodd preferred the translation "expiation" over "propitiation," hoping to downplay the idea that God's wrath is appeased. Replying to Dodd, George Eldon Ladd found that the word in common Greek usage, in the Septuagint, and in the rest of the New Testament means that wrath is placated, and that God is the object of the placation.[40] No historical contextual basis exists to soften the term's translation.

The cultural difficulty for many Westerners derives from modern diffidence to a God whose wrath is turned away by violence. Stephen Holmes found none of the five modern objections to the penal substitutionary view of the atonement can be sustained.[41] Holmes also reminds us the metaphor of substitution, which is supported by the biblical idea of the "sacrifice of propitiation," is one of "many metaphors."[42] Regarding propitiation, we must also note that even when God used violence in the atonement, he first established the new covenant's terms based on his justice. God then fulfilled those terms in himself by virtue of his love. Garrett agrees: Christians "need to take seriously" the Johannine and Pauline doctrine of propitiation, which presents the atonement both as "the removal of wrath and the manifestation of love."[43]

The Blood of Jesus

As in the Old Testament, the New Testament term for *blood* (Greek *haima*, "blood") carries great weight. "In the NT *haima* achieves its greatest theological significance in relation to the death of Christ."[44] Where the blood of bulls and goats in the old covenant could not atone for our high-handed sign, the new covenant promise

40. Dodd focused on the use of the terms in Romans and 1 John. Millard J. Erickson, *Christian Theology*, 2nd ed. (Baker, 1998), 827–29.

41. Holmes, "Penal Substitution," 296–304.

42. Holmes, "Penal Substitution," 304–5, 314.

43. Garrett, *Systematic Theology*, 2:14.

44. Johannes Behm, "Haima, Haimatekchusia," in Gerhard Kittel, Geoffrey W. Bromiley, and Gerhard Friedrich, eds., *Theological Dictionary of the New Testament,* 10 vols. (Eerdmans, 1964–1976), 1:174.

of salvation can. Atonement is provided in the blood of Jesus and memorialized in the cup of his Supper. "For this is my blood of the covenant, which is poured out for many for the forgiveness of sins" (Matt. 26:28; cf. 1 Cor. 11:25).

The cross is where Christ shed his blood for his people (Luke 22:44; John 19:34). Paul warned the elders of the Ephesian church to remember who owns both the church and their elders. Elders are appointed "to shepherd the church of God, which he purchased with his own blood" (Acts 20:28). The apostle Peter reminds us that, above all, Christ's blood is "precious" (Greek *timios*, "of exceptional value; worthy of the highest honor;" 1 Pet. 1:19).[45] Peter also taught that our saving election by the foreknowledge of the Father, and our sanctification by the Holy Spirit, occur through the blood of Christ (1 Pet. 1:2).

The New Testament is replete with references to this central truth of the gospel: Jesus saves us by his atoning blood shed for our sins (Rom. 5:9; Heb. 13:12, 20). The apostle John reminds believers that Christ "loves us and has set us free from our sins by his blood" (Rev. 1:5). The true freedom worked by Christ's sacrifice also grants redeemed humanity participation in the royal priesthood, and the ultimate purpose of this royal priesthood is to give glory to God (v. 6). The individual human person can have his or her conscience made right through Christ's eternal presentation of his blood sacrifice to God by the eternal Spirit (Heb. 9:14).

Thankfully, you and I may now enter the throne room of God by Christ's blood (Heb. 10:19). Our presence with Christ at the throne indicates the blessings of the atonement have been extended to us. The potential of the atonement wrought by Christ's blood can be taken either as general in extent or particular in extent. Scripture certainly indicates the atonement has a universal quality, for Christ's work is powerful enough for everyone (Col. 1:20; 1 John 2:2). On the other hand, there is also a particular quality, for Christ said he laid down his life for those who are "his people" (Matt. 1:21), "the sheep" (John 10:15), "his friends" (John 15:13).[46]

The key to correlating the atonement's general character with its particular character may be found here: Those who will participate in Christ's resurrection life personally receive Christ's atoning

45. Arndt, Danker, Bauer, et al., *A Greek-English Lexicon of the New Testament*, 1005–6.

46. Garrett, *Systematic Theology*, 2:59–61.

blood sacrifice by faith (John 6:56).[47] In the life of the church, to receive communion in the cup is to receive communion with Christ and his people (1 Cor. 10:16). Alternatively, to receive the cup of the Lord's Supper unworthily is to invite judgment. Christians ought not take the memorial blood of the covenant lightly (1 Cor. 11:27; Heb. 10:29). The ethical implications are significant: Christ's blood cleanses us from all sin and enables us to walk in the light (1 John 1:7; Rev. 7:14).

Christ's blood also bears witness to God's eternal love (1 John 5:8). And the Christian's witness to Christ's blood enables him or her to overcome the evil one forever. The Apocalypse prophesies the believers' victory over evil: "They overcame him by the blood of the Lamb, and by the word of their testimony" (Rev. 12:11 KJV). In the end, Christ will wear his blood at his second coming to demonstrate his complete victory over sin, death, and Satan (19:13). The Lamb shall reign "forever and ever" from the divine throne, extending the grace of life by his Spirit to his people forever (22:3–5).

The Significance of the Atonement

The New Testament witnesses in numerous ways to the overarching significance of the atoning work of Christ upon his cross. First, the cross permeates the canon. John Stott recognized "the centrality of the cross" in Scripture,[48] while Leon Morris found "the cross dominates the New Testament."[49] The cross of Christ orients the four Gospels of the New Testament. The narrative of each gospel builds toward and reaches its highpoint in the atoning death of Jesus Christ on the cross. According to G. Campbell Morgan, a literary peak is attained by all four evangelists at the cross (Matt. 27:32–56; Mark 15:22–41; Luke 23:27–49; John 19:17–37).[50]

Second, the atonement as a theme was woven by the Holy Spirit into the "woof and warp" of Scripture. A representative collection of atonement texts from seven apostles clearly demonstrates this truth.

---

47. The historic debate over the extent of the atonement primarily runs through strands of Augustinianism. Garrett, *Systematic Theology*, 2:61–67. Both Erickson and Garrett found the arguments for the general strand more persuasive. Garrett, *Systematic Theology*, 2:67–69.

48. John Stott, *The Cross of Christ* (InterVarsity Press, 1986), 25–40.

49. Leon Morris, *The Cross in the New Testament* (Eerdmans, 1965), 365.

50. G. Campbell Morgan, *The Crises of the Christ: The Seven Greatest Events of His Life* (Kregel, 1989), 195–98.

According to Matthew and Luke, we must take up our crosses like Christ (Matt. 10:38; Luke 9:23). According to Mark, Christ gave his life as a ransom (Mark 10:45). According to John, the high priest spoke more truth than he realized, when he said, "one man should die for the people" (John 11:49–53). John himself realized God "loved us and sent his Son to be the atoning sacrifice for our sins" (1 John 4:10). Paul taught that Christ "redeemed us from the curse of the law by becoming a curse for us" (Gal. 3:13–14; cf. 2 Cor. 5:21; 1 Tim. 2:6). Peter agreed: "For Christ also suffered for sins once for all, the righteous for the unrighteous, that he might bring you to God" (1 Pet. 3:18). And for the apostle who wrote Hebrews, Jesus is "the pioneer and perfecter of our faith," who "endured the cross, despising the shame, and sat down at the right hand of the throne of God" (Heb. 12:2).

Third, the seven last words of Christ from his cross testify to the significance of the atonement. While hanging on his cross, Jesus emphasized the provisions of his atonement: "Father, forgive them; for they do not know what they are doing" (Luke 23:34 NASB1995). "I tell you this: today you shall be with me in Paradise" (v. 43 NEB). "Woman, behold your son!" and "Behold, your mother!" (John 19:26–27 ESV). "My God, my God, why have you forsaken me?" (Matt. 27:46 ESV). "I thirst" (John 19:28 ESV). "It is finished" (John 19:30 ESV). And "Father, into your hands I commit my spirit" (Luke 23:46 ESV). Compelling sermon series have been developed from these sayings alone.[51]

Fourth, the atonement is treated as significant by the New Testament because it required the death of Christ. On the one hand, the unique victory of Christ on the cross is highlighted by such sayings as "It is finished" (John 19:30); "know nothing except Christ and Him crucified" (1 Cor. 2:2); and "glory alone in the cross of Christ" (Gal. 6:14). Some like Erich Sauer have concluded from these texts that "The cross is the greatest event in the history of salvation, greater even than the resurrection. The cross is the victory, the resurrection the triumph; but the victory is more important than the triumph, although the latter necessarily follows from it."[52]

---

51. E.g., Erwin J. Lutzer, *Cries from the Cross: A Journey into the Heart of Jesus* (Moody, 2015); Fulton J. Sheen, *Life of Christ* (Doubleday, 1958), chapter 49.

52. Erich Sauer, *The Triumph of the Crucified: A Survey of Historical Revelation in the New Testament* (Paternoster, 1956), 32.

But the Gospels treat the resurrection as necessary (Matt. 28:1–10; Mark 16:1–8; Luke 24:1–12; John 20:1–18). In his longest theological exposition on the resurrection, written to the church of Corinth, Paul argued forcefully that without the resurrection, "our faith is in vain" (1 Cor. 15:2).[53] It should be clear that there can be no resurrection without the death-dealing crucifixion. Nor, however, is there a crucifixion without the divine plan for the resurrection. Neither the humiliation of the cross nor the exaltation of the resurrection ought to be prioritized over the other.

The gospel of Jesus Christ requires both events. Jesus's summary of what is "necessary" is binary: He must "be betrayed" and "crucified," then he must "rise on the third day" (Luke 24:7). The same binary appears in Paul's gospel: "Christ died" and "was buried," then he "was raised on the third day" and "appeared" (1 Cor. 15:3–5). Elsewhere, Paul grounded our salvation in the twofold paradigm of atonement and resurrection: "He . . . was delivered over because of our transgressions, and was raised because of our justification" (Rom. 4:25 NASB1995). Both Christ's death and his resurrection are foundational for human salvation, so a dialectic tension must be maintained.

A Survey of the New Testament Doctrine

Leon Morris surveyed the entirety of the New Testament witness to the atonement. He found fourteen points of agreement among its various human writers concerning the cross of Christ. (The apostles were, after all, inspired by one Spirit.) Morris began with human sin, explained the divine origin and the divine logic behind the sacrifice of Christ, and concluded with the call for sinners to be saved.

The first two points of agreement from the diverse New Testament witnesses concern human sinfulness: "All men are sinners," and "All sinners are in desperate peril, because of their guilt."[54]

The next two concern the divine origin of salvation: "Salvation takes place only because God in his love wills it and brings it about." And "Salvation depends on what God has done in Christ."[55]

53. First Corinthians 15 is "one of the great theological treasures of the Christian church." Gordon D. Fee, *The First Epistle to the Corinthians*, New International Commentary on the New Testament (Eerdmans, 1987), 717.

54. Morris, *The Cross in the New Testament*, 365–68.

55. Morris, *The Cross in the New Testament*, 368–72.

The next eight points focus on Christ: "Both the Godhead and the manhood of Christ are involved in saving us." "Christ was personally innocent." "While the importance of the life of Christ is not to be minimized, central importance is attached to his death." "In his death Christ made himself one with sinners. He took their place." "By his life, death, resurrection and ascension Christ triumphed over Satan and sin and every conceivable force of evil." "Not only did Christ win a victory, but he secured a verdict." "In his death Christ revealed the nature of God as love." And "In his death Christ is man's supreme example."[56]

Morris concluded with our personal appropriation of the atonement. "Men are invited to make a threefold response in repentance, faith, and holy living." And finally, "There is a cross for the Christian as well as the Christ."[57]

Morris's careful survey of the New Testament helps demonstrate how both testaments emphasize the atonement of sinners by God. Morris also called on theologians to exercise humility regarding the atonement. "The atonement is too big and too complex for our theories. We need not one, but all of them, and even then we have not plumbed the subject to its depths."[58]

Nevertheless, the profundity of the New Testament witness requires us to attempt a theory of atonement. After all, Jesus focused his message on the atonement, revealing the messianic mystery to his disciples (Mark 8:30–31; 9:30–32; 10:32–34; cf. Matt. 16:20–21; Luke 9:21–22).[59] And his prayers to the Father confessed he came into the world precisely to redeem believers by his death (John 12:20–28; 17:1–26; 19:30; cf. Mark 10:45).[60] Christians must do their best to understand the revelation of the cross so they can proclaim it with bold clarity.

---

56. Morris, *The Cross in the New Testament*, 372–90.

57. Morris, *The Cross in the New Testament*, 390–93.

58. Morris, *The Cross in the New Testament*, 401.

59. On the "Messianic Secret" as a means of revelation, see the correction of Wilhelm Wrede by J. D. G. Dunn, "The Messianic Secret in Mark," *Tyndale Bulletin* 21 (1970): 92–117.

60. In his prayer in the garden of Gethsemane, Jesus acknowledged and embraced his cross with great struggle (Matt. 26:36–46; Mark 14:32–42).

Atonement Theories in Christian History

In chapter 10 we learned how Christ's gospel, which centers on his vicarious death and victorious resurrection, makes salvation available to sinners today through proclamation. In chapter 11 we explored Christ's work as human and divine. And in this chapter, we are paying particular attention to his work on the cross.[61] Before turning from Christ's humiliation to his eternal exaltation, we must try to provide a dogmatic account of the atonement. Spiritual wisdom requires us to hear the voices of other Christians.

Seven Atonement Theories

In the history of the Christian church, theologians have explained the cross of Christ according to some theory or another. Seven theories of the doctrine of the atonement have garnered widespread attention in church history.[62] They may be summarily described as follows:

First, the *classical theory*, known as *Christus Victor*, was popular in the early church. It focused on how Christ overcame sin, death, and the devil for humanity by becoming a human being and going to the cross. This theory draws on the biblical ideas of recapitulation (Eph. 1:10), redemption (Mark 10:45; Col. 2:14; 1 Tim. 2:6), and victory (Col. 2:15). Irenaeus of Lyons said Christ recapitulated humanity through his birth, life, and death. Gregory of Nyssa portrayed Christ as conquering Satan, retrieving the keys of death and Hades, and releasing their prisoners. Modern scholars like Hans Boersma and Michael Bird advocate recovering this model as the premiere theory of atonement.[63]

Second, the *satisfaction theory* uses "a rational, non-exegetical approach" to argue that sinful human beings must make satisfaction

61. Aspects of Christ's work will continue to be considered throughout these volumes, for Christian theology is dominated by him. Indeed, our entire religion is uniquely dependent upon and devoted to the rich truth that "Jesus is Lord."

62. Leo Garrett collated the various theories under four categories: "the cross as sacrifice, as propitiation, and as substitution and the righteousness of God," "the cross and the love of God," "the cross as the historic deed of the eternal Son of God," and "the cross/resurrection as a ransom-victory over sin, death, and Satan." Garrett, *Systematic Theology*, chapters 46–48.

63. John S. Hammett and Charles L. Quarles, *The Work of Christ*, Theology for the People of God (B&H Academic, 2024), 208–16.

for failing to honor God with their obedience. Anselm of Canterbury taught that Christ, who is both omnipotent God and sinless man, paid a feudal price on behalf of believers to redeem them from their sin debt. Anselm's theory dominated Western discourse in the late medieval period. Aligning with that shame and honor culture, it emphasized the need to restore God's offended honor. The satisfaction theory shares some ideas with the next theory.[64]

Third, the *penal substitution theory* advocated by John Calvin remains popular with evangelicals. It stresses the placation of divine justice rather than the satisfaction of divine honor. Relevant biblical texts include Exodus 34:6–7, which says God is "compassionate and gracious," but also that he "will not leave the guilty unpunished." Jesus made himself "the atoning sacrifice for our sins, and not only for ours, but for those of the whole world" (1 John 2:2). Only he could serve in this vicarious role, for only he was entirely obedient in his life. This theory locates atonement in Christ receiving the wrath of God intended for sinners. Calvin interpreted the descent in a spiritual rather than literal sense and made the resurrection the locus of Christ's victory. Stott described this theory as "the self-substitution of God."[65]

Fourth, in his *governmental theory* Hugo Grotius argued that Christ died to vindicate the righteous basis of God's rule. Grotius was not concerned with satisfaction of honor or substitution for justice but maintenance of governance. Grotius portrayed God as a benevolent ruler rather than a punishing judge. Christ received punishment to show humanity that God treats sin seriously although he is motivated to bless and forgive.[66]

Fifth, the *moral influence theory* says Christ's personal sacrifice prompts human hearts to act righteously. The medieval theologian Abelard of Paris focused upon Jesus's statement: "No one has greater love than this: to lay down his life for his friends. You are my friends if you do what I command you" (John 15:13–14). Abelard said Christ's sacrificial love fosters "that deeper affection in us which not only frees us from slavery to sin, but also wins for us the true liberty of sons of God, so that we do all things out of love rather

64. Garrett, *Systematic Theology*, 2:21–23.

65. Garrett, *Systematic Theology*, 2:23–34; John Calvin, *Institutes of the Christian Religion*, ed. John T. McNeill, transl. Ford Lewis Battles, Library of Christian Classics (Westminster Press, 1960), 503–34; John Stott, *The Cross of Christ*, 133–63.

66. Garrett, *Systematic Theology*, 2:26–27.

than fear."[67] Both Paul's statement that "the love of Christ compels us" (2 Cor. 5:14) and John's statement that "we love because he first loved us" (1 John 4:19) affirm the atonement will influence character.

Sixth, the *example theory* says that Christ lived sacrificially for God and humbly served others so that he could show us how to live in the same way. The Reformation-era Socinians argued that faith in Christ means not that we believe Christ died for our sins but that we follow his pattern of obedience to come to God. German liberals in the Ritschlian tradition spoke similarly.[68]

Seventh, the *eternal atonement theory* highlights Revelation 13:8, which says the Lamb was "slain from the foundation of the world" (KJV). An alternative translation of the text, however, indicates the names of the redeemed were written down at the world's foundation, rather than that Christ was slain then (CSB). A. H. Strong used the older translation to argue the atonement was performed in eternity and displayed in history. More recently, Donald Baillie used the same text to argue that Christ bore our sins in eternity.[69]

Evaluating the Historic Theories

The various theories tend toward either an objective or a subjective explanation of the atonement. "Objective" theories, like the first four above, teach that the atonement alters God's relation to his temporal human creatures. "Subjective" theories, like the next two, picture the atonement as changing human beings. Evangelicals emphasize the objective theories due to the biblical prominence of objective terms and ideas like "ransom," "sacrifice," "victory," and "propitiation." But Scripture also calls for our subjective appropriation of Christ's cross-bearing humility and service (Mark 10:35–45; Phil. 2:5).

The rhetorical tactics deployed by proponents of various theories may not always translate well, but the objections of opponents may likewise be more cultural than substantial. For instance, Nyssa's ransom theory offends moderns, for he rejoices that Satan was tricked by Christ's visible humanity covering his divine power. Yet, as we shall see, Nyssa's presentation incorporates many biblical

67. Abelard, "Exposition of the Epistle to the Romans," in Eugene R. Fairweather, ed., *A Scholastic Miscellany: Anselm to Ockham* (Westminster Press, 1956), 283–84.

68. Garrett, *Systematic Theology*, 2:43–45.

69. Garrett, *Systematic Theology*, 2:41–42.

ideas. Similarly, Anselm's use of feudal imagery may not be convincing in cultures that downplay shame and honor, but he still offers keen insights. Again, modern revulsion against the violence of penal substitution seems particularly misplaced. Scripture teaches that God's love satisfies God's wrath. The God–Man voluntarily chose to become our "propitiation" (Rom. 3:25; 1 John 2:2; 4:10; cf. Heb. 9:5 NIV). Mere cultural dissonance need not remain insurmountable.

On the other hand, at least one theory requires significant rejection. Socinianism's example theory should be dismissed for failing to maintain the objective aspect of the atonement and for teaching people they have some role in earning their salvation. Finally, the governmental theory need not necessarily be rejected, despite its lack of a direct biblical prooftext. Grotius attempted to operate from a biblical worldview and to defend divine sovereignty.

Why have Christians offered so many different theories of the atonement? Their diverse explanations derive in part from the richness of the biblical testimony about the cross, in part from the various cultural contexts in which Christians reflect on the cross, and in part from the assorted personal and intellectual predilections that individual Christians bring to their work. Moreover, no dogmatic decree on the atonement has been universally received. Ultimately, the diversity of theories derives from the fact that the atonement is an eternal mystery which has been revealed to creatures limited by space and time.

Gustaf Aulén analyzed the historic development of atonement theory and united the various theories under three major headings: victory, substitution, and example. Aulén, however, downplayed both the substitution model and the example model and singularly advocated *Christus Victor*.[70] Contemporary scholars have appropriated Aulén's work but generally agree the best way forward requires synthesis. The various theories of the atonement need not be seen as mutually exclusive, for most develop from biblical exegesis.

The historic theories of the atonement will continue to be debated, because Scripture ultimately has more to say about Christ's work of atoning for our sin than any one human theory can comprehend on its own. It seems best to adopt the penal substitution and victory theories while adapting positive elements from the satisfaction and example theories.

---

70. Gustaf Aulén, *Christus Victor: An Historical Study of the Three Main Types of the Idea of the Atonement*, transl. A. G. Hebert (London: SPCK, 1931).

Honoring the Whole of Christ's Work in the Atonement

The biblical doctrine of the atonement is central to the faith, richly complex in its meaning, and entirely dependent on the Person of Jesus Christ. A good theory of the atonement must emphasize the priestly work of Christ,[71] but it may not merely reflect upon his sacrifice. It should also account for the royal and prophetic consequences of Christ's work as sacrificial Mediator.[72] The best approach to the central act in the work of Christ will honor its wholeness and its mystery. It must therefore include the eternal dimension of Christ's mediation.

First, we may describe the atonement as *royal*, for Christ's cross establishes his right to redeem the saints into his kingdom. Under his royalty, we could include aspects of the satisfaction and governmental theories. However, the most important theory which must be incorporated here is *Christus Victor*. After all, Jesus was crucified for being "the King of the Jews" (Mark 15:2, 9, 12, 18, 26, 32), and his death led to his triumphant resurrection (Col. 2:13–15; Heb. 2:14–18; 1 John 3:4–9; Rev. 12:11).

Second, we must emphasize the atonement as *priestly*, because Christ intervenes for believers. Under his priesthood, we should include the legal and commercial metaphors of the atonement, for they repeatedly appear in the biblical statements about the atonement. We must also account for the cultic context of priesthood and sacrifice. The cultic, legal, and commercial metaphors for the atonement compel us to embrace the penal substitutionary theory.

Third, we should describe the atonement according to Christ's *prophetic* work. Under his prophecy, we may incorporate dimensions of the moral influence and example theories. Christ has the right to demand obedience from those who believe in him and his atonement (Heb. 2:18). Christ and his apostles called upon his disciples

---

71. Hammett and Quarles, *The Work of Christ*, 197.

72. Cf. Henri A. G. Blocher, "Agnus Victor: The Atonement as Victory and Vicarious Punishment," in John G. Stackhouse Jr., ed., *What Does It Mean to Be Saved? Broadening Evangelical Horizons of Salvation* (Wipf and Stock, 2002), 67–91; Graham A. Cole, *God the Peacemaker: How Atonement Brings Shalom* (InterVarsity Press, 2009), 229–31; Sinclair B. Ferguson, "Christus Victor et Propitiator: The Death of Christ, Substitute and Conqueror," in Sam Storms and Justin Taylor, eds., *For the Fame of God's Name* (Crossway, 2010), 171–89; Treat, *The Crucified King*, 45–46.

to live and to die just as he lived and died. The call to carry one's cross in sanctity, service, and humility may be difficult, but it must be proclaimed, and it must be lived (Mark 8:34–38).

Fourth, we should also affirm the *eternality* of the cross. The one Mediator between God and man is both human and divine and is thus infinite as well as finite. Christ's eternal power works to extend the salvation worked in his humanity into eternity.

Each dimension of the atonement requires further elaboration. However, we will wait until the final chapter to address the eternal dimension of Christ's work. The remainder of this chapter develops the royal, priestly, and prophetic contexts of the work of Christ on the cross in a wholistic manner.

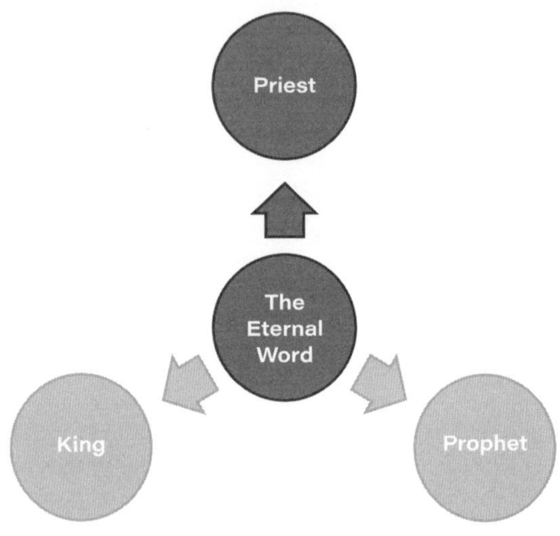

Figure 11: The Atoning Work of the Eternal Word Who Became Man

The King's Victory Through Atonement

Speaking exegetically, biblical theologian R. Alan Streett says Jesus focused on "the good news of the kingdom" (Mark 1:14). After Adam failed to lead, God promised to redeem mankind through Abraham, Moses, and David; that is, through Israel. But Christ alone inaugurated the Kingdom of God by fulfilling God's "kingdom restoration plan."[73] Speaking theologically, Streett says the kingdom provides the framework for the redemption of both individuals and community. He found problems with various atonement theories but embraced both *Christus Victor* and penal substitution.[74]

Several early church fathers, including Irenaeus, Origen, the Cappadocian Fathers, Augustine of Hippo, and John of Damascus, developed the kingdom motif. They rejoiced in the victory of King Jesus over evil.[75] Gregory of Nyssa garnered the most interest with his fishhook analogy, but John McGuckin argues it was a rhetorical flourish.[76] More positively, like other church fathers, Nyssa taught the reconciliation worked by Christ is "deeply personalist," "morally freighted,"[77] and incorporates the whole "economy of salvation."[78]

Gregory focused on the victory that Christ won over the enemy.[79] Psalm 24:8 asked, "Who is this King of Glory?" Nyssa responded, "He who has surpassed all in power. He who has recapitulated all things in himself (Eph 1:10); the One who holds the first place overall, who has restored all things to the primal creation. This is the King of Glory."[80] Christ became man to embrace death and to bestow on human nature "the principle of resurrection."[81] Satan's pride led him to presume Christ was merely a man, but God

73. R. Alan Streett, *Heaven on Earth: Experiencing the Kingdom of God in the Here and Now* (Harvest House, 2013), 14–15, 82–83; idem, "The Work of Christ," in Daniel L. Akin, David S. Dockery, and Nathan A. Finn, eds., *A Handbook of Theology* (B&H Academic, 2023), 340–42.

74. The governmental, example, and satisfaction theories are problematic. Some focus entirely upon individuals and ignore community. Streett, "The Work of Christ," 344–46. Jeremy Treat says the substitutionary work of Christ on the cross necessarily prepares for the coming of the Kingdom. Treat, *Crucified King*, 37–50.

75. Garrett, *Systematic Theology*, 2:48–52.

76. John A. McGuckin, "St. Gregory of Nyssa on the Dynamics of Salvation," in Johnson, ed., *T&T Clark Companion to Atonement,* 166–69.

77. McGuckin, "St. Gregory of Nyssa on the Dynamics of Salvation," 157.

78. McGuckin, "St. Gregory of Nyssa on the Dynamics of Salvation," 170.

79. Through his incarnation, Christ armed himself with humanity. McGuckin, "St. Gregory of Nyssa on the Dynamics of Salvation," 161.

80. Gregory of Nyssa, *Homily on Ascension*, cited in McGuckin, "St. Gregory of Nyssa on the Dynamics of Salvation," 162.

81. McGuckin, "St. Gregory of Nyssa on the Dynamics of Salvation," 164–65.

conquered death in Christ.[82] He defeated the devil and opened the gates of hell to set the enslaved free.[83]

Aulén said the Anselmian theory's dominance over medieval theology was turned back toward *Christus Victor* by Martin Luther.[84] But he faulted both Enlightenment theologians and Protestant Scholastics for failing to give Christ's victory adequate attention.[85] While his study recovered the victory motif, Aulén went too far in concluding it alone answers the problem of evil and alone must be considered "the genuine, authentic Christian faith."[86] Like others, I have affirmed this theory is integral to a biblical view of the work of God,[87] but it cannot stand alone.

The Priest's Sacrifice in Atonement

We may refer to the satisfaction and substitution theories of church history as "priestly," because they draw on the representative aspects of the religious, political, and economic structures both in Scripture and in subsequent periods. These theories focus on how the relationship between fallen human beings on the one hand, and the righteous, holy, and loving God on the other, is reconciled. Christ is the High Priest who offers the sacrifice of his own body in the eternal temple to accomplish humanity's reconciliation with God. Our sins are thereby accounted to him, and his righteousness is thereby accounted to us.

The idea of satisfaction or substitution draws upon themes expressed in Scripture itself, as even the earliest church fathers understood. Take, for instance, this statement from the second- or third-century anonymous Epistle to Diognetus. The author drew upon various biblical themes, such as "the Kingdom of God" and

---

82. Nyssa rejoiced in Christ clothing himself in flesh. "But to look on the clear power of God was beyond Satan's power, and so he could see in him only that fleshly part of the nature which through sin he had so long held in bondage." Christ "hid the Godhead under the veil of our nature, so that just as it is with a ravenous fish, the hook of the Deity might be gulped down with the bait of the flesh." Nyssa, *Catechetical Orations* 23–24, cited in McGuckin, "St. Gregory of Nyssa on the Dynamics of Salvation," 168–69.

83. McGuckin, "St. Gregory of Nyssa on the Dynamics of Salvation," 163.

84. Aulén, *Christus Victor*, 4–7.

85. Aulén, *Christus Victor*, 7–12.

86. Aulén, *Christus Victor*, 159.

87. Malcolm B. Yarnell III, *God the Trinity: Biblical Portraits* (B&H Academic, 2016), 236.

"ransom." The epistle listed several substitutions, including "the blameless One for the wicked" and "the incorruptible One for the corruptible." It then exulted, "O sweet exchange! O unsearchable operation! O benefits surpassing all expectation! That the wickedness of many should be hid in a single righteous One, and that the righteousness of One should justify many transgressors!"[88]

Anselm, the Archbishop of Canterbury at the turn of the twelfth century, went a step further and crafted a highly influential theory.[89] He taught that human sin lays upon humanity a weight it cannot carry.[90] Sin is both personal and objective, for it offends God himself.[91] A "repayment" for the "debt" of human sin must be paid to make "recompense" (Latin *satisfactio*).[92] God has been dishonored, but only God himself can restore that honor. Being just, God must either restore honor or punish the wicked.[93] Thankfully, God is motivated by love.[94] Christ, who is God, became man to pay our sin debt.[95] Only "the God–Man" could overcome sin and Satan so that we can reach the heavenly city.[96] God the Son willingly took the cross upon himself for us.[97]

Liberal critics responded harshly to Anselm. Adolf von Harnack led the charge, arguing Anselm diminished the cross by treating it as a *Wergild*. *Wergild* was money paid to an injured party or a surviving legatee in lieu of the offender being likewise injured or put to death. Theologians have more recently accused Anselm of teaching "a God who demands a cruel and violent end to His own Son as ruthless payment to a Divine, and abstract, justice."[98] However, the

88. Epistle to Diognetus, in Alexander Roberts and James Donaldson, eds., *The Apostolic Fathers, Justin Martyr, Irenaeus, Ante-Nicene Fathers*, vol. 1 (1885; Hendrickson, 1994), 28.

89. He explicitly rejected the idea that a ransom was paid to Satan to redeem humanity from his dominion. Instead, the Anglo-Norman bishop focused on "satisfaction." Katherine Sonderegger, "Anselmian Atonement," in Johnson, ed., *T&T Clark Companion to Atonement*, 191.

90. Anselm of Canterbury, *Why God Became Man*, in Brian Davies and G. R. Evans, eds., *The Major Works* (Oxford University Press, 1998), 305–7.

91. Sonderegger, "Anselmian Atonement," 181.

92. Anselm, *Why God Became Man*, 305.

93. Sonderegger, "Anselmian Atonement," 185.

94. Sonderegger, "Anselmian Atonement," 184.

95. Anselm, *Why God Became Man,* 319–20.

96. Sonderegger, "Anselmian Atonement," 190.

97. Anselm, *Why God Became Man*, 354.

98. Sonderegger, "Anselmian Atonement," 176.

liberal critique misrepresents Anselm, for he clearly saw the cross as a concrete act of divine love. Unlike the liberals, and the Socinians before them, Anselm also maintained Christ's deity.

John Calvin did not advocate "satisfaction," nor did he specifically address Anselm in his catechetical treatment of atonement. Rather, he drew upon Scripture's language of sacrifice, substitution, and propitiation. Calvin found that God sent Christ to redeem humanity, and that he was personally sinless. In his sacrificial mediation, Christ as priest received the punishment for sinners. "This is our acquittal: the guilt that held us liable for punishment has been transferred to the head of the Son of God."[99] Christ's subsequent resurrection is our "victory."[100] Calvin's theory of the atonement remains popular due to its deep grounding in the biblical text.

The Prophet's Call from Atonement

Peter Abelard, a Paris theologian active in the early twelfth century, was attacked in his day for emphasizing the example of Jesus Christ. Theologians today describe Abelard as the "father of exemplarism," but his thought was deeper than the popular definition may allow. Reviewing the historical evidence, Adam Johnson concluded, "Within the broader context of his Commentary, it is evident that Abelard's view included but far transcended an exemplarist understanding of the atonement."[101]

For example, Abelard affirmed the Trinitarian origin of atonement and the threefold office of Christ. And in his comments on Romans, he advocated the exemplary aspect of the atonement alongside its vicarious aspect: Christ's mediatorial sacrifice elicits a desire within us to love God through our obedience. Abelard also agreed the cross was vicarious: "We committed sin, the penalty of which he bore." Again, "he swept away the penalty for sins by the price of his death."[102] But then Abelard went a step further and added that "through the demonstration of so much grace, he drew back our

99. Calvin, *Institutes of the Christian Religion*, 509–10.

100. Calvin, *Institutes of the Christian Religion*, 520.

101. Adam J. Johnson, "Peter Abelard," in idem, ed., *T&T Clark Companion to Atonement*, 357.

102. Peter Abelard, *Commentary on the Epistle to the Romans*, 204, cited in idem, ed., *T&T Clark Companion to Atonement*, 358.

souls from the will to sin and kindled the highest love of himself."[103] Christ's sacrifice thus also transforms our moral character.

A second example theory differs significantly from Abelard's moral transformation theory. Developed by Faustus Socinus and Laelius Socinus in the sixteenth century, then taken up by modern Unitarians and liberals, this theory must be distinguished from the exemplarism propounded by classical theologians. The basic difference between an orthodox approach and a Socinian approach to Christ as example derives from their divergent views of Christ and salvation. For Socinians, Christ is a mere man,[104] and redemption comes as people draw personal inspiration from Christ's human actions. People enter heaven by mimicking Christ's life.[105]

Orthodox exemplarists rightly appeal to texts like Mark 8:34–35, Romans 6:1–15, and Philippians 2:4–11. Christ's atonement fosters Christlike devotion to God, Christlike morality, and Christlike humility. The cross prompts sanctity in true believers. They also understand moral devotion comes only by Trinitarian grace.[106]

Conclusion

All three of the following sentences are true: Christ paid the ransom for our sin through his vicarious death. Christ's death ends in victory over Satan and death. And Christ's call to carry the cross requires moral transformation. The atonement, therefore, is royal and priestly and prophetic. Several New Testament texts even tightly correlate these dimensions of the atonement.

For instance, Colossians 2 affirms Christ makes us alive, paying our debt "by nailing it to the cross" (vv. 13–14). This priestly act results in his royal triumph over "the rulers and authorities" (v. 15) and prophetically calls us to live into his "substance" (vv. 16–17). In

103. Abelard, *Commentary on the Epistle to the Romans*, 204.

104. Thomas Rees, ed., *The Racovian Catechism with Notes and Illustrations* (London: Longman, 1818), 51, 55.

105. "First, he inspires us with a certain hope of salvation, and also incites us both to enter upon the way of salvation and to persevere in it. In the next place, he is with us in every struggle." Rees, ed., *The Racovian Catechism*, 298.

106. The Socinian system affirms the threefold office of Christ but lacks Trinitarian grace. Rees, ed., *The Racovian Catechism*, 33, 169. The treatment of faith by the apostle James must not be construed as works-based salvation. Rather, James taught the type of faith that saves also manifests itself in good works (James 2:14–26).

a second instance, 1 John 3 says Christ revealed himself to "take away sins" (v. 5). And the one who remains in Christ "does not sin" (vv. 6–7), for Christ came to "destroy the devil's work" (v. 8).

In a third instance, Hebrews 2 says Christ became human to destroy "the devil" (v. 14) and "free" us from slavery and death (vv. 15–16). Christ's "atonement for the sins of the people" secured this victory (v. 17). He is thus, effectively and affectively, "able to help those who are tempted" (v. 18). And in a fourth instance, Revelation 12:11 says believers may "conquer" the devil, but only "by the blood of the Lamb," to whom their "testimony" gives witness.

The richness of the biblical atonement prompts four concluding reflections:

1. The kingly, priestly, and prophetic dimensions of the atonement coalesce in the cross. We may not dismiss any revealed aspect of his atonement.
2. The sacrificial mediation of our perfect and sufficient High Priest produced the royal victory for, and the prophetic claim upon the believer. Our High Priest's vicarious sacrifice anchors the atonement through which Christ gained his eternal victory and issues his prophetic call today.[107]
3. Christ's atonement is a work of both human mediation and divine power. The eternal Word assumed our flesh to atone for our sin on his cross. But Christ's personal human death ended neither his Person nor his work. It only ended his humiliation. Instead, by "the power of his indestructible life" (Heb. 7:16), Christ arose from the dead, ascended to heaven, and now sits upon his divine throne. One day, he shall return, bring final judgment, and reign forever, ensuring our eternal

107. The Heidelberg theologians considered Christ's death our propitiation, while Christ's victory over the devil and Christ's gift of the Holy Spirit for our sanctification are the "two benefits" of his death. Caspar Olevianus, *A Firm Foundation: An Aid to Interpreting the Heidelberg Catechism*, transl. Lyle D. Bierma (Baker, 1995), 66–69.

salvation. In the next chapter, we turn to the eternality of his mediation for us.

4. The atonement effected by God in the cross of Christ becomes ours personally by the grace of his Holy Spirit. The Spirit is the divine subject of the third volume in this series. We will address God's extension of Christ's atonement to believers there.

Study Questions

1. Enumerate the preliminary definition of the atonement provided at the beginning of this chapter.

2. Read Isaiah 52:13–53:12. Could you translate this ancient Hebrew poem into a modern hymn for worship?

3. What is the central work of the atonement? Does this central priestly work prompt us to exclude or to include his royal work and his prophetic work? Explain.

Suggested Resources

- Gustaf Aulén, *Christus Victor*
- Leon Morris, *The Cross in the New Testament*
- John Stott, *The Cross of Christ*

CHAPTER THIRTEEN

Who Do You Say That I Am?

◆ ◆

When people encounter Jesus, they are compelled to question who he is and what he is doing. Whatever their religious persuasion, whatever their social status, whoever their person—every human being who meets Christ is driven to wonder about this man. Their queries inevitably center upon the meaning of his Person and work.

Early in his ministry, Jesus healed a paralyzed man, while forgiving his sins. This scandalized the scribes, the academic elite of Israel. The divine implications of his far-reaching claims troubled them: "Why does he speak like this? . . . Who can forgive sins but God alone?" (Mark 2:7).[1] In a private conversation, Jesus inquired of his disciples about what the people said. They said the crowds classed him among the prophets. Christ replied, "But you, who do you say that I am?" (Matt. 16:13–23).[2] Before his passion, Jesus entered Jerusalem like a triumphant lord. And "the whole city was in an uproar, saying, 'Who is this?'" (21:10). During his final trial,

1. Another time, some Gentiles gained an audience with Jesus. He prayed to the Father, and God thundered in response. Jesus explained he is the light who dissipates demonic darkness (John 12:20–36). Startled, the crowds questioned him: "So how can you say, 'The Son of Man must be lifted up'? Who is this Son of Man?" (v. 34).

2. After Peter correctly answered regarding his Person, Jesus revealed his work of death and resurrection. But Peter rejected the suffering and death of the Messiah. Jesus rebuked Peter for his man-centered ideas.

Pilate asked Jesus the key political question: "Are you the king of the Jews?" (John 18:33).[3]

Ironically enough, a Roman soldier provided the most correct answer yet to the many queries about Jesus. The centurion heard all Jesus said upon the cross, felt the turbulent reply of the earth to the death of its Creator, and exclaimed, "Truly this man was the Son of God!" (Matt. 27:54; Mark 15:39).

The question required of every human being by the Spirit of Christ remains the same today: Who do you say Jesus is? The only correct answer is twofold. Regarding his Person, we must confess, "Jesus is Lord." And regarding his work, we must believe, "God raised him from the dead" (Rom. 10:9).

If your salvation depends on the proper worship of God in Christ, and it does, then identifying Christ properly is indeed the most significant issue in theology. Your answer can raise you from death itself, or it can ensure your eternal condemnation. May God in his mercy help us answer correctly. Jesus's own exegesis of Scripture provides the answer:

> While the Pharisees were together, Jesus questioned them, "What do you think about the Messiah? Whose son is he?"
>
> They replied, "David's."
>
> He asked them, "How is it then that David, inspired by the Spirit, calls him 'Lord':
>
> The Lord declared to my Lord, 'Sit at my right hand until I put your enemies under your feet'?
>
> "If David calls him 'Lord,' how, then, can he be his son?" No one was able to answer him at all, and from that day no one dared to question him anymore. (Matt. 22:41–46)[4]

3. Pilate knew he was a "man" (John 19:5) but became afraid after hearing he claimed to be the Son of God. The Roman governor plied, "Where are you from?" (v. 9). Jesus warned him that every authority, including Pilate's, comes from above, and that Jesus himself will personally judge every authority (John 18:36–37; 19:10–11). Pilate shifted the conversation in an abstract direction, hoping to avoid the implications of the truth.

4. The Pharisees were raised to interpret the written Word of God. By referring them to a royal psalm, Jesus explained that the Christ is simultaneously the human

Only after the death and resurrection of Jesus could either the contemporary opponents of Jesus or his own disciples begin comprehending the truth about Christ. Only through his direct teaching could they correctly interpret the Old Testament, which had already revealed Christ is the mediating God–Man (Luke 24:25–27, 44–47). In other words, it is only through the revelation of Christ in his gospel of vicarious death and justifying resurrection that the identity of his Person becomes clear. Conversely, only his divine–human personhood explains the power behind Christ's gospel of salvation.[5]

Let us first consider those who have answered the all-important question about the Christ incorrectly. Second, we will recall the New Testament answer to the question about his divine–human Person from the perspective of his eternally powerful reconstitution of humanity. The eternal Word's work of saving humanity is comprised of his human humiliation and human exaltation. Christ's human acts never compromise the eternal immutability of his divine nature, nor do they destroy the integrity of his divine activity.

Denials, Distortions, and Diminutions of Christ

There have been repeated challenges to the revelation of Jesus Christ since the days he walked the earth. And many of those past challenges have the habit of reappearing. Sadly, even among those claiming to be Christians, the challenges to his personal honor continue unabated, as the woeful results from the most recent survey of American beliefs demonstrate.[6] The early church's reception of the books of the biblical canon and of the gospel as the rule of faith provided the historic church concise answers to this critical question. The rule of faith was later stated clearly by the Apostles' Creed

---

son of David and the divine Son of God (Ps. 110:1; cf. 2 Sam. 7:12, 14). Hearing Christ's equation of God with a man, the Pharisees balked.

5. Many Jews began to receive Jesus as Lord after his resurrection (Acts 2:41), and many Gentiles began to join them in the faith (Acts 10:34–48). However, others continued to reject him.

6. George Barna reports that only 11 percent of Americans and 16 percent of self-proclaimed Christians "believe in the Trinity." Cultural Research Center, "Most Americans—Including Churchgoers—Reject the Trinity," Arizona Christian University, 26 March 2025, https://www.arizonachristian.edu/wp-content/uploads/2025/03/AWVI-2025_03_Most-Americans-Reject-the-Trinity_FINAL_03_26_2025.pdf.

and demarcated from heresy by the Nicene, Chalcedonian, and Athanasian statements of faith about Trinity and Christ.

The classical creeds have long helped true believers address various internal challenges to the identity of Jesus. However, the formalization of the Nicene Creed at the ecumenical council of Constantinople in 381 never entirely stifled these challenges. Nor did the various internal and external denials, distortions, and diminutions of Christ cease after the Christological formula of Chalcedon was crafted in 451. False teachers repeat old heresies, while others combine them with new errors. As noted previously, Jesus and the apostles repeatedly warned that false teachers would proclaim false Christs to try to lead people astray.[7] Apostasy, heresy, and error are rooted in false preaching or teaching about Christ. In reply, we must be careful to uphold his Person, his full deity, and his true humanity.

Because heresy is used by God as a backdrop against which the truth about Christ may shine (1 Cor. 11:18–19), it will prove helpful to rehearse some other major continuing challenges to orthodox Christology, both ancient and modern. Historians and theologians have watched heresies repeat themselves throughout history, down to the present day. Philosophers of history tell us that those who refuse to listen to the lessons of history are apt to repeat its errors. "Nowhere else is this principle more obvious than in the historic heresies of the Christian faith."[8]

One can, for instance, hear ancient Modalism reverberate among modern Oneness Pentecostals. They baptize only in the name of Jesus and believe "Father, Son, and Holy Spirit were simply singular names for Jesus."[9] Similarly, heretical Subordinationism resonates today with Jehovah's Witnesses. Their primary periodical, *The Watchtower*, "has never failed to echo the old Arian heresy."[10]

---

7. See chapter 4 above.

8. Rick Warren, "Foreword," in Alister McGrath, *Heresy: A History of Defending the Truth* (SPCK, 2009), v.

9. George A. Mather, Larry A. Nichols, and Alvin J. Schmidt, *Dictionary of Cults, Sects, Religions and the Occult* (Zondervan, 1993), 215.

10. Walter Martin and Hank Hanegraaff, *The Kingdom of the Cults*, rev. ed. (Bethany House, 1997), 116. Alas, in their zeal to refute Arianism, Martin and Hanegraaff cede the interpretation of *monogenes* to the Arians and deny the eternal generation of the Son, while properly affirming the eternality of the Word. They also deny the ascription of "eternal" to the Father, reducing the Father and the Son to a merely functional relation. They might have consulted Isaiah 9:6. Martin and Hanegraaff, *The Kingdom of the Cults*, 167–70.

Also, incipient "Gnosticism lives on today, not necessarily knowing its real name or even its history. Yet its spoor is unmistakable" in the modern quest for the "real me."[11] Echoes of semi-Arianism may even be heard within contemporary Evangelicalism.

A review of various explicit denials of Christ by those properly considered to belong to other religions, and of the continuing phenomena of Christological heresy and error among those who consider themselves Christian, may benefit the reader. Thankfully, despite every direct denial, every pernicious heresy, and every distracting error, "the faith that was delivered to the saints once for all" (Jude 3) continues to resound among true teachers and preachers in the faithful preaching of the biblical Christ, whom the orthodox churches confess.

Jewish and Pagan Denials

Ancient chronicles report on several major denials of Christ in the first century. These extra-biblical and non-Christian references to Jesus, while sometimes based on secondhand witness and often hostile, yet provide important evidence about explicit rejections of Jesus. Many Jews refused to receive Jesus as Messiah, just as many leading pagans denied the claims of the church about the Person and work of Christ. Both unbelieving Jews and pagan Gentiles often persecuted the early Christians. The early Christians, both Jew and Gentile, found they truly had become one new humanity in Christ (Eph. 2:15).

The New Testament says the council of the Jewish Sanhedrin attempted to suppress the news of Jesus's resurrection by bribery (Matt. 26:57–68; 28:1–15). Nonetheless, a multitude of Jews, including many priests and Pharisees, became believers upon hearing the gospel and coming under conviction (Acts 2:41, 47; 6:7; 15:5). The Sanhedrin then tried to suppress the voice of the early church (4:1–21; 5:17–42). Their efforts led to the stoning of Stephen (6:8–7:60). Saul originally supported this persecution of Christians, but he was transformed by a direct encounter with Christ. Taking the name of Paul, he himself was afterward persecuted by both Jews and Gentiles (Acts 8:1–3; 9:1–30; Gal. 1:13; 2 Cor. 11:22–33).

---

11. McGrath, *Heresy*, 232.

Josephus, the Jewish historian, reported on the high priest's effort to have James, the brother of Jesus, executed in Jerusalem.[12] The Babylonian portion of the Talmud, an important collection of Jewish legal texts, rejected the teachings of the New Testament. Certain fourth and fifth century rabbis beyond the recently Christianized Roman Empire said that Jesus "deserved to be executed because of his blasphemy, that he will sit in hell forever, and that those who follow his example up until today will not, as he has promised, gain eternal life but will share his horrible fate."[13] Through such hostility, it should not surprise us that Judaism and Christianity developed into two different religions.

Ancient Roman pagans opposed the new religion as a "deadly superstition" and "great evil."[14] Concerning events in the year 52, Suetonius records an expulsion of Jews from Rome for "continually making disturbances" about "Chrestus."[15] Pliny the Younger said Christians gathered "to recite a hymn antiphonally to Christ, as to a god." Pliny informed the Emperor Trajan that he forced Christians to worship "your image and the statues of the gods" and to curse Christ.[16] Tacitus reports the same, and that "Christus, from whom their name is derived, was executed at the hand of one of our procurators, Pontius Pilate." Tacitus also reported on the brutal crucifixions and burnings of Christians by the Emperor Nero in 64.[17]

Islamic Distortions

In 632, the founder of Islam, Mohammed of Medina, died. By 638, much of Christian Palestine and Egypt came under the Muslim sword. Muslim rulers showed a semi-tolerance at points to Christians as a people of the book. They appreciated Christ according to their

---

12. The murder of the James mentioned in Acts 12:1–2 concerns the brother of John. Josephus also reported Herod's murder of John the Baptist. A passage in his *Antiquities* refers to Jesus but seems to have been altered later. Everett Ferguson, *Backgrounds of Early Christianity* (Eerdmans, 1987), 387–89.

13. Peter Schäfer, *Jesus in the Talmud* (Princeton University Press, 2007), 129.

14. Ferguson, *Backgrounds of Early Christianity*, 472.

15. Suetonius, *Vita Claudii* 25.4, in Henry Bettenson and Chris Maunder, eds., *Documents of the Christian Church,* 3rd ed. (Oxford University Press, 1999), 2. Cf. Acts 18:2.

16. Pliny the Younger to Trajan (c. 112), in Bettenson and Maunder, eds., *Documents of the Christian Church*, 4.

17. Tacitus, *Annales* 13.32 and 15.44, in Bettenson and Maunder, eds., *Documents of the Christian Church*, 1–2.

understanding of him, even as they demeaned Christian Scripture and theology. Over the centuries, Christians were restrained from expressing their faith and often horribly persecuted.[18]

Islam's holy text, the Koran, recognized Jesus was virgin-born. But it trivialized Christ and subverted his humanity, saying that Jesus talked to Mary from the womb and to others from the crib,[19] and that Jesus miraculously brought a clay bird to life.[20] The Koran also denied the deity of Christ. It subordinated the authority of Jesus entirely to Allah, saying he can only perform miracles "with Allah's permission" or "by my permission."[21] Jesus is merely the "servant," "prophet," and "Messiah" of Allah. He is "not but a messenger."[22]

The Koran also mischaracterized the Christian doctrine of the Trinity. It presumed that Christians believe Mary, the Messiah, and Allah are divine beings and that the church worships Mary and Jesus "as gods."[23] It commanded Muslims that they "shall not ascribe divinity" to Jesus, arguing "the nature of Jesus is as the nature of Adam."[24]

Islam, in other words, affirms a type of human Christ and utterly denies the God–Man of Christian Scripture and history. The Koran, moreover, directly curses anyone who says Jesus is *ibnullâh*, "son of God."[25] Some Christian apologists have thus rejected the title "Son of God" as an apologetic toward Muslims, arguing they want to avoid transmitting carnal understandings.[26] Alas, however, this tactic undermines the integrity of the gospel.[27]

---

18. Philip Jenkins, *The Lost History of Christianity: The Thousand-Year Golden Age of the Church in the Middle East, Africa, and Asia—and How It Died* (HarperCollins, 2008), 207–25; David Wilmshurst, *The Martyred Church: A History of the Church of the East* (London: East and West, 2011).

19. Surahs 3:46; 19:29–31. All citations of the Koran come from Muhammad Asad, *The Message of the Quran: Translated and Explained* (Gibraltar: Dar Al-Andulas, 1980).

20. Surah 3:49.

21. Surahs 3:49; 5:110.

22. Surahs 19:31; 5:75.

23. Surahs 5:72–77; 5:17, 116.

24. Surahs 3:59–64; 4:49; 19:35, 88–89; etc.

25. Surah 9:30.

26. J. Scott Horrell says, "Both terms 'Father' and 'Son' for God are repugnant to the Muslim. Yet they are more than mere metaphors or titles. They are the divine names that most disclose the divine relations." Collin Hansen, "The Son and the Crescent," *Christianity Today* (February 2011).

27. Cf. Ayman S. Ibrahim and Ant Greenham, eds., *Islam and the Bible: Questioning Muslim Idiom Translations* (B&H Academic, 2023).

The Koran affirmed the death of Jesus,[28] but then said it was only apparent. Rather, it said, Allah took Jesus up to himself.[29] Muslim apologists solve this contradiction by arguing somebody other than Jesus died on the cross. One Muslim tradition claims Jesus will return and kill those Christians who have not submitted to Islam.[30]

The Koran speaks positively about the humanity of "Isa" as a prophet. However, it also profoundly distorts the Trinity, explicitly denies the deity of Christ, and diminishes the human work of Jesus. The Koran and Islamic tradition oppose the central dogmas of the Christian faith revealed in Holy Scripture. Christians would be wise not to pervert the truth of Christ in the attempt to build a bridge to Islam. I have learned through personal experience that the best way to win Muslims to faith in Christ is to pray, to love them as fellow image bearers, and to openly share with them the saving truth about the God–Man who died and arose from the dead for us.

Celestial Flesh

In the sixteenth century, Caspar Schwenckfeld derived the essence of Christ's humanity directly from God rather than from Mary. While this Spiritualist theologian tried to preserve the holiness of Christ on the one hand, he undermined the true humanity of Christ on the other. Citing the anti-Apollinarian axiom of Gregory of Nazianzus, a Roman Catholic opponent reminded Schwenckfeld that Christ had to assume our creaturely humanity to save it.[31]

The apocalyptic Anabaptist Melchior Hoffmann adapted Schwenckfeld's celestial flesh doctrine. He made Mary a mere conduit for Christ's heavenly body and embraced Eutychianism: "We have now heard enough that the whole seed of Adam, be it of man, woman, or virgin, is cursed and delivered to eternal death. Now if the

28. Surahs 3:77; 5:17; 19:33.

29. Surah 4:157–58.

30. Sahih al-Bukhari, "Oppressions," *Hadith* 2476, 46, 31, "The Breaking of the Cross and the Killing of the Pigs."

31. Schwenckfeld's undoubted "piety," one scholar wrote, "was considerably more orthodox than his systematics." He also thought Christ's humanity was totally deified in glory, making the communication of attributes to his person impossible. Paul L. Maier, *Caspar Schwenckfeld on the Person and Work of Christ* (Royal VanGorcum, 1959), 106–7.

body of Jesus Christ was also such flesh and of this seed as is openly affirmed, it follows that the redemption has not yet happened."[32]

Like Hoffmann, the early Dutch Anabaptist leader Dirk Phillips was concerned the holiness of Christ could be compromised by the unclean seed of Mary.[33] Unlike Hoffmann, however, Dirk tried to maintain the orthodox Christology of Chalcedon. He said Christ was "truly God" and "truly man."[34] Menno Simons, a former Roman priest whose name was taken by the most populous group of Anabaptists, followed Dirk and Hoffmann in trying to protect Christ from inheriting the taint of sin.[35] But the attempt by Dirk and Menno to combine celestial flesh Christology with Chalcedonian Christology proved unstable.

A second-generation Mennonite leader, Hans de Ries, wrote communal confessions in 1577, 1578, and 1609 that helped move the Dutch Anabaptists toward full Chalcedonian orthodoxy. De Ries confessed that Christ is the divine Son of God through eternal generation. He also confessed that Christ received his humanity from Mary, of the seed of Eve and Abraham.[36] His 1609 confession was translated into English by the Cambridge-educated Baptist, John Smyth. Smyth asked the first Baptist congregation to

---

32. Hoffmann continued, "For the seed of Adam belongs to Satan and is the property of the devil. Satan cannot be paid in his own coin." Melchior Hoffmann, "Truthful Witness" (1533), in Walter Klaassen, ed., *Anabaptism in Outline: Selected Primary Sources* (Herald Press, 1981), 27.

33. Dirk Phillips, "The True Knowledge of Jesus Christ" (1557), in Klaassen, ed., *Anabaptism in Outline*, 37.

34. "He is truly God from everlasting and born of the Father before the foundation of the world. But he became truly man in these last days." Phillips, "The True Knowledge of Jesus Christ," in Klaassen, ed., *Anabaptism in Outline*, 37–38.

35. Abraham Friesen, *Menno Simons: Dutch Reformer between Luther, Erasmus, and the Holy Spirit* (Xlibris, 2015), 199–209.

36. De Ries treated the older Mennonites gently but noted their error. *The First Waterlandian Confession*, arts. II, IV; *The Middelburg Confession*, art. VI; *Short Confession of Faith*, arts. III, VIII, in Cornelius J. Dyck, *Hans de Ries: A Study in Second Generation Dutch Anabaptism* (Pandora Press, 2023), 274–75, 288–89, 297–301.

receive it.[37] Later Mennonite confessions abandoned the celestial flesh Christology of their founders.[38]

The Quests for the Historical Jesus

Academic scholarship, through its novel "historical critical method" of Bible study, has fostered doubt about the special revelation of Jesus Christ since the late seventeenth century. Leo Garrett lamented, "Some practitioners of the historical-critical method have assumed presuppositions for their work that are alien or hostile to the biblical revelation attested to and embodied in the Bible."[39] Andrew Louth agreed, "The whole question of what we know about Christ, and how we know it, has been made complicated—at least at an intellectual level—by three centuries of argument and scholarship in the West."[40]

Rooted in the naturalist philosophy of Baruch Spinoza, the historical critical method tries to go behind the sacred canon affirmed by the church to find a person the critics believe was the true Jesus of history.[41] In the nineteenth century, the Tübingen School of F. C. Baur posited a conflict in the early church between Hebrew Christianity and Pauline Christianity. This conflict, they argued, fostered orthodox Christology.[42] Similarly, in the early twentieth century, Adolf von Harnack claimed classical Christology derived from Hellenism. He

---

37. De Ries pressed the English Baptists to reject Socinian Christology. Unlike most Reformation theologians—including Luther, Calvin, Schwenckfeld, Hoffman, De Ries, and Smyth—the Socinians denied Christ's deity. Dyck, *Hans de Ries*, 164–73, 217–32, 295–97. Thomas Helwys refused to follow Smyth and returned to England to plant the first Baptist church in London. John Smyth, *A Short Confession* (1610), in William L. Lumpkin and Bill J. Leonard, eds., *Baptist Confessions of Faith*, 2nd ed. (Judson Press, 2011), 98; Malcolm B. Yarnell III, "'We Believe with the Heart and with the Mouth Confess': The Engaged Piety of the Early General Baptists," *Baptist Quarterly* 44 (2011): 43.

38. Karl Koop, *Anabaptist-Mennonite Confessions of Faith: The Development of a Tradition* (Pandora Press, 2004), 92–95.

39. James Leo Garrett Jr., *Systematic Theology: Biblical, Historical, and Evangelical*, vol. 1, 2nd ed. (BIBAL Press, 2000), 170.

40. "The sources seem so obvious—principally, the four Gospels that we find in the New Testament—but modern Western scholarship, mostly Protestant, has made what seems obvious shadowy and ambiguous." Andrew Louth, *Introducing Eastern Orthodox Theology* (SPCK, 2013), 50.

41. David S. Dockery and Malcolm B. Yarnell III, *Special Revelation and Scripture* (B&H Academic, 2024), 303–6.

42. Dockery and Yarnell, *Special Revelation and Scripture*, 310.

believed orthodoxy intellectualizes the faith and points Christians away from the life and teachings of the real Jesus. Jesus, he said, was a teacher of ethics who merely called human beings to honor God the Father by loving each other.[43] The historical-critical method of Bible study has long been marked by distrust toward, even disdain for classical Christology.

At least three successive movements may be identified with "the quest for the historical Jesus."[44] The "First Quest" was prominent from the late eighteenth through early twentieth centuries. It began in Hermann Samuel Reimarus's *Wolfenbüttel Fragments* (1774–1778), became solidified in David Friedrich Strauss's *The Life of Jesus Critically Examined* (1835), and concluded with Albert Schweitzer's *Quest of the Historical Jesus* (1906). The "Second Quest," which began in the 1960s and became known as "the Biblical Theology Movement," was led by Rudolf Bultmann, Oscar Cullmann, Ernst Käsemann, and Wolfhart Pannenberg. The "Third Quest" was active in the 1990s, with "The Jesus Seminar" presuming the vanguard. Led by Robert Funk and John Dominic Crossan, the controversial views of the Jesus Seminar were popularized by Marcus Borg and John Spong, among others.[45]

The First Quest rejected both miracles and the special inspiration of revelation. Reimarus said Jesus did not intend to start a new religion. Instead, the New Testament writers committed conscious fraud.[46] Bringing this quest to an end, Schweitzer criticized other liberals for distorting the life of Jesus. Schweitzer himself believed Jesus was not a teacher of ethics, but a deluded apocalyptic who died for claiming to be Messiah. Schweitzer considered the resurrection unimportant.[47] Jesus as a spiritual force supersedes his historical

---

43. Adolf von Harnack, *What Is Christianity?,* transl. Thomas Bailey Saunders (Harper, 1957).

44. Colin Brown expanded the history of the search for the identity of the historical Jesus beyond the three quests, including less skeptical scholars like N. T. Wright. Sadly, Brown restricted the offering of worship to the Father. Colin Brown and Craig A. Evans, *A History of the Quest for the Historical Jesus*, 2 vols. (Zondervan Academic, 2022), 2:688–89.

45. Luke Timothy Johnson, *The Real Jesus: The Misguided Quest for the Historical Jesus and the Truth of the Traditional Gospels* (HarperCollins, 1996).

46. Albert Schweitzer, *The Quest of the Historical Jesus: A Critical Study of Its Progress from Reimarus to Wrede* (1910; Johns Hopkins University Press, 1998), 13–26.

47. Rather, "At midday the same day—it was the 14th Nisan, and in the evening the Paschal lamb would be eaten—Jesus cried aloud and expired. He had chosen to remain fully conscious to the last." Schweitzer, *The Quest of the Historical Jesus,* 397.

person. It only matters how you receive his eschatology, not that he really was Son of God incarnate.[48]

In the Second or "New Quest," Rudolf Bultmann separated the actual events of Jesus's life, *Historie*, from his meaning for Christians, *Geschichte*. Bultmann argued we cannot really know history. Objective historical truth is unobtainable, but a person may still have an existential encounter.[49] Oscar Cullmann likewise deemed ontological concerns about Jesus—whether and how he is God and man—a Greek interposition. Instead, what Jesus does for a person is important. "Christology is the doctrine of an 'event,' not the doctrine of natures."[50]

This Second Quest encouraged scholars to focus on *Heilsgeschichte*, salvation history, to the exclusion of ontology. In reply, we should note that action can never be separated from the agent acting; nor can one's existential experience of a personal act be separated from the person who acts. Neither Bultmann nor Cullmann convincingly demonstrate why we should, nor how we can divorce personal agency from personal action. Personal agents foster personal actions, and personal encounters derive from persons acting upon other persons. The attempt of the Second Quest scholars to divorce personal reality from personal function so contradicts basic human experience and logic that it approaches the fictional.[51]

In the Third Quest, the Jesus Seminar participants used colored beads to vote as to whether a gospel text contained a saying truly uttered by Jesus. If he offered a red bead, it meant the scholar believed the saying was by Jesus. Pink meant it sounds like Jesus. Gray indicated a possibility. The Seminar scholar denied the text was reliable with a black bead. Robert Funk, using this method to look behind the text, concluded that Jesus was "a social gadfly," "no

48. Schweitzer, *The Quest of the Historical Jesus*, 398–403.

49. "I do indeed think that we can now know almost nothing concerning the life and personality of Jesus, since the early Christian sources show no interest in either, are moreover fragmentary and often legendary; and other sources about Jesus do not exist." Bultmann, *Jesus and the Word*, transl. Louise Pettibone Smith and Erminie Huntress Lantero (Charles Scribner, 1958), 14. Bultmann denied Jesus thought he was the Messiah. Bultmann, *Jesus and the Word*, 15.

50. Oscar Cullmann, *The Christology of the New Testament*, rev. ed. (Philadelphia: Westminster, 1963), 9.

51. Moreover, every creaturely action is enabled by divine creation. Brian Davies, *The Thought of Thomas Aquinas* (Oxford University Press, 1992), 159–61.

goody-two-shoes," "something of a party animal," "probably was not celibate," and was "accidentally crucified."[52]

Walter Brueggeman, judging their method "highly subjective," offered this correction: "The Seminar is still trying to get behind the text, and I think that what we need to do is deal with the text."[53] Luke Timothy Johnson found six characteristic traits in the writings of the Jesus Seminar scholars: As a presupposition, they reject the truthfulness of the canonical Gospels. They dismiss other canonical sources as "irrelevant." Jesus pursued "cultural critique" rather than spirituality. Traditional doctrine is a "distortion" of Jesus's thought. And historical knowledge is "normative." Sadly, while most Seminar scholars claimed to be Christian, they yearned for approval from skeptics in the academy.[54]

Rejecting the three quests paradigm, participants in the "Next Quest" argue studies into the historical Jesus require further diversification. They are engaging in reception history, criticizing previous methods, adopting new methods, asking new questions, reconsidering old questions, hearing from diverse viewpoints, and lamenting micro-specialization.[55] Among the interesting new studies in this Fourth Quest is the recovery of a more positive view of the Gospels through appeal to the genre of ancient Greek and Latin biographies.[56] The unorthodoxy of the entire quest project, however, places its continuing utility in grave doubt.

Kenoticism

Kenoticism, a doctrine based on a unique theological reading of Christ's "humbling" (Greek *kenosis*) of himself, "belongs distinctively to modern times."[57] It originated with nineteenth-century German

52. Johnson, *The Real Jesus*, 12.

53. *Atlanta-Journal Constitution* (March 1989), cited in Johnson, *The Real Jesus*, 18.

54. Johnson, *The Real Jesus*, 54–56.

55. They hope studies of class, racism, and gender might provide a more complete picture of Jesus and greater detail about his social context. James Crossley, "Introduction: The Next Quest," in James Crossley and Chris Keith, eds., *The Next Quest for the Historical Jesus* (Zondervan, 2024), 1–14.

56. Helen K. Bond, "Biography," in Crossley and Keith, *The Next Quest for the Historical Jesus*, 62–76.

57. Donald M. Baillie, *God Was in Christ: An Essay on Incarnation and Atonement*, 2nd ed. (Faber and Faber, 1961), 94.

theologian Gottfried Thomasius, a supposed theological conservative. Thomasius tried to answer the historical critical scholar David Strauss, who recognized only the human Jesus.[58] Seeking to explain the human limits of Jesus, Thomasius argued the second Person "laid aside his divine attributes (omnipotence, omniscience, omnipresence) and lived for a period on earth within the limitations of humanity."[59]

Isaak August Dorner criticized Kenoticism for fostering both "theopaschism," wherein the Trinity suffers disruption, and "subordinationism," which makes Christ less than the Father and the Spirit. Thomasius tried to resolve these errors by distinguishing "essential" attributes from "relative" attributes. He said the Son did not surrender his essential attributes of love and holiness, but rather these relative attributes.[60]

Karl Barth said German Kenoticism focused on the wrong question: *How* did God become man? They vainly sought to explain the inexplicable. God has not revealed this detail to man. Theological wisdom must instead focus on *who* Christ is.[61] As we have seen, God certainly has revealed the saving Truth of his Person.

Charles Gore and Peter Forsyth later imported Kenoticism into British theology. Repeating Thomasius's error, they tried to explain how Jesus lacked knowledge. But rather than undergoing ontological loss, they said Christ underwent functional "self-retraction."[62] Donald Baillie replied that functional Kenoticism still either diminishes Christ's deity or makes his humanity temporary. "He had been God, but now He was a man. If taken in all its implications, that seems more like a pagan story of metamorphosis than like the Christian doctrine of incarnation." Recalling our limited knowledge, Baillie replied, "Surely the relation between the divine and the human in the Incarnation is a deeper mystery than this."[63]

---

58. Bruce McCormack, "Kenoticism in Modern Christology," in Francesca Murphy, ed., *The Oxford Handbook of Christology* (Oxford University Press, 2015), 449.

59. Baillie, *God Was in Christ*, 94.

60. This is Karl Barth's critique. McCormack, "Kenoticism in Modern Christology," 451–52.

61. Alan Torrance, "Jesus in Christian Doctrine," in Markus Bockmuehl, ed., *The Cambridge Companion to Jesus* (Cambridge University Press, 2001), 212–14.

62. McCormack, "Kenoticism in Modern Christology," 453.

63. Baillie, *God Was in Christ*, 96–97.

Donald Macleod roundly criticized both ontological Kenoticism and functional Kenoticism: First, Kenoticists fail to explain how the world could be continually upheld by the Word while he supposedly lacked, or supposedly failed to exercise, certain attributes (cf. Heb. 1:3; Col. 1:17). Second, Kenoticism departs from the Chalcedonian Formula, for although it maintains Christ's humanity, it "seriously truncated" his deity. Third, it disrupted the continuity of Christ between his preexistence and Incarnation with a huge mental contraction, thereby driving "a fatal wedge between the Jesus of history and the Christ of faith." Fourth, if Jesus lacks access to divine knowledge, then he cannot really know about his deity or power (cf. John 10:30; 16:15). Kenoticism also makes the Word contradict himself, saying Jesus as a man has fallible knowledge, while he claims to speak God's eternal words (Matt. 4:4; 5:18; John 10:35).[64] A fallible Christ, we might add, emasculates an infallible text.

Paul never uses *kenosis* to diminish Christ's deity. The Greek verb is translated elsewhere as "humbling" or "emptying," with no hint of divine subtraction (Rom. 4:14; 1 Cor. 1:17; 2 Cor. 9:3). There is no worthy exegetical reason for shifting the meaning drastically from a personal act of humility to a loss in divine ontology.[65] In Philippians 2, Christ humbled himself twice: Firstly, at his incarnation, the eternal Word humbled himself by "taking" (Greek *labon*) our servant form, "assuming" (Greek *genomenos*) our human likeness (v. 7), and "being found" (Greek *heuretheis*) in our human form (v. 8a KJV). Secondly, he humbled himself in his humanity by "becoming obedient to the point of death—even to death on a cross" (v. 8b). Taking human nature does not mutate the immutable nature of the divine Person. Nor does human death threaten his sovereign deity. While human minds try to explain that which seems weak, the eyes of faith understand Christ's humility displays divine virtue.

Historically, orthodox theologians have long argued the eternal Word's "self-emptying" entailed no suspension of deity. Christ remained God and upheld the universe even as he took human flesh, died, and arose.[66] Cyril of Alexandria argued the two natures

---

64. Donald Macleod, *The Person of Christ, Contours of Christian Theology* (InterVarsity Press, 1998), 209–12.

65. The functional Kenoticist attempt to ascribe a loss of function to the divine Word while ascribing a continuity of ontology is theologically untenable. God the Word, being simple, immutable, and eternal, is "pure act."

66. McCormack, "Kenoticism in Modern Christology," 445.

of Jesus Christ were united in his one Person without diminishing either. "He remained Lord of all things, even when he came, for the economy, in the form of a slave, and this is why the mystery of Christ is truly wonderful."[67] Cyril's excellent twelfth anathema against Nestorianism was affirmed at the ecumenical Council of Ephesus in 431: "If anyone does not recognize that the Word of God suffered in the flesh and was crucified in the flesh and tasted death in the flesh and became the firstborn of the dead, although as God he is life and life-giving, let him be anathema."[68]

Among contemporary Kenoticists, Bruce McCormack claims that Christ limited the display of his divine glory.[69] In reply, we can note that just because human beings may not see Christ in his deity, this diminishes the light of his glory not one bit (John 1:11). Rather, human blindness demonstrates divine incomprehensibility. Christ displayed his glory when he wished (Mark 9:2–9).[70] Some American evangelicals also teach Kenoticism.[71] Stephen Wellum discovered evidence of "Evangelical Kenoticism" in both its ontological and functional forms.[72]

Leo Garrett lamented how Kenoticism compromised "the simultaneous union of the human and the divine in Jesus,"[73] and

---

67. Cyril of Alexandria, *On the Unity of Christ*, transl. John Anthony McGuckin (St. Vladimir's Seminary Press, 1995), 61.

68. Council of Ephesus (431), in Norman P. Tanner, ed., *Decrees of the Ecumenical Councils*, 2 vols. (Georgetown University Press, 1990), 1:*61.

69. McCormack, "Kenoticism in Modern Christology," 447–48.

70. Robert Kolb and Timothy J. Wengert, eds., *The Book of Concord: The Confessions of the Evangelical Lutheran Church*, transl. Charles Arand et al. (Fortress Press, 2000), 511.

71. Answering the question, "Did the Son of God Give Up His Deity at the Incarnation?" R. Albert Mohler agreed "it is true in no sense that Jesus gave up His deity," but then limited Christ's divine privileges and communion with God. "But what the Son of God did give up was the sublime infinite pleasure of being with the Father in communion in heaven with God without taking on the burden of human flesh and obedience to the will of the Father. The Son of God gave up some of the privileges He had with the Father in order to come to be one of us, among us." Mohler, *The Briefing* (22 December 2023), part ix. Cf. Millard J. Erickson, *Christian Theology*, 2nd ed. (Baker, 1998), 751; Mohler, *The Briefing (*13 December 2024), part iii; Mohler, *The Briefing* (21 March 2025), part iv; J. P. Moreland and William Lane Craig, *Philosophical Foundations for a Christian Worldview*, 2nd ed. (IVP Academic, 2017), 607–8.

72. Stephen J. Wellum, *The Person of Christ: An Introduction* (Crossway, 2021), 128–34.

73. Garrett, *Systematic Theology*, 1:695.

"threatened the loss of the divine nature." Garrett reminded his evangelical colleagues, "The unity of the person of Jesus Christ means that in assuming human nature the eternal Word did not abandon his divine nature."[74] In his recent detailed evaluation of Kenoticism, James E. Dolezal strongly criticized Kenoticism's diminishing of Christ by "subtraction." He also correctly rejected the ascription of a "real addition" to Christ.[75]

In conclusion, the early church fathers faced variants of what later became known as Kenoticism and found it wanting. More recently, Dorner, Baillie, Macleod, Garrett, and Dolezal commended a careful theological exegesis of Scripture and informed reception of the creeds while rejecting Kenoticism in both its ontological and functional forms. We must teach the divine Word became truly human. The Word remained God even when he became a man, and he continues to act as God even as he also acts as man. Christ's divine nature, which necessarily encompasses his divine activity, should be compromised neither by the subtraction advocated by some evangelicals nor the addition advocated by others. We must learn to say with Scripture, "Jesus Christ is the same yesterday, today, and forever" (Heb. 13:8).

The "God Incarnate" Debate

While German, British, and American conservatives propagated Kenoticism, liberal theologians became adept at creating numerous mythologies of Jesus. As mentioned above, Adolf von Harnack, the last great liberal theologian, accused orthodox theologians in the early church of having "Hellenized" the gospel. He preferred a Jesus who was merely a great preacher of love for others and reverence for God as Father.[76]

The origin of liberalism's redefined Jesuses can be traced back to the naturalistic and rationalist approach to biblical interpretation fostered by Baruch Spinoza coupled with the epistemological principles of Gerhard Lessing (1646–1716). Lessing detected an "ugly,

74. Garrett, *Systematic Theology*, 1:715–16.

75. Cf. Stephen J. Wellum, *God the Son Incarnate: The Doctrine of Christ* (Crossway, 2016), 177. Dolezal appreciated Wellum's intent, but criticized trading "substantive mutation for accidental mutation, at least implicitly." James E. Dolezal, "Neither Subtraction, Nor Addition: The Word's Terminative Assumption of a Human Nature," *Nova et Vetera* 20 (2022): 143–45.

76. See the section above on the Quests.

broad ditch which I cannot get across, however often and however earnestly I have tried to make the leap."[77] For Lessing, that ditch separated historical events on the one side from divine reality on the other. The result of detaching knowledge of God from historical evidence later led some theologians to view the accounts of Jesus in Scripture as comprised of myths.

For instance, rather than looking to an inspired Word for his understanding of Jesus, Strauss argued that human beings should recognize their own sense of divinity. "The father of myth theory" thus rejected Christ's unique deity.[78] Scholars after Strauss increasingly dealt with the biblical texts according to acidic historical critical methods and deemed Scripture a mythology. George Tyrrell said liberal biographers of Jesus "looked into the deep well of history and saw there only the reflections of their own faces."[79]

While the liberal quests continued, the clash between liberal mythologies and the orthodox hermeneutic came to a head in 1977 with rival publications. The liberals, led by John Hick, published first. Contributors to *The Myth of God Incarnate* said the doctrine of the incarnation defined by Nicaea and Chalcedon required change "in order to be believable," and said Christ can no longer be accepted as the Son of God.[80] Some authors argued that Nicene doctrine was "harmful," because it denies salvation through other religions. The myth of the incarnation may be helpful only for personal inspiration.[81]

Orthodox evangelicals, led by Michael Green, replied with *The Truth of God Incarnate* later that same year. Green said the demise of incarnational Christology occurred in stages: First, Scripture's inspiration and trustworthiness were "abandoned." Second, the virgin birth of Christ was doubted. "Next came a rejection of miracles." Fourth, the "death of God" theologians lost faith in God while still speaking of him. Fifth, the resurrection was scorned. Finally, the Incarnation was attacked. The critics thereby dismantled the very

---

77. Gotthold Lessing, *Lessing's Theological Writings,* ed. Henry Chadwick (Stanford University Press, 1957), 55.

78. Torrance, "Jesus in Christian Doctrine," 214–16.

79. George Tyrrell, *Christianity at the Cross-Roads* (Longmans, Green, 1909), 44.

80. John Hick, ed., *The Myth of God Incarnate* (SCM Press, 1977), ix–x.

81. Don Cupitt, "The Christ of Christendom," in *The Myth of God Incarnate*, 133–47; John Hick, "Jesus and the World Religions," in *The Myth of God Incarnate*, 167–85.

"chassis" which holds Christian theology together.[82] *The Truth of God Incarnate* authors defended the revelation of Jesus in Scripture, examined various uses of "myth" in church and academy, and provided historical and theological defenses of the Incarnation.[83]

In the modern period, the Quests for the historical Jesus challenged orthodox Christology from the left side of the theological spectrum. Next, Kenoticism undermined Christology from the right. Afterward, the mythologists challenged Christology, again from the left. It should not surprise us, therefore, that a fourth challenge to orthodox Christology in Modernity has come from the right.

A Lesser Lordship

Attempting to align his novel doctrine of "eternal functional subordination" (EFS) with Nicene orthodoxy, Wayne Grudem divided eternal functional subordination from eternal ontological subordination.[84] Bruce Ware, developing a similar theology, posited "eternal relations of authority and submission" between the divine Father and his Son (ERAS). Deeply concerned for personal authority, these EFS/ERAS theologians buttressed their anthropology of submission with submission in God.[85]

Grudem cited 1 Corinthians 11:3, which states, "But I want you to know that Christ is the head of every man, and the man is the head of the woman, and God is the head of Christ." He interpreted the Greek word *kephale* to mean "head" only in the sense of "authority," rather than "source" or "origin." He then levied a hierarchy of "roles" upon God and humanity: God has authority over Christ, Christ over man, and man over woman.[86] However, in the

---

82. Michael Green, "Skepticism in the Church," in Michael Green, ed., *The Truth of God Incarnate* (Hodder and Stoughton, 1977), 9–11.

83. I had the privilege of meeting and hearing John Hick in the University Schools at Oxford University and worshiped often with Michael Green at St. Andrew's Church in Oxford. Green possessed the superior hermeneutic.

84. Wayne Grudem, *Systematic Theology: An Introduction to Biblical Doctrine*, 2nd ed. (Zondervan Academic, 2020), 299–307. Modernist biblical scholarship often separates ontology from function, limiting discussion of divine being. Dockery and Yarnell, *Special Revelation and Scripture*, 106–8, 320–21.

85. See chapter 2 above.

86. Grudem, *Systematic Theology*, 318–19, 585–87. Cf. Wayne Grudem, "Appendix 1," in George W. Knight III, *The Role Relationship of Men and Women: New Testament Teaching*, rev. ed. (Presbyterian and Reformed, 1985), 49–80. The original orderings (Christ–man; man–woman; God–Christ) are typically recast by EFS/ERAS

same passage, Paul indicated man and woman are dependent sources of one another, so "source" or "origin" remains a proper interpretation (1 Cor. 11:8–12). Moreover, Paul elsewhere clearly teaches that Christ, as *kephale*, is both the source of the growth of his body, the church (Eph. 4:15–16; Col. 2:19), and originates all authorities (Col. 2:10).

Ware cites 1 Corinthians 15:28 to limit the kingship of the Lord Jesus Christ in a dimension he names "eternity future."[87] However, if we follow the Reformation hermeneutical principle that Scripture interprets Scripture, 1 Corinthians 15:24–28 must be interpreted with reference to Ephesians 1:20–23, also written by Paul, as well as Hebrews 2:4–10. In all three New Testament passages, Psalm 8 is quoted to demonstrate how God saves humanity through the "Son of Man." Both the humanity of Christ and the eternal power of his Person are required to work the salvation of humanity, certainly at the cross but also through the eternal reign of Christ upon the divine throne.

In Ephesians 1, Paul said God exercises his power "in Christ," that is in his Person, by raising his humanity from death and seating him at the right hand of the Father (v. 20). God thereby "subjected everything under his feet" (Eph. 1:22; cf. Ps. 8:6), which Paul takes to mean God "appointed him as head over everything for the church" (Eph. 1:22). The gift of the fullness of divine sovereignty to Christ is reinforced by Paul's further statement that Christ is now "the one who fills all things in every way" (v. 23). Similarly, "Colossians 1:19 and 2:9 speak of all the divine fullness indwelling Christ himself, that is to say he is filled by, and is the full expression of, the Godhead."[88] The one Person of Christ possesses universal sovereignty in his Person and thereby applies his power for our salvation through his humanity.

---

theologians to justify a hierarchical chain (God–Christ–man–woman). As he often does in 1 Corinthians, Paul may be citing a Corinthian proverb requiring correction.

87. Ware asserts God is delimited by "structures," which he names "eternity past" and "eternity future." Bruce A. Ware, *Father, Son, and Holy Spirit: Relationships, Roles, and Relevance* (Crossway, 2005), 76–77, 83–85; Bruce A. Ware, "Unity and Distinction of the Trinitarian Persons," in Keith S. Whitfield, ed., *Trinitarian Theology: Theological Models and Doctrinal Applications* (B&H Academic, 2019), 54. Arius delimited Christ to a temporal dimension between eternity and creation. See above chapter 4.

88. Francis Foulkes, *Ephesians: An Introduction and Commentary*, Tyndale New Testament Commentaries (InterVarsity Press, 1989), 74.

The author of the epistle to the Hebrews reinforces Paul's portrayal of the eternal reign of Christ as the source of human salvation. Three claims relevant to this discussion are advanced in Hebrews 2. First, through the Son's incarnation as man, which was followed by his human ascension above the angels, God subjected everything to the Son of Man. He did this to demonstrate his divine sovereignty over angels through his divine–human Son (Ps. 8:4–6; Heb. 2:5–9).

Second, the incarnation became the vehicle by which humanity was redeemed through the death and resurrection of the Son of Man. God appropriately chose to "make the pioneer of their salvation perfect through sufferings" (Heb. 2:10). The perfection of humanity, which Paul described as a recapitulation (Eph. 1:10),[89] occurs only in the humanity of Christ. He shared in our "flesh and blood," so that "he might destroy the one holding the power of death—that is, the devil" (Heb. 2:14). Christ served as our "high priest" to make atonement for our sins (v. 17).

Third, moreover, he continues to help us as our eternal high priest (v. 18). In other words, the eternal power of God in Christ secures human salvation through the humanity of the eternal Person of Christ. "The Son and the sons belong together and point to one another. . . . Humanity and Messiah stand in close, indissoluble union with one another."[90] It is through redeemed humanity's union with Christ in the Spirit by the grace of faith, and through Christ's personal union of humanity with God by the grace of his incarnation, that humanity is granted access to God. Our access has past, present, and future dimensions, dimensions that are possible only in the humanity of the eternal priest-king, Jesus Christ (cf. Ps. 110:4; Heb. 7:17, 21).

We may not limit the lordship of Christ by reference to the subjection of all things in Christ to God. Rather, Christ reconstituted humanity by fulfilling the priest-king role the first Adam failed to accomplish (Gen. 1:28).[91] This is why Paul in 1 Corinthians 15 identifies Christ as the second or "last" Adam: "For just as in Adam

89. Regarding *anakephalaiosasthai*, "recapitulate" or "sum up," Foulkes says, "Three ideas are present in the word here—restoration, unity, and the headship of Christ." Foulkes, *Ephesians*, 61.

90. J. Kögel, cited in Paul Ellingworth, *The Epistle to the Hebrews: A Commentary on the Greek Text*, New International Greek Testament Commentary (Eerdmans, 1993), 152.

91. G. K. Beale, *A New Testament Biblical Theology: The Unfolding of the Old Testament in the New* (Baker Academic, 2011), 46.

all die, so also in Christ all will be made alive" (1 Cor. 15:22, 45; cf. Rom. 5:12–21). God is subjecting everything to Christ, the new Adam. When Christ completes his human task of abolishing "all rule and all authority and power," every creaturely thing will be submitted through his humanity "to God the Father" (1 Cor. 15:24). The recapitulation of all angelic and human creatures through the headship of Christ in the judgment will finally restore the divine "kingdom" to its original creational intent.[92]

Paul's Corinthian statement, "When everything is subject to Christ, then the Son himself will also be subject to the one who subjected everything to him, so that God may be all in all" (v. 28), thus does not limit the authority of Christ's deity but subjects our humanity. Paul summarizes here what Scripture expounds in Hebrews 2 and Ephesians 1: That is, that in the unity of his own Person, Christ submits humanity to God again. The one Lord Jesus Christ remains truly divine in authority while perfecting humanity through his human obedience (Heb. 2:10). The Son's divine nature and divine work are coextensive with the Trinity. Divine authority is unqualified, for the Son as for the Father and the Spirit. Essentially, Christ is named "the power of God" (1 Cor. 1:24), as is the Holy Spirit (Zech. 4:6; Acts 1:8; 2 Tim. 1:7).

Christ's Eternal Work in Human Salvation

By his divine nature, the Lord Jesus Christ eternally dominates the universe, from its creation through its redemption to his complete and continual rule over the world. In our doctrine of Christ's work, we must include every divine work, for he is God who came in human flesh.[93] We must also include his every human work, for he is the one who recapitulates our humanity (Eph. 1:10). Having perfected our humanity by his own obedience and suffering (Heb. 2:10), Christ became "the source of eternal salvation for all who obey him" (Heb. 5:9).

92. Beale, *A New Testament Biblical Theology*, 261–62, 913–14.

93. From a Trinitarian perspective, the Incarnation is Christ's proper work, for only the Word became man.

Figure 12: The Eternal Immutability of the Divine Word and the Historical Progress of His Creaturely Humanity

Through his human nature, the Lord Jesus Christ saves us. Christ in his humanity suffered humiliation unto death, and he now enjoys eternal exaltation. But even as he descended and ascended, Christ remained God without diminution. Moreover, Christ's eternal deity empowers him to serve as the divine–human Mediator of our eternal salvation. As Lord, Christ's authority is universal and eternal. These four truths require further exploration.

Christ's Human Humiliation and Exaltation

The Son's assumption of human nature obliges us to confess both his human humiliation and his human exaltation. His *humiliation* included both his incarnation and his perfection of humanity through suffering and obedience. His humiliation ended with his voluntary death on the cross to atone for human sin, as detailed in the last chapter. The subsequent *exaltation* of Christ, which we must also explore, includes his resurrection, ascension, and heavenly session, as well as his second coming, final judgment, and eternal reign. The doctrine of exaltation does not mean his eternal Person was changed in his bodily resurrection, although his humanity certainly experienced renewal of life and ascension to the right hand of the Father. Rather, through his human exaltation, God himself "declared" the deity of Christ (Matt. 22:44; Mark 12:36; Luke 20:42; Acts 2:34; Heb. 5:10; cf. Ps. 110:1, 4).

The extraordinary power of the work of Christ is not provided by his humanity, although it is manifested through his humanity in his Person. Rather, the life-giving principle in Christ derives from his eternal nature as God (John 5:26; 1 Cor. 15:45). The author of Hebrews united Christ's deity, which he proved at length from the Old Testament (Heb. 1), with Christ's humanity, which he likewise proved at length from the Hebrew text (Heb. 2). Christ's unity of deity with humanity in his Person enables him to engage in his priestly work (Heb. 2:17; 7:17; etc.). The eternally effective mediation provided by the uniquely powerful divine–human Christ dominates the remainder of Hebrews through its praise of Christ as superior (Heb. 3:1; 4:14; etc.).

In the middle of his discourse on Christ's priesthood, the inspired author of that epistle drops an important statement about Christ that connects his divine power to his humanity in his Person. Christ, it is written, "did not become a priest based on a legal regulation about physical descent but based on the power of an indestructible life" (Heb. 7:16). In other words, just as the humanity of Christ was created by the power of God at work in his bodily conception (10:5),[94] so also his human body was raised from death by the power of God at work in his eternal Person (11:19).[95] He is one Person, truly God, who assumed to himself our humanity, which he alone perfects. His divine power unites our humanity with his Person, whereby he perfects us through his human submission (2:10).

The personal union of deity and humanity in Christ, which requires us to proclaim both his divine nature and his human nature, as well as his divine working and his human working, has a mysterious quality, because God does not explain exactly how this union works. He does, however, reveal the truth of this union. We trust his personal union does work, because he is the eternally sovereign God, and he can and does assume our creaturely humanity to himself. We must hold in tension the unity of Christ's Person with the distinction of his two natures as displayed in his powerful work as God and in his saving work as man. In his eternal Person Christ provides the foundation for our salvation through his eternal mediation.[96]

---

94. Rhyne R. Putman, *Conceived by the Holy Spirit: The Virgin Birth in Scripture and Theology* (B&H Academic, 2024), 301.

95. Power belongs to the nature of God, so the resurrection of Christ is an inseparable operation of the Three.

96. In the Afterword, we offer an historical summary of his work of exaltation.

The Eternal Foundation of Our Salvation

We previously alluded to the eternal dimension of the atonement. The cross of Christ is based not only in history but in eternity. The eternality of Christ's provision of human salvation pervades the book of Hebrews.[97] For instance, Christ's covenant is superior, because it is "everlasting" (Greek *aionios*; Heb. 13:20). Again, Christ's priesthood is superior, for he holds it "permanently" (Greek *aparabatos*; 7:24). Moreover, Christ's sacrifice of himself upon his cross for our sins was superior, because it was enacted "once for all time" (Greek *ephapax*; 10:10) with the result that it "perfects forever" (Greek *eis to dianekes*, "into perpetuity"; 10:14). Also, Christ's presentation of his sacrifice must be deemed superior, since he offered himself "through the eternal Spirit" (Greek *pneumatos aioniou*; 9:14). Finally, the power in the atonement derives from divine eternity, for the "indestructible" (Greek *akatalutos*, "endless"; 7:16) nature of the life of Christ enabled his resurrection from human death. Christ's personal divine eternity provides perpetual saving power through his assumed humanity.

Leading theologians across the Christian communions have highlighted the importance of the eternity of Christ in providing our eternal salvation. It will be remembered that Maximus the Confessor (580–662) received the early orthodox exegesis of Scripture's revelation of the Person and work of Jesus Christ. His essay, "On the Cosmic Mystery of Jesus Christ," frames the atonement by locating both its origin and its end in eternity. Expositing the biblical text with care, Maximus offered a stable and comprehensive Christology that avoided human transgression of the limits of revelation in our perceiving the eternal mystery.

First, Maximus honored the biblical paradigm for relating Christ's divine eternality to his work in time and history. Relying primarily upon 1 Peter 1:20 ("He was foreknown before the foundation of the world but was revealed in these last times") and Colossians 1:26 ("the mystery hidden for ages and generations but now revealed"), Maximus argued that Christ performed his work in history according to "the grand plan of God, a super-infinite plan

---

97. "Christ's priesthood is mentioned explicitly and implicitly in all thirteen chapters." Simon J. Kistemaker, "Atonement in Hebrews: 'A Merciful and Faithful High Priest,'" in Charles E. Hill and Frank A. James III, eds., *The Glory of the Atonement: Biblical, Historical, and Practical Perspectives* (InterVarsity Press, 2004), 163.

infinitely preexisting the ages."[98] This plan, a "mystery" to man, is the indivisible work of the eternal Trinity. "The mystery was known solely to the Father, the Son, and the Holy Spirit before all the ages."[99]

The eternal Christ's personal union with humanity in time is the key historic event determined by the mystery planned by God. "This union draws his humanity into perfect identity, in every way, through the principle of person (*hypostasis*); it is a union that realizes one person composite of both natures, inasmuch as it in no way diminishes the essential difference between those natures."[100] Human salvation through Christ's personal union is "the preconceived goal for which everything exists."[101] God sovereignly grants human beings the gift of participation in the blessedness and eternity of God, but only through the humanity of Christ.[102] Finally, Christ is the end of all things, for "the termination of time is fixed within Christ."[103] The eternal Word is the personal foundation for abiding human salvation.

Our Eternal Divine–Human Mediator

During the sixteenth century, Reformed theologians in Heidelberg, Germany, also recognized the significance of Christ's eternal nature for our salvation. In his commentary on the *Heidelberg Catechism*, Caspar Olevianus repeatedly grounded our salvation in the eternal Person and work of Christ. First, he argued, the only possible person who could perform our salvation was a "mediator" who

---

98. Maximus the Confessor, *Ad Thalassium* 60, in Paul M. Blowers and Robert Louis Wilken, eds., *On the Cosmic Mystery of Jesus Christ: Selected Writings of Maximus the Confessor* (St. Vladimir's Seminary Press, 2003), 124–25.

99. "It was known to the Father by his approval, to the Son by his carrying out, and to the Holy Spirit by his cooperation in it." Maximus grounds both the attributes of knowledge and of power in divine simplicity. "For there is only one knowledge shared by the Father, the Son, and the Holy Spirit because they also share one essence and power." Maximus, *On the Cosmic Mystery of Jesus Christ*, 127.

100. Maximus, *On the Cosmic Mystery of Jesus Christ*, 123.

101. Salvation may be described as "deification" insofar as union with God is the experience of human "creatures," but this union is only "by grace." Maximus, *On the Cosmic Mystery of Jesus Christ*, 124.

102. Salvation does not involve man becoming the eternal God "by nature." Maximus, *On the Cosmic Mystery of Jesus Christ*, 128.

103. Maximus, *On the Cosmic Mystery of Jesus Christ*, 128.

could bear "the infinite, eternal wrath of God."[104] Only Jesus Christ can be that person, for he is the only "One who is at the same time truly human and righteous and yet more powerful than any creature, that is, true, eternal God."[105]

Olevianus placed the saving work of Christ in a covenantal frame. An "eternal covenant" is necessary so that humanity can have "lasting, eternal peace and friendship between God and us." Our reconciliation with God is made by Christ's "one offering" wherein he "perfected forever those who are being sanctified."[106] The gospel must be eternal, or we will face "eternal death."[107] The covenant assures us that "eternal life" comes by grace through faith. We are "pardoned from eternity" and our sins are "forever forgotten." Christ's sacrifice is presented to God eternally, so that in Christ we access "forever its efficacy for our full redemption."[108]

The effectiveness of the human office of Christ as Mediator thoroughly depends upon his personal reign with eternal and universal power. Christ performed our salvation once on the cross and has applied its benefits to us, but he must also "continue to do so forever."[109] Olevianus then correlated the temporal work of Christ as Man with his eternal work as God through a protracted discussion of Christ's threefold office as King, Prophet, and Priest. We may summarize his argument in three paragraphs.

In his *kingdom*, the "one head," Jesus Christ both "rules" his people and "produces eternal salvation" in them forever. He does this by incorporating the elect into his body, by not imputing our sins to us, and by daily purifying us through "living" in us with his Spirit. "This is in order that in this life they might live happily in the Lord, have peace with God, and at last in eternity live and reign with their King."[110]

Through his *priestly* work, Christ established his kingdom. "The foundation on which the Kingdom of Christ rests is the priesthood of Christ, which in God's eternal decree was established

---

104. Caspar Olevianus, *A Firm Foundation: An Aid to Interpreting the Heidelberg Catechism*, transl. Lyle D. Bierma (Baker, 1995), 3.

105. Olevianus, *A Firm Foundation*, 4.

106. Olevianus, *A Firm Foundation*, 5.

107. Olevianus, *A Firm Foundation*, 8.

108. Olevianus, *A Firm Foundation*, 9.

109. Olevianus, *A Firm Foundation*, 37.

110. Olevianus, *A Firm Foundation*, 37.

and confirmed with an oath of God."[111] The priesthood of Christ is comprised of two parts, first by his sacrifice. Afterward, Christ "presented Himself henceforth before the face of the Father."[112] Olevianus dwells upon the presentation, for it demonstrates "that in the Son there is an unvarying, eternal will to redeem and represent us, which agrees with the unvarying, immutable will of the Father." Our sins are thereby "wiped away—not only until death but forever."[113] Christ's eternal presence on the divine throne guarantees our salvation will last.

Finally, Christ fulfills his *prophetic* work forever. He was "anointed in his human nature with the fullness of the Holy Spirit so that, full of grace and truth, He might clearly and intelligibly reveal to us the eternal will and counsel of God."[114] The benefits for us of his eternal human teaching office include removing any doubt about God's saving will. God's will to save us is rendered "immutable" in the Person of Christ.[115] A second benefit to believers is found in the "complete wisdom" of Christ. A third comes from the Spirit's power "to transfigure them into that which they learned from Him."[116]

After Maximus and Olevianus, several modern authors grounded Christ's human work for us in his eternal Person. Augustus Hopkins Strong wrote, "The historical work of atonement was finished upon the Cross, but that historical work only revealed to men the atonement made both before and since by the extra-mundane Logos."[117] Donald Baillie affirmed Christ's eternal provision of our salvation: "And if we then go on to speak of an eternal Atonement in the very being and life of God, it is not by way of reducing the significance of the historical moment of the Incarnation, but by way of realizing the relation of the living God to every historical moment."[118] W. T. Conner agreed: "His eternal existence was necessary to explain his

---

111. Olevianus, *A Firm Foundation*, 40.

112. Olevianus, *A Firm Foundation*, 40.

113. Olevianus, *A Firm Foundation*, 41.

114. Olevianus, *A Firm Foundation*, 42–43.

115. Olevianus, *A Firm Foundation*, 43.

116. Olevianus, *A Firm Foundation*, 43–44.

117. Extra-mundane means "above this world." Strong argued from Hebrews 9:11–14 and Revelation 13:8. Augustus Hopkins Strong, *Systematic Theology: A Compendium Designed for the Use of Theological Students* (Fleming H. Revell, 1907), 762.

118. Baillie, *God Was in Christ*, 191.

redeeming power."[119] Our Mediator can save us forever, because he is eternal God who became man.

Our Eternal King

The qualification of sovereignty, therefore, belongs to the economy of human salvation, which is worked in the humanity of Christ. Christ's lordship is, by contrast, both eternal and universal. John Chrysostom reminded the early church that it must distinguish the divine nature from the economy of salvation when interpreting 1 Corinthians 15:28.[120] Leon Morris agreed with this Nicene logic: "Paul is not speaking of the essential nature of either the Son or the Father. He is speaking of the work that Christ has accomplished and will accomplish."[121] However, the confusion of the human economy of Christ with the eternal divine nature of Christ in some dogmatic systems, ancient and modern, limits our Lord, even if unintentionally.

Numerous other biblical statements, as well as numerous creedal, confessional, and contemporary statements support the universality and eternality of Christ's authority. Both Scripture and tradition teach us that no limit may be placed upon Christ's kingship, or lordship, vis-à-vis the Father and divine eternity. First, the Bible repeatedly prophesies that the Messiah's "kingdom will have no end" (Luke 1:33; cf. Isa. 9:7), and that "he will reign forever and ever" (Rev. 11:15; cf. 2 Sam. 7:13, 16; Dan. 7:14; also Ps. 110:4; Heb. 7:17, 21). In the Revelation, John saw the risen Lamb inhabiting the eternal throne. The Son rules indivisibly, apocalyptically, and eternally with the Father and the Spirit (Rev. 1:17–18; 5:5–10; 7:9–10, 17; 22:3–5). The scriptural evidence for the universal, entire, and unremitting authority of Christ as messianic Priest-King and divine Lord is overwhelming.

Second, in the fourth century, Marcellus of Ancyra limited Christ's kingdom. Marcellus was corrected through a clause added to the Nicene Creed by the ecumenical council of Constantinople:

---

119. Walter Thomas Conner, *Revelation and God: An Introduction to Christian Doctrine* (Broadman Press, 1936), 176.

120. John Chrysostom, *Homilies on the Epistles of Paul to the Corinthians*, ed. Philipp Schaff, Nicene and Post-Nicene Fathers, First Series, vol. 12 (1889; reprint Hendrickson, 1994), 237.

121. Leon Morris, *1 Corinthians: An Introduction and Commentary*, Tyndale New Testament Commentaries (InterVarsity Press, 1985), 208.

"his kingdom shall have no end."[122] Grounding universal authority and lordship in the divine nature, the Athanasian Creed likewise confesses "there are not three almighty beings; there is but one almighty being," and "there are not three lords; there is but one Lord." The Apostles' Creed agrees, confessing unqualified belief in Jesus Christ as "our Lord." The fourth great Christian creed, the Chalcedonian Formula, distinguishes Christ's deity from his humanity, without compromising either Trinitarian unity or Christ's personal unity.[123] The ecumenical creeds afford no room for a division of divine authority.

Third, evangelical confessions typically locate eternal sovereignty in the being of God, which encompasses the Son, rather than by sundering the Persons: According to Lutherans, "the characteristics of the divine nature" include that Christ is "almighty, eternal, infinite."[124] According to the Reformed, "being yesterday and today the same, and forever," Christ purchased "an everlasting inheritance in the kingdom of heaven" for the redeemed.[125] And according to the Baptists, the Son is "ever present Lord."[126] The recent 1,700th anniversary of the Nicene Creed reminded evangelicals of the continuing challenge to orthodoxy within our own communities.[127]

Finally, John Fesko and Craig Carter connect the contemporary theology of EFS/ERAS to the "semi-Arians" of the fourth

122. See the discussion in chapter 4 above. During the second ecumenical council of Constantinople in 553 the twelfth anathema against Origen read, "If anyone shall say the Kingdom of Christ shall have an end: let him be anathema." Cf. https://www.newadvent.org/fathers/3812.htm; Tanner, ed., *Decrees of the Ecumenical Councils*, 1:106.

123. Chad Van Dixhoorn, ed., *Creeds, Confessions, and Catechisms* (Crossway, 2022), 13, 21, 27.

124. Kolb and Wengert, eds., *The Book of Concord*, 510.

125. *The Westminster Confession of Faith*, in Van Dixhoorn, ed., *Creeds, Confessions, and Catechisms*, 199. The last paragraph of the Second Helvetic Confession is even stronger: "Damnanus item omnes haereses atque haereticos, docentes, Filium et Spiritus Sanctum nuncupatione esse Deum; item creatum ac serviens aut alteri officiale esse in trinitate. . . ." ("We condemn all heresies and heretics who teach that the Son and the Holy Spirit are God in name only, also that there is something creaturely and subservient or an official of another in the Trinity. . . .") *Confessio Helvetica Posterior* (1544), in Philip Schaff and David A. Schaff, eds., *Creeds of Christendom*, 6th ed., 3 vols. (Harper and Row, 1931), 3:241.

126. *The Baptist Faith and Message*, article II.

127. Malcolm B. Yarnell III, "The Contemporary Relevance of the Nicene Creed: The Need for and Challenges to Its Retrieval," *Bibliotheca Sacra* 183.

century.[128] Proponents of EFS/ERAS disavow the Arian label,[129] but dividing the authority of God into parts by eternally subordinating the Son to the Father nonetheless similarly diminishes Christ's Lordship. It also undermines divine unity, divine simplicity, and the inseparable operations. In reply, we must proclaim that the Son is truly Lord, and that his kingdom has no limit, neither in creaturely time nor in divine eternity.

In history, the deity of Christ has faced repeated challenges, directly and indirectly. But the apostle Paul reminds us that there is "one Lord" (Eph. 4:5–6) and that "Jesus is Lord" (Rom. 10:9; 1 Cor. 12:3). Jesus is truly God. He lacks no divine perfection, nor is he absent from any divine work. Our theologies may never limit the eternal Word's divine sovereignty. Christ himself proclaimed not only that "everything the Father has is mine" (John 16:15), but that he possesses all authority everywhere (Matt. 28:18). His eternal kingship is why, "at the name of Jesus every knee will bow—in heaven and on earth and under the earth—and every tongue will confess that Jesus Christ is Lord, to the glory of God the Father" (Phil. 2:10–11).

Jesus Is Lord

Let us return to the critical question raised at the start of this chapter: Who do you say that Jesus is? For myself, I believe he is Lord, and that by truly confessing him as Lord we appropriate saving truth. Literally and simply, "Jesus is Lord" means this man, "Jesus," is the one true God, the "Lord." "The confession 'Jesus is Lord' (*Kyrios Christos*) has been from the very beginning the central

---

128. J. V. Fesko, "The New Adventures of Old Trinitarian Heresies," *Tabletalk* (December 2019): 22–25; Craig A. Carter, "The Decline of Nicene Orthodoxy," *First Things* (January 2022). Over the last decade, I gently encouraged teachers of EFS/ERAS, in person and in writing, to reconsider. E.g., Malcolm B. Yarnell III and Karen A. Yarnell, "Trinity and Authority," *Musings on Christ*, June 2016, https://www.malcolmyarnell.com/2016/06/trinity-and-authority-part-five-of-five.html; Malcolm B. Yarnell III, "Response to Bruce A. Ware, Matthew Y. Emerson, and Luke Stamps," in Whitfield, ed., *Trinitarian Theology*, 145–48, 153–55.

129. Early Arians denied being Arian. R. P. C. Hanson, *The Search for the Christian Doctrine of God: The Arian Controversies, 318–381* (Baker Academic, 2005), xvii.

confession of the community."[130] Divine eternity and universal history are united in his Person, and his deity ensures his human acts have saving significance. The gospel of salvation is summarized in a twofold faith statement: "Jesus is Lord" and "God has raised him from the dead" (Rom. 10:9).[131] I beg you so to confess Jesus.

Like the other apostles, Luke supports our confession of Christ as God and Man. Luke's first book alternates between presenting Christ from above (Luke 1:32a, 33b, 35) and from below (vv. 31, 32b, 33a). "Jesus is at one and the same time a particular historical figure and an eternal type." He is transcendent above history, yet also "the centre" within history.[132] Interested in "orderly sequence" (v. 3), Luke reported at length on the human birth, life, and death of Christ, before considering his exaltation.[133] Christ's exaltation began with his resurrection, which was verified to his disciples in three major encounters (Luke 24:3–8, 15–35, 36–49). His subsequent bodily ascent into heaven (vv. 50–51) "marks the limit of his stay on earth and the beginning of his heavenly reign."[134]

Luke's second book begins with another report of the startling ascension of Jesus Christ (Acts 1:9), followed soon after by the spectacular arrival of the Holy Spirit (Acts 1:5, 8; 2:1–4). These historic events of Christ's Ascension and of the Spirit's Coming at Pentecost launched "the epoch" of the church. Today, the church prepares the world for the coming judgment by proclaiming Christ in the power of the Spirit. Decision is required of those who hear the message of the church about Christ's resurrection.[135] At present, Christ is "seated at the right hand of God." But in the "future," he will come to judge the living and the dead.[136]

---

130. Helmut Thielicke, *The Doctrine of God and of Christ,* transl. Geoffrey W. Bromiley, *The Evangelical Faith*, vol. 2 (Eerdmans, 1977), 290. "In this figure we encounter two dimensions, a universal cosmological dimension on the one side and an individual historical dimension on the other." Thielicke, *The Doctrine of God and of Christ,* 306.

131. See chapter 10 above.

132. Hans Conzelmann, *The Theology of St. Luke*, transl. Geoffrey Buswell (Fortress Press, 1961), 185. The kingdom is both historical and "metaphysical," above the world. Conzelmann, *The Theology of St. Luke*, 113. Christ centers the story of salvation within history by connecting the first epoch, Israel, with the second epoch, the church. Conzelmann, *The Theology of St. Luke*, 170.

133. Conzelmann, *The Theology of St. Luke*, 199–204.

134. Conzelmann, *The Theology of St. Luke*, 204.

135. Conzelmann, *The Theology of St. Luke*, 205–6.

136. Conzelmann, *The Theology of St. Luke*, 187.

Across the canon, then, Scripture compels us to recognize that both history and eternity are oriented from Christ, in Christ, and toward Christ. Indeed, our salvation is entirely dependent upon Christ in both his Person and his work.[137] Again, in his great Christological hymn, Paul first established the theological ground (Phil. 2:6), then rehearsed the historical dimension of Christ's work (v. 7). Christ's descent from heaven to earth led Paul to portray Christ's assumed human life as a progression of humiliation (v. 8) and exaltation (vv. 9–10). This progress is bookended by his origin in eternity and by his temporal human ascent to eternity (vv. 6, 11). In the end, every knee shall bow before the eternal throne of Christ and every tongue shall confess, without equivocation, "Jesus Christ is Lord" (v. 11)!

We ended the last chapter, which considered Christ in his *humiliation*, by focusing on his death on the cross. In this chapter, we have reminded ourselves of the need to affirm his *eternal deity* during his human humiliation. As difficult as the tension may be to our limited minds, we must never compromise Christ's personal unity, divine nature, or human nature. In the Afterword that follows, we conclude our Christology by portraying the *exaltation* of Christ in his humanity.

Study Questions

1. What is the most critical question that can be asked about Jesus Christ? What is your answer to that question?

2. Describe three modern heresies or errors which present challenges to a full confession of Christ's deity. How might you reply to each challenge?

3. Is Christ's eternal deity necessary for humanity's salvation? Why?

137. Thielicke, *The Doctrine of God and of Christ*, 291, 300–1.

Suggested Resources

- G. K. Beale, *A New Testament Biblical Theology*
- Donald Macleod, *The Person of Christ*
- Caspar Olevianus, *A Firm Foundation*

AFTERWORD

Our Exalted Lord Jesus

THIS BOOK FOCUSES ON THE eternal Word who became man, Jesus Christ. Over the last several chapters, we have explored his work. In chapter 10, we surveyed Scripture's description of his gospel of salvation. In chapter 11, we learned that the one Person who is God and man necessarily works in divine and human ways. In chapter 12, we discovered the riches of his atoning work upon his cross. And in the last chapter, we recognized our Lord will reign forever, thereby ensuring our salvation lasts forever. Christ even now works powerfully and will perform yet more wonders in the final consummation. To a summary of the present and future dimensions of Christ's work, often treated under the rubric of exaltation, we now turn.

For my second master's degree, at Duke University, I dove deep into the preaching of the early church, the Middle Ages, and the Reformation. I was shocked to realize how contemporary evangelical preaching fails to stress Christ's works like our forefathers did. Conservative sermons rightly focus on Christ's death for sinners and his bodily resurrection. Also, we prepare homilies about his second coming and final judgment. More rarely do we hear of Christ's ascent, victory over the devil, and heavenly session. And almost never do we hear about his presentation of his sacrifice, much less his eternal reign. Yet each aspect of his exaltation is both established by Scripture and significant for our salvation. Out of this realization I commissioned the painting below to remind myself to preach of our universal calling to exalt Jesus Christ (Phil. 2:10–11).

Figure 13: "Every Knee Shall Bow" by Mellinda Gay Hansen (1995)[1]

Historically, theologians covered the life of Christ in various ways: John of Damascus defended Christ's twofold work as the God–Man rather than outlining his humiliation and exaltation.[2] By contrast, Thomas Aquinas traced Christ's life chronologically, from his birth, through his crucifixion and resurrection, to his final judgment.[3] Martin Luther, more interested in calling for faith in Christ, nevertheless perceived a fourfold movement in his human

1. Author commissioned and owns the painting and gives permission to use.

2. John of Damascus, *On the Orthodox Faith*, transl. Norman Russell (St. Vladimir's Seminary Press, 2022), 198–210.

3. Thomas Aquinas, *Compendium of Theology*, transl. Richard J. Regan (Oxford University Press, 2009), 177–85, 185–200, 200–8.

life: "birth, passion, resurrection, and ascension."[4] Like Aquinas, the Westminster Larger Catechism emphasized the details. In Christ's exaltation, it detected four events: "his resurrection, ascension, sitting at the right hand of the Father, and his coming again."[5] Among modern scholars, Michael Bird discerned a twofold movement in his exaltation: resurrection, then ascension and session.[6] While treating the works of Christ individually, Robert Peterson saw "three grand movements" determined by his two comings.[7] John Hammett and Charles Quarles discussed four acts in his exaltation: descent, resurrection, ascension, and second coming.[8]

We shall follow a Reformed, Anabaptist, and early Baptist model for the exaltation of our Lord Jesus Christ:[9] After his descent, Christ's exaltation began when he arose bodily from the dead. His appearances verified his resurrection and concluded in the Great Commission. Second, Christ's ascent inaugurated his eternal reign as Messiah. His ascent brought to heaven his priestly presentation of his sacrifice by the Spirit to the Father and cast Satan to the earth. Third, Christ's present session upon the divine throne began with the gift of his Holy Spirit to the church. His mediatorial office continues as he intercedes for his church and prophesies through her. Fourth, while Christ's resurrection sealed his triumph over evil, his bodily return to earth will complete his victory through the final judgment. He will then unveil his new creation over which he will continue to reign eternally.

---

4. Martin Luther, *The Large Catechism*, transl. Robert H. Fischer (Fortress Press, 1959), 59.

5. *Westminster Larger Catechism*, q. 51, in Chad Van Dixhoorn, ed., *Creeds, Confessions, and Catechisms* (Crossway, 2022), 351.

6. Michael F. Bird, *Evangelical Theology: A Biblical and Systematic Introduction*, 2nd ed. (Zondervan Academic, 2020), 494–516.

7. Robert A. Peterson, *Salvation Accomplished by the Son: The Work of Christ* (Crossway, 2012), 183.

8. John S. Hammett and Charles L. Quarles, *The Work of Christ*, Theology for the People of God (B&H Academic, 2024), 2–326.

9. The signal Anabaptist confession of Hans de Ries, translated into English by the first leader of the Baptist movement, also discerned four movements in Christ's exaltation: his resurrection (art. XV), his ascension (art. XVI), his threefold office in glory (arts. XVII–XIX), and his return to raise the dead and judge the world (art. XL). *The Short Confession of Faith and the Essential Elements of Christian Doctrine* (1610), in Karl Koop, ed., *Confessions of Faith in the Anabaptist Tradition 1527–1660*, transl. Cornelius J. Dyck et al. (Plough, 2019), 144–47, 155–56.

Figure 14: The Human Exaltation of Our Lord Jesus Christ

Christ's Descent

Some theologians begin Christ's post-crucifixion work with his descent to the dead. Two of the four great symbols of the universal Christian faith—the Apostles' Creed and the Athanasian Creed—portray the descent as Christ's triumph over "principalities and powers" (Col. 2:15 NKJV; cf. Eph. 4:8–10).[10] Collating Christ's victory over the fallen angels with other references in Scripture (cf. Matt. 27:50–53; Luke 16:19–31; Acts 2:27, 31; Heb. 11:39; 1 Pet. 3:18–20; 4:6), early church theologians provided the doctrine of Holy Saturday with details.[11]

The descent doctrine gained widespread approval during the Middle Ages.[12] Aquinas said Christ's human body remained in the grave without decaying, while his soul descended to the abode of the dead. Christ went there "not to suffer punishment" but "to show himself liberator of the living and the dead." He freed those who looked to his coming but left the rebellious behind.[13] John Calvin, doubting a literal descent, spiritualized it to mean Christ suffered

10. Van Dixhoorn, *Creeds, Confessions, and Catechisms*, 13, 22.

11. Malcolm B. Yarnell III, "Holy Saturday: A Baptist Reflects on Holy Week," *Musings on Christ,* 23 April 2011, https://www.malcolmyarnell.com/search?q=holy+saturday.

12. E.g., *Formula of Concord*, art. IX, in Robert Kolb and Timothy J. Wengert, eds., *The Book of Concord: The Confessions of the Evangelical Lutheran Church* (Fortress Press, 2000), 634–35; Matthew Y. Emerson, *"He Descended to the Dead": An Evangelical Theology of Holy Saturday* (InterVarsity Press, 2019), 82.

13. Aquinas, *Compendium of Theology*, 194.

torment.[14] However, many theologians across the traditions interpret the descent literally.[15]

Proponents of Christ's descent to the dead believe they have a biblical case. However, the allusive dispersal of the scriptural references to the descent fosters diverse opinions among orthodox Christians. If the descent truly happened, which seems likely, Christ both demonstrated his kingship over the angels and declared freedom to the Old Testament saints who were once disobedient but expected him by faith (1 Pet. 3:20; 4:6). Their eternal freedom (and ours) was secured by Christ's victory over Satan.[16] That the Nicene Creed fails to mention the descent suggests the early church recognized the doctrine was a matter of theological freedom.

Christ's Bodily Resurrection

Beyond any doubt whatsoever, Scripture establishes and emphasizes Christ's bodily resurrection from death. Placed alongside his atoning death in the New Testament definition of the saving gospel (Rom. 10:9; 1 Cor. 15:3–11), Christ's resurrection is a fundamental article of the Christian faith.[17] Scripture credits the resurrection of Jesus not only to the Son (John 2:19–21; 10:18), but also the Father (Rom. 6:4; Acts 2:32) and the Holy Spirit (Rom. 1:4; 1 Pet. 3:18; 1 Tim. 3:16b). The inseparable operations of the three Persons are thus evident in every divine work, from creation through the resurrection to the new creation.

All four canonical Gospels highlight the transformative effect of the astonishing news of our Lord's resurrection on the third day. Its reality was first revealed to his women disciples, both by angelic messengers and by the risen Lord himself (Matt. 28:5–10;

---

14. John Calvin, *Institutes of the Christian Religion*, ed. John T. McNeill, transl. Ford Lewis Battles (Westminster Press, 1960), 512–20.

15. The descent of Christ will be investigated further in volume 3 of Theology for Every Person.

16. Lutherans, while not deeming the article necessary, argue its primary purpose was to defeat the devil. Kolb and Wengert, *The Book of Concord*, 635.

17. The propositional definition of the gospel as centered in, first, Christ's death and, second, Christ's resurrection, is affirmed by all four of the primary classical creeds.

Mark 16:5–7; Luke 24:1–10; John 20:11–18).[18] Paul considered the bodily resurrection of Jesus so critical that without it "our proclamation is in vain, and so is your faith" (1 Cor. 15:14).[19] By his resurrection, Christ overcame the devil (Heb. 2:14), death, and the grave (Rom. 6:9; 1 Cor. 15:54–57). Human beings may appropriate the life-giving benefits of his resurrection by faith (John 11:25–26).

Sadly, unbelievers deny his resurrection, while some believers diminish its importance. James Ware replies to such attempts to denigrate the resurrection: "The implications of Jesus's resurrection" are "extraordinary." Above all, it "warrants belief in him as the incarnate Son of God."[20] The further implications of Christ's resurrection are manifold and significant. According to Augustine, Christ's bodily resurrection does not merely guarantee our future resurrection. He was raised so "that the life which the Christian leads here might be modelled" upon his life, death, and resurrection.[21] According to Martin Luther, Christ became a man and suffered for human sin, but not "for himself." Rather, by his resurrection, the holy and divine Christ "swallowed up and devoured death" for us.[22]

According to Calvin, the bodily resurrection of Jesus Christ assures us "that we are reborn into righteousness through his power."[23] According to Hammett and Quarles, the implications of Christ's resurrection continue. It "vindicates Jesus's identity," "completes the work of salvation," "inaugurates new creation," "empowers Christian living," and "shapes the mission of the church."[24] Finally, according to the Anabaptists, the resurrection comes after the

18. I cannot but weep for joy as I read these accounts again. His humblest disciples from a human perspective were the first to be divinely graced with the knowledge of this most exalted and saving truth.

19. Paul's defense of the resurrection and its meaning in 1 Corinthians 15 makes that chapter a vital text in Christology.

20. James P. Ware, *The Final Triumph of God: Jesus, the Eyewitnesses, and the Resurrection of the Body in 1 Corinthians 15* (Eerdmans, 2025), 151. Cf. Malcolm B. Yarnell III, "Seven Reasons You Can Rejoice in the Resurrection," *Baptist Press*, 28 March 2024, https://www.baptistpress.com/resource-library/bptoolbox/seven-reasons-you-can-rejoice-in-the-resurrection-of-jesus-christ/.

21. Those incorporated into his resurrection "also should walk in newness of life." Augustine, *Enchiridion on Faith, Hope, and Love*, ed. Thomas S. Hibbs (Regnery, 1996), 64.

22. Luther, *The Large Catechism*, 58.

23. Calvin, *Institutes of the Christian Religion*, 522.

24. It also "marks the transition from Christ's humiliation to his exaltation." Hammett and Quarles, *The Work of Christ*, 310–14.

suffering of Christ to remind his true disciples that we can follow Christ "through the cross into the light" (Latin *per crucem ad lucem*).[25]

Christ verified the truth of his resurrection by appearing to the apostles. All four canonical Gospels provide detailed and diverse yet numerous and corroborative reports of his bodily appearances between his resurrection and his ascension (Matt. 28; Mark 16; Luke 24; John 20–21), as do other texts (e.g., Acts 9:1–6; 22:6–10; 26:12–18; 1 John 1:1–2). During his appearances, Jesus demonstrated the truth of his bodily resurrection to the disciples beyond any shadow of doubt (e.g., John 20:24–29). Paul spoke of the transformative effect upon the once-fearful disciples, who then became bold witnesses: "He appeared to Cephas, then to the Twelve. Then he appeared to over five hundred brothers and sisters at one time; most of them are still alive, but some have fallen asleep. Then he appeared to James, then to all the apostles. Last of all, as to one born at the wrong time, he also appeared to me" (1 Cor. 15:5–8). The title "apostle" was thus granted to those who saw and bore witness to Christ's life after death (Acts 1:22–26).

Christ also gave his Great Commission to the church through his apostles (Matt. 28:16–20; Luke 24:48–49). He left his church on the earth to warn its rebellious inhabitants of the final judgment and the general resurrection of the dead, and to win the nations to saving faith in Christ through their witness. The Lord also taught the apostles to interpret the Old Testament correctly through a Christological hermeneutic rather than some "foolish" hermeneutic (Luke 24:25–27, 32, 44–47). He also promised to send the Holy Spirit to them, so that he could be present with them until his bodily return (John 20:21–23; Acts 1:4–8).

Christ's Ascension

After his resurrection and appearances to the disciples, Jesus ascended to heaven. His ascension to the divine throne demonstrates he is the eternal King. Christ's right to rule was always his as God, but now he places his humanity on the exalted throne. The sequence is important. By his death, the human Christ atoned for our sins; by

25. Malcolm Yarnell, "Anabaptist Spirituality," in G. Stephen Weaver and Ian Hugh Clary, eds., *The Pure Flame of Devotion: The History of Christian Spirituality* (Joshua Press, 2013), 151–75.

his resurrection, he defeated the devil and death; and by his ascension, it was declared the eternal Lord had become the human King. At his ascension, Christ also presented his atoning blood sacrifice to the Father to gain humanity access to the throne and purified heaven by casting Satan out and down.

Significant Old Testament prophecies foretold this historic moment. Hebrews 1 collates the prophets' declaration that Christ is the Lord: God promised David that his human son would be God's own Son, and that he would reign forever (2 Sam. 7:14; Heb. 1:5b). God likewise revealed in the first royal psalm the Messiah's dual divine–human sonship (Ps. 2:7; Heb. 1:5a). God also instructed the angels to worship the Son (Ps. 97:7; Heb. 1:6), for the Son created them (Ps. 104:4; Heb. 1:7). God declared his Son to be the Anointed Messiah, both by virtue of his divine nature and the ascension of his perfect humanity (Ps. 45:6–7; Heb. 1:8–9). God also proclaimed both that Christ created all things and that all things conclude in Christ. Creation grows old and wears out, but Christ remains, for he, too, is the immutable God (Ps. 102:25–27; Heb. 1:10–12). Finally, God told his Son to sit upon the divine throne while he makes everyone submit to him (Ps. 110:1; Heb. 1:13).

Hebrews 2 tracks the human Christ through his incarnation and cross into glory: God the Father, speaking to "the Son," calls the Son, "God." God also declares the Son's eternal kingship: "Your throne, God, is forever and ever; and the scepter of your kingdom is a scepter of justice" (Ps. 45:6; Heb. 2:8). By divine right, the Son possesses complete and eternal authority. "The enthronement sequence is not, of course, to be construed as the Son's acquisition of a status not previously possessed or exercised, but as the definitive irrefutable declaration of his inherent dignity."[26] In other words, after taking humanity to himself in the incarnation and perfecting it through his own obedience, suffering, and death (Heb. 2:10), Christ ascended to set his humanity upon the divine throne where he continually intercedes for his brothers and sisters (v. 17).

The declaration of Christ's eternal kingship was accompanied by his priestly presentation of his own blood. "Sacrifice in the Old Testament was not completed solely by slaughtering the sacrificial offering but also included the presentation of this offering

26. "In it, the eternal lordship of Jesus Christ is vindicated and his detractors are covered with shame." John Webster, *The Domain of the Word: Scripture and Theological Reason* (T&T Clark, 2012), 32.

before God (Lev. 1–7, 16)."[27] So Christ presented his self-offering "through the eternal Spirit" to the Father. The importance of the eternal presentation cannot be underplayed, for by offering himself "without blemish to God," Christ made it possible to "cleanse our consciences from dead works" (Heb. 9:14). Christ presents his sacrifice—performed upon the cross in time—to the Father in eternity. The sacrifice occurred "once" in history, but by virtue of the heavenly presentation, its effect is "for all" (Greek *ephapax*; v. 12).[28] Through the blood of his self-sacrifice, Christ obtained "an eternal redemption" (v. 12). And the eternal reign of the perfect man upon the divine throne guarantees believers have "an eternal inheritance" (v. 15).

The eternal priesthood of Christ upon the divine throne is emphasized in Hebrews 4–8. The author quotes Psalm 110:4 three times: "You are a priest forever according to the pattern of Melchizedek" (Heb. 5:6; 7:17, 21). After the third instance, the Holy Spirit explains, "Because he remains forever, he holds his priesthood permanently. Therefore, he is able to save completely those who come to God through him, since he always lives to intercede for them" (7:24–25).[29] Human salvation requires the eternal presence of Christ upon the throne.[30] "His once-completed self-offering is utterly acceptable and efficacious; his contact with the Father is immediate and unbroken; his priestly ministry on his people's behalf is never ending, and therefore the salvation which he secures to them is absolute."[31]

Moreover, in his ascension, the victorious Christ cast the devil out and down from appearing before the council of the heavenly angels. Through his self-presentation of his blood, the eternal high priest "purified" the heavens themselves (Heb. 9:23). Douglas

---

27. Peterson, *Salvation Accomplished by the Son*, 180–81.

28. Evangelicals, with a wary eye toward the Roman Mass, emphasize there is nothing repetitive in Christ's sacrifice. Christ's once-for-all sacrifice is propitiatory. The Christian's spiritual sacrifices are never propitiatory. Malcolm B. Yarnell III, *Royal Priesthood in the English Reformation* (Oxford University Press, 2013), 231–38.

29. Hebrews 3:7 makes it clear that where Scripture speaks, the Holy Spirit speaks.

30. John Dunhill says this reminds us of our continual need for divine grace. John Dunhill, *Covenant and Sacrifice in the Letter to the Hebrews*, Society for New Testament Studies (Cambridge University Press, 1992), 259.

31. F. F. Bruce, *The Epistle to the Hebrews*, rev. ed., New International Commentary on the New Testament (Eerdmans, 1990), 175.

Farrow distinguishes the heavens cleansed by Christ from the unapproachable light of the Father and the Son. "The heaven to which Hebrews refers . . . is the place from which God's rule over the world is affected through the angels, the place where God's presence to and for creation is manifested and known, the place around which all creation is therefore ordered and arranged."[32] Christ begins the new creation by ridding the devil of any presence in heaven. Christ also shares this power with his disciples (Luke 10:18–20; Rev. 12:9, 11), but it is only ever exercised by absolute reference to Christ (Zech. 3:2; Jude 9).

Christ's Heavenly Session

The Word who became man and arose from the dead, Jesus Christ, then "sat down at the right hand of the Majesty on high" (Heb. 1:3). The heavenly session of Jesus began only "after" he endured his cross, conquered the devil, overcame death, and made purification for sins by presenting his offering (Heb. 1:3; 8:3; 10:12; 12:2; Rev. 3:21). The place of Christ's session is the divine throne, a throne which can be described only in apocalyptic terms (e.g., Isa. 6; Dan. 7; Rev. 4–5; 21–22), for it both exceeds time and includes time.[33] The one Lord Jesus Christ as God transcends history, but as man he lives within history. As God he reigns eternally, but as man he ascends in time. The heavenly session compromises neither Christ's divine reality nor his human nature. Instead, during his session, he both establishes his rule over the heavens and continues to bring humanity salvation.

The *Westminster Larger Catechism* confesses Christ on his throne is "God–man" and "has all fullness of joy, glory, and power." This Reformed symbol sees three works within his session: First, he "doth gather and defend his church, and subdue their enemies." Second, he "furnisheth his ministers and people with gifts and graces." Third, he

32. Douglas Farrow, *Ascension Theology* (T&T Clark, 2011), 124.

33. T. C. Vriezen described apocalyptic eschatology as "historical and at the same time supra-historical. It takes place within the framework of history but is caused by forces that transcend history." Quoted in G. E. Ladd, "Apocalyptic Literature," in G. W. Bromiley, ed., *The International Standard Bible Encyclopedia*, rev. ed., vol. 1 (Eerdmans, 1979), 152.

"maketh intercession for them."[34] The Anabaptists and the Baptists agreed. Moreover, Christ's work as priest and king continues into glory, indeed "forever" and "in all eternity."[35] Christ also sends his Spirit to apply to believers the benefits Christ has worked.[36]

The coming of the Holy Spirit upon the church joins Christ in his heavenly session, where his body resides on the throne, with his people in their earthly sojourn. The promised descent of the Spirit on the church at Pentecost constituted the church and empowered believers to live the Christian life and proclaim the gospel (John 20:21–23; Acts 2:1–4, 37–40).[37] Earlier, Jesus said the Spirit would be sent to make Christ present to his disciples by residing within them (John 14:16–18), to help the apostles remember what Jesus told them and reveal to them yet more truth (John 14:26; 15:26–27; 16:12–14), and to empower them to witness to Christ (Acts 1:8; 2:38; 5:9; etc.). The Holy Spirit brings life through regeneration as people believe in the Word (John 3:5; Rom. 8:8–11). He also fills the Christian life with fruitful graces (Gal. 5:22–25) and diverse gifts for building up Christ's body (Rom. 12:3–8; 1 Cor. 12:4–11, 27–31; Eph. 4:7–16).

Peter confirms Christ's royal victory over the rebellious authorities and powers in his session. He "has gone into heaven and is at the right hand of God with angels, authorities, and powers subject to him" (1 Pet. 3:22). Even now, he is bringing the rebels to heel. He offers rebellious human beings the hope of reconciliation "by making peace through his blood" (Col. 1:20). But the rebellious angels, over whom he gained victory (Rev. 5:5–7), face rebuke and defeat (Luke 10:17–19; Jude 9; cf. Isa. 14:12). A series of battles characterize Christ's resubmission of all things to God, and believers participate in this warfare (Matt. 16:18–19; Eph. 6:12; Rev. 12:11). The Apocalypse of John details the process of resubmission, which will culminate in Christ's second coming, the imprisonment of the ancient serpent, and the final judgment (Rev. 19:11–20:3, 7–11).

34. *Westminster Larger Catechism*, in Van Dixhoorn, *Creeds, Confessions, and Catechisms*, 352. Cf. Hammett and Quarles, *The Work of Christ*, 321.

35. *Short Confession*, in Koop, *Confessions of Faith in the Anabaptist Tradition*, 144–45.

36. *Westminster Larger Catechism*, in Dixhoorn, *Creeds, Confessions, and Catechisms*, 353; Short Confession, in Koop, *Confessions of Faith in the Anabaptist Tradition*, 145.

37. Peterson, *Salvation Accomplished by the Son*, 225–26.

Satan's time of leading rebellion on earth, after being cast out of heaven, is "short" (12:12).

In his prophetic work, Christ continues to proclaim judgment and redemption from his eternal throne in and through his church. The book of Acts provides an early record of what Christ taught "by his Spirit in the apostles after his ascension."[38] Indeed, the books of the New Testament together perfectly and powerfully deliver his prophetic voice to the church.[39] When it is understood the eternal Word came to the prophets of the Old Testament, we recognize Christ speaks through the entire canon, then and now and forever.[40] The prophetic work of Christ continues today as the church teaches the apostolic writings externally to human ears and his Spirit moves internally in human hearts.[41]

In his priestly work during his session Christ intercedes for believers. Robert Peterson summarizes the biblical implications of Christ's intercession well: First, his intercession saves us by enabling our faith to continue (Rom. 8:29–30). Second, Christ intercedes to the Father for us in heaven (v. 34) as the Spirit intercedes in our hearts (v. 26). Third, Christ's intercession applies to us the sacrifice he made on the cross. Fourth, Christ's intercession continues unabated. Fifth, his intercession ensures our victory. Sixth, Christ intercedes for his own people.[42] The Anabaptist confession adopted by the first Baptists emphasized Christ's continuing priestly work through his two ordinances: They first affirmed his baptism of us by the Holy Spirit and fire. They then confessed Christ's spiritual presence. "He celebrates his spiritual Supper with believing souls, making them partakers of the living food and drink of the soul. In these holy sacraments alone is appropriated the fruit, power, work, and worth of his cross."[43]

---

38. F. F. Bruce, *The Acts of the Apostles* (Eerdmans, 1951), 66.

39. They are God's "living words still speaking to us" and "the crystallized voice of God." B. B. Warfield, *Revelation and Inspiration* (Oxford University Press, 1932), 300–1.

40. David S. Dockery and Malcolm B. Yarnell III, *Special Revelation and Scripture* (B&H Academic, 2024), 175–76.

41. Malcolm B. Yarnell III, *The Formation of Christian Doctrine* (B&H Academic, 2007), 79–90.

42. Peterson, *Salvation Accomplished by the Son*, 248–50.

43. *Short Confession*, in Koop, *Confessions of Faith in the Anabaptist Tradition*, 145–46.

Christ's Second Coming

There is much still to be said about the future work of Christ in his second coming: his eschatological warfare with the devil and his followers, his resurrection of dead believers to join those who remain upon the earth, his victory over the evil one, his millennial reign, his final judgment, the casting of the devil and his followers into the eternal lake of fire, the unveiling of the new creation where heaven and earth are joined in the new Jerusalem, and his continual reign over and blessing of his people from the divine throne. But these awesome truths await the final volume of Theology for Every Person, which focuses on the Spirit while continuing to honor the Lord Jesus, who has the unqualified authority to name himself, "the Alpha and the Omega, the first and the last, the beginning and the end" (Rev. 22:13).

The eternal Word's human exaltation in and through his second coming does not, therefore, conclude or terminate either his divine authority or his human priesthood. Rather, Christ's human exaltation will bring together eternity and time in the new creation, a creation eternally ruled by God in Christ by his Spirit. Redeemed humanity will have Christ forever as the eternal priest who grants us the privilege to approach the eternal throne and experience the blessed vision of the One who is Father and Son and Holy Spirit. In preparation for those earth-changing eschatological events, may I encourage you to sing from your heart with me a few verses from the great contemporary hymn, "He Is Lord"?

Humbled and rejected, beaten, and despised;
Upon the cross the Son of God was slain.
Just like a lamb to slaughter, a sinless sacrifice;
But, by His death His loss became our gain.

Satan's forces crumbled like a mighty wall;
The stone that held Him in was rolled aside.
The Prince of Life in glory was lifted over all;
Now earth and heaven echo with the cry.

He is Lord, He is Lord!
He is risen from the dead and He is Lord!
Ev'ry knee shall bow, ev'ry tongue confess
That Jesus Christ is Lord.[44]

44. Linda Lee Johnson, Claire Cloninger, and Tom Fettke, "He Is Lord," in Wesley L. Forbis, ed., *The Baptist Hymnal* (Convention Press, 1991), 178. Thanks to W. Madison Grace for recently reminding me of this hymn and how it has deeply shaped both our hearts.

Acknowledgments

◆ ◆

Appreciation is expressed to all those who helped this volume come to completion. First, of course, come the preachers and teachers through whom Christ the Prophet has spoken to me throughout my life, in word and in deed. These include ancient defenders of the Word like Athanasius of Alexandria, Martin Luther, and Thomas Helwys, whose writings have enlightened my mind and whose lives have inspired my soul. Such preachers and teachers also include modern leaders like Wayne L. DuBose, James Leo Garrett Jr., and John Webster, each of whom took personal interest in my intellectual, spiritual, and professional growth as a young man. Five of these six leaders have now preceded me to glory, and I see the sixth too little in this life. I treasure the introductions, reunions, and conversations we shall one day have with one another in the presence and worship of our Lord and Savior, Jesus Christ.

Second, I value the thousands of students who allowed me the honor to teach them, primarily at Southwestern Baptist Theological Seminary, but also at theological institutions around the world, from Missouri and North Carolina to China and Germany to Grand Cayman and Ukraine, and beyond. While no single lecture or course of lectures in a dynamic environment can convey everything that needs to be said about the Lord, my students will recognize the content and spirit of these lectures. Some students, like Derrick Bledsoe, Madison Grace, Chris Kim, Wang Yong Lee, John Mann, Clayton Ross, Travis Trawick, Sufnat Wasti, and Sean Wegener, have provided detailed interaction with these lectures. Countless others have engaged passionately with me and the other students of God's Word in numerous live and online classrooms, graduate seminar conference rooms, and coffee shop conversations. We learned from one another, as God the Father guided us by his Holy Spirit, that Jesus the Christ is our only Mediator, our God, and our eternal King.

Third, thanks are extended to the many others who have blessed me personally in the construction of this book, especially through worshipful exegesis, theological conversation, and international mission in various private ventures. These include the Commission on Baptist Doctrine and Christian Unity with Paul Fiddes, Curtis Freeman, Steve Harmon, Beth Newman, and many international theologians in the Baptist World Alliance; the Emmaus Way project with Andy Brown, Jason Lee, Stephen Lorance, and Steve McKinion at the First Baptist Church of Starkville; the Going Deeper podcast with Brad Humphrey, Debbie McKinnon, Karen Yarnell, and the PTL Class at Lakeside Baptist Church of Granbury; the Nicene Creed project with the world-renowned scholars gathered by Matthew Barrett to contribute to the thenicenecreed.org website funded by Lakeside; the Philip Teaching Ministry with Brad Humphrey, Sid McCormick, and Bryan Yarnell; and the Trinity Project with Matt Sanders and the Alec and Belle Waterhouse Lecture Series at the Waialae Baptist Church of Honolulu.

Special thanks are extended to my patient and ever-encouraging editor, Mary Wiley, and to Devin Maddox, Michael McEwen, and the other fine leaders at Lifeway Christian Resources. It is a great blessing to work with you and so many other Christian theologians who are dedicated to declaring that to the risen Lamb belongs glory and honor and majesty and power forever and ever. Amen.

Malcolm B. Yarnell III
April 30, 2025

Scripture Index